Picture Books to Enhance the Curriculum

□ ■ □ ■ □ ■ □ ■

Picture Books
to Enhance
the Curriculum

■　□　■　□　■

Jeanne McLain Harms
Lucille J. Lettow

The H. W. Wilson Company / 1996

Visit our Web site at: http://www.hwwilson.com

Library of Congress Cataloging-in-Publication Data

Harmes, Jeanne McLain.
  Picture books to enhance the curriculum / Jeanne McLain Harmes, Lucille J. Lettow.
    p. cm.
  ISBN 0-8242-0867-6
  1. Picture books for children—Educational aspects—Indexes. 2. Picture books for children—Educational aspects—Bibliography. I. Lettow, Lucille. II. Title.
LB1044.9.P49H37   1996
371.3′3—dc20   94-42653
                                                             CIP

Printed in the United States of America

Dedicated to Carol Jean Porter (1932–1992)
Children's Librarian and Friend
Her Dream Fulfilled

Contents

Introduction

In schools today, much attention is being given to expanding the literature base in all areas of the curriculum. Rather than limiting study to a textbook, all types of literature are provided, offering children opportunities for in-depth learning experiences.

Those involved in program enrichment are finding picture book experiences with texts representing different genres most valuable. These short pieces with illustrations that amplify the text not only offer quality literature experiences, but because of their brevity, lend to the exploration of a theme. In-depth learning can be promoted by making connections with different works of a common theme and then comparing and contrasting the points of view and messages of the works.

Many librarians, teachers, and curriculum consultants are energized by the prospect of enriching the school program through an extended literature base. As school personnel begin instructional development activity, their enthusiasm often wanes when they come to grips with the problem of finding materials related to a common theme. Ready access to works can greatly facilitate their efforts. Also, literature-based programs tend to expand children's reading activity. In fulfilling their requests for books on a particular theme, students, teachers, and librarians in school and public library collections for young people need user-friendly references.

This book offers an index of picture books organized by themes to extend the literature base of the elementary school curricular areas (language arts, graphic and performing arts, social studies, and science). Enriching the instructional program through literature is one way to implement the whole language concept. This instructional concept focuses on children creating meaning through the language processes within the functions of language. These functions, or reasons to listen, speak, read, and write, are found across the curriculum. This picture book index offers easy reference to common themes found throughout the curriculum. It is designed to assist curriculum coordinators, teachers, librarians, and students to identify picture books that meet their particular needs.

The index does not present an exhaustive collection but focuses on titles typically found in children's literature collections. The selection of titles and themes is based on the authors' extensive study of professional resources in children's literature and curriculum development as well as their many years of experience in school classrooms and library media centers. Criteria for picture books listed in the index include literary and artistic quality, curriculum application, appeal to youth, and availability. Standard retrospective bibliographies, including *Children's Catalog*, sixteenth edition, edited by Juliette Yaakov, and *Children's Literature in the Elementary School*, third edition and third update edition by Charlotte S. Huck and fourth and fifth editions by Huck, Susan Hepler, and Janet Hickman, served as reference sources for determining respected titles for inclusion in the index. Review sources, including *School Library Journal*, *Booklist*, *Horn Book Magazine*, and *Bulletin of the Center for Children's Books*, were used to select recently published volumes. Also, annual lists of recommended books appearing in *The Reading Teacher*, *Social Education*, and *Science and Children* were consulted.

Some volumes in the index can be shared with a wide range of age groups for different purposes. Some have more than one level of meaning that provoke different responses from children at different stages of development.

The index has two major sections: (1) An index of themes with accompanying lists of related titles is organized into as many as three levels (e.g., **ANIMALS—Farm, sheep**). The themes are cross-referenced to guide readers to the theme heading selected for the listing; for example, **ADOPTION** *See* **FAMILIES—Adoption.** Works can be found in other sections of the index when the entries are connected with the phrase "*See also*"; for example, **ANIMALS—Marine life** (*See also* other **ANIMALS—Small creatures, turtles/tortoises**). (2) Individual works can be further surveyed in the second section, which offers full bibliographic information, a brief annotation reviewing the content, and a list of themes developed in the text. The index of titles at the end of the volume can serve as another means of locating a book in the index.

Acknowledgments

We wish to thank the teachers and librarians who shared their instructional programs with us as they participated in our classes, workshops, and graduate programs. We are especially appreciative to Carol Jean Porter for pointing out that a picture book index of this type would assist teachers and librarians in extending the literature base of their programs.

To Dr. James Bodensteiner, Director of Credit Programs, and Dr. Glenn Hansen, Dean, Division of Continuing Education at the University of Northern Iowa, we extend our gratitude for providing us with many opportunities to work with teachers and librarians through courses, workshops and graduate programs offered in the field.

We are grateful to Judy O'Malley, our editor, who gave much support as she guided us through the publication process. It was a pleasure to work with her.

A special thanks also goes to Beverly Bauer, who typed the manuscript and, as always, provided her expertise and good cheer.

JMH and LJL

Key to Themes

elephants
foxes
hippopotami
lions
moose
tigers
wolves
others
Marine life *See also* ANIMALS—Small creatures, turtles/tortoises
alligators
aquariums
crocodiles
fishes
frogs
whales
others
Personified
Pets
cats
dogs
others
Prehistoric
Reptiles *See also* ANIMALS—Marine life, alligators; ANIMALS—Marine life, crocodiles; ANIMALS—Small creatures, turtles/tortoises
lizards/chameleons
snakes
Small creatures
butterflies/moths/caterpillars
insects
mice
monkeys
rabbits
spiders
squirrels
turtles/tortoises
others
Zoo *See also* ANIMALS—Large animals
APPLES
ARTS AND ARTISTS *See* GRAPHIC AND PERFORMING ARTS
ASIAN AMERICANS *See* UNITED STATES—Specific cultures, Asian American
ASTRONOMY *See also* SPACE
Earth *See* ECOLOGY/ENVIRONMENTAL PROBLEMS
Moon
Stars

Sun
Other
AUTOMOBILES *See* TRANSPORTATION—Cars

BABYSITTING
BALLOONS
BEHAVIOR
  Ambitious/Persistent
  Apprehensive
  Boastful
  Bored
  Bossy
  Bullying
  Competitive
  Cooperative
  Courageous
  Crying
  Curious
  Destructive/Violent
  Disobedient
  Evil
  Excited
  Fighting/Quarreling
  Foolish
  Forgetful
  Greedy
  Heroic
  Hiding
  Imitating
  Impatient
  Lazy
  Loyal
  Lying
  Mischievous
  Obedient
  Patient
  Pretending
  Problem-solving
  Proud
  Resourceful
  Responsible
  Revengeful
  Ridiculing
  Rude
  Running away *See also* PERSONAL PROBLEMS—Running away

Searching
Selfish
Sharing
Shy
Stealing
Teasing
Tricking
Wise
BELLS
BICYCLES *See* TRANSPORTATION—Bicycles; TOYS—Bicycles
BIOGRAPHY/LIFE STORIES *See also* GRAPHIC AND PERFORMING ARTS
BIRDS *See* ANIMALS—Birds
BIRTH
BIRTHDAYS
BOATS *See* TRANSPORTATION
BODY
  Parts of body
    eyes
    hair
    noses
    teeth
  Shape and size
BOTTLES/JARS *See* STRUCTURES—Boxes and Containers
BUILDINGS *See* STRUCTURES—Buildings
BUSES *See* TRANSPORTATION

CAMPING *See also* VACATIONS
CAROUSELS
CARS *See* TRANSPORTATION
CHANGES *See also* TRANSFORMATION
CHRISTMAS *See* HOLIDAYS AND CELEBRATIONS
CIRCUS
CLOCKS *See* TIME—Clocks and other time-telling methods
CLOTHING
  Buttons
  Coats
  Costumes
  Dresses
  Hats
  Mittens
  Pockets
  Shoes/Boots
  Others
COLORS
COMMUNICATION
  Newspapers

Signs *See also* WRITING—Signs
Telephones
Televisions
COMMUNITIES *See* NEIGHBORHOODS AND COMMUNITIES
CONSTRUCTION
COWBOYS/COWGIRLS *See also* RANCHES

DANCE AND DANCERS *See* GRAPHIC AND PERFORMING ARTS
DANGER *See* SAFETY/DANGER
DAYS OF THE WEEK *See* TIME—Cycles, days of the week
DEATH
DINOSAURS *See also* HISTORICAL PERIODS—Prehistoric
DISABILITIES
DISASTERS *See also* WEATHER—Storms, WATER AND BODIES OF WA-
    TER—Floods
DRAGONS *See* IMAGINATION—Imaginary creatures
DRAMA *See* GRAPHIC AND PERFORMING ARTS
DREAMS

ECOLOGY/ENVIRONMENTAL PROBLEMS
ELDERLY *See also* FAMILIES—Grandparents
EMOTIONS
    Anger
    Disappointment
    Embarrassment
    Fear
    Happiness
    Hate
    Jealousy
    Loneliness
    Love
    Sadness
ENEMIES
ENVIRONMENTAL PROBLEMS *See* ECOLOGY/ENVIRONMENTAL PROB-
    LEMS
ESKIMOS *See* UNITED STATES—Specific cultures, American Indians/Eskimos
ETHNIC CULTURES
    Jewish
    Others
EVERYDAY EXPERIENCES
    Seasonal activities *See* TIME—Specific seasons
    Time of day
        awakening for the day
        bedtime *See also* SLEEPING
        daytime
        nighttime *See also* SLEEPING
        sleeping *See* SLEEPING

EXPLORATION

FAIRS *See also* NEIGHBORHOODS AND COMMUNITIES—Social gatherings
FAMILIES
  Adoption
  Babies and young siblings
  Family gatherings/Outings
  Grandparents
  Husbands and wives
  Marriage
  Orphans
  Other relatives
  Parents
  Problems *See* FAMILY PROBLEMS
  Siblings
  Twins
FAMILY PROBLEMS *See also* PERSONAL PROBLEMS
  Death *See* DEATH
  Homelessness
  Moving *See* MOVING
  New siblings
  Separation
  Others
FARMS *See also* ANIMALS—Farm; RANCHES
FEAR *See* EMOTIONS—Fear
FIRE
FISHING *See also* ANIMALS—Marine life
FLOWERS *See* PLANTS
FLYING
  Aviation
  Fantasy
FOOD AND EATING
  Cookies
  Fruits *See* PLANTS—Fruits
  Soup
  Vegetables *See* PLANTS—Vegetables
FRIENDSHIP
  Imaginary friends
  Relationships
FRUITS *See* PLANTS; APPLES
FURNITURE
  Beds
  Chairs

GAMES/PUZZLES/TRICKS
GARDENS *See also* PLANTS; PUMPKINS

GHOSTS *See* IMAGINATION—Imaginary creatures
GIFTS
GOALS
GOBLINS *See* IMAGINATION—Imaginary creatures, others
GRAPHIC AND PERFORMING ARTS
    Art and artists
    Dance and dancers
    Drama and actors *See also* STORYTELLING
    Music and musicians

HALLOWEEN *See* HOLIDAYS AND CELEBRATIONS
HARBORS *See* WATER AND BODIES OF WATER—Harbors
HEALTH
    Bathing
    Health care
    Human body *See* BODY
    Illness and injury
HISPANIC AMERICANS *See* UNITED STATES—Specific cultures, Hispanic
    American
HISTORICAL PERIODS
    Across time *See also* TIME—Across time
    Colonial
    Exploration of the New World
    Medieval/Renaissance *See also* TIME–Across time
    Nineteenth Century
        early
        late
        pioneer/westward movement
    Prehistoric
    Twentieth Century
        early
        World War II
        modern/contemporary
HOBBIES
HOLIDAYS AND CELEBRATIONS
    April Fool's Day
    Celebrations around the World
    Christmas
    Easter
    Halloween
    Hanukkah
    Kwanzaa
    New Year
    Thanksgiving
    Valentine's Day
HOT-AIR BALLOONS *See* TRANSPORTATION

HOUSES *See* STRUCTURES—Buildings, houses and other dwellings
HUMAN BODY *See* BODY
HUMOR

IDENTITY
  Gender roles
  Geographic identity
  Relationships
  Self-worth
IMAGINATION
  Imaginary creatures
    dragons
    ghosts
    monsters
    witches
    others
  Imaginary friends *See* FRIENDSHIP—Imaginary friends
  Imaginary objects
  Imaginary worlds
IMMIGRANTS/REFUGEES
INDIVIDUALITY
INSECTS *See* ANIMALS—Small creatures
INVENTIONS
ISLANDS

JEWELS/JEWELRY

KITES
KNIGHTS

LANGUAGE
  Alphabet
  Names
  Sayings and special language
  Words
LIGHT AND SHADOWS/REFLECTIONS
LOST AND FOUND *See also* PERSONAL PROBLEMS—Getting lost
LUCK

MACHINES *See also* FARMS
  Wheels
MAGIC
MAPS
MASKS
MATHEMATICS
  Classification

Counting
Measurement
  length
  mass
  volume
Numbers
  ideas
  ordinal
  processes
Shapes
Size
MEMORIES
MIGRANTS
MONEY
MONSTERS *See* IMAGINATION—Imaginary creatures, monsters
MOON *See* ASTRONOMY
MOUNTAIN CLIMBING
MOVEMENT/SPEED
MOVING
MUSIC *See* GRAPHIC AND PERFORMING ARTS—Music and musicians
MYSTERY

NEIGHBORHOODS AND COMMUNITIES
  General
  Moving *See* MOVING
  Parks
  Social gatherings
  Specific
    rural
    urban

OBSERVATION *See also* STORIES—Minimal or no text
OCCUPATIONS *See also* GRAPHIC AND PERFORMING ARTS
ORPHANS *See* FAMILIES—Orphans

PARADES
PARKS *See* NEIGHBORHOODS AND COMMUNITIES—Parks
PARTIES *See also* FAMILIES—Family gatherings/Outings
PATHS *See* TRAILS
PEACE *See also* WAR
PERSONAL PROBLEMS
  Breaking promises
  Fearing to try something new
  Getting lost
  Giving up security objects
  Name-calling

Running away
Others
PETS *See* ANIMALS—Pets
PHOTOGRAPHY
PILGRIMS *See* HOLIDAYS AND CELEBRATIONS—Thanksgiving
PIONEERS *See* HISTORICAL PERIODS—Nineteenth Century
PIRATES
PLANTS *See also* GARDENS
  Cycles
  Flowers
  Fruits *See also* APPLES
  Seeds
  Trees
  Vegetables *See also* PUMPKINS
  Others
PLAY *See also* GAMES/PUZZLES/TRICKS
POST OFFICE *See* WRITING—Letters
POVERTY
PRESENTS *See* GIFTS
PUMPKINS
PUPPETS

QUILTS

RACES *See* MOVEMENT/SPEED
RAIN *See* WEATHER—Rain
RANCHES *See also* FARMS
READING
REFLECTIONS *See* LIGHT AND SHADOWS/REFLECTIONS
REFUGEES *See* IMMIGRANTS/REFUGEES
RELIGION
RIDDLES
ROADS
ROCKS AND MINERALS
ROOMS
  Attics
  Bathrooms
  Bedrooms
  Others
ROYALTY *See also* KNIGHTS

SAFETY/DANGER
SAND
SCARECROWS
SCHOOL EXPERIENCES
SEASONS *See* TIME—Specific seasons

SECRETS
SEEDS *See* PLANTS—Seeds
SELF-IDENTITY *See* IDENTITY—Self-worth
SENSES
  Sight *See also* OBSERVATION
  Smell and taste
  Sound
  Touch
SEWING *See also* QUILTS
SHADOWS *See* LIGHT AND SHADOWS/REFLECTIONS
SHOPPING/MARKETING
SIGNS *See* **COMMUNICATIONS—Signs;** WRITING—Signs
SLAVERY
SLEEPING *See also* EVERYDAY EXPERIENCES—Time of day, bedtime;
    EVERYDAY EXPERIENCES—Time of day, nighttime
SNOW *See* WEATHER—Snow
SOUNDS *See* SENSES
SPACE *See also* ASTRONOMY
SPORTS *See also* FISHING, MOUNTAIN CLIMBING
STATUES
STORIES
  Minimal or no text *See also* OBSERVATION
  Predictable text
STORYTELLING
STRANGERS
STRUCTURES
  Boxes and containers
  Bridges
  Buildings
    barns
    cabins
    castles/palaces
    churches
    houses and other dwellings *See also* ROOMS
    libraries
    museums
    schools
    stores
    others
  Caves
  Tunnels
  Others
SUN *See* ASTRONOMY
SURPRISES
SURVIVAL

TEACHERS *See* SCHOOL EXPERIENCES
TEETH *See* BODY—Parts of body, teeth
TIME
   Across time *See also* HISTORICAL PERIODS—Across time
   Clocks and other time-telling methods
   Cycles
      day and night
      days of the week
      months of the year
      seasons
   Daytime
   Nighttime
   Specific seasons
      spring
      summer
      fall
      winter
TOYS
   Balloons *See* BALLOONS
   Bears
   Bicycles *See also* TRANSPORTATION—Bicycles
   Dolls
   Kites *See* KITES
   Others
TRAILS
TRAINS *See* TRANSPORTATION—Trains
TRANSFORMATION
TRANSPORTATION
   Airplanes
   Bicycles *See also* TOYS—Bicycles
   Boats
   Buses
   Cars
   Horses
   Hot-air balloons
   Sleighs
   Spaceships *See* SPACE
   Trains
   Trucks
   Wagons
   Others
TRAVEL
TREASURES
TREES *See* PLANTS—Trees
TRICKERY *See* BEHAVIOR—Tricking

TRUCKS *See* TRANSPORTATION—Trucks
TWINS *See* FAMILIES

UNITED STATES
  Cross cultural
  General
  Regions
    Alaska
    Appalachia
    Hawaii
    Middle Atlantic
    Midwest
    Northeast
    Northwest/Alaska
    South
    Southwest
    West Coast
    Western Mountain
  Specific cultures
    African American
    American Indian/Eskimo *See also* WORLD CULTURES—North America,
      Canada
    Asian American
    Hispanic American

VACATIONS
VEGETABLES *See* GARDENS; PLANTS

WAR *See also* PEACE
WATER AND BODIES OF WATER *See also* WEATHER—Rain
  Floods
  Harbors
  Lakes
  Oceans
  Ponds
  Rivers
WEATHER
  Clouds
  Drought
  Fog
  Rain
  Rainbows
  Snow
  Storms
  Sunshine
  Wind

WEAVING
WEDDINGS *See* FAMILIES—Marriage
WHEELS *See* MACHINES
WISHES
WITCHES *See also* IMAGINATION—Imaginary creatures, witches
WORLD CULTURES/COUNTRIES
  Africa
    Eastern
    Northern
    Southern
    Western
  Asia
    China
    Japan
    others
  Australia and the Pacific Islands
  Central America
    Caribbean Islands
    Mexico
  Cross cultures
  Europe
    Central/Eastern
    Northern
    Southern
  Middle East
  North America (not United States)
    Canada
  Polar regions
  South America
WORLD REGIONS
  Desert
  Forest
  Mountain
  Plain
  Rain forest/Jungle
  Seashore
WRITING
  Diaries
  Letters
  Poems
  Signs
  Others

ZOOS *See also* ANIMALS—zoo

Themes Index

ACTORS *See* **GRAPHIC AND PERFORMING ARTS—Drama and actors**
ADOPTION *See* **FAMILIES—Adoption**
ADVENTURES

Agee, Jon. *The Return of Freddy LeGrand.*
Arnold, Tedd. *Green Wilma.*
Asch, Frank. *Mooncake.*
Babbitt, Natalie. *Nellie: A Cat on Her Own.*
Bang, Molly. *Yellow Ball.*
Blegvad, Lenore. *Anna Banana and Me.*
Brett, Jan. *Armadillo Rodeo.*
Briggs, Raymond. *The Snowman.*
Brown, Marc. *Arthur's Halloween.*
Browne, Anthony. *Tunnel.*
Brunhoff, Jean de. *The Story of Babar.*
Burningham, John. *Come Away from the Water, Shirley.*
———. *Hey! Get Off Our Train.*
———. *Mr. Gumpy's Motor Car.*
———. *Mr. Gumpy's Outing.*
———. *Time to Get Out of the Bath, Shirley.*
———. *Where's Julius?*
Calhoun, Mary. *High-Wire Henry.*
Christiansen, Candace. *Calico and Tin Horns.*
Cole, Joanna. *The Magic School Bus in the Time of the Dinosaurs.*
———. *The Magic School Bus Inside a Hurricane.*
Conrad, Pam. *The Lost Sailor.*
Cox, David. *Bossyboots.*
Crews, Donald. *Shortcut.*
Day, Alexandra. *Frank and Ernest.*
Dodds, Dayle Ann. *Wheel Away!*
Ernst, Lisa Campbell. *A Colorful Adventure of the Bee, Who Left Home One Monday Morning and What He Found Along the Way.*
Farber, Norma. *Return of the Shadows.*
Fleischman, Paul. *Time Train.*
Freeman, Don. *A Pocket for Corduroy.*
Garland, Michael. *Dinner at Magritte's.*
Geisert, Arthur. *Pigs from 1 to 10.*

————. *Winter Whale.*
Sadler, Marilyn. *Alistair in Outer Space.*
San Souci, Robert. *Kate Shelley: Bound for Legend.*
Sara. *Across Town.*
Say, Allen. *El Chino.*
————. *Grandfather's Journey.*
Shaw, Nancy. *Sheep in a Jeep.*
Sis, Peter. *A Small, Tall Tale from the Far, Far North.*
Spier, Peter. *Father, May I Come?*
Steig, William. *The Amazing Bone.*
————. *Amos & Boris.*
————. *Gorky Rises.*
Tafuri, Nancy. *Have You See My Duckling?*
————. *Junglewalk.*
————. *Rabbit's Morning.*
Testa, Fulvio. *If You Take a Pencil.*
Van Allsburg, Chris. *The Garden of Abdul Gasazi.*
————. *Jumanji.*
————. *The Polar Express.*
————. *Two Bad Ants.*
————. *The Wreck of the Zephyr.*
————. *The Wretched Stone.*
Wahl, Jan. *My Cat Ginger.*
Weller, Frances Ward. *Riptide.*
Wiesner, David. *Free Fall.*
————. *Hurricane.*
Wilkon, Piotr. *Rosie the Cool Cat.*
Williams, Sue. *I Went Walking.*
Winter, Jeanette. *Follow the Drinking Gourd.*
Woodruff, Elvira. *The Wing Shop.*

AESTHETIC APPRECIATION

dePaola, Tomie. *The Art Lesson.*
Dunrea, Olivier. *The Painter Who Loved Chickens.*
Ernst, Lisa Campbell. *Sam Johnson and the Blue Ribbon Quilt.*
Garland, Michael. *Dinner at Magritte's.*
Lionni, Leo. *Frederick.*
————. *Matthew's Dream.*
Moss, Lloyd. *Zin! Zin! Zin! A Violin.*
Purdy, Carol. *Mrs. Merriwether's Musical Cat.*
Shea, Pegi Deitz. *The Whispering Cloth: A Refugee's Story.*
Yorinks, Arthur. *Bravo, Minski.*

AMERICAN AMERICANS *See* **UNITED STATES—Specific cultures, African American**
AIRPLANES *See* **TRANSPORTATION—Airplanes**

ALPHABET *See* **LANGUAGE—Alphabet**
AMERICAN INDIANS *See* **UNITED STATES—Specific cultures, American Indian**
ANIMALS

    Bunting, Eve. *A Turkey for Thanksgiving.*
    Dragonwagon, Crescent. *Half a Moon and One Whole Star.*
    Grossman, Bill. *Donna O'Neeshuck Was Chased by Some Cows.*
    Hoban, Tana. *Big Ones, Little Ones.*
    Hutchins, Pat. *1 Hunter.*
    Kitchens, Bert. *Animal Numbers.*
    Lewin, Hugh. *Jafta.*
    Martin, Bill. *Brown Bear, Brown Bear, What Do You See?*
    McCloskey, Robert. *One Morning in Maine.*
    Spier, Peter. *Gobble, Growl, Grunt.*
    ———. *Peter Spier's Circus!*
    Weiss, Nicki. *Where Does the Brown Bear Go?*

Babies

    Asch, Frank. *The Last Puppy.*
    Cannon, Janell. *Stellaluna.*
    Carle, Eric. *The Very Quiet Cricket.*
    Dana, Katharine Floyd. *Over in the Meadow.*
    dePaola, Tomie. *Jingle: The Christmas Clown.*
    Fisher, Aileen. *Listen, Rabbit.*
    Heinz, Brian. *The Alley Cat.*
    Hoban, Tana. *Big Ones, Little Ones.*
    Keats, Ezra Jack. *Over in the Meadow.*
    Kellogg, Steven. *Pinkerton, Behave!*
    Rand, Gloria. *Prince William.*
    Rogers, Jean. *Runaway Mittens.*
    Tafuri, Nancy. *Rabbit's Morning.*
    Wahl, Jan. *My Cat Ginger.*
    Walsh, Ellen Stoll. *You Silly Goose.*

Birds *See also* **STRUCTURES—Nests**

    Baker, Keith. *The Dove's Letter.*
    Bang, Molly. *The Paper Crane.*
    Baylor, Byrd. *Hawk, I'm Your Brother.*
    Bunting, Eve. *Fly Away Home.*
    ———. *The Man Who Could Call Down Owls.*
    Cannon, Janell. *Stellaluna.*
    Coerr, Eleanor. *Sadako.*
    Dillon, Jana. *Jeb Scarecrow's Pumpkin Patch.*
    Ehlert, Lois. *Feathers for Lunch.*
    Fleming, Denise. *In the Tall, Tall Grass.*
    Haugaard, Erik Christian. *Prince Boghole.*
    Hutchins, Pat. *Good Night, Owl!*

Heine, Helme. *The Most Wonderful Egg in the World.*
James, Betsy. *Mary Ann.*
Kellogg, Steven. *The Mysterious Tadpole.*
Leedy, Loreen. *Tracks in the Sand.*
Polacco, Patricia. *Chicken Sunday.*
———. *Rechenka's Eggs.*
Ryder, Joanne. *Where Butterflies Grow.*
Scamell, Ragnhild. *Solo Plus One.*
Seuss, Dr. *Horton Hatches the Egg.*
Wildsmith, Brian. *The Little Wood Duck.*
———. *Pelican.*

Endangered species
Burningham, John. *Hey! Get Off Our Train.*
Jonas, Ann. *Aardvarks, Disembark!*

Fantasy
Arnold, Tedd. *Green Wilma.*
Asch, Frank, and Vladimir Vagin. *Here Comes the Cat! = Siuda idet kot!*
Barrett, Judi. *Animals Should Definitely Not Act Like People.*
———. *Animals Should Definitely Not Wear Clothing.*
Burningham, John. *Aldo.*
Cazet, Denys. *I'm Not Sleepy.*
Cohen, Miriam. *Lost in the Museum.*
Jonas, Ann. *The Trek.*
Leaf, Margaret. *Eyes of the Dragon.*
Lionni, Leo. *Matthew's Dream.*
Martin, Rafe. *Will's Mammoth.*
Mayer, Mercer. *There's an Alligator Under My Bed.*
Ryder, Joanne. *The Bear on the Moon.*
———. *The Night Flight.*
———. *One Small Fish.*
Teague, Mark. *The Field Beyond the Outfield.*
Van Allsburg, Chris. *The Garden of Abdul Gasazi.*
———. *Jumanji.*
Wegen, Ronald. *Sky Dragon.*

Farm
Carle, Eric. *The Very Busy Spider.*
Dunbar, Joyce. *Four Fierce Kittens.*
Ehlert, Lois. *Color Farm.*
Fleischman, Paul. *The Animal Hedge.*
Fleming, Denise. *Barnyard Banter.*
Griffith, Helen V. *Grandaddy's Place.*
Martin, Bill, and John Archambault. *Barn Dance!*
Martin, Jacqueline Briggs. *Good Times on Grandfather Mountain.*
Polacco, Patricia. *Thunder Cake.*
Tafuri, Nancy. *Early Morning in the Barn.*

webs

    Carle, Eric. *The Very Busy Spider.*

    Koralek, Jenny. *The Cobweb Curtain: A Christmas Story.*

Hibernation

    Asch, Frank. *Moon Bear.*

    ———. *Mooncake.*

    Bunting, Eve. *The Valentine Bears.*

    Freeman, Don. *Bearymore.*

    Kesey, Ken. *Little Tricker the Squirrel Meets Big Double the Bear.*

Insects *See* **ANIMALS—Small creatures**

Large animals

    Bowen, Betsy. *Antler, Bear, Canoe. A Northwoods Alphabet Year.*

    Cherry, Lynne. *The Great Kapok Tree. A Tale of the Amazon Rain Forest.*

    Luenn, Nancy. *Nessa's Fish.*

    Ryder, Joanne. *The Night Flight.*

  bears

    Asch, Frank. *Bear Shadow.*

    ———. *Happy Birthday, Moon.*

    ———. *Just Like Daddy.*

    ———. *Moon Bear.*

    ———. *Mooncake.*

    ———. *Moondance.*

    ———. *Sand Cake.*

    ———. *Skyfire.*

    Brett, Jan. *Berlioz the Bear.*

    Browne, Anthony. *Bear Hunt.*

    Bunting, Eve. *The Valentine Bears.*

    Carle, Eric. *The Honeybee and the Robber.*

    Freeman, Don. *Bearymore.*

    Gage, Wilson. *Cully Cully and the Bear.*

    Graham, Thomas. *Mr. Bear's Chair.*

    Gregory, Valiska. *Through the Mickle Woods.*

    Isaacs, Anne. *Swamp Angel.*

    Kasza, Keiko. *A Mother for Choco.*

    Kesey, Ken. *Little Tricker the Squirrel Meets Big Double the Bear.*

    Kraus, Robert. *Milton the Early Riser.*

    Luenn, Nancy. *Nessa's Fish.*

    McCloskey, Robert. *Blueberries for Sal.*

    Minarik, Else Holmelund. *A Kiss for Little Bear.*

    ———. *Little Bear.*

    ———. *Little Bear's Friend.*

    ———. *Little Bear's Visit.*

    Murphy, Jill. *Peace at Last.*

    ———. *What Next, Baby Bear?*

    Rosen, Michael. *We're Going on a Bear Hunt.*

Ryder, Joanne. *The Bear on the Moon.*
———. *White Bear, Ice Bear.*
Vincent, Gabrielle. *Feel Better, Ernest!*
———. *Smile, Ernest and Celestine.*
Wildsmith, Brian. *The Lazy Bear.*

deer

Owens, Mary Beth. *A Caribou Alphabet.*
Van Allsburg, Chris. *The Polar Express.*
Wild, Margaret. *Thank You, Santa.*

elephants

Brunhoff, Jean de. *The Story of Babar.*
Lobel, Arnold. *Uncle Elephant.*
Murphy, Jill. *All in One Piece.*
Mwenye Hadithi. *Tricky Tortoise.*
Paxton, Tom. *Engelbert the Elephant.*
Sadler, Marilyn. *Alistair's Elephant.*
Seuss, Dr. *Horton Hatches the Egg.*
Steig, William. *Gorky Rises.*
Tsuchiya, Yukio. *Faithful Elephants.*

foxes

Fox, Mom. *Hattie and the Fox.*
Hartley, Deborah. *Up North in Winter.*
Hutchins, Pat. *Rosie's Walk.*
Kent, Jack. *Silly Goose.*
Luenn, Nancy. *Nessa's Fish.*
Sharmat, Marjorie Weinman. *The Best Valentine in the World.*
Steig, William. *The Amazing Bone.*
———. *Doctor De Soto.*
Tejima, Keizaburo. *Fox's Dream.*
Walsh, Ellen Stoll. *You Silly Goose.*
Wildsmith, Brian. *The Little Wood Duck.*

hippopotami

Marshall, James. *George and Martha.*
———. *George and Martha Back in Town.*
———. *George and Martha, One Fine Day.*
———. *George and Martha 'Round and 'Round.*
———. *George and Martha, Tons of Fun.*

lions

Fatio, Louise. *The Happy Lion.*
Freeman, Don. *Dandelion.*
Mwenye Hadithi. *Lazy Lion.*

moose

Alexander, Martha. *Even That Moose Won't Listen to Me.*
Bunting, Eve. *A Turkey for Thanksgiving.*

Brunhoff, Jean de. *The Story of Babar.*

Bunting, Eve. *The Mother's Day Mice.*

———. *A Turkey for Thanksgiving.*

———. *The Valentine Bears.*

Burningham, John. *Mr. Gumpy's Motor Car.*

———. *Mr. Gumpy's Outing.*

Calhoun, Mary. *High-Wire Henry.*

Cannon, Janell. *Stellaluna.*

Carle, Eric. *Do You Want to Be My Friend?*

Carlstrom, Nancy White. *I'm Not Moving, Mama!*

———. *Jesse Bear, What Will You Wear?*

Castle, Caroline, and Peter Weevers. *Herbert Binns & the Flying Tricycle.*

Cohen, Caron Lee. *Whiffle Squeek.*

Cole, Babette. *Hurray for Ethelyn.*

Day, Alexandra. *Frank and Ernest.*

Dillon, Jana. *Jeb Scarecrow's Pumpkin Patch.*

Duvoisin, Roger. *Petunia.*

Fox, Mem. *Koala Lou.*

———. *Possum Magic.*

Freeman, Don. *Dandelion.*

Freeman, Lydia. *Pet of the Met.*

Gray, Libba Moore. *Small Green Snake.*

Geisert, Arthur. *Pigs from A to A.*

———. *Pigs from 1 to 10.*

Gerstein, Mordicai. *Roll Over!*

Glass, Andrew. *Jackson Makes His Move.*

Goodall, John S. *The Adventures of Paddy Pork.*

———. *Naughty Nancy Goes to School.*

———. *Paddy to the Rescue.*

———. *Paddy's New Hat.*

———. *Shrewbettina's Birthday.*

Graham, Thomas. *Mr. Bear's Chair.*

Gregory, Valiska. *Through the Mickle Woods.*

Hayes, Sarah. *The Grumpalump.*

Henkes, Kevin. *Chester's Way.*

———. *Chrysanthemum.*

———. *Julius, the Baby of the World.*

———. *Owen.*

———. *Sheila Rae, the Brave.*

Hoban, Lillian. *Arthur's Great Big Valentine.*

Hoban, Russell. *A Baby Siter for Frances.*

———. *A Bargain for Frances.*

———. *Emmet Otter's Jug-Band Christmas.*

———. *The Mole Family's Christmas.*

Kasza, Keiko. *A Mother for Choco.*

rabbits
 Bolliger, Max. *The Lonely Prince.*
 Brown, Marc. *The Bionic Bunny Show.*
 Carlstrom, Nancy White. *Who Gets the Sun Out of Bed?*
 Fisher, Aileen. *Listen, Rabbit.*
 McBratney, Sam. *Guess How Much I Love You.*
 Potter, Beatrix. *The Tale of Peter Rabbit.*
 Tafuri, Nancy. *Rabbit's Morning.*
 Zolotow, Charlotte. *Mr. Rabbit and the Lovely Present.*
spiders
 Carle, Eric. *The Very Busy Spider.*
 Koralek, Jenny. *The Cobweb Curtain: A Christmas Story.*
 McNulty, Faith. *The Lady and the Spider.*
 Ryder, Joanne. *The Spiders Dance.*
squirrels
 Kesey, Ken. *Little Tricker the Squirrel Meets Big Double the Bear.*
 Wildsmith, Brian. *Squirrels.*
turtles/tortoises
 Asch, Frank. *Turtle Tale.*
 Leedy, Loreen. *Tracks in the Sand.*
 Mwenye Hadithi. *Tricky Tortoise.*
 Oppenheim, Joanne. *You Can't Catch Me!*
others
 Baylor, Byrd. *Amigo.*
 Brett, Jan. *Armadillo Rodeo.*
 Cannon, Janell. *Stellaluna.*
 Duke, Kate. *Guinea Pigs Far and Near.*
 Fox, Mem. *Koala Lou.*
 ———. *Possum Magic.*
 Hoban, Russell. *Emmet Otter's Jug-Band Christmas.*
 ———. *The Mole Family's Christmas.*
 Lionni, Leo. *The Biggest House in the World.*
 ———. *Inch by Inch.*
 Lobel, Arnold. *Days with Frog and Toad.*
 Ryder, Joanne. *Chipmunk Song.*
 ———. *The Snail's Spell.*
 Schoenherr, John. *The Barn.*
 Williams, Barbara. *A Valentine for Cousin Archie.*
Zoo *See also* **ANIMALS—Large animals**
 Carle, Eric. *The Mixed-Up Chameleon.*
 ———. *1, 2, 3 to the Zoo.*
 de Regniers, Beatrice Schenk. *May I Bring a Friend?*
 Ehlert, Lois. *Color Zoo.*
 Fatio, Louise. *The Happy Lion.*
 Gauch, Patricia Lee. *Tanya and Emily in a Dance for Two.*

Kitchens, Bert. *Animal Alphabet.*
Martin, Bill. *Polar Bear, Polar Bear, What Do You Hear?*
Munari, Bruno. *Bruno Munari's Zoo.*
Rey, H. A. *Curious George.*
Rice, Eve. *Sam Who Never Forgets.*
Sadler, Marilyn. *Alistair's Elephant.*
Wild, Margaret. *Thank You, Santa.*

APPLES

Asch, Frank. *Turtle Tale.*
dePaola, Tomie. *An Early American Christmas.*
Scheer, Julian, and Marvin Bileck. *Rain Makes Applesauce.*

ART AND ARTISTS *See* **GRAPHIC AND PERFORMING ARTS**

ASIAN AMERICANS *See* **UNITED STATES—Specific cultures, Asian American**

ASTRONOMY *See also* **SPACE**

Cole, Joanna. *The Magic School Bus in the Time of the Dinosaurs.*
———. *The Magic School Bus Lost in the Solar System.*
Duran, Cheli. *Hildilid's Night.*
Henkes, Kevin. *The Biggest Boy.*
Isaacs, Anne. *Swamp Angel.*
Testa, Fulvio. *If You Look Around You.*

Earth *See* **ECOLOGY/ENVIRONMENTAL PROBLEMS**

Moon

Asch, Frank. *Happy Birthday, Moon.*
———. *Mooncake.*
———. *Moondance.*
Babbitt, Natalie. *Nellie: A Cat on Her Own.*
Berger, Barbara. *Grandfather Twilight.*
Carlstrom, Nancy White. *Who Gets the Sun Out of Bed?*
Dragonwagon, Crescent. *Half a Moon and One Whole Star.*
Lobel, Arnold. *Owl at Home.*
Martin, Bill, and John Archambault. *Barn Dance!*
McBratney, Sam. *Guess How Much I Love You.*
Minarik, Else Holmelun. *Little Bear.*
Murphy, Jill. *What Next, Baby Bear!*
Ormerod, Jan. *Moonlight.*
Ryder, Joanne. *The Bear on the Moon.*
———. *Under the Moon.*
Schertle, Alice. *Witch Hazel.*
Wildsmith, Brian. *What the Moon Saw.*

Stars

Dragonwagon, Crescent. *Half a Moon and One Whole Star.*
Griffith, Helen V. *Grandaddy's Stars.*
Hoban, Russell. *The Mole Family's Christmas.*
Levinson, Riki. *Watch the Stars Come Out.*

Turner, Ann Warren. *Stars for Sarah.*
Winter, Jeanette. *Follow the Drinking Gourd.*

Sun

Baylor, Byrd. *The Way to Start a Day.*
Carle, Eric. *Walter the Baker.*
Carlstrom, Nancy White. *Who Gets the Sun Out of Bed?*
Dragonwagon, Crescent. *Half a Moon and One Whole Star.*
Ormerod, Jan. *Sunshine.*
Shepperson, Rob. *The Sandman.*
Tejima, Keizaburo. *Swan Sky.*
Wildsmith, Brian. *What the Moon Saw.*

Other

Polacco, Patricia. *Meteor!*
Tejima, Keizaburo. *Swan Sky.*

AUTOMOBILES *See* **TRANSPORTATION—Cars**

BABYSITTING

Brown, Marc. *Arthur Babysits.*
———. *Arthur's Baby.*
MacLachlan, Patricia. *All the Places to Love.*
Murphy, Jill. *All in One Piece.*
Rayner, Mary. *Mr. and Mrs. Pig's Evening Out.*
Waggoner, Karen. *The Lemonade Babysitter.*

BALLOONS

Bang, Molly. *Yellow Ball.*
Gray, Nigel. *A Balloon for Grandad.*
Rey, H. A. *Curious George.*

BEHAVIOR

Ambitious/Persistent

Agee, Jon. *The Return of Freddy LeGrand.*
Alexander, Sue. *Nadia the Willful.*
Asch, Frank. *Bear Shadow.*
———. *Moondance.*
Bartone, Elisa. *Peppe the Lamplighter.*
Brown, Marc. *Arthur's Teacher Trouble.*
———. *Arthur's TV Trouble.*
Burton, Virginia Lee. *Mike Mulligan and His Steam Shovel.*
Carle, Eric. *The Very Busy Spider.*
Charlip, Remy. *Fortunately.*
Coerr, Eleanor. *Sadako.*
Cooney, Barbara. *Hattie and the Wild Waves.*
dePaola, Tomie. *The Art Lesson.*
———. *Oliver Button Is a Sissy.*
Dillon, Jana. *Jeb Scarecrow's Pumpkin Patch.*
Dunrea, Olivier. *The Painter Who Loved Chickens.*

Ernst, Lisa Campbell. *Sam Johnson and the Blue Ribbon Quilt.*

Flournoy, Valerie. *The Patchwork Quilt.*

Garland, Sherry. *The Lotus Seed.*

Gauch, Patricia Lee. *Tanya and Emily in a Dance for Two.*

Hoban, Russell. *Emmet Otter's Jug-Band Christmas.*

Hoffman, Mary. *Amazing Grace.*

Howard, Elizabeth Fitzgerald. *Papa Tells Chita a Story.*

Johnston, Tony. *Amber on the Mountain.*

———. *Pages of Music.*

Isaacs, Anne. *Swamp Angel.*

Keats, Ezra Jack. *Whistle for Willie.*

Lawson, Julie. *The Dragon's Pearl.*

Lionni, Leo. *Matthew's Dream.*

Lobel, Arnold. *Days with Frog and Toad.*

———. *On the Day Peter Stuyvesant Sailed into Town.*

McCully, Emily Arnold. *The Amazing Felix.*

Olalye, Isaac O. *Bitter Bananas.*

Ray, Mary Lyn. *Pianna.*

Sadler, Marilyn. *Alistair's Elephant.*

Say, Allen. *El Chino.*

Schroeder, Alan. *Ragtime Tumpie.*

Shea, Pegi Deitz. *The Whispering Cloth: A Refugee's Story.*

Shefelman, Janice Jordan. *A Peddler's Dream.*

Speed, Toby. *Hattie Baked a Wedding Cake.*

Steig, William. *Brave Irene.*

Van Allsburg, Chris. *The Wreck of the Zephyr.*

Wellner, Frances Ward. *Matthew Wheelock's Wall.*

Williams, Sherley Anne. *Working Cotton.*

Wittman, Patricia. *Go Ask Giorgio!*

Yamaka, Sara. *The Gift of Driscoll Lipscomb.*

Yorinks, Arthur. *Bravo, Minski.*

Apprehensive

Alexander, Martha. *When the New Baby Comes, I'm Moving Out.*

Allard, Harry. *Miss Nelson Is Missing.*

Asch, Frank. *Moon Bear.*

———. *Skyfire.*

Bang, Molly. *Delphine.*

Benjamin, Amanda. *Two's Company.*

Bennett, Jill. *Teeny Tiny.*

Blegvad, Lenore. *Anna Banana and Me.*

Brett, Jan. *Berlioz the Bear.*

Briggs, Raymond. *Father Christmas.*

Brown, Marc. *Arthur Babysits.*

———. *Arthur's April Fool.*

———. *Arthur's Baby.*

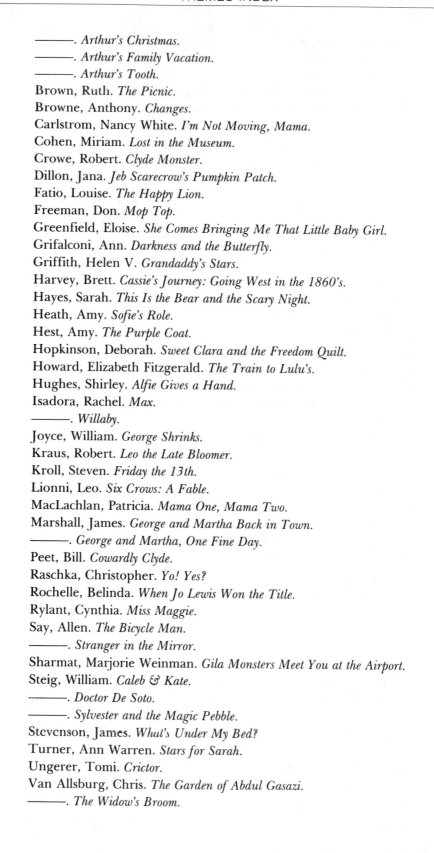

Viorst, Judith. *Alexander and the Terrible, Horrible, No Good, Very Bad Day.*

Wells, Rosemary. *Timothy Goes to School.*

Williams, Vera B. *Something Special for Me.*

Winter, Jeanette. *Follow the Drinking Gourd.*

Woodruff, Elvira. *The Wing Shop.*

Yorinks, Arthur. *Louis the Fish.*

Zolotow, Charlotte. *A Tiger Called Thomas.*

Boastful

Bohdal, Susi. *Bird Adalbert.*

Dillon, Jana. *Jeb Scarecrow's Pumpkin Patch.*

Ernst, Lisa Campbell. *Zinnia and Dot.*

Gershator, Phyllis. *Sambalena Show-Off.*

Grifalconi, Ann. *Osa's Pride.*

Henkes, Kevin. *Chester's Way.*

————. *Sheila Rae, the Brave.*

Johnston, Tony. *The Cowboy and the Black-eyed Pea.*

Kent, Jack. *Silly Goose.*

McCully, Emily Arnold. *First Snow.*

McKissack, Patricia. *A Million Fish—More or Less.*

McPhail, David. *Pig Pig Rides.*

Meddaugh, Susan. *Hog-Eye.*

Oppenheim, Joanne. *You Can't Catch Me!*

Peet, Bill. *Cowardly Clyde.*

Schwartz, Amy. *Her Majesty, Aunt Essie.*

Sharmat, Marjorie Weinman. *The Best Valentine in the World.*

Stolz, Mary. *Storm in the Night.*

Waber, Bernard. *Ira Says Goodbye.*

Williams, Linda. *The Little Old Lady Who Was Not Afraid of Anything.*

Bored

Carle, Eric. *The Mixed-Up Chameleon.*

de Regniers, Beatrice Schenk. *Waiting for Mama.*

Flournoy, Valerie. *Tanya's Reunion.*

Garland, Michael. *Dinner at Magritte's.*

Ketteman, Helen. *The Year of No More Corn.*

Kroll, Steven. *The Tyrannosaurus Game.*

Noble, Trinka Hakes. *Meanwhile Back at the Ranch.*

Oram, Hiawyn. *In the Attic.*

Polacco, Patricia. *The Bee Tree.*

Raskin, Ellen. *Nothing Ever Happens on My Block.*

Van Allsburg, Chris. *Jumanji.*

Vincent, Gabrielle. *Feel Better, Ernest!*

Bossy

Allard, Henry. *Miss Nelson Is Missing.*

Browne, Anthony. *Piggybook.*

Cox, David. *Bossyboots.*

Leaf, Margaret. *Eyes of the Dragon.*

Lobel, Arnold. *On the Day Peter Stuyvesant Sailed into Town.*

Mwenye Hadithi. *Lazy Lion.*

Schwartz, Amy. *Her Majesty, Aunt Essie.*

Sendak, Maurice. *Where the Wild Things Are.*

Bullying

Brown, Marc. *Arthur's April Fool.*

Dillon, Jana. *Jeb Scarecrow's Pumpkin Patch.*

Keats, Ezra Jack. *Goggles.*

Kesey, Ken. *Little Tricker the Squirrel Meets Big Double the Bear.*

Mayer, Mercer, and Marianna Mayer. *One Frog Too Many.*

Peet, Bill. *The Spooky Tail of Prewitt Peacock.*

Rosenberg, Liz. *Monster Mama.*

Stevenson, James. *That Dreadful Day.*

Wildsmith, Brian. *The Lazy Bear.*

Yorinks, Arthur. *Whitefish Rides Again!*

Competitive

Allard, Henry. *Miss Nelson Has a Field Day.*

Brown, Marc. *Arthur's Chicken Pox.*

———. *Arthur's Teacher Trouble.*

Burton, Virginia Lee. *Mike Mulligan and His Steam Shovel.*

Crews, Donald. *Bicycle Race.*

Ernst, Lisa Campbell. *Sam Johnson and the Blue Ribbon Quilt.*

———. *Zinnia and Dot.*

Fox, Mem. *Koala Lou.*

Friedman, Aileen. *A Cloak for the Dreamer.*

Haugaard, Erik Christian. *Prince Boghole.*

Heine, Helme. *The Most Wonderful Egg in the World.*

Heinz, Brian. *The Alley Cat.*

Henkes, Kevin. *Julius, the Baby of the World.*

Hoffman, Mary. *Amazing Grace.*

Hutchins, Pat. *The Very Worst Monster.*

Isaacs, Anne. *Swamp Angel.*

Johnston, Tony. *Farmer Mack Measures His Pig.*

Keats, Ezra Jack. *Pet Show!*

Mahy, Margaret. *The Queen's Goat.*

Martin, Bill, and John Archambault. *Chicka Chicka Boom Boom.*

McBratney, Sam. *Guess How Much I Love You.*

McKissack, Patricia. *Mirandy and Brother Wind.*

Say, Allen. *El Chino.*

Schroeder, Alan. *Ragtime Tumpie.*

Cooperative

Day, Alexandra. *Frank and Ernest.*

Emberley, Barbara. *Drummer Hoff.*

Fair, Sylvia. *The Bedspread.*

Khalsa, Dayal Kaur. *Cowboy Dreams.*
Kimmel, Eric A. *Hershel and the Hanukkah Goblins.*
Leighton, Maxinne Rhea. *An Ellis Island Christmas.*
Luenn, Nancy. *Nessa's Fish.*
Marshall, James. *George and Martha Back in Town.*
Martin, Bill, and John Archambault. *Knots on a Counting Rope.*
Marzollo, Jean. *In 1492.*
McCully, Emily Arnold. *The Amazing Felix.*
———. *Mirette on the High Wire.*
Meddaugh, Susan. *Hog-Eye.*
Mendez, Phil. *The Black Snowman.*
Peet, Bill. *Cowardly Clyde.*
Pilkey, Dav. *Hallo-Weiner.*
———. *When Cats Dream.*
Polacco, Patricia. *Pink and Say.*
Pryor, Bonnie. *Lottie's Dream.*
Rosen, Michael. *We're Going on a Bear Hunt.*
San Souci, Robert. *Kate Shelley: Bound for Legend.*
Say, Allen. *El Chino.*
Shefelman, Janice Jordan. *A Peddler's Dream.*
Sis, Peter. *Follow the Dream.*
———. *A Small, Tall Tale from the Far, Far North.*
Smith, Barry. *The First Voyage of Christopher Columbus, 1492.*
Spier, Peter. *Father, May I Come?*
Steig, William. *Brave Irene.*
———. *Doctor De Soto.*
Turkle, Brinton. *Do Not Open.*
Ungerer, Toni. *Crictor.*
Van Allsburg, Chris. *Bad Day at Riverbend.*
Williams, Linda. *The Little Old Lady Who Was Not Afraid of Anything.*
Winter, Jeanette. *Follow the Drinking Gourd.*

Crying
Birdseye, Tom. *Airmail to the Moon.*
Bolliger, Max. *The Lonely Prince.*
Brunhoff, Jean de. *The Story of Babar.*
Bunting, Eve. *Smoky Night.*
———. *The Wall.*
Coerr, Eleanor. *The Josefina Story Quilt.*
Cohen, Miriam. *Lost in the Museum.*
dePaola, Tomie. *Nana Upstairs & Nana Downstairs.*
Garland, Sherry. *The Lotus Seed.*
Hathorn, Elizabeth. *Grandma's Shoes.*
Henkes, Kevin. *Sheila Rae, the Brave.*
Keller, Holly. *Furry.*
———. *The New Boy.*

Lawson, Julie. *The Dragon's Pearl.*
Lewin, Hugh. *Jafta—the Town.*
Lobel, Arnold. *Owl at Home.*
————. *Uncle Elephant.*
MacLachlan, Patricia. *Mama One, Mama Two.*
Marshall, James. *George and Martha.*
Maruki, Toshi. *Hiroshima No Pika.*
McCully, Emily Arnold. *The Christmas Gift.*
Neitzel, Shirley. *The Jacket I Wear in the Snow.*
Pollaco, Patricia. *Pink and Say.*
Potter, Beatrix. *The Tale of Peter Rabbit.*
Shea, Pegi Deitz. *The Whispering Cloth: A Refugee's Story.*
Sonnenschein, Harriet. *Harold's Runaway Nose.*
Speed, Toby. *Hattie Baked a Wedding Cake.*
Steig, William. *The Amazing Bone.*
————. *Brave Irene.*
————. *Doctor De Soto.*
Turner, Ann Warren. *Katie's Trunk.*
Uchida, Yoshiko. *The Bracelet.*
Waber, Bernard. *The House on East 88th Street.*
Williams, Vera B. *Something Special for Me.*
Yashima, Taro. *Crow Boy.*
Yolen, Jane. *Grandad Bill's Song.*

Curious

Andrews, Jan. *Very First Time.*
Aylesworth, Jim. *Shenandoah Noah.*
Bedard, Michael. *Emily.*
Brett, Jan. *Armadillo Rodeo.*
Gray, Libba Moore. *Small Green Snake.*
Grifalconi, Ann. *Darkness and the Butterfly.*
Hoban, Russell. *The Mole Family's Christmas.*
Krahn, Fernando. *The Secret in the Dungeon.*
Kroll, Virginia L. *Africa Brothers and Sisters.*
Marshall, James. *George and Martha Back in Town.*
————. *George and Martha, One Fine Day.*
McCully, Emily Arnold. *Mirette on the High Wire.*
Melmed, Laura. *The First Song Ever Sung.*
Norman, Philip Ross. *A Mammoth Imagination.*
Rey, H. A. *Curious George.*
Ringgold, Faith. *Dinner at Aunt Connie's House.*
Ryder, Joanne. *The Bear on the Moon.*
Say, Allen. *Stranger in the Mirror.*
Sheldon, Dyan. *Under the Moon.*
Soto, Gary. *Too Many Tamales.*
Steig, William. *The Amazing Bone.*

Tafuri, Nancy. *Rabbit's Morning.*
Wildsmith, Brian. *Goat's Trail.*
Williams, Barbara. *A Valentine for Cousin Archie.*

Destructive/Violent

Alexander, Martha. *Even That Moose Won't Listen to Me.*
Arnold, Tedd. *No Jumping on the Bed!*
————. *No More Water in the Tub.*
————. *The Signmaker's Assistant.*
Bang, Molly. *Dawn.*
Brown, Ruth. *The Big Sneeze.*
Bunting, Eve. *The Man Who Could Call Down Owls.*
————. *Smoky Night.*
Cleaver, Elizabeth. *Petrouchka.*
Cohen, Caron Lee. *Whiffle Squeek.*
Cole, Babette. *Hurray for Ethelyn.*
Dillon, Jana. *Jeb Scarecrow's Pumpkin Patch.*
Ernst, Lisa Campbell. *Zinnia and Dot.*
Gantos, Jack. *Rotten Ralph.*
Goodall, John S. *The Adventures of Paddy Pork.*
Hathorn, Elizabeth. *Way Home.*
Hutchins, Pat. *The Very Worst Monster.*
————. *Where's the Baby?*
Innocenti, Roberto. *Rose Blanche.*
Keats, Ezra Jack. *Hi, Cat!*
Keller, Holly. *The New Boy.*
Kellogg, Steven. *Pinkerton, Behave!*
Kesey, Ken. *Little Tricker the Squirrel Meets Big Double the Bear.*
Lawson, Julie. *The Dragon's Pearl.*
Le Guin, Ursula K. *A Ride on the Red Mare's Back.*
Lobel, Arnold. *The Rose in My Garden.*
Mattingley, Christobel. *The Angel with a Mouth-Organ.*
Mayer, Mercer. *Frog Goes to Dinner.*
Noble, Trinka Hakes. *The Day Jimmy's Boa Ate the Wash.*
————. *Jimmy's Boa Bounces Back.*
Peet, Bill. *The Spooky Tail of Prewitt Peacock.*
Polacco, Patricia. *Pink and Say.*
————. *Rechenka's Eggs.*
Rosenberg, Liz. *Monster Mama.*
Scamell, Ragnhild. *Solo Plus One.*
Seuss, Dr. *The Cat in the Hat.*
Steig, William. *Brave Irene.*
Turner, Ann Warren. *Katie's Trunk.*
Van Allsburg, Chris. *Just a Dream.*
————. *The Widow's Broom.*
Ward, Cindy. *Cookie's Week.*

Fighting/Quarreling

Cleaver, Elizabeth. *Petrouchka.*
Ernst, Lisa Campbell. *Zinnia and Dot.*
Gág, Wanda. *Millions of Cats.*
Heinz, Brian. *The Alley Cat.*
Hoban, Lillian. *Arthur's Great Big Valentine.*
Isaacs, Anne. *Swamp Angel.*
Keats, Ezra Jack. *Goggles.*
Marshall, James. *George and Martha 'Round and 'Round.*
Peet, Bill. *Cowardly Clyde.*
Sendak, Maurice. *Where the Wild Things Are.*
Steig, William. *Caleb & Kate.*
Turner, Ann Warren. *Katie's Trunk.*

Foolish

Duvoisin, Roger. *Petunia.*
Steig, William. *Sylvester and the Magic Pebble.*
Van Allsburg, Chris. *The Wretched Stone.*
Walsh, Ellen Stoll. *You Silly Goose.*

Forgetful

Bahr, Mary. *The Memory Box.*
Baker, Betty. *The Turkey Girl.*
Hayes, Sarah. *This Is the Bear and the Scary Night.*
Isadora, Rachel. *Willaby.*
Jonas, Ann. *Where Can It Be?*
King-Smith, Dick. *Farmer Bungle Forgets.*
Rice, Eve. *Sam Who Never Forgets.*
Rogers, Jean. *Runaway Mittens.*
Sharmat, Marjorie Weinman. *The Best Valentine in the World.*

Greedy

Bang, Molly. *Dawn.*
Chetwin, Grace. *Box and Cox.*
Christiansen, Candace. *Calico and Tin Horns.*
Coomb, Patricia. *The Magic Pot.*
Lawson, Julie. *The Dragon's Pearl.*
Lester, Helen. *Me First.*
Mwenye Hadithi. *Greedy Zebra.*
Van Allsburg, Chris. *The Sweetest Fig.*
Yee, Paul. *Roses Sing on New Snow.*

Heroic

Arnold, Tedd. *No More Water in the Tub!*
Bodkin, Odds. *The Banshee Train.*
Brown, Marc. *The True Francine.*
Browne, Anthony. *Tunnel.*
Calhoun, Mary. *High-Wire Henry.*
Carle, Eric. *The Honeybee and the Robber.*
Goodall, John S. *Paddy's New Hat.*

———. *Shrewbettina's Birthday.*

Hathorn, Elizabeth. *Way Home.*

Henkes, Kevin. *Sheila Rae, the Brave.*

Howard, Elizabeth Fitzgerald. *Papa Tells Chita a Story.*

Isaacs, Anne. *Swamp Angel.*

Kroll, Steven. *Friday the 13th.*

Le Guin, Ursula K. *A Ride on the Red Mare's Back.*

Lionni, Leo. *Frederick.*

McCully, Emily Arnold. *The Amazing Felix.*

Mendez, Phil. *The Black Snowman.*

Peet, Bill. *Cowardly Clyde.*

Pilkey, Dav. *Hallo-Wiener.*

Polacco, Patricia. *Appelemando's Dreams.*

San Souci, Robert. *Kate Shelley: Bound for Legend.*

Small, David. *Paper John.*

Steig, William. *The Amazing Bone.*

———. *Amos & Boris.*

Ungerer, Tomi. *Crictor.*

Walsh, Ellen Stoll. *You Silly Goose.*

Wildsmith, Brian. *The Little Wood Duck.*

Winter, Jeanette. *Follow the Drinking Gourd.*

Hiding

Ackerman, Karen. *The Tin Heart.*

Asch, Frank. *Turtle Tale.*

Baker, Keith. *Hide and Snake.*

Baylor, Byrd. *Amigo.*

Bedard, Michael. *Emily.*

Bennett, Jill. *Teeny Tiny.*

Brown, Ruth. *The Picnic.*

Bunting, Eve. *Fly Away Home.*

Christiansen, Candace. *Calico and Tin Horns.*

Coerr, Eleanor. *The Josefina Story Quilt.*

Freeman, Don. *Mop Top.*

Geisert, Arthur. *Pigs from A to Z.*

Gerstein, Mordicai. *William, Where are You?*

Houston, Gloria. *But No Candy.*

Hughes, Shirley. *The Big Alfie and Annie Rose Storybook.*

Jonas, Ann. *The Quilt.*

Keats, Ezra Jack. *Goggles.*

Koralek, Jenny. *The Cobweb Curtain: A Christmas Story.*

Marion, Jeff Daniel. *Hello, Crow.*

Marshall, James. *George and Martha, One Fine Day.*

Mayer, Mercer. *Frog Goes to Dinner.*

———. *There's an Alligator Under My Bed.*

Potter, Beatrix. *The Tale of Peter Rabbit.*

Steig, William. *Brave Irene.*
Turner, Ann Warren. *Katie's Trunk.*

Lying

Aylesworth, Jim. *Hanna's Hog.*
Brown, Marc. *The True Francine.*
McDonald, Megan. *The Great Pumpkin Switch.*
Ness, Evaline. *Sam, Bangs, & Moonshine.*
Polacco, Patricia. *Appelemando's Dreams.*
Yee, Paul. *Roses Sing on New Snow.*

Mischievous

Brown, Marc. *Arthur Babysits.*
Browne, Anthony. *Tunnel.*
Marshall, James. *George and Martha 'Round and 'Round.*
Mayer, Mercer. *Frog Goes to Dinner.*
Oppenheim, Joanne. *You Can't Catch Me!*
Sendak, Maurice. *Where the Wild Things Are.*
Slobodkina, Esphyr. *Caps for Sale.*
Van Allsburg, Chris. *The Garden of Abdul Gasazi.*
Ward, Cindy. *Cookie's Week.*
Wildsmith, Brian. *Goat's Trail.*

Obedient

Arnold, Tedd. *The Signmaker's Assistant.*
de Regniers, Beatrice Schenk. *Waiting for Mama.*
Grifalconi, Ann. *Flyaway Girl.*
Ness, Evaline. *Sam, Bangs, & Moonshine.*
Schwartz, Amy. *Oma and Bobo.*
Yolen, Jane. *Owl Moon.*

Patient

Adoff, Arnold. *Hard to Be Six.*
Alexander, Martha. *When the New Baby Comes, I'm Moving Out.*
Baylor, Byrd. *Amigo.*
———. *The Other Way to Listen.*
Bunting, Eve. *How Many Days to America? A Thanksgiving Story.*
Burningham, John. *Time to Get Out of the Bath, Shirley.*
Carlstrom, Nancy White. *I'm Not Moving, Mama!*
de Regniers, Beatrice Schenk. *Waiting for Mama.*
Flournoy, Valerie. *The Patchwork Quilt.*
Hayes, Sarah. *This Is the Bear and the Scary Night.*
Isadora, Rachel. *At the Crossroads.*
Kovalski, Maryann. *The Wheels on the Bus.*
Kraus, Robert. *Leo the Late Bloomer.*
Purdy, Carol. *Mrs. Merriwether's Musical Cat.*
Rudolph, Marguerita. *How a Shirt Grew in the Field.*
Schertle, Alice. *Witch Hazel.*
Shea, Pegi Deitz. *The Whispering Cloth: A Refugee's Story.*

Ketteman, Helen. *The Year of No More Corn.*
Kimmel, Eric A. *Hershel and the Hanukkah Goblins.*
Kovalski, Maryann. *The Wheels on the Bus.*
Krahn, Fernando. *Arthur's Adventure in the Abandoned House.*
Kraus, Robert. *Whose Mouse Are You?*
Lawson, Julie. *The Dragon's Pearl.*
Le Guin, Ursula K. *A Ride on the Red Mare's Back.*
Lionni, Leo. *Six Crows: A Fable.*
———. *Swimmy.*
Lobel, Arnold. *Ming Lo Moves the Mountain.*
———. *On the Day Peter Stuyvesant Sailed into Town.*
Luenn, Nancy. *Nessa's Fish.*
Mahy, Margaret. *The Queens' Goat.*
McDonald, Megan. *The Great Pumpkin Switch.*
Meddaugh, Susan. *Hog-Eye.*
———. *Martha Speaks.*
Mellecker, Judith. *Randolph's Dream.*
Norman, Howard A. *The Owl-Scatterer.*
Olaleye, Isaac O. *Bitter Bananas.*
Phillips, Mildred. *The Sign in Mendel's Window.*
Rand, Gloria. *Prince William.*
Reddix, Valerie. *Dragon-Kite of the Autumn Moon.*
Rice, Eve. *Peter's Pockets.*
Schwartz, Amy. *Her Majesty, Aunt Essie.*
Scott, Ann Herbert. *Sam.*
Small, David. *Paper John.*
Speed, Toby. *Hattie Baked a Wedding Cake.*
Steig, William. *Amos & Boris.*
———. *Brave Irene.*
Stevenson, James. *What's Under My Bed?*
Stewart, Sarah. *The Library.*
Tompert, Ann. *The Silver Whistle.*
Turkle, Brinton. *Do Not Open.*
Van Allsburg, Chris. *Bad Day at River Bend.*
———. *Jumanji.*
Vaughan, Marcia K., and Patricia Mullins. *The Sea-Breeze Hotel.*
Vincent, Gabrielle. *Feel Better, Ernest!*
———. *Smile, Ernest and Celestine.*
Wellner, Frances Ward. *Matthew Wheelock's Wall.*
Wild, Margaret. *The Very Best of Friends.*
Wildsmith, Brian. *Pelican.*
Williams, Vera B. *Music, Music for Everyone.*
Winter, Jeanette. *Follow the Drinking Gourd.*
Yolen, Jane. *The Seeing Stick.*
Yorinks, Arthur. *Bravo, Minski.*

————. *The Widow's Broom.*

Wildsmith, Brian. *The Lazy Bear.*

Ridiculing

Cole, Babette. *Hurray for Ethelyn.*

dePaola, Tomie. *Oliver Button Is a Sissy.*

Ernst, Lisa Campbell. *Sam Johnson and the Blue Ribbon Quilt.*

Gantos, Jack. *Rotten Ralph.*

Henkes, Kevin. *Chrysanthemum.*

Isadora, Rachel. *Ben's Trumpet.*

Keats, Ezra Jack. *Louie.*

Kent, Jack. *Silly Goose.*

Kroll, Steven. *Friday the 13th.*

Martin, Bill, and John Archambault. *The Ghost-Eye Tree.*

Turner, Ann Warren. *Katie's Trunk.*

Wells, Rosemary. *Timothy Goes to School.*

Wildsmith, Brian. *The Little Wood Duck.*

Yashima, Taro. *Crow Boy.*

Rude

Hughes, Shirley. *Alfie Gives a Hand.*

Lester, Helen. *Me First.*

Rosenberg, Liz. *Monster Mama.*

Running away *See also* **PERSONAL PROBLEMS—Running away**

Arnold, Tedd. *Green Wilma.*

Farber, Norma. *Return of the Shadows.*

Goodall, John S. *The Adventures of Paddy Pork.*

Johnston, Tony. *Farmer Mack Measures His Pig.*

Mahy, Margaret. *The Queen's Goat.*

Martin, Jacqueline Briggs. *Good Times on Grandfather Mountain.*

Ringgold, Faith. *Aunt Harriet's Underground Railroad in the Sky.*

Winter, Jeanette. *Follow the Drinking Gourd.*

Searching

Ackerman, Karen. *The Banshee.*

Albert, Burton. *Where Does the Trail Lead?*

Asch, Frank. *Happy Birthday, Moon.*

Baker, Keith. *Who Is the Beast?*

Baylor, Byrd. *Amigo.*

————. *The Other Way to Listen.*

Birdseye, Tom. *Airmail to the Moon.*

Brown, Marc. *Arthur's Christmas.*

Browne, Anthony. *Tunnel.*

Bunting, Eve. *Fly Away Home.*

————. *A Turkey for Thanksgiving.*

————. *The Wall.*

Carle, Eric. *The Rooster Who Set Out to See the World.*

Cohen, Miriam. *Lost in the Museum.*

Cole, Joanna. *The Magic School Bus in the Time of the Dinosaurs.*
———. *The Magic School Bus Inside the Earth.*
———. *The Magic School Bus Inside the Human Body.*
———. *The Magic School Bus Lost in the Solar System.*
———. *The Magic School Bus on the Ocean Floor.*
Dunbar, Joyce. *Four Fierce Kittens.*
Fatio, Louise. *The Happy Lion.*
Fisher, Aileen. *Listen, Rabbit.*
Fleming, Denise. *Barnyard Banter.*
Fox, Mem. *Possum Magic.*
———. *Wilfrid Gordon McDonald Partridge.*
Freeman, Don. *Corduroy.*
———. *A Pocket for Corduroy.*
Gág, Wanda. *Millions of Cats.*
Geisert, Arthur. *Pigs from 1 to 10.*
Gerstein, Mordicai. *William, Where are You?*
Glass, Andrew. *Jackson Makes His Move.*
Greenfield, Eloise. *Africa Dream.*
Haseley, Dennis. *The Old Banjo.*
Hathorn, Elizabeth. *Grandma's Shoes.*
Heinz, Brian. *The Alley Cats.*
Hutchins, Pat. *1 Hunter.*
———. *Where's the Baby?*
Inkpen, Mick. *Kipper.*
Johnston, Tony. *The Cowboy and the Black-eyed Pea.*
———. *Farmer Mack Measures His Pig.*
Jonas, Ann. *The Quilt.*
———. *The 13th Clue.*
———. *Where Can It Be?*
Joyce, William. *A Day with Wilbur Robinson.*
Kasza, Keiko. *A Mother for Choco.*
Keats, Ezra Jack. *Pet Show!*
Keller, Holly. *Horace.*
Kent, Jack. *There's No Such Thing as a Dragon.*
Krahn, Fernando. *The Mystery of the Giant Footprints.*
Kroll, Virginia L. *Africa Brothers and Sisters.*
Legge, David. *Bamboozled.*
Le Guin, Ursula K. *A Ride on the Red Mare's Back.*
Levitin, Sonia. *The Man Who Kept His Heart in a Bucket.*
Martin, Bill, and John Archambault. *Knots on a Counting Rope.*
Mayer, Mercer, and Marianna Mayer. *One Frog Too Many.*
McCloskey, Robert. *Blueberries for Sal.*
———. *Make Way for Ducklings.*
Moss, Thylias. *I Want to Be.*
Mwenye Hadithi. *Lazy Lion.*

Ness, Evaline. *Sam, Bangs, & Moonshine.*

Noble, Trinka Hakes. *Meanwhile Back at the Ranch.*

Norman, Philip Ross. *A Mammoth Imagination.*

Polacco, Patricia. *The Bee Tree.*

Ray, Deborah Kogan. *The Cloud.*

Ringgold, Faith. *Tar Beach.*

Rogers, Jean. *Runaway Mittens.*

Rosen, Michael. *We're Going on a Bear Hunt.*

Rylant, Cynthia. *An Angel for Solomon Singer.*

Say, Allen. *Grandfather's Journey.*

———. *Stranger in the Mirror.*

Schwartz, Amy. *Her Majesty, Aunt Essie.*

Scott, Ann Herbert. *Sam.*

Sheldon, Dyan. *Under the Moon.*

Sis, Peter. *An Ocean World.*

Sonnenschein, Harriet. *Harold's Runaway Nose.*

Steig, William. *Caleb & Kate.*

———. *Sylvester and the Magic Pebble.*

Tafuri, Nancy. *Have You Seen My Duckling?*

Tejima, Keizaburo. *Fox's Dream.*

———. *Owl Lake.*

Van Allsburg, Chris. *Bad Day at River Bend.*

———. *Two Bad Ants.*

Wahl, Jan. *My Cat Ginger.*

Wild, Margaret. *The Very Best of Friends.*

Wildsmith, Brian. *Give a Dog a Bone.*

Winter, Jeanette. *Follow the Drinking Gourd.*

Wood, Audrey. *Heckedy Peg.*

Woodruff, Elvira. *The Wing Shop.*

Yolen, Jane. *Grandad Bill's Song.*

———. *Owl Moon.*

———. *The Seeing Stick.*

Zolotow, Charlotte. *Mr. Rabbit and the Lovely Present.*

Selfish

Hoban, Russell. *A Birthday for Frances.*

Sharing

Aliki. *The Two of Them.*

Asch, Frank. *Happy Birthday, Moon.*

Bang, Molly. *The Paper Crane.*

Baylor, Byrd. *The Way to Start a Day.*

Baylor, Byrd, and Peter Parnall. *Your Own Best Place.*

Benjamin, Amanda. *Two's Company.*

Bolliger, Max. *The Lonely Prince.*

Browne, Anthony. *Piggybook.*

Bunting, Eve. *Smoky Night.*

dePaola, Tomie. *Jingle: The Christmas Clown.*

———. *Pancakes for Breakfast.*

———. *Watch Out for Chicken Feet in Your Soup.*

Ernst, Lisa Campbell. *Zinnia and Dot.*

Franklin, Kristine L. *The Old, Old Man and the Very Little Boy.*

Greenfield, Eloise. *She Comes Bringing Me That Little Baby Girl.*

Griffith, Helen V. *Grandaddy's Stars.*

Hathorn, Elizabeth. *Grandma's Shoes.*

———. *Way Home.*

Heinz, Brian. *The Alley Cat.*

Henkes, Kevin. *Chester's Way.*

Hill, Elizabeth Starr. *Evan's Corner.*

Hoban, Russell. *A Bargain for Frances.*

Hopkinson, Deborah. *Sweet Clara and the Freedom Quilt.*

Howard, Elizabeth Fitzgerald. *Papa Tells Chita a Story.*

Hutchins, Pat. *The Doorbell Rang.*

———. *You'll Soon Grow into Them, Titch.*

Innocenti, Roberto. *Rose Blanche.*

Isadora, Rachel. *Ben's Trumpet.*

Johnston, Tony. *Pages of Music.*

Keats, Ezra Jack. *Louie.*

Lawson, Julie. *The Dragon's Pearl.*

Lionni, Leo. *Cornelius: A Fable.*

———. *Frederick.*

Marshall, James. *George and Martha Back in Town.*

———. *George and Martha 'Round and 'Round.*

Mills, Lauren. *The Rag Coat.*

Minarik, Else Holmelund. *A Kiss for Little Bear.*

Mora, Pat. *A Birthday Basket for Tia.*

Ness, Evaline. *Sam, Bangs, & Moonshine.*

Pilkey, Dav. *Hallo-Weiner.*

Polacco, Patricia. *The Bee Tree.*

———. *Chicken Sunday.*

Reddix, Valerie. *Dragon-Kite of the Autumn Moon.*

Ringgold, Faith. *Dinner at Aunt Connie's House.*

Rosenberg, Liz. *Monster Mama.*

Rylant, Cynthia. *All I See.*

Say, Allen. *The Bicycle Man.*

———. *Tree of Cranes.*

Schwartz, Amy. *Annabelle Swift, Kindergartner.*

Scott, Ann Herbert. *On Mother's Lap.*

Shelby, Anne. *Potluck.*

Silverman, Erica. *Big Pumpkin.*

Steig, William. *Amos & Boris.*

Stevenson, James. *The Worst Person's Christmas.*

Stolz, Mary. *Storm in the Night.*

Titherington, Jeanne. *A Place for Ben.*

Tompert, Ann. *The Silver Whistle.*

Tyler, Anne. *Tumble Tower.*

Van Allsburg, Chris. *The Polar Express.*

Vincent, Gabrielle. *Merry Christmas, Ernest and Celestine.*

Wildsmith, Brian. *The Lazy Bear.*

Williams, Vera B. *Something Special for Me.*

Yolen, Jane. *Owl Moon.*

Zolotow, Charlotte. *Do You Know What I'll Do?*

Shy

Aylesworth, Jim. *Shenandoah Noah.*

Browne, Anthony. *Tunnel.*

Burningham, John. *Aldo.*

Hughes, Shirley. *Alfie Gives a Hand.*

Johnston, Tony. *Amber on the Mountain.*

Keats, Ezra Jack. *Louie.*

McCully, Emily Arnold. *First Snow.*

Rylant, Cynthia. *All I See.*

Say, Allen. *The Bicycle Man.*

Yashima, Taro. *Crow Boy.*

Stealing

Agee, Jon. *The Incredible Painting of Felix Clousseau.*

Aylesworth, Jim. *Hanna's Hog.*

Bunting, Eve. *The Man Who Could Call Down Owls.*

———. *Smoky Night.*

Cox, David. *Bossyboots.*

Ernst, Lisa Campbell. *Zinnia and Dot.*

Goodall, John S. *Paddy to the Rescue.*

———. *Shrewbettina's Birthday.*

Kellogg, Steven. *Pinkerton, Behave!*

McDonald, Megan. *The Potato Man.*

Meddaugh, Susan. *Martha Speaks.*

Olaleye, Isaac O. *Bitter Bananas.*

Phillips, Mildred. *The Sign in Mendel's Window.*

Seuss, Dr. *How the Grinch Stole Christmas.*

Small, David. *Paper John.*

Steig, William. *The Amazing Bone.*

———. *Caleb & Kate.*

Turner, Ann Warren. *Katie's Trunk.*

Ungerer, Tomi. *Crictor.*

Wildsmith, Brian. *Pelican.*

Wolff, Ferida. *The Woodcutter's Coat.*

Teasing

Asch, Frank. *Sand Cake.*

Brown, Marc. *Arthur's Chicken Pox.*

Olaleye, Isaac O. *Bitter Bananas.*
Price, Leontyne. *Aïda.*
Sis, Peter. *A Small, Tall Tale from the Far, Far North.*
Slobodkina, Esphyr. *Caps for Sale.*
Small, David. *Paper John.*
Soto, Gary. *Chato's Kitchen.*
Steig, William. *Doctor De Soto.*
Stevenson, James. *That Terrible Halloween Night.*
Van Allsburg, Chris. *The Mysteries of Harris Burdick.*
———. *The Sweetest Fig.*
———. *The Widow's Broom.*
Waggoner, Karen. *The Lemonade Babysitter.*
Wildsmith, Brian. *The Lazy Bear.*
Wood, Audrey. *Heckedy Peg.*
Yolen, Jane. *No Bath Tonight.*

Wise

Asch, Frank. *Turtle Tale.*
Carlstrom, Nancy White. *I'm Not Moving, Mama!*
Duvoisin, Roger. *Petunia.*
Franklin, Kristine L. *The Old, Old Man and the Very Little Boy.*
Grifalconi, Ann. *Darkness and the Butterfly.*
Lionni, Leo. *The Biggest House in the World.*
———. *Six Crows: A Fable.*
Lobel, Arnold. *Ming Lo Moves the Mountain.*

BELLS

Ehlert, Lois. *Feathers for Lunch.*
Van Allsburg, Chris. *The Polar Express.*

BICYCLES *See* **TRANSPORTATION—Bicycles**
BIOGRAPHY/LIFE STORIES *See also* **GRAPHIC AND PERFORMING ARTS**

Aliki. *The Two of Them.*
Conrad, Pam. *The Lost Sailor.*
Cooney, Barbara. *Hattie and the Wild Waves.*
———. *Island Boy.*
———. *Miss Rumphius.*
dePaola, Tomie. *The Art Lesson.*
Franklin, Kristine L. *The Old, Old Man and the Very Little Boy.*
Garland, Sherry. *The Lotus Seed.*
Golenbock, Peter. *Teammates.*
Houston, Gloria. *My Great-Aunt Arizona.*
Johnston, Tony. *Pages of Music.*
———. *Yonder.*
Lionni, Leo. *Matthew's Dream.*
Morimoto, Junko. *My Hiroshima.*
Oberman, Sheldon. *The Always Prayer Shawl.*
Provensen, Alice. *The Glorious Flight Across the Channel with Louis Bleriot, July 25, 1909.*

Pryor, Bonnie. *Lottie's Dream.*
Ray, Mary Lynn. *Pianna.*
Ringgold, Faith. *Aunt Harriet's Underground Railroad in the Sky.*
———. *Dinner at Aunt Connie's House.*
Say, Allen. *El Chino.*
———. *Grandfather's Journey.*
Schroeder, Alan. *Ragtime Tumpie.*
Shefelman, Janice Jordan. *A Peddler's Dream.*
Sis, Peter. *A Small, Tall Tale from the Far, Far North.*
Stewart, Sarah. *The Library.*
Wellner, Frances Ward. *Matthew Wheelock's Wall.*
Yolen, Jane. *Grandad Bill's Song.*
Zolotow, Charlotte. *This Quiet Lady.*

BIRDS *See* **ANIMALS—Birds**
BIRTH
Aliki. *The Two of Them.*
Asch, Frank. *The Last Puppy.*
Brown, Marc. *Arthur's Baby.*
Carle, Eric. *The Very Quiet Cricket.*
Ernst, Lisa Campbell. *Zinnia and Dot.*
Ginsburg, Mirra. *Good Morning, Chick.*
Leedy, Loreen. *Tracks in the Sand.*
MacLachlan, Patricia. *All the Places to Love.*
Martin, Bill, and John Archambault. *Knots on a Counting Rope.*
Polacco, Patricia. *Rechenka's Eggs.*
Scamell, Ragnhild. *Solo Plus One.*
Wilkon, Piotr. *Rosie the Cool Cat.*
Zolotow, Charlotte. *My Grandson Lew.*
———. *This Quiet Lady.*

BIRTHDAYS
Asch, Frank. *Happy Birthday, Moon.*
Bunting, Eve. *The Wednesday Surprise.*
Charlip, Remy. *Fortunately.*
Freeman, Don. *Mop Top.*
Goodall, John S. *Shrewbettina's Birthday.*
Hoban, Russell. *A Birthday for Frances.*
Hughes, Shirley. *Alfie Gives a Hand.*
———. *The Big Alfie and Annie Rose Storybook.*
Jonas, Ann. *The 13th Clue.*
Keats, Ezra Jack. *A Letter to Amy.*
Kellogg, Steven. *The Mysterious Tadpole.*
Lobel, Arnold. *Days with Frog and Toad.*
Lydon, Kerry Raines. *A Birthday for Blue.*
MacLachlan, Patricia. *All the Places to Love.*
Marshall, James. *George and Martha, Tons of Fun.*
Mayer, Mercer, and Marianna Mayer. *One Frog Too Many.*

Minarik, Else Holmelund. *Little Bear.*
Mora, Pat. *A Birthday Basket for Tia.*
Van Allsburg, Chris. *Just a Dream.*
Williams, Vera B. *Something Special for Me.*
Yamaka, Sara. *The Gift of Driscoll Lipscomb.*
Yashima, Taro. *Umbrella.*
Zion, Gene. *No Roses for Harry.*
Zolotow, Charlotte. *Mr. Rabbit and the Lovely Present.*

BOATS *See* **TRANSPORTATION**
BODY
Parts of body
Baker, Keith. *Who Is the Beast?*
Carle, Eric. *The Very Quiet Cricket.*
Cole, Joanna. *The Magic School Bus Inside the Human Body.*
Gershator, Phillis. *Sambalena Show-Off.*
Levitin, Sonia. *The Man Who Kept His Heart in a Bucket.*
Peet, Bill. *The Whingdingdilly.*
Polacco, Patricia. *Mrs. Katz and Tush.*
Ryder, Joanne. *My Father's Hands.*
Say, Allen. *Stranger in the Mirror.*
Woodruff, Elvira. *The Wing Shop.*
eyes
Brown, Marc. *Arthur's Eyes.*
Bunting, Eve. *Scary Scary Halloween.*
Ehlert, Lois. *Fish Eyes.*
Hoban, Russell. *The Mole Family's Christmas.*
Leaf, Margaret. *Eyes of the Dragon.*
Yolen, Jane. *The Seeing Stick.*
hair
Freeman, Don. *Mop Top.*
Nesbit, E. *Melisande.*
Yarbrough, Camille. *Cornrows.*
noses
Brown, Ruth. *The Big Sneeze.*
Sonnenschein, Harriet. *Harold's Runaway Nose.*
teeth
Birdseye, Tom. *Airmail to the Moon.*
Brown, Marc. *Arthur's Tooth.*
Joyce, William. *A Day with Wilbur Robinson.*
Kellogg, Steven. *Prehistoric Pinkerton.*
Marshall, James. *George and Martha.*
McCloskey, Robert. *One Morning in Maine.*
Steig, William. *Doctor De Soto.*
shape and size
Adoff, Arnold. *Hard to Be Six.*

Gerard, Roy. *Sir Cedric.*
Heide, Florence Parry. *The Shrinking of Treehorn.*
Henkes, Kevin. *The Biggest Boy.*
Hest, Amy. *The Purple Coat.*
Isaacs, Anne. *Swamp Angel.*
Joyce, William. *George Shrinks.*
Mitchell, Rita Phillips. *Hue Boy.*
Pilkey, Dav. *Hallo-Weiner.*
Steig, William. *Amos & Boris.*
Turkle, Brinton. *Do Not Open.*
Yolen, Jane. *All Those Secrets of the World.*

BUILDINGS *See* **STRUCTURES—Buildings**

BUSES *See* **TRANSPORTATION**

CAMPING *See also* **VACATIONS**
Baker, Jeannie. *Where the Forest Meets the Sea.*
Harvey, Brett. *Cassie's Journey: Going West in the 1860's.*
Locker, Thomas. *Where the River Begins.*
Ray, Deborah Kogan. *The Cloud.*
Shulevitz, Peter. *Dawn.*
Van Leeuwen, Jean. *Going West.*

CAROUSELS
Crews, Donald. *Carousel.*
Khalsa, Dayal Kaur. *Cowboy Dreams.*
Wildsmith, Brian. *Carousel.*

CARS *See* **TRANSPORTATION**

CHANGES *See also* **TRANSFORMATION**
Ackerman, Karen. *Araminta's Paintbox.*
Aliki. *The Two of Them.*
Allard, Harry. *Miss Nelson Is Missing!*
Anno, Mitsumasa. *Anno's Counting House.*
Asch, Frank. *Moon Bear.*
Benjamin, Amanda. *Two's Company.*
Brown, Marc. *Arthur's Eyes.*
Browne, Anthony. *Changes.*
Burton, Virginia Lee. *The Little House.*
———. *Mike Mulligan and His Steam Shovel.*
Carle, Eric. *The Mixed-Up Chameleon.*
Crews, Donald. *Sail Away.*
Finchler, Judy. *Miss Malarkey Doesn't Live in Room 10.*
Freeman, Don. *Dandelion.*
Gershator, Phillis. *Sambalena Show-Off.*
Goodall, John S. *The Story of a Castle.*
———. *The Story of a Farm.*
———. *The Story of a Main Street.*

Wilkon, Piotr. *Rosie the Cool Cat.*

Wolff, Ferida. *The Woodcutter's Coat.*

Woodruff, Elvira. *The Wing Shop.*

Yolen, Jane. *Letting Swift River Go.*

CHRISTMAS *See* **HOLIDAYS AND CELEBRATIONS**

CIRCUS

Blos, Joan. *Lottie's Circus.*

Brown, Marc. *Arthur's Chicken Pox.*

Chwast, Seymour. *The Twelve Circus Rings.*

dePaola, Tomie. *Jingle: The Christmas Clown.*

Ehlert, Lois. *Circus.*

Freeman, Don. *Bearymore.*

Gantos, Jack. *Rotten Ralph.*

Goodall, John S. *The Adventures of Paddy Pork.*

Marion, Jeff Daniel. *Hello, Crow.*

McCully, Emily Arnold. *Mirette on the High Wire.*

Munari, Bruno. *The Circus in the Mist.*

Spier, Peter. *Peter Spier's Circus!*

Wildsmith, Brian. *Brian Wildsmith's Circus.*

CLOCKS *See* **TIME—Clocks and other time-telling methods**

CLOTHING

Ackerman, Karen. *Song and Dance Man.*

Baker, Betty. *The Turkey Girl.*

Barrett, Judi. *Animals Should Definitely Not Act Like People.*

———. *Animals Should Definitely Not Wear Clothing.*

Brunhoff, Jean de. *The Story of Babar.*

Carlstrom, Nancy White. *Jesse Bear, What Will You Wear?*

Fleischman, Sid. *The Scarebird.*

Fox, Mem. *Shoes from Grandpa.*

Freeman, Don. *Dandelion.*

Henkes, Kevin. *The Biggest Boy.*

Houston, Gloria. *The Year of the Perfect Christmas Tree.*

Hutchins, Pat. *You'll Soon Grow into Them, Titch.*

Jonas, Ann. *Color Dance.*

Kuskin, Karla. *The Philharmonic Gets Dressed.*

Lobel, Arnold. *Uncle Elephant.*

Mahy, Margaret. *The Queen's Goat.*

Minarik, Else Holmelund. *Little Bear.*

Murphy, Jill. *All in One Piece.*

Neitzel, Shirley. *The Dress I'll Wear to the Party.*

———. *The Jacket I Wear in the Snow.*

Noble, Trinka Hakes. *Jimmy's Boa Bounces Back.*

Potter, Beatrix. *The Tale of Peter Rabbit.*

Schwartz, Amy. *Her Majesty, Aunt Essie.*

Steig, William. *The Amazing Bone.*

Mittens

Rogers, Jean. *Runaway Mittens.*

Pockets

Freeman, Don. *A Pocket for Corduroy.*

Rice, Eve. *Peter's Pockets.*

Van Allsburg, Chris. *The Polar Express.*

Shoes

Brett, Jan. *Armadillo Rodeo.*

Daly, Niki. *Not So Fast, Songololo.*

dePaola, Tomie. *Oliver Button Is a Sissy.*

Others

Ackerman, Karen. *The Tin Heart.*

Briggs, Raymond. *Father Christmas.*

Brown, Craig McFarland. *The Patchwork Farmer.*

Henkes, Kevin. *Owen.*

Hughes, Shirley. *The Big Alfie and Annie Rose Storybook.*

Keats, Ezra Jack. *Goggles.*

Kent, Jack. *Socks for Supper.*

Legge, David. *Bamboozled.*

Mendez, Phil. *The Black Snowman.*

Oberman, Sheldon. *The Always Prayer Shawl.*

Rudolph, Marguerita. *How a Shirt Grew in the Field.*

Spier, Peter. *Peter Spier's Rain.*

Tompert, Ann. *The Silver Whistle.*

Uchida, Yoshiko. *The Bracelet.*

Wells, Rosemary. *Timothy Goes to School.*

Yashima, Taro. *Umbrella.*

Zion, Gene. *No Roses for Harry.*

COLORS

Bang, Molly. *Yellow Ball.*

Baylor, Byrd. *Guess Who My Favorite Person Is.*

Brett, Jan. *Armadillo Rodeo.*

Brown, Craig McFarland. *The Patchwork Farmer.*

Carle, Eric. *The Mixed-Up Chameleon.*

Crews, Donald. *Bicycle Race.*

———. *Freight Train.*

Dunrea, Oliver. *The Broody Hen.*

Ehlert, Lois. *Color Farm.*

———. *Color Zoo.*

———. *Planting a Rainbow.*

Ernst, Lisa Campbell. *A Colorful Adventure of the Bee, Who Left Home One Monday Morning and What He Found Along the Way.*

Friedman, Aileen. *A Cloak for the Dreamer.*

Hest, Amy. *The Purple Coat.*

——. *The Bionic Bunny Show.*

Rathmann, Peggy. *Officer Buckle and Gloria.*

Wilkon, Piotr. *Rosie the Cool Cat.*

COMMUNITIES *See* **NEIGHBORHOODS AND COMMUNITIES**

CONSTRUCTION

Anno, Mitsumasa. *Anno's Alphabet.*

Agee, Jon. *The Return of Freddy LeGrand.*

Alexander, Martha. *Even That Moose Won't Listen to Me.*

Asch, Frank. *Mooncake.*

Baker, Jeannie. *Window.*

Blegvad, Lenore. *Anna Banana and Me.*

Briggs, Raymond. *The Snowman.*

Burton, Virginia Lee. *The Little House.*

——. *Mike Mulligan and His Steam Shovel.*

Carle, Eric. *The Very Hungry Caterpillar.*

Crews, Donald. *Ten Black Dots.*

Emberley, Barbara. *Drummer Hoff.*

Fleischman, Sid. *The Scarebird.*

Geisert, Arthur. *Pigs from A to Z.*

——. *Pigs from 1 to 10.*

Graham, Thomas. *Mr. Bear's Chair.*

Hoban, Tana. *Dig, Drill, Dump, Fill.*

Houghton, Eric. *The Backwards Watch.*

Hughes, Shirley. *The Big Concrete Lorry: A Tale of Trotter Street.*

Hutchins, Pat. *Changes, Changes.*

Johnston, Tony. *Amber on the Mountain.*

Keats, Ezra Jack. *Louie.*

——. *The Trip.*

Khalsa, Dayal Kaur. *Cowboy Dreams.*

Lobel, Arnold. *Ming Lo Moves the Mountain.*

McCloskey, Robert. *Make Way for Ducklings.*

McLerran, Alice. *Roxaboxen.*

Murphy, Jill. *What Next, Baby Bear!*

Mwenye Hadithi. *Lazy Lion.*

Provensen, Alice. *The Glorious Flight: Across the Channel with Louis Bleriot, July 25, 1909.*

Ringgold, Faith. *Tar Beach.*

Rounds, Glen. *Sod Houses on the Great Plains.*

Schertle, Alice. *Witch Hazel.*

Shecter, Ben. *Conrad's Castle.*

Small, David. *Paper John.*

Steig, William. *Amos & Boris.*

Turner, Ann Warren. *Heron Street.*

Vaughan, Marcia K., and Patricia Mullins. *The Sea-Breeze Hotel.*

Wegen, Ronald. *Sky Dragon.*
Wellner, Frances Ward. *Matthew Wheelock's Wall.*
Westcott, Nadine Bernard. *Peanut Butter and Jelly: A Play Rhyme.*

COWBOYS/COWGIRLS *See also* **RANCHES**

Brett, Jan. *Armadillo Rodeo.*
Johnston, Tony. *The Cowboy and the Black-eyed Pea.*
Khalsa, Dayal Kaur. *Cowboy Dreams.*
Rounds, Glen. *Cowboys.*
Van Allsburg, Chris. *Bad Day at Riverbend.*
Yorkins, Arthur. *Whitefish Will Rides Again!*

DANCE AND DANCERS *See* **GRAPHIC AND PERFORMING ARTS**
DANGER *See* **SAFETY/DANGER**
DAYS OF THE WEEK *See* **TIME—Cycles, days of the week**
DEATH

Adoff, Arnold. *Hard to Be Six.*
Alexander, Sue. *Nadia the Willful.*
Aliki. *The Two of Them.*
Brunhoff, Jean de. *The Story of Babar.*
Bunting, Eve. *Fly Away Home.*
————. *The Wall.*
Carrick, Carol. *The Foundling.*
Clifton, Lucille. *Everett Anderson's Goodbye.*
Coerr, Eleanor. *The Josefina Story Quilt.*
————. *Sadako.*
Cohen, Barbara. *Gooseberries to Oranges.*
Cooney, Barbara. *Island Boy.*
dePaola, Tomie. *Nana Upstairs & Nana Downstairs.*
Gould, Deborah Lee. *Grandpa's Slide Show.*
Gregory, Valiska. *Through the Mickle Woods.*
Hathorn, Elizabeth. *Grandma's Shoes.*
Lewin, Hugh. *Jafta—the Town.*
Maruki, Toshi. *Hiroshima No Pika.*
Mattingley, Christobel. *The Angel with a Mouth-Organ.*
Miles, Miska. *Annie and the Old One.*
Mills, Lauren. *The Rag Coat.*
Morimoto, Junko. *My Hiroshima.*
Oppenheim, Joanne. *You Can't Catch Me!*
Polacco, Patricia. *Mrs. Katz and Tush.*
————. *Pink and Say.*
Rand, Gloria. *Prince William.*
Shea, Pegi Deitz. *The Whispering Cloth: A Refugee's Story.*
Tejima, Keizaburo. *Swan Sky.*
Tsuchiya, Yukio. *Faithful Elephants.*

Viorst, Judith. *The Tenth Good Thing about Barney.*
Wild, Margaret. *The Very Best of Friends.*
Wilhelm, Hans. *I'll Always Love You.*
Yolen, Jane. *Grandad Bill's Song.*
Zolotow, Charlotte. *My Grandson Lew.*

DINOSAURS *See also* **HISTORICAL PERIODS—Prehistoric**

Carmine, Mary. *Daniel's Dinosaurs.*
Cohen, Miriam. *Lost in the Museum.*
Cole, Joanna. *The Magic School Bus in the Time of the Dinosaurs.*
Fleischman, Paul. *Time Train.*
Kellogg, Steven. *Prehistoric Pinkerton.*
Kroll, Steven. *The Tyrannosaurus Game.*

DISABILITIES

Bahr, Mary. *The Memory Box.*
Brown, Marc. *Arthur's Eyes.*
dePaola, Tomie. *Now One Foot, Now the Other.*
Fox, Mem. *Wilfrid Gordon McDonald Partridge.*
Lobel, Arnold. *On the Day Peter Stuyvesant Sailed into Town.*
MacLachlan, Patricia. *Through Grandpa's Eyes.*
Martin, Bill, and John Archambault. *Knots on a Counting Rope.*
McDonald, Megan. *The Potato Man.*
Roy, Ron. *Three Ducks Went Wandering.*
Wildsmith, Brian. *The Little Wood Duck.*
Winter, Jeanette. *Follow the Drinking Gourd.*
Yolen, Jane. *The Seeing Stick.*

DISASTERS *See also* **WEATHER—Storms; WATER AND BODIES OF WA-TER—Floods**

Alexander, Martha. *Even That Moose Won't Listen to Me.*
Arnold, Tedd. *No Jumping on the Bed!*
———. *No More Water in the Tub.*
———. *The Singmaker's Assistant.*
Brown, Ruth. *The Big Sneeze.*
Burningham, John. *Mr. Gumpy's Motor Car.*
———. *Mr. Gumpy's Outing.*
Coerr, Eleanor. *Sadako.*
———. *The Josefina Story Quilt.*
Conrad, Pam. *The Lost Sailor.*
Duvoisin, Roger. *Petunia.*
Ernst, Lisa Campbell. *Sam Johnson and the Blue Ribbon Quilt.*
Garland, Sherry. *The Lotus Seed.*
Hutchins, Pat. *Rosie's Walk.*
Lent, Blair. *Molasses Flood.*
Maruki, Toshi. *Hiroshima No Pika.*
Morimoto, Junko. *My Hiroshima.*
Noble, Trinka Hakes. *The Day Jimmy's Boa Ate the Wash.*

Paxton, Tom. *Engelbert the Elephant.*

Polacco, Patricia. *Rechenka's Eggs.*

Rand, Gloria. *Prince William.*

San Souci, Robert. *Kate Shelley: Bound for Legend.*

Speed, Toby. *Hattie Baked a Wedding Cake.*

Spier, Peter. *Father, May I Come?*

Tyler, Anne. *Tumble Tower.*

Van Allsburg, Chris. *The Alphabet Theatre Proudly Presents: The Z Was Zapped.*

———. *Two Bad Ants.*

———. *The Wreck of the Zephyr.*

Ward, Cindy. *Cookie's Week.*

Williams, Vera B. *A Chair For My Mother.*

DRAGONS *See* **IMAGINATION—Imaginary creatures**
DRAMA *See* **GRAPHIC AND PERFORMING ARTS**
DREAMS

Arnold, Tedd. *Green Wilma.*

Baylor, Byrd. *Guess Who My Favorite Person Is.*

Berger, Barbara. *The Donkey's Dream.*

Briggs, Raymond. *The Snowman.*

Brown, Marc. *Arthur's April Fool.*

Burningham, John. *Hey! Get Off Our Train.*

Carle, Eric. *The Rooster who Set Out to See the World.*

Carrick, Carol. *The Foundling.*

Cohen, Caron Lee. *Whiffle Squeek.*

Cooney, Barbara. *Miss Rumphius.*

Dragonwagon, Crescent. *Half a Moon and One Whole Star.*

Freeman, Don. *Bearymore.*

Friedman, Aileen. *A Cloak for the Dreamer.*

Ginsburg, Mirra. *Across the Stream.*

Greenfield, Eloise. *Africa Dream.*

Grifalconi, Ann. *Darkness and the Butterfly.*

Haley, Gail E. *Sea Tale.*

Henkes, Kevin. *The Biggest Boy.*

———. *Chrysanthemum.*

Jonas, Ann. *The Quilt.*

Joyce, William. *George Shrinks.*

Keats, Ezra Jack. *Dreams.*

———. *Louie.*

———. *The Snowy Day.*

Kellogg, Steven. *Pinkerton, Behave!*

Lionni, Leo. *Matthew's Dream.*

Lobel, Arnold. *On the Day Peter Stuyvesant Sailed into Town.*

Lyon, George Ella. *Cecil's Story.*

Mellecker, Judith. *Randolph's Dream.*

Mendez, Phil. *The Black Snowman.*
Ness, Evaline. *Sam, Bangs, & Moonshine.*
Peet, Bill. *The Spooky Tail of Prewitt Peacock.*
Pilkey, Dav. *When Cats Dream.*
Polacco, Patricia. *Appelemando's Dreams.*
Ryder, Joanne. *The Night Flight.*
Rylant, Cynthia. *An Angel for Solomon Singer.*
Sendak, Maurice. *Where the Wild Things Are.*
Sheldon, Dyan. *Under the Moon.*
Sis, Peter. *Follow the Dream.*
Steig, William. *Doctor De Soto.*
Stevenson, James. *Could Be Worse!*
Tafuri, Nancy. *Junglewalk.*
Turner, Ann Warren. *Nettie's Trip South.*
Twining, Edith. *Sandman.*
Van Allsburg, Chris. *Just a Dream.*
———. *The Sweetest Fig.*
Wiesner, David. *Free Fall.*
Yamaka, Sara. *The Gift of Driscoll Lipscomb.*
Yolen, Jane. *Encounter.*
Yorinks, Arthur. *Louis the Fish.*
Zion, Gene. *The Plant Sitter.*

ECOLOGY/ENVIRONMENTAL PROBLEMS

Baker, Jeannie. *Where the Forest Meets the Sea.*
———. *Window.*
Baylor, Byrd. *The Desert Is Theirs.*
Blos, Joan. *Old Henry.*
Bunting, Eve. *Someday a Tree.*
Burningham, John. *Hey! Get Off Our Train.*
Burton, Virginia Lee. *The Little House.*
Cherry, Lynne. *The Great Kapok Tree: A Tale of the Amazon Rain Forest.*
Cole, Joanna. *The Magic School Bus on the Ocean Floor.*
Cooney, Barbara. *Miss Rumphius.*
Lobel, Arnold. *On the Day Peter Stuyvesant Sailed into Town.*
Lydon, Kerry Raines. *A Birthday for Blue.*
McNulty, Faith. *The Lady and the Spider.*
Rand, Gloria. *Prince William.*
Ryder, Joanne. *My Father's Hands.*
———. *When the Woods Hum.*
Seuss, Dr. *The Lorax.*
Sis, Peter. *An Ocean World.*
Thompson, Colin. *The Paper Bag Prince.*
Turner, Ann Warren. *Heron Street.*

EMOTIONS
Anger

Disappointment

Bartone, Elisa. *Peppe the Lamplighter.*
Briggs, Raymond. *The Snowman.*
Brown, Marc. *Arthur's TV Trouble.*
dePaola, Tomie. *The Art Lesson.*
————. *Oliver Button Is a Sissy.*
————. *Pancakes for Breakfast.*
————. *Sing, Pierrot, Sing.*
Ernst, Lisa Campbell. *Sam Johnson and the Blue Ribbon Quilt.*
Fleischman, Paul. *The Animal Hedge.*
Flournoy, Valerie. *Tanya's Reunion.*
Freeman, Don. *Dandelion.*
Gomi, Taro. *Coco Can't Wait.*
Goodall, John S. *The Adventures of Paddy Pork.*
Henkes, Kevin. *Chrysanthemum.*
Keats, Ezra Jack. *Jennie's Hat.*
————. *The Snowy Day.*
Lionni, Leo. *Cornelius: A Fable.*
Mayer, Mercer. *A Boy, a Dog, and a Frog.*
McCully, Emily Arnold. *The Christmas Gift.*
Meddaugh, Susan. *Martha Speaks.*
Mills, Lauren. *The Rag Coat.*
Mitchell, Rita Phillips. *Hue Boy.*
Polacco, Patricia. *Rechenka's Eggs.*
Ray, Deborah Kogan. *The Cloud.*
Reddix, Valerie. *Dragon-Kite of the Autumn Moon.*
Sharmat, Marjorie Weinman. *The Best Valentine in the World.*
Shefelman, Janice Jordan. *A Peddler's Dream.*
Sonnenschein, Harriet. *Harold's Runaway Nose.*
Speed, Toby. *Hattie Baked a Wedding Cake.*
Van Allsburg, Chris. *The Polar Express.*
Viorst, Judith. *Alexander, Who Used to be Rich Last Sunday.*

Embarrassment

Birdseye, Tom. *Airmail to the Moon.*
Brown, Marc. *Arthur's Eyes.*
dePaola, Tommie. *Watch Out for Chicken Feet in Your Soup.*
Gershator, Phillis. *Sambalena Show-Off.*
Kroll, Steven. *Friday the 13th.*
Mayer, Mercer. *Frog Goes to Dinner.*
Meddaugh, Susan. *Martha Speaks.*
Pilkey, Dav. *Hallo-Weiner.*
Rathmann, Peggy. *Officer Buckle and Gloria.*
Rochelle, Belinda. *When Jo Louis Won the Title.*
Wells, Rosemary. *Timothy Goes to School.*
Wilkon, Piotr. *Rosie the Cool Cat.*
Yashima, Taro. *Crow Boy.*
Zion, Gene. *No Roses for Harry.*

Fear

Waber, Bernard. *The House on East 88th Street.*

———. *Ira Says Goodbye.*

Wild, Margaret. *The Very Best of Friends.*

Wilhelm, Hans. *I'll Always Love You.*

Wilkon, Piotr. *Rosie the Cool Cat.*

Williams, Karen Lynn. *When Africa Was Home.*

Williams, Vera B. *Something Special for Me.*

Winter, Jeanette. *Follow the Drinking Gourd.*

Wood, Audrey. *Heckedy Peg.*

Yolen, Jane. *Grandad Bill's Song.*

———. *The Seeing Stick.*

Yorinks, Arthur. *Louis the Fish.*

Zolotow, Charlotte. *A Tiger Called Thomas.*

ENEMIES

Asch, Frank. *Turtle Tale.*

Asch, Frank, and Vladimir Vagin. *Here Comes the Cat! = Siuda idet kot!*

Brunhoff, Jean de. *The Story of Babar.*

Bunting, Eve. *How Many Days to America? A Thanksgiving Story.*

Carle, Eric. *The Mixed-Up Chameleon.*

Christiansen, Candace. *Calico and Tin Horns.*

Coerr, Eleanor. *The Josefina Story Quilt.*

Cohen, Caron Lee. *Whiffle Squeek.*

Cole, Babette. *Hurray for Ethelyn.*

Ehlert, Lois. *Feathers for Lunch.*

Ernst, Lisa Campbell. *Zinnia and Dot.*

Fox, Mem. *Hattie and the Fox.*

Freeman, Lydia. *Pet of the Met.*

Ginsburg, Mirra. *Across the Stream.*

Goodall, John S. *The Adventures of Paddy Pork.*

Gray, Libba Moore. *Small Green Snake.*

Hathorn, Elizabeth. *Way Home.*

Hayes, Sarah. *This Is the Bear and the Scary Night.*

Heinz, Brian. *The Alley Cat.*

Hoban, Russell. *The Mole Family's Christmas.*

Hutchins, Pat. *1 Hunter.*

———. *Rosie's Walk.*

Isaacs, Anne. *Swamp Angel.*

Innocenti, Roberto. *Rose Blanche.*

Joyce, William. *George Shrinks.*

Keats, Ezra Jack. *Goggles.*

Krahn, Fernando. *Arthur's Adventure in the Abandoned House.*

Lionni, Leo. *Swimmy.*

Lobel, Arnold. *Uncle Elephant.*

Mattingley, Christobel. *The Angel with a Mouth-Organ.*

Mwenye Hadithi. *Crafty Chameleon.*

ENVIRONMENTAL PROBLEMS *See* **ECOLOGY/ENVIRONMENTAL PROBLEMS**

ESKIMOS *See* **UNITED STATES—Specific cultures, American Indians/Eskimos**

ETHNIC CULTURES

Jewish

Others

EVERYDAY EXPERIENCES

Seasonal activities *See* **TIME—Specific seasons**

Time of day

  awakening for the day

daytime

Adoff, Arnold. *Hard to Be Six.*

Arnold, Tedd. *The Signmaker's Assistant.*

Aylesworth, Jim. *The Folks in the Valley: A Pennsylvania Dutch ABC.*

Brown, Ruth. *The Picnic.*

Burningham, John. *Mr. Gumpy's Motor Car.*

———. *Mr. Gumpy's Outing.*

Carlstrom, Nancy White. *Jesse Bear, What Will You Wear?*

Clifton, Lucille. *Some of the Days of Everett Anderson.*

Cutler, Jane. *Darcy and Gran Don't Like Babies.*

Ehlert, Lois. *Growing Vegetable Soup.*

———. *Planting a Rainbow.*

———. *Red Leaf, Yellow Leaf.*

Fleming, Denise. *In the Tall, Tall Grass.*

Giganti, Paul. *How Many Snails? A Counting Book.*

Hellen, Nancy. *The Bus Stop.*

Henkes, Kevin. *Chester's Way.*

Hoban, Tana. *All About Where.*

Hoopes, Lyn Littlefield. *Wing-a-Ding.*

Hutchins, Pat. *Tidy Titch.*

———. *You'll Soon Grow into Them, Titch.*

Joyce, William. *George Shrinks.*

Keats, Ezra Jack. *Hi, Cat!*

———. *The Snowy Day.*

Kroll, Steven. *Friday the 13th.*

Lester, Alison. *Clive Eats Alligators.*

Lotz, Karen E. *Snowsong Whistling.*

Mayer, Mercer. *A Boy, a Dog, and a Frog.*

McCloskey, Robert. *One Morning in Maine.*

McKissack, Patricia. *A Million Fish—More or Less.*

Numeroff, Laura Joffe. *If You Give a Mouse a Cookie.*

Rogers, Jean. *Runaway Mittens.*

Ryder, Joanne. *Hello, Tree!*

———. *My Father's Hands.*

———. *A Wet and Sandy Day.*

Schwartz, Amy. *Bea and Mr. Jones.*

Tafuri, Nancy. *Rabbit's Morning.*

Viorst, Judith. *Alexander and the Terrible, Horrible, No Good, Very Bad Day.*

Westcott, Nadine Bernard. *Peanut Butter and Jelly: A Play Rhyme.*

Yolen, Jane. *No Bath Tonight.*

nighttime *See also* **SLEEPING**

Ackerman, Karen. *The Banshee.*

Adoff, Arnold. *Hard to Be Six.*

Asch, Frank. *Happy Birthday, Moon.*

Bennett, Jill. *Teeny Tiny.*

Berger, Barbara. *Grandfather Twilight.*
Cazet, Denys. *I'm Not Sleepy.*
Clifton, Lucille. *Some of the Days of Everett Anderson.*
Dillon, Jana. *Jeb Scarecrow's Pumpkin Patch.*
Fleming, Denise. *In the Tall, Tall Grass.*
Giganti, Paul. *How Many Snails? A Counting Book.*
Grifalconi, Ann. *Darkness and the Butterfly.*
Horwitz, Elinor Lander. *When the Sky Is Like Lace.*
Murphy, Jill. *Peace at Last.*
Rylant, Cynthia. *Night in the Country.*
Schertle, Alice. *Witch Hazel.*
Silverman, Erica. *Big Pumpkin.*
Wiesner, David. *Free Fall.*
Zolotow, Charlotte. *My Grandson Lew.*
sleeping *See* **SLEEPING**
EXPLORATION
Albert, Burton. *Where Does the Trail Lead?*
Baylor, Byrd. *The Other Way to Listen.*
————. *Your Own Best Secret Place.*
Blegvad, Lenore. *Anna Banana and Me.*
Burningham, John. *Come Away from the Water, Shirley.*
Carle, Eric. *The Mixed-Up Chameleon.*
Cole, Joanna. *The Magic School Bus in the Time of the Dinosaurs.*
————. *The Magic School Bus Inside the Earth.*
————. *The Magic School Bus Inside the Human Body.*
————. *The Magic School Bus Inside a Hurricane.*
————. *The Magic School Bus Lost in the Solar System.*
————. *The Magic School Bus on the Ocean Floor.*
Columbus, Christopher. *The Log of Christopher Columbus.*
Fatio, Louise. *The Happy Lion.*
Fritz, Jean. *The Great Adventure of Christopher Columbus.*
Jonas, Ann. *The 13th Clue.*
Keats, Ezra Jack. *The Snowy Day.*
Kellogg, Steven. *The Mysterious Tadpole.*
Krahn, Fernando. *The Secret in the Dungeon.*
Kraus, Robert. *Owliver.*
Lionni, Leo. *Fish Is Fish.*
————. *Inch by Inch.*
Locker, Thomas. *Where the River Begins.*
Marzollo, Jean. *In 1492.*
McCully, Emily Arnold. *School.*
Rice, Eve. *Peter's Pockets.*
Sis, Peter. *Follow the Dream.*
————. *An Ocean World.*
————. *A Small, Tall Tale from the Far, Far North.*

Hutchins, Pat. *The Very Worst Monster.*
———. *Where's the Baby?*
———. *You'll Soon Grow into Them, Titch.*
Joyce, William. *George Shrinks.*
Keats, Ezra Jack. *Peter's Chair.*
Kraus, Robert. *Whose Mouse Are You?*
MacLachlan, Patricia. *All the Places to Love.*
Polacco, Patricia. *The Keeping Quilt.*
Tafuri, Nancy. *The Ball Bounced.*
Titherington, Jeanne. *A Place for Ben.*
Wells, Rosemary. *Noisy Nora.*
Wilkon, Piotr. *Rosie the Cool Cat.*
Zolotow, Charlotte. *Do You Know What I'll Do?*

Family gatherings/Outings
Albert, Burton. *Where Does the Trail Lead?*
Asch, Frank. *Sand Cake.*
Benjamin, Amanda. *Two's Company.*
Brown, Marc. *Arthur's Family Vacation.*
Brown, Ruth. *The Picnic.*
Brunhoff, Jean de. *The Story of Babar.*
Bunting, Eve. *The Wall.*
———. *The Wednesday Surprise.*
Crews, Donald. *Bigmama's.*
———. *Sail Away.*
dePaola, Tomie. *An Early American Christmas.*
Dragonwagon, Crescent. *Home Place.*
Flournoy, Valerie. *Tanya's Reunion.*
Gould, Deborah Lee. *Grandpa's Slide Show.*
Hest, Amy. *The Purple Coat.*
Hoban, Russell. *Best Friends for Frances.*
———. *The Mole Family's Christmas.*
Houston, Gloria. *But No Candy.*
Howard, Elizabeth Fitzgerald. *Chita's Christmas Tree.*
Krahn, Fernando. *The Secret in the Dungeon.*
Lewin, Hugh. *Jafta and the Wedding.*
Locker, Thomas. *Where the River Begins.*
Martin, Bill, and John Archambault. *Knots on a Counting Rope.*
Mayer, Mercer. *Frog Goes to Dinner.*
McCully, Emily Arnold. *The Amazing Felix.*
———. *The Christmas Gift.*
———. *First Snow.*
———. *Picnic.*
Minarik, Else Holmelund. *Little Bear's Friend.*
Nesbit, E. *Melisande.*
Polacco, Patricia. *Chicken Sunday.*

Steig, William. *The Amazing Bone.*
———. *Brave Irene.*
———. *Sylvester and the Magic Pebble.*
Stevenson, James. *Don't You Know There's a War On?*
Tafuri, Nancy. *Follow Me!*
———. *Have You See My Duckling?*
Teague, Mark. *The Field Beyond the Outfield.*
Thomas, Jane Resh. *Lights on the River.*
Titherington, Jeanne. *Sophy and Auntie Pearl.*
Turner, Ann Warren. *Stars for Sarah.*
Twining, Edith. *Sandman.*
Tyler, Anne. *Tumble Tower.*
Viorst, Judith. *The Tenth Good Thing about Barney.*
Weller, Frances Ward. *Riptide.*
Wells, Rosemary. *Noisy Nora.*
Wiesner, David. *Hurricane.*
Wilkon, Piotr. *Rosie the Cool Cat.*
Williams, Karen Lynn. *When Africa Was Home.*
Williams, Sherley Anne. *Working Cotton.*
Williams, Vera B. *A Chair For My Mother.*
———. *Music, Music for Everyone.*
———. *Something Special for Me.*
Wood, Audrey. *Heckedy Peg.*
Yarbrough, Camille. *Cornrows.*
Yee, Paul. *Roses Sing on New Snow.*
Yolen, Jane. *All Those Secrets of the World.*
———. *Grandad Bill's Song.*
———. *Letting Swift River Go.*
———. *Owl Moon.*
———. *The Seeing Stick.*
Ziefert, Harriet. *A New Coat for Anna.*
Zion, Gene. *The Plant Sitter.*
Zolotow, Charlotte. *Mr. Rabbit and the Lovely Present.*
———. *My Grandson Lew.*
———. *This Quiet Lady.*
———. *A Tiger Called Thomas.*

Problems *See* **FAMILY PROBLEMS**
Siblings

Adoff, Arnold. *Hard to Be Six.*
Alexander, Martha. *Even That Moose Won't Listen to Me.*
———. *When the New Baby Comes, I'm Moving Out.*
Alexander, Sue. *Nadia the Willful.*
Arnold, Tedd. *No More Water in the Tub!*
Bartone, Elisa. *Peppe the Lamplighter.*
Birdseye, Tom. *Airmail to the Moon.*

Hopkinson, Deborah. *Sweet Clara and the Freedom Quilt.*
Houston, Gloria. *The Year of the Perfect Christmas Tree.*
Hughes, Shirley. *Alfie Gets in First.*
Isadora, Rachel. *At the Crossroads.*
Joyce, William. *George Shrinks.*
Kraus, Robert. *Whose Mouse Are You?*
Leighton, Maxinne Rhea. *An Ellis Island Christmas.*
Levinson, Riki. *Watch the Stars Come Out.*
Lewin, Hugh. *Jafta—the Journey.*
———. *Jafta—the Town.*
———. *Jafta's Father.*
Lobel, Arnold. *Uncle Elephant.*
Lyon, George Ella. *Cecil's Story.*
MacLachlan, Patricia. *Mama One, Mama Two.*
Mattingley, Christobel. *The Angel with a Mouth-Organ.*
Meddaugh, Susan. *Hog-Eye.*
Mellecker, Judith. *Randolph's Dream.*
Mitchell, Rita Phillips. *Hue Boy.*
Polacco, Patricia. *Pink and Say.*
Rayner, Mary. *Garth Pig and the Ice-Cream Lady.*
Ringgold, Faith. *Aunt Harriet's Underground Railroad in the Sky.*
Say, Allen. *Stranger in the Mirror.*
Schroeder, Alan. *Ragtime Tumpie.*
Shea, Pegi Deitz. *The Whispering Cloth: A Refugee's Story.*
Steig, William. *Gorky Rises.*
———. *Sylvester and the Magic Pebble.*
Stevenson, James. *Don't You Know There's a War On?*
Tafuri, Nancy. *Have You See My Duckling?*
Turner, Ann Warren. *Nettie's Trip South.*
Wilkon, Piotr. *Rosie the Cool Cat.*
Wood, Audrey. *Heckedy Peg.*
Yolen, Jane. *All Those Secrets of the World.*

Others

Bahr, Mary. *The Memory Box.*
Bartone, Elisa. *Peppe the Lamplighter.*
Browne, Anthony. *Piggybook.*
Christiansen, Candace. *Calico and Tin Horns.*
Lyon, George Ella. *Come a Tide.*
Murphy, Jill. *Peace at Last.*
Turner, Ann Warren. *Katie's Trunk.*
Tyler, Anne. *Tumble Tower.*
Uchida, Yoshiko. *The Bracelet.*

FARMS *See also* **ANIMALS—Farm; RANCHES**

Aylesworth, Jim. *The Folks in the Valley: A Pennsylvania Dutch ABC.*
———. *Hanna's Hog.*
Azarian, Mary. *A Farmer's Alphabet.*

Birdseye, Tom. *Airmail to the Moon.*
Brown, Craig McFarland. *The Patchwork Farmer.*
Brown, Ruth. *The Big Sneeze.*
Christiansen, Candace. *Calico and Tin Horns.*
Crews, Donald. *Bigmama's.*
Domanska, Janina. *Busy Monday Morning.*
Dunbar, Joyce. *Four Fierce Kittens.*
Dunrea, Oliver. *The Broody Hen.*
———. *The Painter Who Loved Chickens.*
Ernst, Lisa Campbell. *When Bluebell Sang.*
Fleischman, Paul. *The Animal Hedge.*
Fleischman, Sid. *The Scarebird.*
Fleming, Denise. *Barnyard Banter.*
Flournoy, Valerie. *Tanya's Reunion.*
Fox, Mem. *Hattie and the Fox.*
Garland, Michael. *My Cousin Katie.*
Ginsburg, Mirra. *Good Morning, Chick.*
Goodall, John S. *The Story of a Farm.*
Griffith, Helen V. *Georgia Music.*
———. *Grandaddy's Place.*
Hall, Donald. *The Farm Summer 1942.*
———. *Ox-Cart Man.*
Haseley, Dennis. *The Old Banjo.*
Herriot, James. *Blossom Comes Home.*
———. *Bonny's Big Day.*
Johnston, Tony. *Amber on the Mountain.*
———. *Farmer Mack Measures His Pig.*
———. *Yonder.*
Ketteman, Helen. *The Year of No More Corn.*
King-Smith, Dick. *Farmer Bungle Forgets.*
Lionni, Leo. *Six Crows: A Fable.*
Lobel, Arnold. *A Treeful of Pigs.*
Lyon, George Ella. *Cecil's Story.*
MacLachlan, Patricia. *All the Places to Love.*
Marion, Jeff Daniel. *Hello, Crow.*
Martin, Bill, and John Archambault. *Barn Dance!*
Martin, Jacqueline Briggs. *Good Times on Grandfather Mountain.*
Murphy, Shirley Rousseau. *Tattie's River Journey.*
Noble, Trinka Hakes. *The Day Jimmy's Boa Ate the Wash.*
Peet, Bill. *The Whingdingdilly.*
Pryor, Bonnie. *Lottie's Dream.*
Rylant, Cynthia. *Night in the Country.*
Schoenherr, John. *The Barn.*
Tafuri, Nancy. *Early Morning in the Barn.*
Turner, Ann Warren. *Dakota Dugout.*
Van Allsburg, Chris. *The Stranger.*

Baker, Keith. *The Dove's Letter.*
Briggs, Raymond. *Father Christmas.*
———. *The Snowman.*
Browne, Anthony. *Bear Hunt.*
Cazet, Denys. *I'm Not Sleepy.*
Dorros, Arthur. *Abuela.*
Grifalconi, Ann. *Darkness and the Butterfly.*
Hathorn, Elizabeth. *Grandma's Shoes.*
Joyce, William. *George Shrinks.*
Keats, Ezra Jack. *The Trip.*
Lyon, George Ella. *Together.*
Mellecker, Judith. *Randolph's Dream.*
Minarik, Else Holmelund. *Little Bear.*
Murphy, Jill. *What Next, Baby Bear!*
Ringgold, Faith. *Aunt Harriet's Underground Railroad in the Sky.*
———. *Tar Beach.*
Ryder, Joanne. *Catching the Wind.*
———. *The Night Flight.*
Sadler, Marilyn. *Alistair in Outer Space.*
Steig, William. *Gorky Rises.*
Titherington, Jeanne. *Sophy and Auntie Pearl.*
Van Allsburg, Chris. *The Widow's Broom.*
———. *The Wreck of the Zephyr.*
Wiesner, David. *Free Fall.*
———. *Tuesday.*
Wildsmith, Brian. *Carousel.*
Woodruff, Elvira. *The Wing Shop.*

FOOD AND EATING

Abolafia, Yossi. *A Fish for Mrs. Gardenia.*
Andrews, Jan. *Very First Time.*
Arnold, Tedd. *Green Wilma.*
Asch, Frank. *Moon Bear.*
———. *Mooncake.*
———. *Sand Cake.*
Bang, Molly. *The Paper Crane.*
Barrett, Judi. *Cloudy with a Chance of Meatballs.*
Baylor, Byrd. *Guess Who My Favorite Person Is.*
Bennett, Jill. *Teeny Tiny.*
Brown, Marc. *Arthur's Christmas.*
Brown, Ruth. *The Picnic.*
Bunting, Eve. *A Turkey for Thanksgiving.*
———. *The Valentine Bears.*
Burningham, John. *Where's Julius?*
Carle, Eric. *The Mixed-Up Chameleon.*
———. *The Very Hungry Caterpillar.*

———. *The Very Best of Friends.*
Wildsmith, Brian. *Carousel.*
———. *The Lazy Bear.*
Wilhelm, Hans. *I'll Always Love You.*
Wilkon, Piotr. *Rosie the Cool Cat.*
Williams, Karen Lynn. *When Africa Was Home.*
Williams, Vera B. *Music, Music for Everyone.*
Yamaka, Sara. *The Gift of Driscoll Lipscomb.*
Yolen, Jane. *Letting Swift River Go.*
Zolotow, Charlotte. *A Tiger Called Thomas.*
———. *The Unfriendly Book.*

FRUITS *See* **PLANTS; APPLES**

FURNITURE

Beds
Arnold, Tedd. *No Jumping on the Bed!*
Bennett, Jill. *Teeny Tiny.*
Carlstrom, Nancy White. *Who Gets the Sun Out of Bed?*
Christelow, Eileen. *Five Little Monkeys Jumping on the Bed.*
Dragonwagon, Crescent. *Half a Moon and One Whole Star.*
Fair, Sylvia. *The Bedspread.*
Gerstein, Mordicai. *Roll Over!*
Mayer, Mercer. *There's an Alligator Under My Bed.*
Rosen, Michael. *We're Going on a Bear Hunt.*
Stevenson, James. *What's Under My Bed?*
Wiesner, David. *Free Fall.*
Williams, Vera B. *Music, Music for Everyone.*
Wood, Audrey. *The Napping House.*

Chairs
Bunting, Eve. *A Turkey for Thanksgiving.*
Graham, Thomas. *Mr. Bear's Chair.*
Keats, Ezra Jack. *Peter's Chair.*
Scott, Ann Herbert. *On Mother's Lap.*
Williams, Vera B. *A Chair For My Mother.*
———. *Music, Music for Everyone.*

GAMES/PUZZLES/TRICKS
Anno, Mitsumasa. *Anno's Alphabet.*
Asch, Frank. *Sand Cake.*
Baker, Keith. *Hide and Snake.*
Bang, Molly. *Ten, Nine, Eight.*
Baylor, Byrd. *Guess Who My Favorite Person Is.*
Chwast, Seymour. *The Twelve Circus Rings.*
dePaola, Tomie. *Jingle: The Christmas Clown.*
Fleischman, Sid. *The Scarebird.*
Gardner, Beau. *What Is It? A Spin-About Book.*

Geisert, Arthur. *Pigs from A to Z.*

———. *Pigs from 1 to 10.*

Gerstein, Mordicai. *Roll Over!*

Goodall, John S. *The Adventures of Paddy Pork.*

Grindley, Sally. *Knock, Knock! Who's There?*

Heide, Florence Parry. *The Shrinking of Treehorn.*

Houston, Gloria. *My Great-Aunt Arizona.*

Hughes, Shirley. *The Big Alfie and Annie Rose Storybook.*

Hutchins, Pat. *What Game Shall We Play?*

Jonas, Ann. *The 13th Clue.*

———. *The Trek.*

Joyce, William. *George Shrinks.*

Kimmel, Eric A. *Hershel and the Hanukkah Goblins.*

Kroll, Steven. *The Tyrannosaurus Game.*

Kroll, Virginia L. *Africa Brothers and Sisters.*

Legge, David. *Bamboozled.*

Lester, Alison. *Clive Eats Alligators.*

———. *Magic Beach.*

———. *Tessa Snaps Snakes.*

Marshall, James. *George and Martha, One Fine Day.*

———. *George and Martha, Tons of Fun.*

McBratney, Sam. *Guess How Much I Love You.*

McCully, Emily Arnold. *The Amazing Felix.*

Mwenye Hadithi. *Tricky Tortoise.*

Pinkney, Brian. *Max Found Two Sticks.*

Polacco, Patricia. *The Bee Tree.*

Say, Allen. *The Bicycle Man.*

Seuss, Dr. *The Cat in the Hat.*

Van Allsburg, Chris. *Jumanji.*

Waber, Bernard. *The House on East 88th Street.*

Westcott, Nadine Bernard. *Peanut Butter and Jelly: A Play Rhyme.*

Wildsmith, Brian. *Puzzles.*

Williams, Barbara. *A Valentine for Cousin Archie.*

GARDENS *See also* **PLANTS; PUMPKINS**

Alexander, Martha. *Even That Moose Won't Listen to Me.*

Ehlert, Lois. *Eating the Alphabet: Fruits and Vegetables from A to Z.*

———. *Growing Vegetable Soup.*

———. *Planting a Rainbow.*

Gray, Libba Moore. *Small Green Snake.*

Lobel, Arnold. *Frog and Toad Together.*

———. *The Rose in My Garden.*

———. *Uncle Elephant.*

McNulty, Faith. *The Lady and the Spider.*

Potter, Beatrix. *The Tale of Peter Rabbit.*

Ryder, Joanne. *My Father's Hands.*

———. *The Snail's Spell.*

———. *Where Butterflies Grow.*

Schertle, Alice. *Witch Hazel.*

Titherington, Jeanne. *Pumpkin, Pumpkin.*

Van Allsburg, Chris. *The Garden of Abdul Gasazi.*

Williams, Linda. *The Little Old Lady Who Was Not Afraid of Anything.*

GHOSTS *See* **IMAGINATION—Imaginary creatures**

GIFTS

Ackerman, Karen. *Araminta's Paintbox.*

Aliki. *The Two of Them.*

Asch, Frank. *Happy Birthday, Moon.*

Asch, Frank, and Vladimir Vagin. *Here Comes the Cat! = Siuda idet kot!*

Aylesworth, Jim. *McGraw's Emporium.*

Bang, Molly. *Delphine.*

———. *The Paper Crane.*

Baylor, Byrd. *The Way to Start a Day.*

Bedard, Michael. *Emily.*

Brown, Marc. *Arthur's Christmas.*

Bunting, Eve. *The Mother's Day Mice.*

———. *The Valentine Bears.*

———. *The Wednesday Surprise.*

Coomb, Patricia. *The Magic Pot.*

dePaola, Tomie. *Jingle: The Christmas Clown.*

Flournoy, Valerie. *The Patchwork Quilt.*

Fox, Mem. *Shoes from Grandpa.*

———. *Wilfrid Gordon McDonald Partridge.*

Graham, Thomas. *Mr. Bear's Chair.*

Haley, Gail E. *Sea Tale.*

Herriot, James. *The Christmas Day Kitten.*

Hoban, Lillian. *Arthur's Great Big Valentine.*

Hoban, Russell. *A Birthday for Frances.*

———. *Emmet Otter's Jug-Band Christmas.*

———. *The Mole Family's Christmas.*

Horwitz, Elinor Lander. *When the Sky Is Like Lace.*

Houston, Gloria. *The Year of the Perfect Christmas Tree.*

Howard, Elizabeth Fitzgerald. *Chita's Christmas Tree.*

Hughes, Shirley. *Alfie Gives a Hand.*

Johnston, Tony. *Amber on the Mountain.*

———. *Pages of Music.*

Keats, Ezra Jack. *Jennie's Hat.*

———. *Louie.*

Keller, Holly. *Geraldine's Blanket.*

Kellogg, Steven. *The Mysterious Tadpole.*

Kent, Jack. *Socks for Supper.*

Lobel, Anita. *Alison's Zinnia.*

———. *Days with Frog and Toad.*
Lydon, Kerry Raines. *A Birthday for Blue.*
Marshall, James. *George and Martha 'Round and 'Round.*
———. *George and Martha, Tons of Fun.*
Mayer, Mercer, and Marianna Mayer. *One Frog Too Many.*
McCully, Emily Arnold. *The Christmas Gift.*
McDonald, Megan. *The Potato Man.*
McLerran, Alice. *I Want to Go Home.*
Mills, Lauren. *The Rag Coat.*
Minarik, Else Holmelund. *A Kiss for Little Bear.*
———. *Little Bear's Friend.*
Mora, Pat. *A Birthday Basket for Tia.*
Nones, Eric Jon. *Caleb's Friend.*
Numeroff, Laura Joffe. *If You Give a Mouse a Cookie.*
Polacco, Patricia. *Chicken Sunday.*
———. *Mrs. Katz and Tush.*
———. *Rechenka's Eggs.*
Rylant, Cynthia. *All I See.*
Say, Allen. *Tree of Cranes.*
Seuss, Dr. *How the Grinch Stole Christmas.*
Small, David. *Paper John.*
Stevenson, James. *The Night After Christmas.*
———. *The Worst Person's Christmas.*
Stewart, Sarah. *The Library.*
Tompert, Ann. *The Silver Whistle.*
Uchida, Yoshiko. *The Bracelet.*
Ungerer, Tomi. *Crictor.*
Van Allsburg, Chris. *The Polar Express.*
Wild, Margaret. *Thank You, Santa.*
Wildsmith, Brian. *Carousel.*
Williams, Barbara. *A Valentine for Cousin Archie.*
Williams, Vera B. *A Chair For My Mother.*
———. *Something Special for Me.*
Wood, Audrey. *Heckedy Peg.*
Yamaka, Sara. *The Gift of Driscoll Lipscomb.*
Yashima, Taro. *Umbrella.*
Zion, Gene. *No Roses for Harry.*
Zolotow, Charlotte. *Mr. Rabbit and the Lovely Present.*
———. *A Rose, A Bridge, and a Wild Black Horse.*

GOALS

Abolafia, Yossi. *A Fish for Mrs. Gardenia.*
Agee, Jon. *The Return of Freddy LeGrand.*
Arnold, Tedd. *The Signmaker's Assistant.*
Asch, Frank. *Moondance.*
Aylesworth, Jim. *Hanna's Hog.*

Bahr, Mary. *The Memory Box.*

Baker, Jeannie. *Window.*

Baker, Keith. *The Dove's Letter.*

Bang, Molly. *Dawn.*

Bartone, Elisa. *Peppe the Lamplighter.*

Baylor, Byrd. *Amigo.*

———. *Hawk, I'm Your Brother.*

Blos, Joan. *Lottie's Circus.*

———. *Old Henry.*

Brown, Marc. *Arthur's Teacher Trouble.*

———. *Arthur's TV Trouble.*

Browne, Anthony. *Piggybook.*

Bunting, Eve. *How Many Days to America? A Thanksgiving Story.*

———. *The Mother's Day Mice.*

———. *The Wednesday Surprise.*

Burton, Virginia Lee. *Mike Mulligan and His Steam Shovel.*

Castle, Caroline, and Peter Weevers. *Herbert Binns & the Flying Tricycle.*

Coerr, Eleanor. *Sadako.*

Cole, Babette. *Hurray for Ethelyn.*

Columbus, Christopher. *The Log of Christopher Columbus.*

Cooney, Barbara. *Miss Rumphius.*

Crews, Donald. *Bicycle Race.*

dePaola, Tomie. *The Art Lesson.*

Dillon, Jana. *Jeb Scarecrow's Pumpkin Patch.*

Ehlert, Lois. *Growing Vegetable Soup.*

———. *Planting a Rainbow.*

———. *Red Leaf, Yellow Leaf.*

Ernst, Lisa Campbell. *Sam Johnson and the Blue Ribbon Quilt.*

Fox, Mem. *Koala Lou.*

———. *Wilfrid Gordon McDonald Partridge.*

French, Fiona. *Anancy and Mr. Dry-Bone.*

Friedman, Aileen. *A Cloak for the Dreamer.*

Fritz, Jean. *The Great Adventure of Christopher Columbus.*

Gomi, Taro. *Coco Can't Wait.*

Graham, Thomas. *Mr. Bear's Chair.*

Grifalconi, Ann. *Flyaway Girl.*

———. *Osa's Pride.*

Griffith, Helen V. *Georgia Music.*

Haley, Gail E. *Sea Tale.*

Harvey, Brett. *Cassie's Journey: Going West in the 1860's.*

Hathorn, Elizabeth. *Grandma's Shoes.*

Haugaard, Erik Christian. *Prince Boghole.*

Heine, Helme. *The Most Wonderful Egg in the World.*

Hoffman, Mary. *Amazing Grace.*

Hopkinson, Deborah. *Sweet Clara and the Freedom Quilt.*

Houston, Gloria. *My Great-Aunt Arizona.*

————. *The Year of the Perfect Christmas Tree.*

Hughes, Shirley. *The Big Concrete Lorry: A Tale of Trotter Street.*

Isadora, Rachel. *Ben's Trumpet.*

Johnson, Angela. *When I Am Old With You.*

Johnston, Tony. *Amber on the Mountain.*

————. *Pages of Music.*

Keats, Ezra Jack. *Whistle for Willie.*

Lester, Alison. *The Journey Home.*

Lionni, Leo. *Matthew's Dream.*

Martin, Bill, and John Archambault. *Knots on A Counting Rope.*

Marzollo, Jean. *In 1492.*

Mattingley, Christobel. *The Angel with a Mouth-Organ.*

McKissack, Patricia. *Mirandy and Brother Wind.*

Mills, Lauren. *The Rag Coat.*

Noll, Sally. *Watch Where You Go.*

Polacco, Patricia. *The Bee Tree.*

————. *Chicken Sunday.*

————. *Thunder Cake.*

Provensen, Alice. *The Glorious Flight: Across the Channel with Louis Bleriot, July 25, 1909.*

Ringgold, Faith. *Aunt Harriet's Underground Railroad in the Sky.*

Rylant, Cynthia. *The Relatives Came.*

Sadler, Marilyn. *Alistair in Outer Space.*

Say, Allen. *El Chino.*

Schroeder, Alan. *Ragtime Tumpie.*

Shecter, Ben. *Conrad's Castle.*

Shefelman, Janice Jordan. *A Peddler's Dream.*

Silverman, Erica. *Big Pumpkin.*

Sis, Peter. *Follow the Dream.*

Smith, Barry. *The First Voyage of Christopher Columbus 1492.*

Soto, Gary. *Chato's Kitchen.*

Tafuri, Nancy. *Have You See My Duckling?*

Titherington, Jeanne. *A Place for Ben.*

————. *Pumpkin, Pumpkin.*

Tompert, Ann. *The Silver Whistle.*

Van Allsburg, Chris. *Jumanji.*

————. *The Wreck of the Zephyr.*

Wellner, Frances Ward. *Matthew Wheelock's Wall.*

Williams, Karen Lynn. *When Africa Was Home.*

Winter, Jeanette. *Follow the Drinking Gourd.*

Yee, Paul. *Roses Sing on New Snow.*

Yorinks, Arthur. *Bravo, Minski.*

Ziefert, Harriet. *A New Coat for Anna.*

GOBLINS *See* **IMAGINATION—Imaginary creatures, others**

GRAPHIC AND PERFORMING ARTS
Art and artists

Ackerman, Karen. *Araminta's Paintbox.*

Agee, Jon. *The Incredible Painting of Felix Clousseau.*

Asch, Frank. *Sand Cake.*

Bang, Molly. *The Paper Crane.*

Browne, Anthony. *Bear Hunt.*

Coerr, Eleanor. *Sadako.*

Cole, Joanna. *The Magic School Bus Inside the Earth.*

———. *The Magic School Bus Inside the Human Body.*

———. *The Magic School Bus Lost in the Solar System.*

———. *The Magic School Bus on the Ocean Floor.*

Cooney, Barbara. *Hattie and the Wild Waves.*

dePaola, Tomie. *The Art Lesson.*

———. *An Early American Christmas.*

Dunrea, Oliver. *The Painter Who Loved Chickens.*

Ernst, Lisa Campbell. *Sam Johnson and the Blue Ribbon Quilt.*

Freeman, Don. *Norman the Doorman.*

Garland, Michael. *Dinner at Magritte's.*

Glass, Andrew. *Jackson Makes His Move.*

Grifalconi, Ann. *Osa's Pride.*

Hoban, Lillian. *Arthur's Great Big Valentine.*

Hunt, Jonathan. *Illuminations.*

Isadora, Rachel. *The Pirates of Bedford Street.*

———. *Willaby.*

Johnston, Tony. *Pages of Music.*

Keats, Ezra Jack. *Dreams.*

———. *Louie.*

———. *The Trip.*

Ketteman, Helen. *The Year of No More Corn.*

Leaf, Margaret. *Eyes of the Dragon.*

Lionni, Leo. *Matthew's Dream.*

Marshall, James. *George and Martha 'Round and 'Round.*

Martin, Jacqueline Briggs. *Good Times on Grandfather Mountain.*

Miles, Miska. *Annie and the Old One.*

Minarik, Else Holmelund. *A Kiss for Little Bear.*

Modell, Frank. *One Zillion Valentines.*

Polacco, Patricia. *Appelemando's Dreams.*

———. *Chicken Sunday.*

———. *Rechenka's Eggs.*

Radin, Ruth Yaffe. *A Winter Place.*

Reddix, Valeria. *Dragon-Kite of the Autumn Moon.*

Ringgold, Faith. *Dinner At Aunt Connie's House.*

———. *Tar Beach.*

Rylant, Cynthia. *All I See.*

Say, Allen. *Tree of Cranes.*
Sharmat, Marjorie Weinman. *The Best Valentine in the World.*
Shea, Pegi Deitz. *The Whispering Cloth: A Refugee's Story.*
Small, David. *Paper John.*
Testa, Fulvio. *If You Take a Pencil.*
Tompert, Ann. *The Silver Whistle.*
Van Allsburg, Chris. *Bad Day at Riverbend.*
Walsh, Ellen Stoll. *Mouse Paint.*
Wild, Margaret. *Thank You, Santa.*
Yamaka, Sara. *The Gift of Driscoll Lipscomb.*
Yolen, Jane. *The Seeing Stick.*

Dance and dancers

Ackerman, Karen. *Song and Dance Man.*
Asch, Frank. *Moondance.*
Babbitt, Natalie. *Nellie: A Cat on Her Own.*
Baker, Betty. *The Turkey Girl.*
Bang, Molly. *The Paper Crane.*
Brett, Jan. *Armadillo Rodeo.*
———. *Berlioz the Bear.*
Cleaver, Elizabeth. *Petrouchka.*
dePaola, Tomie. *Oliver Button Is a Sissy.*
Freeman, Lydia. *Pet of the Met.*
Gauch, Patricia Lee. *Tanya and Emily in a Dance for Two.*
Gershator, Phillis. *Sambalena Show-Off.*
Isadora, Rachel. *At the Crossroads.*
———. *Max.*
———. *Opening Night.*
Johnston, Tony. *Amber on the Mountain.*
Jonas, Ann. *Color Dance.*
Lobel, Arnold. *Ming Lo Moves the Mountain.*
Martin, Bill, and John Archambault. *Barn Dance!*
McKissack, Patricia. *Mirandy and Brother Wind.*
Moss, Thylias. *I Want to Be.*
Paxton, Tom. *Engelbert the Elephant.*
Schroeder, Alan. *Ragtime Tumpie.*
Sendak, Maurice. *Where the Wild Things Are.*
Steig, William. *Brave Irene.*
Vincent, Gabrielle. *Merry Christmas, Ernest and Celestine.*
Waggoner, Karen. *The Lemonade Babysitter.*
Walsh, Ellen Stoll. *Hop Jump.*
Williams, Vera B. *Music, Music for Everyone.*

Drama and actors *See also* **STORYTELLING**

Brown, Marc. *Arthur's April Fool.*
———. *Arthur's Thanksgiving.*
dePaola, Tomie. *Sing, Pierrot, Sing.*

Luenn, Nancy. *Nessa's Fish.*
Marshall, James. *George and Martha, Tons of Fun.*
Martin, Bill, and John Archambault. *Barn Dance!*
Martin, Jacqueline Briggs. *Good Times on Grandfather Mountain.*
Mattingley, Christobel. *The Angel with a Mouth-Organ.*
Mayer, Mercer. *Frog Goes to Dinner.*
McCully, Emily Arnold. *The Amazing Felix.*
Melmed, Laura. *The First Song Ever Sung.*
Moss, Lloyd. *Zin! Zin! Zin! A Violin.*
Moss, Thylias. *I Want to Be.*
Pinkney, Brian. *Max Found Two Sticks.*
Polacco, Patricia. *Chicken Sunday.*
Price, Leontyne. *Aïda.*
Purdy, Carol. *Mrs. Merriwether's Musical Cat.*
Ray, Mary Lyn. *Pianna.*
Rydell, Katy. *Wind Says Good Night.*
Rylant, Cynthia. *All I See.*
Schroeder, Alan. *Carolina Shout!*
Speed, Toby. *Hattie Baked a Wedding Cake.*
Steig, William. *The Amazing Bone.*
Thomas, Jane Resh. *Lights on the River.*
Vincent, Gabrielle. *Merry Christmas, Ernest and Celestine.*
Wildsmith, Brian. *Goat's Trail.*
Wilkon, Piotr. *Rosie the Cool Cat.*
Williams, Vera B. *Music, Music for Everyone.*
————. *Something Special for Me.*
Winter, Jeanette. *Follow the Drinking Gourd.*
Yorinks, Arthur. *Bravo, Minski.*
————. *Whitefish Will Rides Again!*

HALLOWEEN *See* HOLIDAYS AND CELEBRATIONS
HARBORS *See* WATER AND BODIES OF WATER—Harbors
HEALTH
Bathing
Allen, Pamela. *Mr. Archimedes' Bath.*
Arnold, Tedd. *No More Water in the Tub!*
Aylesworth, Jim. *Shenandoah Noah.*
Burningham, John. *Time to Get Out of the Bath, Shirley.*
Kuskin, Karla. *The Philharmonic Gets Dressed.*
Marshall, James. *George and Martha.*
Mayer, Mercer. *A Boy, a Dog, and a Frog.*
Murphy, Jill. *What Next, Baby Bear!*
Schwartz, Amy. *Her Majesty, Aunt Essie.*
Yolen, Jane. *No Bath Tonight.*
Zion, Gene. *Harry, the Dirty Dog.*

Cohen, Barbara. *Gooseberries to Oranges.*
Cooney, Barbara. *Hattie and the Wild Waves.*
De Paola, Tomie. *An Early American Christmas.*
Dragonwagon, Crescent. *Home Place.*
Goodall, John S. *An Edwardian Christmas.*
Howard, Elizabeth Fitzgerald. *Papa Tells Chita a Story.*
Houston, Gloria. *My Great-Aunt Arizona.*
Leighton, Maxinne Rhea. *An Ellis Island Christmas.*
Levinson, Riki. *Watch the Stars Come Out.*
Lyon, George Ella. *Cecil's Story.*
Polacco, Patricia. *Pink and Say.*
Radin, Ruth Yaffe. *A Winter Place.*
Rudolph, Marguerita. *How a Shirt Grew in the Field.*
San Souci, Robert. *Kate Shelley: Bound for Legend.*
Sis, Peter. *A Small, Tall Tale from the Far, Far North.*
Stone, Bernard. *A Day to Remember.*
Turner, Ann Warren. *Nettie's Trip South.*

pioneer/westward movement

Ackerman, Karen. *Araminta's Paintbox.*
Aylesworth, Jim. *The Folks in the Valley: A Pennsylvania Dutch ABC.*
Coerr, Eleanor. *The Josefina Story Quilt.*
Harvey, Brett. *Cassie's Journey: Going West in the 1860's.*
Johnston, Tony. *The Quilt Story.*
————. *Yonder.*
Lydon, Kerry Raines. *A Birthday for Blue.*
Pryor, Bonnie. *Lottie's Dream.*
Rounds, Glen. *Sod Houses on the Great Plains.*
Turner, Ann Warren. *Dakota Dugout.*
Van Allsburg, Chris. *Bad Day at Riverbend.*
Van Leeuwen, Jean. *Going West.*
Yorkins, Arthur. *Whitefish Will Rides Again!*

Prehistoric

Baylor, Byrd. *The Way to Start a Day.*
Cole, Joanna. *The Magic School Bus in the Time of the Dinosaurs.*
Fleischman, Paul. *Time Train.*
Sheldon, Dyan. *Under the Moon.*

Twentieth Century

early

Aylesworth, Jim. *Country Crossing.*
Bartone, Elisa. *Peppe the Lamplighter.*
Bodkin, Odds. *The Banshee Train.*
Ernst, Lisa Campbell. *Sam Johnson and the Blue Ribbon Quilt.*
Hartley, Deborah. *Up North in Winter.*
Hendershot, Judith. *In Coal Country.*
Houston, Gloria. *My Great-Aunt Arizona.*
————. *The Year of the Perfect Christmas Tree.*

Howard, Elizabeth Fitzgerald. *Aunt Flossie's Hats (And Crab Cakes Later)*.

————. *Chita's Christmas Tree*.

————. *The Train to Lulu's*.

Isadora, Rachel. *Ben's Trumpet*.

Ketteman, Helen. *The Year of No More Corn*.

McCully, Emily Arnold. *The Amazing Felix*.

————. *Mirette on the High Wire*.

McDonald, Megan. *The Great Pumpkin Switch*.

————. *The Potato Man*.

Provensen, Alice. *The Glorious Flight: Across the Channel with Louis Bleriot, July 25, 1909*.

Ringgold, Faith. *Tar Beach*.

Schroeder, Alan. *Carolina Shout!*

————. *Ragtime Tumpie*.

Shefelman, Janice Jordan. *A Peddler's Dream*.

Yee, Paul. *Roses Sing on New Snow*.

World War II

Coerr, Eleanor. *Sadako*.

Friedman, Ina R. *How My Parents Learned to Eat*.

Hall, Donald. *The Farm Summer 1942*.

Houston, Gloria. *But No Candy*.

Innocenti, Roberto. *Rose Blanche*.

Maruki, Toshi. *Hiroshima No Pika*.

Mattingley, Christobel. *The Angel with a Mouth-Organ*.

Mellecker, Judith. *Randolph's Dream*.

Morimoto, Junko. *My Hiroshima*.

Say, Allen. *The Bicycle Man*.

Stevenson, James. *Don't You Know There's a War On?*

Tsuchiya, Yukio. *Faithful Elephants*.

Uchida, Yoshiko. *The Bracelet*.

Yolen, Jane. *All Those Secrets of the World*.

Ziefert, Harriet. *A New Coat for Anna*.

modern/contemporary

Bunting, Eve. *The Wall*.

HOBBIES

Bottner, Barbara. *Hurricane Music*.

dePaola, Tomie. *The Art Lesson*.

Marshall, James. *George and Martha, One Fine Day*.

————. *George and Martha, Tons of Fun*.

McCully, Emily Arnold. *The Amazing Felix*.

Pinkney, Brian. *Max Found Two Sticks*.

Steig, William. *Sylvester and the Magic Pebble*.

Stewart, Sarah. *The Library*.

HOLIDAYS AND CELEBRATIONS

April Fool's Day

Brown, Marc. *Arthur's April Fool*.

Celebrations around the World
  Coerr, Eleanor. *Sadako.*
  Ets, Marie Hall, and Aurora Labastida. *Nine Days to Christmas.*
  Lewin, Hugh. *Jafta and the Wedding.*
Christmas
  Berger, Barbara. *The Donkey's Dream.*
  Briggs, Raymond. *Father Christmas.*
  Brown, Marc. *Arthur's Christmas.*
  dePaola, Tomie. *An Early American Christmas.*
  ———. *Jingle: The Christmas Clown.*
  Ets, Marie Hall, and Aurora Labastida. *Nine Days to Christmas.*
  Goodall, John S. *An Edwardian Christmas.*
  Heath, Amy. *Sofie's Role.*
  Herriot, James. *The Christmas Day Kitten.*
  Hoban, Russell. *Emmet Otter's Jug-Band Christmas.*
  ———. *The Mole Family's Christmas.*
  Houston, Gloria. *My Great-Aunt Arizona.*
  ———. *The Year of the Perfect Christmas Tree.*
  Howard, Elizabeth Fitzgerald. *Chita's Christmas Tree.*
  Johnston, Tony. *Pages of Music.*
  Koralek, Jenny. *The Cobweb Curtain: A Christmas Story.*
  Leighton, Maxinne Rhea. *An Ellis Island Christmas.*
  Mattingley, Christobel. *The Angel with a Mouth-Organ.*
  McCully, Emily Arnold. *The Christmas Gift.*
  McDonald, Megan. *The Potato Man.*
  Mendez, Phil. *The Black Snowman.*
  Say, Allen. *Tree of Cranes.*
  Seuss, Dr. *How the Grinch Stole Christmas.*
  Soto, Gary. *Too Many Tamales.*
  Spier, Peter. *Peter Spier's Christmas!*
  Stevenson, James. *The Night After Christmas.*
  ———. *The Worst Person's Christmas.*
  Stone, Bernard. *A Day to Remember.*
  Thomas, Jane Resh. *Lights on the River.*
  Tompert, Ann. *The Silver Whistle.*
  Van Allsburg, Chris. *The Polar Express.*
  Vincent, Gabrielle. *Merry Christmas, Ernest and Celestine.*
  Wild, Margaret. *Thank You, Santa.*
  Ziefert, Harriet. *A New Coat for Anna.*
Easter
  Polacco, Patricia. *Chicken Sunday.*
  ———. *Rechenka's Eggs.*
Halloween
  Brown, Marc. *Arthur's Halloween.*
  Bunting, Eve. *Scary Scary Halloween.*

IDENTITY
Gender roles

Asch, Frank. *Just Like Daddy.*
Aylesworth, Jim. *Hanna's Hog.*
Blegvad, Lenore. *Anna Banana and Me.*
Brown, Craig McFarland. *The Patchwork Farmer.*
Browne, Anthony. *Piggybook.*
———. *Tunnel.*
Carle, Eric. *The Very Quiet Cricket.*
Cooney, Barbara. *Hattie and the Wild Waves.*
———. *Miss Rumphius.*
Cox, David. *Bossyboots.*
dePaola, Tomie. *Oliver Button Is a Sissy.*
Ernst, Lisa Campbell. *Sam Johnson and the Blue Ribbon Quilt.*
Gerrard, Roy. *Sir Cedric.*
Goodall, John S. *Naughty Nancy Goes to School.*
Grifalconi, Ann. *Flyaway Girl.*
Henkes, Kevin. *Chester's Way.*
Hoban, Russell. *Best Friends for Frances.*
Hoffman, Mary. *Amazing Grace.*
Isaacs, Anne. *Swamp Angel.*
Isadora, Rachel. *Max.*
Keats, Ezra Jack. *A Letter to Amy.*
Noble, Trinka Hakes. *Meanwhile Back at the Ranch.*
Ringgold, Faith. *Dinner at Aunt Connie's House.*
San Souci, Robert. *Kate Shelley: Bound for Legend.*
Yee, Paul. *Roses Sing on New Snow.*
Zolotow, Charlotte. *This Quiet Lady.*
———. *William's Doll.*

Geographic identity
Alexander, Sue. *Nadia the Willful.*
Andrews, Jan. *Very First Time.*
Anno, Mitsumasa. *Anno's Britain.*
———. *Anno's Italy.*
———. *Anno's Journey.*
———. *Anno's U.S.A.*
Aylesworth, Jim. *The Folks in the Valley: A Pennsylvania Dutch ABC.*
Baker, Jeannie. *Where the Forest Meets the Sea.*
———. *Window.*
Baylor, Byrd. *The Desert Is Theirs.*
———. *Your Own Best Secret Place.*
Baylor, Byrd, and Peter Parnall. *Your Own Best Secret Place.*
Bowen, Betsy. *Antler, Bear, Canoe: A Northwoods Alphabet Year.*
Burton, Virginia Lee. *The Little House.*
Cooney, Barbara. *Island Boy.*
Garland, Sherry. *The Lotus Seed.*
Greenfield, Eloise. *Africa Dream.*

Hathorn, Elizabeth. *Way Home.*
Hill, Elizabeth Starr. *Evan's Corner.*
Isaacs, Anne. *Swamp Angel.*
Keats, Ezra Jack. *The Trip.*
Khalsa, Dayal Kaur. *Cowboy Dreams.*
Kroll, Virginia L. *Africa Brothers and Sisters.*
MacLachlan, Patricia. *All the Places to Love.*
Morimoto, Junko. *My Hiroshima.*
Murphy, Jill. *What Next, Baby Bear!*
Owens, Mary Beth. *A Caribou Alphabet.*
Polacco, Patricia. *The Keeping Quilt.*
Price, Leontyne. *Aïda.*
Rand, Gloria. *Prince William.*
Rounds, Glen. *Cowboys.*
Rylant, Cynthia. *An Angel for Solomon Singer.*
———. *Appalachia: The Voices of Sleeping Birds.*
———. *When I Was Young in the Mountains.*
Schroeder, Alan. *Carolina Shout!*
Sharmat, Marjorie Weinman. *Gila Monsters Meet You at the Airport.*
Sheldon, Dyan. *Under the Moon.*
Sis, Peter. *A Small, Tall Tale from the Far, Far North.*
Spier, Peter. *Father, May I Come?*
Tejima, Keizaburo. *Swan Sky.*
Thompson, Colin. *The Paper Bag Prince.*
Turner, Ann Warren. *Dakota Dugout.*
Van Allsburg, Chris. *Bad Day at Riverbend.*
Wild, Margaret. *Thank You, Santa.*
Williams, Karen Lynn. *When Africa Was Home.*
Yorinks, Arthur. *Whitefish Will Rides Again!*

Relationships
Alexander, Martha. *When the New Baby Comes, I'm Moving Out.*
Bahr, Mary. *The Memory Box.*
Baylor, Byrd. *Hawk, I'm Your Brother.*
———. *The Other Way to Listen.*
———. *The Way to Start a Day.*
Benjamin, Amanda. *Two's Company.*
Brown, Marc. *Arthur's Baby.*
———. *Arthur's Eyes.*
Bunting, Eve. *Fly Away Home.*
———. *The Wall.*
Calhoun, Mary. *High-Wire Henry.*
Carle, Eric. *Do You Want to Be My Friend?*
Carrick, Carol. *The Foundling.*
Crowe, Robert. *Clyde Monster.*
Cutler, Jane. *Darcy and Gran Don't Like Babies.*

Rathmann, Peggy. *Officer Buckle and Gloria.*

Rice, Eve. *Sam Who Never Forgets.*

Ringgold, Faith. *Aunt Harriet's Underground Railroad in the Sky.*

Rosenberg, Liz. *Monster Mama.*

Ryder, Joanne. *Hello, Tree!*

———. *My Father's Hands.*

———. *Under Your Feet.*

Say, Allen. *The Bicycle Man.*

———. *Grandfather's Journey.*

Schwartz, Amy. *Her Majesty, Aunt Essie.*

Scott, Ann Herbert. *On Mother's Lap.*

Seuss, Dr. *Horton Hatches the Egg.*

Shea, Pegi Deitz. *The Whispering Cloth: A Refugee's Story.*

Sis, Peter. *An Ocean World.*

Steig, William. *Brave Irene.*

Thomas, Jane Resh. *Lights on the River.*

Titherington, Jeanne. *Sophy and Auntie Pearl.*

Turner, Ann Warren. *Katie's Trunk.*

Waber, Bernard. *Ira Says Goodbye.*

Wahl, Jan. *My Cat Ginger.*

Weller, Frances Ward. *Riptide.*

Yolen, Jane. *Grandad Bill's Song.*

———. *The Seeing Stick.*

Zolotow, Charlotte. *This Quiet Lady.*

Self-worth

Ackerman, Karen. *Song and Dance Man.*

Adoff, Arnold. *Hard to Be Six.*

Agee, Jon. *The Incredible Painting of Felix Clousseau.*

Arnold, Tedd. *The Signmaker's Assistant.*

Asch, Frank. *Moondance.*

———. *Turtle Tale.*

Babbitt, Natalie. *Nellie: A Cat on Her Own.*

Baker, Keith. *The Dove's Letter.*

Bartone, Elisa. *Peppe the Lamplighter.*

Blegvad, Lenore. *Anna Banana and Me.*

Blos, Joan. *Old Henry.*

Brown, Marc. *Arthur Babysits.*

———. *Arthur's Halloween.*

———. *Arthur's Teacher Trouble.*

Burningham, John. *Aldo.*

Burton, Virginia Lee. *Mike Mulligan and His Steam Shovel.*

Calhoun, Mary. *High-Wire Henry.*

Carle, Eric. *A House for Hermit Crab.*

———. *The Mixed-Up Chameleon.*

Carlstrom, Nancy White. *Baby-O.*

Norman, Philip Ross. *A Mammoth Imagination.*
Peet, Bill. *Cowardly Clyde.*
————. *The Spooky Tail of Prewitt Peacock.*
————. *The Whingdingdilly.*
Pilkey, Dav. *Hallo-Weiner.*
Pinkney, Brian. *Max Found Two Sticks.*
Polacco, Patricia. *Appelemando's Dreams.*
Pomerantz, Charlotte. *Flap Your Wings and Try.*
Rathmann, Peggy. *Officer Buckle and Gloria.*
Ringgold, Faith. *Tar Beach.*
Rochelle, Belinda. *When Jo Louis Won the Title.*
Rylant, Cynthia. *All I See.*
Say, Allen. *El Chino.*
Schroeder, Alan. *Ragtime Tumpie.*
Schwartz, Amy. *Bea and Mr. Jones.*
Scott, Ann Herbert. *Sam.*
Shecter, Ben. *Conrad's Castle.*
Shefelman, Janice Jordan. *A Peddler's Dream.*
Teague, Mark. *The Field Beyond the Outfield.*
Thomas, Jane Resh. *Lights on the River.*
Tompert, Ann. *The Silver Whistle.*
Tyler, Anne. *Tumble Tower.*
Viorst, Judith. *Alexander and the Terrible, Horrible, No Good, Very Bad Day.*
Welch, Willy. *Playing Right Field.*
Yamaka, Sara. *The Gift of Driscoll Lipscomb.*
Wellner, Frances Ward. *Matthew Wheelock's Wall.*
Wells, Rosemary. *Timothy Goes to School.*
Wilkon, Piotr. *Rosie the Cool Cat.*
Yashima, Taro. *Crow Boy.*
Yolen, Jane. *Encounter.*
————. *Owl Moon.*
Yorinks, Arthur. *Bravo, Minski.*
————. *Louis the Fish.*
Zolotow, Charlotte. *A Tiger Called Thomas.*
————. *The Unfriendly Book.*

IMAGINATION

Adoff, Arnold. *Hard to Be Six.*
Ahlberg, Janet. *The Jolly Postman.*
Alexander, Martha. *When the New Baby Comes, I'm Moving Out.*
Asch, Frank. *Moondance.*
————. *Sand Cake.*
Baker, Jeannie. *Where the Forest Meets the Sea.*
Barrett, Judi. *Animals Should Definitely Not Wear Clothing.*
Blos, Joan. *Lottie's Circus.*
Bottner, Barbara. *Hurricane Music.*

Henkes, Kevin. *The Biggest Boy.*
Hoban, Russell. *A Baby Sister for Frances.*
Ichikawa, Satomi. *Nora's Castle.*
Isadora, Rachel. *The Pirates of Bedford Street.*
Jonas, Ann. *The Quilt.*
Joyce, William. *A Day with Wilbur Robinson.*
————. *George Shrinks.*
Keats, Ezra Jack. *Dreams.*
————. *Louie.*
————. *The Trip.*
Khalsa, Dayal Kaur. *Cowboy Dreams.*
Legge, David. *Bamboozled.*
Lent, Blair. *Molasses Flood.*
Lester, Alison. *The Journey Home.*
Lester, Helen. *Me First.*
Lionni, Leo. *Fish Is Fish.*
Martin, Rafe. *Will's Mammoth.*
McLerran, Alice. *Roxaboxen.*
Murphy, Jill. *What Next, Baby Bear!*
Oram, Hiawyn. *In the Attic.*
Pilkey, Dav. *When Cats Dream.*
Ringgold, Faith. *Aunt Harriet's Underground Railroad in the Sky.*
————. *Tar Beach.*
Ryder, Joanne. *The Bear on the Moon.*
Sendak, Maurice. *Where the Wild Things Are.*
Shecter, Ben. *Conrad's Castle.*
Shepperson, Rob. *The Sandman.*
Stevenson, James. *That Terrible Halloween Night.*
Teague, Mark. *The Field Beyond the Outfield.*
Testa, Fulvio. *If You Take a Pencil.*
Twining, Edith. *Sandman.*
Van Allsburg, Chris. *Bad Day at Riverbend.*
————. *The Garden of Abdul Gasazi.*
————. *Just a Dream.*
————. *The Polar Express.*
————. *The Wreck of the Zephyr.*
Wahl, Jan. *My Cat Ginger.*
Wiesner, David. *Free Fall.*
————. *Hurricane.*
————. *Tuesday.*
Zolotow, Charlotte. *Someday.*

IMMIGRANTS/REFUGEES
Bartone, Elisa. *Peppe the Lamplighter.*
Bunting, Eve. *How Many Days to America? A Thanksgiving Story.*
Cohen, Barbara. *Gooseberries to Oranges.*

dePaola, Tomie. *An Early American Christmas.*

Garland, Sherry. *The Lotus Seed.*

Leighton, Maxinne Rhea. *An Ellis Island Christmas.*

Levinson, Riki. *Watch the Stars Come Out.*

Oberman, Sheldon. *The Always Prayer Shawl.*

Polacco, Patricia. *Chicken Sunday.*

———. *The Keeping Quilt.*

———. *Mrs. Katz and Tush.*

———. *Thunder Cake.*

Say, Allen, *Grandfather's Journey.*

Shea, Pegi Deitz. *The Whispering Cloth: A Refugee's Story.*

Shefelman, Janice Jordan. *A Peddler's Dream.*

Winter, Jeanette. *Follow the Drinking Gourd.*

Yee, Paul. *Roses Sing on New Snow.*

INDIVIDUALITY

Baylor, Byrd, and Peter Parnall. *Your Own Best Place.*

Blos, Joan. *Old Henry.*

Brown, Anthony. *Tunnel.*

Burningham, John. *Would You Rather . . .*

dePaola, Tomie. *The Art Lesson.*

Dunbar, Joyce. *Four Fierce Kittens.*

Dunrea, Oliver. *The Painter Who Loved Chickens.*

Ernst, Lisa Campbell. *Sam Johnson and the Blue Ribbon Quilt.*

———. *When Bluebell Sang.*

Fair, Sylvia. *The Bedspread.*

Finchler, Judy. *Miss Malarkey Doesn't Live in Room 10.*

Fleischman, Paul. *Rondo in C.*

Friedman, Aileen. *A Cloak for the Dreamer.*

Garland, Michael. *Dinner at Magritte's.*

Gauch, Patricia Lee. *Tanya and Emily in a Dance for Two.*

Glass, Andrew. *Jackson Makes His Move.*

Hall, Donald, *I Am the Dog, I Am the Cat.*

Heine, Helme. *The Most Wonderful Egg in the World.*

Hest, Amy. *The Purple Coat.*

Isaacs, Anne. *Swamp Angel.*

Isadora, Rachel. *Willaby.*

Kraus, Robert. *Owliver.*

Lester, Alison. *Clive Eats Alligators.*

———. *Tessa Snaps Snakes.*

Lionni, Leo. *Cornelius: A Fable.*

Mora, Pat. *A Birthday Basket for Tia.*

Moss, Thylias. *I Want to Be.*

Pinkney, Brian. *Max Found Two Sticks.*

Pryor, Bonnie. *Lottie's Dream.*

Purdy, Carol. *Mrs. Merriwether's Musical Cat.*

Ray, Mary Lyn. *Pianna.*
Rosenberg, Liz. *Monster Mama.*
Sharmat, Mitchell. *Gregory, the Terrible Eater.*
Stewart, Sarah. *The Library.*
Thompson, Colin. *The Paper Bag Prince.*
Tyler, Anne. *Tumble Tower.*
Walsh, Ellen Stoll. *Hop Jump.*
Wilkon, Piotr. *Rosie the Cool Cat.*
Yee, Paul. *Roses Sing on New Snow.*

INSECTS *See* **ANIMALS—Small creatures**

INVENTIONS

Brown, Marc. *Arthur's TV Trouble.*
Carle, Eric. *Walter The Baker.*
Castle, Caroline and Peter Weevers. *Herbert Binns & the Flying Tricycle.*
Provensen, Alice. *The Glorious Flight: Across the Channel with Louis Bleriot, July 25, 1909.*
Steig, William. *Gorky Rises.*
Yorinks, Arthur. *Bravo, Minski.*

ISLANDS

Albert, Burton. *Where Does the Trail Lead?*
Conrad, Pam. *The Lost Sailor.*
Cooney, Barbara. *Island Boy.*
Gershator, Phillis. *Rata-pata-scata-fata.*
Johnston, Tony. *Pages of Music.*
McCloskey, Robert. *One Morning in Maine.*
————. *Time of Wonder.*
Ness, Evaline. *Sam, Bangs, & Moonshine.*
Sis, Peter. *Komodo!*
Van Allsburg, Chris. *The Wretched Stone.*

JEWELS/JEWELRY

Goodall, John S. *Paddy to the Rescue.*
Gregory, Valiska. *Through the Mickle Woods.*
Haley, Gail E. *Sea Tale.*
Lawson, Julie. *The Dragon's Pearl.*
Neitzel, Shirley. *The Dress I'll Wear to the Party.*
Soto, Gary. *Too Many Tamales.*

KITES

Ets, Marie Hall. *Gilberto and the Wind.*
Fort, Patrick. *Redbird.*
Lionni, Leo. *Six Crows: A Fable.*
Lobel, Arnold. *Days with Frog and Toad.*
Reddix, Valerie. *Dragon-Kite of the Autumn Moon.*
Say, Allen. *Tree of Cranes.*
Seuss, Dr. *The Cat in the Hat.*

Small, David. *Paper John.*
Steig, William. *Gorky Rises.*
Vaughan, Marcia K., and Patricia Mullins. *The Sea-Breeze Hotel.*
KNIGHTS
dePaola, Tomie. *The Knight and the Dragon.*
Gerrard, Roy. *Sir Cedric.*
Peet, Bill. *Cowardly Clyde.*

LANGUAGE
Alphabet
Anno, Mitsumasa. *Anno's Alphabet.*
Aylesworth, Jim. *The Folks in the Valley: A Pennsylvania Dutch ABC.*
Azarian, Mary. *A Farmer's Alphabet.*
Bowen, Betsy. *Antler, Bear, Canoe: A Northwoods Alphabet Year.*
Brown, Marcia. *All Butterflies: An ABC.*
Duke, Kate. *The Guinea Pig ABC.*
Ehlert, Lois. *Eating the Alphabet: Fruits and Vegetables from A to Z.*
Feelings, Muriel. *Jambo Means Hello: Swahili Alphabet Book.*
Geisert, Arthur. *Pigs from A to Z.*
Hoban, Russell. *Bedtime for Frances.*
Hoban, Tana. *A, B, See!*
———. *26 Letters and 99 Cents.*
Hunt, Jonathan. *Illuminations.*
Jonas, Ann. *Aardvarks, Disembark!*
Kitchens, Bert. *Animal Alphabet.*
Lobel, Anita. *Alison's Zinnia.*
———. *On Market Street.*
MacDonald, Suse. *Alphabatics.*
Martin, Bill, and John Archambault. *Chicka Chicka Boom Boom.*
Meddaugh, Susan. *Martha Speaks.*
Munari, Bruno. *ABC.*
Owens, Mary Beth. *A Caribou Alphabet.*
Shelby, Anne. *Potluck.*
Ungerer, Tomi. *Crictor.*
Van Allsburg, Chris. *The Alphabet Theatre Proudly Presents: The Z Was Zapped.*
Wells, Ruth. *A to Zen: A Book of Japanese Culture.*
Wildsmith, Brian. *ABC.*
Names
Abolafia, Yossi. *A Fish for Mrs. Gardenia.*
Bang, Molly. *Delphine.*
Benjamin, Amanda. *Two's Company.*
Birdseye, Tom. *Airmail to the Moon.*
Burningham, John. *John Patrick Norman McHennessy: The Boy Who Was Always Late.*
Daly, Niki. *Not So Fast, Songololo.*

Emberley, Barbara. *Drummer Hoff*.

Fox, Mem. *Wilfrid Gordon McDonald Partridge*.

Hathorn, Elizabeth. *Way Home*.

Heide, Florence Parry, and Judith Heide Gilliland. *The Day of Ahmed's Secret*.

Henkes, Kevin. *Chrysanthemum*.

Houston, Gloria. *My Great-Aunt Arizona*.

Howard, Elizabeth Fitzgerald. *Papa Tells Chita a Story*.

Isaacs, Anne. *Swamp Angel*.

James, Betsy. *May Ann*.

Keller, Holly. *Furry*.

Kellogg, Steven. *The Mysterious Tadpole*.

King-Smith, Dick. *Farmer Bungle Forgets*.

Lester, Alison. *The Journey Home*.

Lobel, Anita. *Alison's Zinnia*.

MacLachlan, Patricia. *All the Places to Love*.

Martin, Bill, and John Archambault. *Knots on a Counting Rope*.

Oberman, Sheldon. *The Always Prayer Shawl*.

Pilkey, Dav. *Hallo-Weiner*.

Polacco, Patricia. *Mrs. Katz and Tush*.

———. *Rechenka's Eggs*.

Ray, Mary Lyn. *Pianna*.

Rochelle, Belinda. *When Jo Louis Won the Title*.

Schwartz, Amy. *Annabelle Swift, Kindergartner*.

Sharmat, Marjorie Weinman. *The Best Valentine in the World*.

Steig, William. *Amos & Boris*.

Waber, Bernard. *The House on East 88th Street*.

Weller, Frances Ward. *Riptide*.

Wood, Audrey. *Heckedy Peg*.

Yashima, Taro. *Crow Boy*.

———. *Umbrella*.

Sayings and special language

Birdseye, Tom. *Airmail to the Moon*.

Burningham, John. *Granpa*.

Coomb, Patricia. *The Magic Pot*.

Day, Alexandra. *Frank and Ernest*.

Fort, Patrick. *Redbird*.

Gershator, Phillis. *Rata-pata-scata-fata*.

Gray, Libba Moore. *Small Green Snake*.

Hathorn, Elizabeth. *Grandma's Shoes*.

Hoban, Tana. *Exactly the Opposite*.

Houston, Gloria. *But No Candy*.

Hughes, Shirley. *The Big Alfie and Annie Rose Storybook*.

Hutchins, Pat. *What Game Shall We Play?*

Kraus, Robert. *Whose Mouse Are You?*

Lawson, Julie. *The Dragon's Pearl*.

Lester, Helen. *Me First.*

McBratncy, Sam. *Guess How Much I Love You.*

Neitzel, Shirley. *The Dress I'll Wear to the Party.*

Olaleye, Isaac O. *Bitter Bananas.*

Peet, Bill. *The Whingdingdilly.*

Rosenberg, Liz. *Monster Mama.*

Scheer, Julian and Marvin Bileck. *Rain Makes Applesauce.*

Schroeder, Alan. *Carolina Shout!*

Shea, Pegi Deitz. *The Whispering Cloth: A Refugee's Story.*

Soto, Gary. *Chato's Kitchen.*

Steig, William. *The Amazing Bone.*

———. *Caleb & Kate.*

Stevenson, James. *Could Be Worse!*

Thomas, Jane Resh. *Lights on the River.*

Viorst, Judith. *Alexander and the Terrible, Horrible, No Good, Very Bad Day.*

Wilhelm, Hans. *I'll Always Love You.*

Winter, Jeanette. *Follow the Drinking Gourd.*

Words

Allen, Pamela. *Mr. Archimedes' Bath.*

Andrews, Jan. *Very First Time.*

Bang, Molly. *Yellow Ball.*

Brown, Marc. *Arthur's Teacher Trouble.*

Bunting, Eve. *A Turkey for Thanksgiving.*

Carle, Eric. *Walter the Baker.*

Charlip, Remy. *Fortunately.*

Cole, Joanna. *The Magic School Bus Inside the Earth.*

———. *The Magic School Bus Inside the Human Body.*

dePaola, Tomie. *Jingle: The Christmas Clown.*

Dodds, Dayle Ann. *Wheel Away!*

Duke, Kate. *The Guinea Pig ABC.*

———. *Guinea Pigs Far and Near.*

Ehlert, Lois. *Color Farm.*

———. *Color Zoo.*

———. *Eating the Alphabet: Fruits and Vegetables from A to Z.*

———. *Feathers for Lunch.*

———. *Growing Vegetable Soup.*

———. *Planting a Rainbow.*

———. *Red Leaf, Yellow Leaf.*

Fatio, Louise. *The Happy Lion.*

Feelings, Muriel. *Jambo Means Hello: Swahili Alphabet Book.*

———. *Moja Means One: Swahili Counting Book.*

Fleming, Denise. *In the Small, Small Pond.*

———. *In the Tall, Tall Grass.*

Gardner, Beau. *What Is It? A Spin-About Book.*

Gauch, Patricia Lee. *Tanya and Emily in a Dance for Two.*

Hoban, Tana. *All About Where.*

——. *Over, Under & Through, and Other Spatial Concepts.*

——. *Push, Pull, Empty, Fill: A Book of Opposites.*

Hutchins, Pat. *Rosie's Walk.*

Johnston, Tony. *Yonder.*

Jonas, Ann. *Aardvarks, Disembark!*

——. *Color Dance.*

Levitin, Sonia. *The Man Who Kept His Heart in a Bucket.*

Lionni, Leo. *Frederick.*

——. *Six Crows: A Fable.*

Miller, Margaret. *Whose Hat?*

Mora, Pat. *A Birthday Basket for Tia.*

Moss, Lloyd. *Zin! Zin! Zin! A Violin.*

Neitzel, Shirley. *The Jacket I Wear in the Snow.*

Ness, Evaline. *Sam, Bangs, & Moonshine.*

Reiss, John. *Colors.*

Rice, Eve. *City Night.*

Sonnenschein, Harriet. *Harold's Runaway Nose.*

Spier, Peter. *Crash! Bang! Boom!*

——. *Fast-Slow, High-Low: A Book of Opposites.*

Steig, William. *The Amazing Bone.*

Tafuri, Nancy. *The Ball Bounced.*

Van Allsburg, Chris. *The Alphabet Theatre Proudly Presents: The Z Was Zapped.*

Wildsmith, Brian. *Birds.*

——. *What the Moon Saw.*

Williams, Sue. *I Went Walking.*

Zolotow, Charlotte. *Some Things Go Together.*

LIGHT AND SHADOWS/REFLECTIONS

Andrews, Jan. *Very First Time.*

Asch, Frank. *Bear Shadow.*

——. *Moondance.*

Asch, Frank, and Vladimir Vagin. *Here Comes the Cat! = Siuda idet kot!*

Aylesworth, Jim. *Country Crossing.*

Bartone, Elisa. *Peppe the Lamplighter.*

Bunting, Eve. *Ghost's Hour, Spook's Hour.*

Farber, Norma. *Return of the Shadows.*

Hoban, Tana. *Shadows and Reflections.*

Jonas, Ann. *The 13th Clue.*

Keats, Ezra Jack. *Dreams.*

——. *Hi, Cat!*

Kimmel, Eric A. *Hershel and the Hanukkah Goblins.*

Maruki, Toshi. *Hiroshima No Pika.*

Reddix, Valerie. *Dragon-Kite of the Autumn Moon.*

Rylant, Cynthia. *All I See.*

Say, Allen. *Stranger in the Mirror.*

——. *Tree of Cranes.*

Uchida, Yoshiko. *The Bracelet.*
Van Allsburg, Chris. *The Polar Express.*
Wildsmith, Brian. *Goat's Trail.*
Wolff, Ferida. *The Woodcutter's Coat.*
Zion, Gene. *No Roses for Harry.*

LUCK

Coerr, Eleanor. *Sadako.*
dePaola, Tomie. *An Early American Christmas.*
Garland, Sherry. *The Lotus Seed.*
Hutchins, Pat. *Rosie's Walk.*
Johnston, Tony. *The Cowboy and the Black-eyed Pea.*
Kroll, Steven. *Friday the 13th.*
Lawson, Julie. *The Dragon's Pearl.*
Roy, Ron. *Three Ducks Went Wandering.*
Williams, Sherley Anne. *Working Cotton.*

MACHINES *See also* **FARMS**

Brown, Marc. *Arthur's TV Trouble.*
Burton, Virginia Lee. *The Little House.*
————. *Mike Mulligan and His Steam Shovel.*
Crews, Donald. *Carousel.*
Emberley, Barbara. *Drummer Hoff.*
Hoban, Tana. *Dig, Drill, Dump, Fill.*
Hughes, Shirley. *The Big Concrete Lorry: A Tale of Trotter Street.*
Lionni, Leo. *Alexander and the Wind-up Mouse.*
Polacco, Patricia. *Meteor!*
Steig, William. *Doctor De Soto.*

Wheels

Dodds, Dayle Ann. *Wheel Away!*
Freeman, Don. *Bearymore.*

MAGIC

Agee, Jon. *The Incredible Painting of Felix Clousseau.*
Babbitt, Natalie. *Nellie: A Cat on Her Own.*
Bang, Molly. *The Paper Crane.*
Blos, Joan. *Lottie's Circus.*
Bohdal, Susi. *Bird Adalbert.*
Brown, Marc. *Arthur's April Fool.*
Bunting, Eve. *The Man Who Could Call Down Owls.*
Cleaver, Elizabeth. *Petrouchka.*
Cole, Joanna. *The Magic School Bus in the Time of the Dinosaurs.*
————. *The Magic School Bus Inside the Earth.*
————. *The Magic School Bus Inside the Human Body.*
————. *The Magic School Bus Inside a Hurricane.*
————. *The Magic School Bus Lost in the Solar System.*
————. *The Magic School Bus on the Ocean Floor.*

Cooney, Barbara. *Island Boy*.
Ernst, Lisa Campbell. *Sam Johnson and the Blue Ribbon Quilt*.
Feelings, Muriel. *Jambo Means Hello: Swahili Alphabet Book*.
————. *Moja Means One: Swahili Counting Book*.
Friedman, Aileen. *A Cloak for the Dreamer*.
Harvey, Brett. *Cassie's Journey: Going West in the 1860's*.
Howard, Elizabeth Fitzgerald. *The Train to Lulu's*.
Kroll, Virginia L. *Africa Brothers and Sisters*.
Provensen, Alice, and Martin Provensen. *Shaker Lane*.
Ringgold, Faith. *Aunt Harriet's Underground Railroad in the Sky*.
San Souci, Robert. *Kate Shelley: Bound for Legend*.
Shea, Pegi Deitz. *The Whispering Cloth: A Refugee's Story*.
Sis, Peter. *Follow the Dream*.
————. *Komodo!*
————. *A Small, Tall Tale from the Far, Far North*.
Smith, Barry. *The First Voyage of Christopher Columbus, 1492*.
Spier, Peter. *Father, May I Come?*
Wiesner, David. *Free Fall*.

MASKS

de Regniers, Beatrice Schenk. *May I Bring a Friend?*
Grifalconi, Ann. *Flyaway Girl*.
Waggoner, Karen. *The Lemonade Babysitter*.

MATHEMATICS

Classification

Anno, Mitsumasa. *Anno's Counting Book*.
————. *Anno's Counting House*.
Baer, Gene. *Thump, Thump, Rat-a-tat-tat*.
Baker, Keith. *Hide and Snake*.
Chwast, Seymour. *The Twelve Circus Rings*.
Giganti, Paul. *How Many Snails? A Counting Book*.
Hoban, Tana. *Of Colors and Things*.
Lester, Alison. *Clive Eats Alligators*.
————. *Tessa Snaps Snakes*.
Lionni, Leo. *Fish Is Fish*.
Lobel, Anita. *On Market Street*.
Spier, Peter. *Crash! Bang! Boom!*
Walsh, Ellen Stoll. *Mouse Paint*.

Counting

Anno, Mitsumasa. *Anno's Counting Book*.
————. *Anno's Counting House*.
Bang, Molly. *Ten, Nine, Eight*.
Carle, Eric. *1, 2, 3 to the Zoo*.
————. *The Rooster Who Set Out to See the World*.
————. *The Very Hungry Caterpillar*.

Christelow, Eileen. *Five Little Monkeys Jumping on the Bed.*
Chwast, Seymour. *The Twelve Circus Rings.*
Coerr, Eleanor. *Sadako.*
Crews, Donald. *Bicycle Race.*
——. *Ten Black Dots.*
Dana, Katharine Floyd. *Over in the Meadow.*
Dunrea, Oliver. *Deep Down Underground.*
Ehlert, Lois. *Fish Eyes.*
Feelings, Muriel. *Moja Means One: Swahili Counting Book.*
Geisert, Arthur. *Pigs from 1 to 10.*
Giganti, Paul. *How Many Snails? A Counting Book.*
Hoban, Tana. *Count and See.*
——. *26 Letters and 99 Cents.*
Hutchins, Pat. *1 Hunter.*
Kitchens, Bert. *Animal Numbers.*
Lobel, Arnold. *Uncle Elephant.*
MacDonald, Suse, and Bill Oakes. *Numbers.*
Moss, Lloyd. *Zin! Zin! Zin! A Violin.*
Keats, Ezra Jack. *Over in the Meadow.*
Polacco, Patricia. *Thunder Cake.*
Pomerantz, Charlotte. *One Duck, Another Duck.*
Reiss, John. *Numblers.*
Sis, Peter. *Waving: A Counting Book.*
Testa, Fulvio. *If You Take a Pencil.*
Ungerer, Tomi. *Crictor.*
Wildsmith, Brian. *Brian Wildsmith's 1, 2, 3's.*
Zemach, Harve. *The Judge: An Untrue Tale.*

Measurement

length

Hest, Amy. *The Purple Coat.*
Howard, Elizabeth Fitzgerald. *Train to Lulu's.*
Johnston, Tony. *Farmer Mack Measures His Pig.*
Lester, Alison. *The Journey Home.*
Lionni, Leo. *Inch by Inch.*
McBratney, Sam. *Guess How Much I Love You.*
McCully, Emily Arnold. *Mirette on the High Wire.*
Mitchell, Rita Phillips. *Hue Boy.*
Miwenye Hadithi. *Tricky Tortoise.*
Nesbit, E. *Melisande.*
Schwartz, David M. *How Much Is a Million?*
Teague, Mark. *The Field Beyond the Outfield.*
Williams, Karen Lynn. *When Africa Was Home.*
Woodruff, Elvira. *The Wing Shop.*
Ziefert, Harriet. *A New Coat for Anna.*

mass

Anno, Mitsumasa. *The King's Flower.*

Bodecker, N. M. *Carrot Holes and Frisbee Trees.*

Carle, Eric. *A House for Hermit Crab.*

dePaola, Tomie. *The Quicksand Book.*

Hayes, Sarah. *The Grumpalump.*

Hutchins, Pat. *The Doorbell Rang.*

Lionni, Leo. *The Biggest House in the World.*

McDonald, Megan. *The Great Pumpkin Switch.*

Scott, Ann Herbert. *On Mother's Lap.*

Seuss, Dr. *Horton Hatches the Egg.*

Speed, Toby. *Hattie Baked a Wedding Cake.*

Williams, Vera B. *A Chair For My Mother.*

————. *Music, Music for Everyone.*

Wood, Audrey. *The Napping House.*

volume

Allen, Pamela. *Mr. Archimedes' Bath.*

Ehlert, Lois. *Growing Vegetable Soup.*

Lawson, Julie. *The Dragon's Pearl.*

Lent, Blair. *Molasses Flood.*

Lyon, George Ella. *Come a Tide.*

Murphy, Shirley Rousseau. *Tattie's River Journey.*

Polacco, Patricia. *Thunder Cake.*

Numbers

Anno, Mitsumasa. *Anno's Counting House.*

Bang, Molly. *Ten, Nine, Eight.*

Crews, Donald. *Bicycle Race.*

ideas

Gag, Wanda. *Millions of Cats.*

Geisert, Arthur. *Pigs from A to Z.*

Haugaard, Erik Christian. *Prince Boghole.*

James, Betsy. *Mary Ann.*

Levitin, Sonia. *The Man Who Kept His Heart in a Bucket.*

MacDonald, Suse, and Bill Oakes. *Numblers.*

McKissack, Patricia. *A Million Fish—More or Less.*

Modell, Frank. *One Zillion Valentines.*

Moss, Lloyd. *Zin! Zin! Zin! A Violin.*

Say, Allen. *Tree of Cranes.*

Schwartz, David M. *How Much Is a Million?*

ordinal

Asch, Frank. *The Last Puppy.*

Chwast, Seymour. *The Twelve Circus Rings.*

Hellen, Nancy. *The Bus Stop.*

Hughes, Shirley. *Alfie Gets in First.*

Moss, Thylias. *I Want to Be.*

Mwenye Hadithi. *Tricky Tortoise.*

Oppenheim, Joanne. *You Can't Catch Me!*

Ryder, Joanne. *The Snail's Spell.*

Steig, William. *Amos & Boris.*

Wellner, Frances Ward. *Matthew Wheelock's Wall.*

Yolen, Jane. *All Those Secrets of the World.*

Ziefert, Harriet. *A New Coat for Anna.*

MEMORIES

Ackerman, Karen. *Song and Dance Man.*

Alexander, Sue. *Nadia the Willful.*

Aliki. *The Two of Them.*

Bahr, Mary. *The Memory Box.*

Blos, Joan. *Old Henry.*

Bunting, Eve. *The Wall.*

Carlstrom, Nancy White. *I'm Not Moving, Mama!*

Carrick, Carol. *The Foundling.*

Cohen, Barbara. *Gooseberries to Oranges.*

dePaola, Tomie. *Nana Upstairs & Nana Downstairs.*

Dragonwagon, Crescent. *Home Place.*

Fair, Sylvia. *The Bedspread.*

Fleischman, Paul. *The Animal Hedge.*

———. *Rondo in C.*

Flournoy, Valerie. *The Patchwork Quilt.*

———. *Tanya's Reunion.*

Fox, Mem. *Wilfrid Gordon McDonald Partridge.*

Franklin, Kristine L. *The Old, Old Man and the Very Little Boy.*

Garland, Sherry. *The Lotus Seed.*

Gerstein, Mordicai. *The Room.*

Gould, Deborah Lee. *Grandpa's Slide Show.*

Griffith, Helen V. *Georgia Music.*

Haseley, Dennis. *The Old Banjo.*

Hathorn, Elizabeth. *Grandma's Shoes.*

Hendershot, Judith. *In Coal Country.*

Hest, Amy. *The Purple Coat.*

Hoban, Russell. *A Bargain for Frances.*

Hopkinson, Deborah. *Sweet Clara and the Freedom Quilt.*

Houghton, Eric. *The Backwards Watch.*

Houston, Gloria. *My Great-Aunt Arizona.*

———. *The Year of the Perfect Christmas Tree.*

Howard, Elizabeth Fitzgerald. *Aunt Flossie's Hats (And Crab Cakes Later).*

———. *Papa Tells Chita a Story.*

Hughes, Shirley. *The Big Alfie and Annie Rose Storybook.*

Johnson, Angela. *Tell Me a Story, Mama.*

Johnston, Tony. *Pages of Music.*

MIGRANTS
> Thomas, Jane Resh. *Lights on the River.*
> Williams, Sherley Anne. *Working Cotton.*

MONEY
> Brown, Marc. *Arthur's TV Trouble.*
> Cohen, Barbara. *Gooseberries to Oranges.*
> Freeman, Don. *Mop Top.*
> Hoban, Tana. *26 Letters and 99 Cents.*
> Lawson, Julie. *The Dragon's Pearl.*
> Lester, Alison. *Tessa Snaps Snakes.*
> McCully, Emily Arnold. *The Amazing Felix.*
> McDonald, Megan. *The Great Pumpkin Switch.*
> Modell, Frank. *One Zillion Valentines.*
> Noble, Trinka Hakes. *Meanwhile Back at the Ranch.*
> Phillips, Mildred. *The Sign in Mendel's Window.*
> Schroeder, Alan. *Ragtime Tumpie.*
> Schwartz, David M. *If You Made a Million.*
> Tompert, Ann. *The Silver Whistle.*
> Vincent, Gabrielle. *Merry Christmas, Ernest and Celestine.*
> Viorst, Judith. *Alexander, Who Used to be Rich Last Sunday.*
> Williams, Vera B. *A Chair For My Mother.*
> ———. *Music, Music for Everyone.*
> ———. *Something Special for Me.*
> Zion, Gene. *The Plant Sitter.*

MONSTERS *See* **IMAGINATION—Imaginary creatures, monsters**
MOON *See* **ASTRONOMY**
MOUNTAIN CLIMBING
> Bang, Molly. *Delphine.*
> Conrad, Pam. *The Tub People.*
> Ray, Deborah Kogan. *The Cloud.*
> Van Allsburg, Chris. *Two Bad Ants.*

MOVEMENT/SPEED
> Agee, Jon. *The Incredible Painting of Felix Clousseau.*
> Arnold, Tedd. *Green Wilma.*
> ———. *No More Water in the Tub.*
> Aylesworth, Jim. *Country Crossing.*
> Baer, Gene. *Thump, Thump, Rat-a-tat-tat.*
> Bang, Molly. *The Paper Crane.*
> ———. *Yellow Ball.*
> Baylor, Byrd. *Hawk, I'm Your Brother.*
> Bodkin, Odds. *The Banshee Train.*
> Briggs, Raymond. *Father Christmas.*
> Brown, Ruth. *The Big Sneeze.*
> Burningham, John. *Mr. Grumpy's Outing.*
> Christelow, Eileen. *Five Little Monkeys Jumping on the Bed.*

Pomerantz, Charlotte. *Flap Your Wings and Try.*
Rayner, Mary. *Garth Pig and the Ice-Cream Lady.*
Rosen, Michael. *We're Going on a Bear Hunt.*
Rosenberg, Liz. *Monster Mama.*
Ryder, Joanne. *Dancers in the Garden.*
————. *One Small Fish.*
————. *Where Butterflies Grow.*
Sara. *Across Town.*
Say, Allen. *Stranger in the Mirror.*
Scott, Ann Herbert. *On Mother's Lap.*
Shaw, Nancy. *Sheep in a Jeep.*
Sis, Peter. *Waving: A Counting Book.*
Stevenson, James. *What's Under My Bed?*
Tafuri, Nancy. *The Ball Bounced.*
Tejima, Keizaburo. *Owl Lake.*
————. *Swan Sky.*
Walsh, Ellen Stoll. *Hop Jump.*
Westcott, Nadine Bernard. *Peanut Butter and Jelly: A Play Rhyme.*
Wildsmith, Brian. *The Lazy Bear.*
————. *The Little wood Duck.*
————. *Squirrels.*
Williams, Linda. *The Little Old Lady Who Was Not Afraid of Anything.*
Williams, Sherley Anne. *Working Cotton.*
Wood, Audrey. *The Napping House.*

MOVING

Ackerman, Karen. *Araminta's Paintbox.*
Anno, Mitsumasa. *Anno's Counting House.*
Babbitt, Natalie. *Nellie: A Cat on Her Own.*
Blos, Joan. *Old Henry.*
Bunting, Eve. *How Many Days to America? A Thanksgiving Story.*
Burton, Virginia Lee. *The Little House.*
Carle, Eric. *A House for Hermit Crab.*
Carlstrom, Nancy White. *I'm Not Moving, Mama!*
Chetwin, Grace. *Box and Cox.*
Coerr, Eleanor. *The Josefina Story Quilt.*
Cohen, Barbara. *Gooseberries to Oranges.*
Finchler, Judy. *Miss Malarkey Doesn't Live in Room 10.*
Garland, Sherry. *The Lotus Seed.*
Gerstein, Mordicai. *The Room.*
Glass, Andrew. *Jackson Makes His Move.*
Harvey, Brett. *Cassie's Journey: Going West in the 1860's.*
Henkes, Kevin. *Chester's Way.*
Hughes, Shirley. *The Big Concrete Lorry: A Tale of Trotter Street.*
James, Betsy. *Mary Ann.*

Johnson, Angela. *The Leaving Morning.*
Johnston, Tony. *The Quilt Story.*
Keats, Ezra Jack. *The Trip.*
Keller, Holly. *The New Boy.*
Leighton, Maxinne Rhea. *An Ellis Island Christmas.*
Levinson, Riki. *Watch the Stars Come Out.*
Lobel, Arnold. *Ming Lo Moves the Mountain.*
Lyon, George Ella. *Come a Tide.*
Mattingley, Christobel. *The Angel with a Mouth-Organ.*
McCloskey, Robert. *Time of Wonder.*
McLerran, Alice. *I Want to Go Home.*
Oberman, Sheldon. *The Always Prayer Shawl.*
Provensen, Alice, and Martin Provensen. *Shaker Lane.*
Rochelle, Belinda. *When Jo Louis Won the Title.*
Say, Allen. *Grandfather's Journey.*
Sharmat, Marjorie Weinman. *Gila Monsters Meet You at the Airport.*
Turner, Ann Warren. *Dakota Dugout.*
————. *Stars for Sarah.*
Uchida, Yoshiko. *The Bracelet.*
Waber, Bernard. *Ira Says Goodbye.*
Williams, Karen Lynn. *When Africa Was Home.*
Woodruff, Elvira. *The Wing Shop.*
Yolen, Jane. *Letting Swift River Go.*
Zolotow, Charlotte. *A Tiger Called Thomas.*

MUSIC *See* **GRAPHIC AND PERFORMING ARTS—Music and musicians**
MYSTERY

Allard, Harry. *Miss Nelson Is Missing!*
Bedard, Michael. *Emily.*
Bodkin, Odds. *The Banshee Train.*
Brown, Marc. *Arthur's Valentine.*
Garland, Michael. *Dinner at Magritte's.*
Jonas, Ann. *The 13th Clue.*
Kellogg, Steven. *The Mysterious Tadpole.*
Krahn, Fernando. *The Mystery of the Giant Footprints.*
Lyon, George Ella. *Who Came Down That Road?*
Marion, Jeff Daniel. *Hello, Crow.*
Say, Allen. *Stranger in the Mirror.*
Schertle, Alice. *Witch Hazel.*
Steig, William. *Caleb & Kate.*
Van Allsburg, Chris. *The Garden of Abdul Gasazi.*
————. *Jumanji.*
————. *The Mysteries of Harris Burdick.*
————. *The Stranger.*
————. *The Widow's Broom.*

Radin, Ruth Yaffe. *A Winter Place*.
Rand, Gloria. *Prince William*.
Ray, Mary Lyn. *Pianna*.
Robbins, Ken. *City/Country*.
Rudolph, Marguerita. *How a Shirt Grew in the Field*.
Rylant, Cynthia. *All I See*.
———. *An Angel for Solomon Singer*.
———. *Appalachia: The Voices of Sleeping Birds*.
———. *Miss Maggie*.
———. *Night in the Country*.
———. *The Relatives Came*.
———. *When I Was Young in the Mountains*.
San Souci, Robert. *Kate Shelley: Bound for Legend*.
Schertle, Alice. *Witch Hazel*.
Schoenherr, John. *The Barn*.
Spier, Peter. *Father, May I Come?*
Thompson, Colin. *The Paper Bag Prince*.
Van Allsburg, Chris. *The Stranger*.
———. *The Widow's Broom*.
Wellner, Frances Ward. *Matthew Wheelock's Wall*.
Williams, Sherley Anne. *Working Cotton*.
Yolen, Jane. *Letting Swift River Go*.
———. *Owl Moon*.
Zolotow, Charlotte. *The Storm Book*.

urban

Abolafia, Yossi. *A Fish for Mrs. Gardenia*.
Arnold, Tedd. *No Jumping on the Bed!*
———. *No More Water in the Tub!*
———. *The Signmaker's Assistant*.
Bartone, Elisa. *Peppe the Lamplighter*.
Bedard, Michael. *Emily*.
Blegvad, Lenore. *Anna Banana and Me*.
Brown, Marc. *Arthur's Halloween*.
Browne, Anthony. *Tunnel*.
Brunhoff, Jean de. *The Story of Babar*.
Bunting, Eve. *Smoky Night*.
Burton, Virginia Lee. *The Little House*.
Chetwin, Grace. *Box and Cox*.
Cooney, Barbara. *Hattie and the Wild Waves*.
Daly, Niki. *Not So Fast, Songololo*.
DiSalvo-Ryan, DyAnne. *Uncle Willie and the Soup Kitchen*.
Dorros, Arthur. *Abuela*.
Fatio, Louise. *The Happy Lion*.
Finchler, Judy. *Miss Malarkey Doesn't Live in Room 10*.
Florian, Douglas. *The City*.

Raskin, Ellen. *Nothing Ever Happens on My Block.*
Rice, Eve. *City Night.*
———. *Goodnight, Goodnight.*
Ringgold, Faith. *Tar Beach.*
Robbins, Ken. *City/Country.*
Rochelle, Belinda. *When Jo Louis Won the Title.*
Ryder, Joanne. *The Night Flight.*
Rylant, Cynthia. *An Angel for Solomon Singer.*
Sara. *Across Town.*
Schroeder, Alan. *Carolina Shout!*
———. *Ragtime Tumpie.*
Sharmat, Marjorie Weinman. *Gila Monsters Meet You at the Airport.*
Sis, Peter. *Waving: A Counting Book.*
Stevenson, James. *The Worst Person's Christmas.*
Tsuchiya, Yukio. *Faithful Elephants.*
Ungerer, Tomi. *Crictor.*
Waber, Bernard. *The House on East 88th Street.*
Wildsmith, Brian. *Goat's Trail.*
Williams, Vera B. *A Chair For My Mother.*
———. *Something Special for Me.*
Woodruff, Elvira. *The Wing Shop.*
Yee, Paul. *Roses Sing on New Snow.*
Zolotow, Charlotte. *The Storm Book.*

OBSERVATION *See also* **STORIES—Minimal or No text**
Anno, Mitsumasa. *Anno's Alphabet.*
———. *Anno's Britain.*
———. *Anno's Counting Book.*
———. *Anno's Counting House.*
———. *Anno's Italy.*
———. *Anno's Journey.*
———. *Anno's U.S.A.*
Arnold, Tedd. *The Signmaker's Assistant.*
Asch, Frank. *Bear Shadow.*
Aylesworth, Jim. *Country Crossing.*
Baer, Gene. *Thump, Thump, Rat-a-tat-tat.*
Baker, Jeannie. *Window.*
Baker, Keith. *Hide and Snake.*
———. *Who Is the Beast?*
Bang, Molly. *Delphine.*
———. *Yellow Ball.*
Barrett, Judi. *Animals Should Definitely Not Act Like People.*
Baylor, Byrd. *We Walk in Sandy Places.*
Bohdal, Susi. *Bird Adalbert.*
Brown, Craig McFarland. *The Patchwork Farmer.*

Yamaka, Sara. *The Gift of Driscoll Lipscomb.*
Zemach, Harve. *The Judge: An Untrue Tale.*
Zolotow, Charlotte. *This Quiet Lady.*

OCCUPATIONS *See also* **GRAPHIC AND PERFORMING ARTS**

Ahlberg, Janet. *The Jolly Postman.*
Allard, Harry. *Miss Nelson Has a Field Day.*
Arnold, Tedd. *Green Wilma.*
——. *The Signmaker's Assistant.*
Aylesworth, Jim. *Hanna's Hog.*
——. *The Folks in the Valley: A Pennsylvania Dutch ABC.*
——. *McGraw's Emporium.*
Baker, Keith. *The Dove's Letter.*
Bang, Molly. *Dawn.*
——. *Delphine.*
——. *The Paper Crane.*
Bartone, Elisa. *Peppe the Lamplighter.*
Bodkin, Odds. *The Banshee Train.*
Brown, Craig McFarland. *The Patchwork Farmer.*
Brown, Marc. *Arthur's Teacher Trouble.*
——. *The Bionic Bunny Show.*
——. *The True Francine.*
Brown, Ruth. *The Big Sneeze.*
Browne, Anthony. *Piggybook.*
Bunting, Eve. *Fly Away Home.*
——. *Smoky Night.*
Burningham, John. *John Patrick Norman McHennessy: The Boy Who Was Always Late.*
Burton, Virginia Lee. *Mike Mulligan and His Steam Shovel.*
Carle, Eric. *Walter the Baker.*
Castle, Caroline, and Peter Weevers. *Herbert Binns & the Flying Tricycle.*
Chetwin, Grace. *Box and Cox.*
Christelow, Eileen. *Five Little Monkeys Jumping on the Bed.*
Cohen, Miriam. *Lost in the Museum.*
Cole, Babette. *Hurray for Ethelyn.*
Cole, Joanna. *The Magic School Bus in the Time of the Dinosaurs.*
——. *The Magic School Bus Inside the Earth.*
——. *The Magic School Bus Lost in the Solar System.*
——. *The Magic School Bus on the Ocean Floor.*
Conrad, Pam. *The Lost Sailor.*
——. *The Tub People.*
Cooney, Barbara. *Island Boy.*
——. *Miss Rumphius.*
Crews, Donald. *Parade.*
Day, Alexandra. *Frank and Ernest.*
dePaola, Tomie. *The Art Lesson.*
——. *Charlie Needs a Cloak.*

Waggoner, Karen. *The Lemonade Babysitter.*
Weller, Frances Ward. *Riptide.*
Williams, Sherley Anne. *Working Cotton.*
Williams, Vera B. *A Chair For My Mother.*
———. *Something Special for Me.*
Wittman, Patricia. *Go Ask Giorgio!*
Wolff, Ferida. *The Woodcutter's Coat.*
Yashima, Taro. *Crow Boy.*
Yee, Paul. *Roses Sing on New Snow.*
Yolen, Jane. *The Seeing Stick.*
Yorinks, Arthur. *Louis the Fish.*
———. *Whitefish Will Rides Again!*
Zemach, Harve. *The Judge: An Untrue Tale.*
Ziefert, Harriet. *A New Coat for Anna.*
Zion, Gene. *The Plant Sitter.*

ORPHANS *See* **FAMILIES—Orphans**

PARADES

Baer, Gene. *Thump, Thump, Rat-a-tat-tat.*
Crews, Donald. *Parade.*
Hutchins, Pat. *The Wind Blew.*
Jonas, Ann. *Aardvarks, Disembark!*
Mahy, Margaret. *The Queen's Goat.*
Pinkney, Brian. *Max Found Two Sticks.*
Polacco, Patricia. *Meteor!*

PARKS *See* **NEIGHBORHOODS AND COMMUNITIES—Parks**
PARTIES *See also* **FAMILIES—Family gatherings/Outings**

Adoff, Arnold. *Hard to Be Six.*
Babbitt, Natalie. *Nellie: A Cat on Her Own.*
Baker, Betty. *The Turkey Girl.*
Brown, Marc. *Arthur's Halloween.*
dePaola, Tomie. *An Early American Christmas.*
Ets, Marie Hall and Aurora Labastida. *Nine Days to Christmas.*
Finchler, Judy. *Miss Malarkey Doesn't Live in Room 10.*
Freeman, Don. *Dandelion.*
Gershator, Phillis. *Sambalena Show-Off.*
Hoban, Lillian. *Arthur's Great Big Valentine.*
Hoban, Russell. *A Birthday for Frances.*
Hughes, Shirley. *Alfie Gives a Hand.*
Ichikawa, Satomi. *Nora's Castle.*
Jonas, Ann. *The 13th Clue.*
Keats, Ezra Jack. *A Letter to Amy.*
Kherdian, David. *The Cat's Midsummer Jamboree.*
Martin, Jacqueline Briggs. *Good Times on Grandfather Mountain.*
McKissack, Patricia. *Mirandy and Brother Wind.*

Minarik, Else Holmelund. *Little Bear's Friend.*
Mora, Pat. *A Birthday Basket for Tia.*
Murphy, Jill. *All in One Piece.*
Neitzel, Shirley. *The Dress I'll Wear to the Party.*
Noble, Trinka Hakes. *Jimmy's Boa Bounces Back.*
Paxton, Tom. *Engelbert the Elephant.*
Polacco, Patricia. *The Keeping Quilt.*
Steig, William. *Brave Irene.*
Stevenson, James. *The Worst Person's Christmas.*
Vincent, Gabrielle. *Merry Christmas, Ernest and Celestine.*
Williams, Vera B. *Music, Music for Everyone.*

PATHS *See* **TRAILS**

PEACE *See also* **WAR**

Asch, Frank, and Vladimir Vagin. *Here Comes the Cat! = Siuda idet kot!*
Christiansen, Candace. *Calico and Tin Horns.*
Coerr, Eleanor. *Sadako.*
Lionni, Leo. *Six Crows: A Fable.*
Say, Allen. *Tree of Cranes.*

PERSONAL PROBLEMS

Breaking promises

Bang, Molly. *Dawn.*
Gray, Libba Moore. *Small Green Snake.*
Lobel, Arnold. *A Treeful of Pigs.*
Marshall, James. *George and Martha, Tons of Fun.*
McCully, Emily Arnold. *The Amazing Felix.*
Van Allsburg, Chris. *Jumanji.*

Fearing to try something new

Alexander, Martha. *When the New Baby Comes, I'm Moving Out.*
Bang, Molly. *Delphine.*
Carrick, Carol. *The Foundling.*
Freeman, Don. *Mop Top.*
Hest, Amy. *The Purple Coat.*
Howard, Elizabeth Fitzgerald. *The Train to Lulu's.*
McCully, Emily Arnold. *First Snow.*
Pomerantz, Charlotte. *Flap Your Wings and Try.*
Sharmat, Marjorie Weinman. *Gila Monsters Meet You at the Airport.*

Getting lost

Andrews, Jan. *Very First Time.*
Bahr, Mary. *The Memory Box.*
Cohen, Miriam. *Lost in the Museum.*
Conrad, Pam. *The Lost Sailor.*
Freeman, Don. *A Pocket for Corduroy.*
Henkes, Kevin. *Sheila Rae, the Brave.*
Hutchins, Pat. *Where's the Baby?*
Krahn, Fernando. *The Secret in the Dungeon.*

McCully, Emily Arnold. *The Amazing Felix.*
———. *Picnic.*
Steig, William. *Sylvester and the Magic Pebble.*

Giving up security objects

Henkes, Kevin. *Owen.*
Hughes, Shirley. *Alfie Gives a Hand.*
Inkpen, Mick. *Kipper.*
Keller, Holly. *Geraldine's Blanket.*
Waber, Bernard. *Ira Sleeps Over.*

Name-calling

Pilkey, Dav. *Hallo-Weiner.*
Rosenberg, Liz. *Monster Mama.*

Running away

Ackerman, Karen. *The Tin Heart.*
Hoban, Russell. *A Baby Sister for Frances.*
Hopkinson, Deborah. *Sweet Clara and the Freedom Quilt.*
Keats, Ezra Jack. *Peter's Chair.*
Polacco, Patricia. *Pink and Say.*
Sendak, Maurice. *Where the Wild Things Are.*
Seuss, Dr. *Horton Hatches the Egg.*
Wells, Rosemary. *Noisy Nora.*
Wilkon, Piotr. *Rosie the Cool Cat.*
Winter, Jeanette. *Follow the Drinking Gourd.*
Zion, Gene. *Harry, the Dirty Dog.*

Others

Ackerman, Karen. *The Tin Heart.*
Gershator, Phillis. *Sambalena Show-Off.*
McCully, Smily Arnold. *Mirette on the High Wire.*
Mitchell, Rita Phillips. *Hue Boy.*
Uchida, Yoshiko. *The Bracelet.*

PETS *See* **ANIMALS—Pets**

PHOTOGRAPHY

Brunhoff, Jean de. *The Story of Babar.*
Gould, Deborah Lee. *Grandpa's Slide Show.*
Vincent, Gabrielle. *Smile, Ernest and Celestine.*
Willard, Nancy. *Simple Pictures Are Best.*
Williams, Vera B. *Something Special for Me.*
Zolotow, Charlotte. *This Quiet Lady.*

PILGRIMS *See* **HOLIDAYS AND CELEBRATIONS—Thanksgiving**
PIONEERS *See* **HISTORICAL PERIODS—Nineteenth Century**
PIRATES

Burningham, John. *Come Away from the Water, Shirley.*
Isadora, Rachel. *The Pirates of Bedford Street.*

PLANTS *See also* **GARDENS**

Alexander, Martha. *Even That Moose Won't Listen to Me.*
Baylor, Byrd. *The Other Way to Listen.*

Geisert, Arthur. *Pigs from A to Z.*
Hoopes, Lyn Littlefield. *Wing-a-Ding.*
Houston, Gloria. *The Year of the Perfect Christmas Tree.*
Howard, Elizabeth Fitzgerald. *Chita's Christmas Tree.*
Johnston, Tony. *Yonder.*
Ketteman, Helen. *The Year of No More Corn.*
Kherdian, David. *The Cat's Midsummer Jamboree.*
Lydon, Kerry Raines. *A Birthday for Blue.*
Martin, Bill, and John Archambault. *Chicka Chicka Boom Boom.*
———. *The Ghost-Eye Tree.*
Minarik, Else Holmelund. *Little Bear's Friend.*
Polacco, Patricia. *The Bee Tree.*
Ryder, Joanne. *Hello, Tree!*
Say, Allen. *Tree of Cranes.*
Schertle, Alice. *Witch Hazel.*
Seuss, Dr. *The Lorax.*
Van Allsburg, Chris. *Just a Dream.*
Wiesner, David. *Hurricane.*
Yolen, Jane. *Owl Moon.*
Vegetables *See also* **PUMPKINS**
Ehlert, Lois. *Eating the Alphabet: Fruits and Vegetables from A to Z.*
———. *Growing Vegetable Soup.*
McNulty, Faith. *The Lady and the Spider.*
Meddaugh, Susan. *Hog-Eye.*
Potter, Beatrix. *The Tale of Peter Rabbit.*
Others
Domanska, Janina. *Busy Monday Morning.*
Fleischman, Paul. *The Animal Hedge.*
Keats, Ezra Jack. *Clementina's Cactus.*
Lawson, Julie. *The Dragon's Pearl.*
Meddaugh, Susan. *Hog-Eye.*
Williams, Sherley Anne. *Working Cotton.*
Zion, Gene. *The Plant Sitter.*
PLAY *See also* **GAMES/PUZZLES/TRICKS**
Adoff, Arnold. *Hard to Be Six.*
Asch, Frank. *Sand Cake.*
Blos, Joan. *Lottie's Circus.*
Briggs, Raymond. *The Snowman.*
Brown, Marc. *Arthur Babysits.*
Burningham, John. *Where's Julius?*
Cutler, Jane. *Darcy and Gran Don't Like Babies.*
Ets, Marie Hall. *Play with Me.*
Freeman, Don. *Mop Top.*
Grifalconi, Ann. *Osa's Pride.*
Henkes, Kevin. *The Biggest Boy.*
———. *Jessica.*

———. *Owen.*

Hoban, Lillian. *Arthur's Great Big Valentine.*

Hoban, Russell,. *A Bargain for Frances.*

———. *Best Friends for Frances.*

Hoffman, Mary. *Amazing Grace.*

Hoopes, Lyn Littlefield. *Wing-a-Ding.*

Houghton, Eric. *The Backwards Watch.*

Howard, Elizabeth Fitzgerald. *Aunt Flossie's Hats (And Crab Cakes Later).*

Hughes, Shirley. *The Big Alfie and Annie Rose Storybook.*

———. *The Big Concrete Lorry: A Tale of Trotter Street.*

Keats, Ezra Jack. *The Snowy Day.*

Keller, Holly. *Geraldine's Big Snow.*

Khalsa, Dayal Kaur. *Cowboy Dreams.*

———. *The Snow Cat.*

Kraus, Robert. *Milton the Early Riser.*

Lester, Alison. *Clive Eats Alligators.*

———. *The Journey Home.*

———. *Magic Beach.*

———. *Tessa Snaps Snakes.*

Martin, Rafe. *Will's Mammoth.*

McLerran, Alice. *Roxaboxen.*

Miller, Margaret. *Whose Hat?*

Minarik, Else Holmelund. *Little Bear's Friend.*

Moss, Thylias. *I Want to Be.*

Neitzel, Shirley. *The Jacket I Wear in the Snow.*

Ness, Evaline. *Sam, Bangs, & Moonshine.*

Norman, Philip Ross. *A Mammoth Imagination.*

Oram, Hiawyn. *In the Attic.*

Rayner, Mary. *Garth Pig and the Ice-Cream Lady.*

Rice, Eve. *Goodnight, Goodnight.*

Ringgold, Faith. *Dinner at Aunt Connie's House.*

Ryder, Joanne. *A House by the Sea.*

———. *A Wet and Sandy Day.*

Scott, Ann Herbert. *Sam.*

Seuss, Dr. *The Cat in the Hat.*

Shulevitz, Uri. *Rain Rain Rivers.*

Spier, Peter. *Peter Spier's Rain.*

Tresselt, Alvin R. *Hide and Seek Fog.*

Twining, Edith. *Sandman.*

Van Allsburg, Chris. *Jumanji.*

Wegen, Ronald. *Sky Dragon.*

Wildsmith, Brian. *The Lazy Bear.*

POST OFFICE *See* **WRITING—Letters**

POVERTY

Baker, Betty. *The Turkey Girl.*

Bang, Molly. *The Paper Crane.*

Bartone, Elisa. *Peppe the Lamplighter*.
Baylor, Byrd. *Amigo*.
Bunting, Eve. *Fly Away Home*.
Chaffin, Lillie. *We Be Warm Till Springtime Comes*.
Coomb, Patricia. *The Magic Pot*.
DiSalvo-Ryan, DyAnne. *Uncle Willie and the Soup Kitchen*.
Fleischman, Paul. *The Animal Hedge*.
French, Fiona. *Anancy and Mr. Dry-Bones*.
Haseley, Dennis. *The Old Banjo*.
Hathorn, Elizabeth. *Way Home*.
Hoban, Russell. *Emmet Otter's Jug-Band Christmas*.
Isadora, Rachel. *At the Crossroads*.
Johnston, Tony. *Pages of Music*.
Kent, Jack. *Socks for Supper*.
Lawson, Julie. *The Dragon's Pearl*.
Mendez, Phil. *The Black Snowman*.
Mills, Lauren. *The Rag Coat*.
Phillips, Mildred. *The Sign in Mendel's Window*.
Polacco, Patricia. *Pink and Say*.
Ringgold, Faith. *Tar Beach*.
Rylant, Cynthia. *An Angel for Solomon Singer*.
———. *Miss Maggie*.
———. *When I Was Young in the Mountains*.
Schroeder, Alan. *Ragtime Tumpie*.
Thomas, Jane Resh. *Lights on the River*.
Tompert, Ann. *The Silver Whistle*.
Williams, Sherley Anne. *Working Cotton*.
Ziefert, Harriet. *A New Coat for Anna*.

PRESENTS *See* **GIFTS**

PUMPKINS

Dillon, Jana. *Jeb Scarecrow's Pumpkin Patch*.
McDonald, Megan. *The Great Pumpkin Switch*.
Schertle, Alice. *Witch Hazel*.
Silverman, Erica. *Big Pumpkin*.
Titherington, Jeanne. *Pumpkin, Pumpkin*.
Williams, Linda. *The Little Old Lady Who Was Not Afraid of Anything*.

PUPPETS

Babbitt, Natalie. *Nellie: A Cat on Her Own*.
Cleaver, Elizabeth. *Petrouchka*.
Fleischman, Paul. *Shadow Play*.
Keats, Ezra Jack. *Louie*.

QUILTS

Coerr, Eleanor. *The Josefina Story Quilt*.
Ernst, Lisa Campbell. *Sam Johnson and the Blue Ribbon Quilt*.

Fair, Sylvia. *The Bedspread.*
Flournoy, Valerie. *The Patchwork Quilt.*
Hopkinson, Deborah. *Sweet Clara and the Freedom Quilt.*
Johnston, Tony. *The Quilt Story.*
Jonas, Ann. *The Quilt.*
Mills, Lauren. *The Rag Coat.*
Polacco, Patricia. *The Keeping Quilt.*
Ringgold, Faith. *Aunt Harriet's Underground Railroad in the Sky.*
———. *Dinner at Aunt Connie's House.*
———. *Tar Beach.*

RACES *See* **MOVEMENT/SPEED**
RAIN *See* **WEATHER—RAIN**
RANCHES *See also* **FARMS**
Brett, Jon. *Armadillo Rodeo.*
Johnston, Tony. *The Cowboy and the Black-eyed Pea.*
Noble, Trinka Hakes. *Meanwhile Back at the Ranch.*
Rounds, Glen. *Cowboys.*
Sharmat, Marjorie Weinman. *Gila Monsters Meet You at the Airport.*
Yorinks, Arthur. *Whitefish Will Rides Again!*
READING
Adoff, Arnold. *Hard to Be Six.*
Arnold, Tedd. *The Signmaker's Assistant.*
Baker, Keith. *The Dove's Letter.*
Bunting, Eve. *The Wednesday Surprise.*
Cole, Joanna. *The Magic School Bus Inside the Human Body.*
———. *The Magic School Bus Lost in the Solar System.*
———. *The Magic School Bus on the Ocean Floor.*
dePaola, Tomie. *The Knight and the Dragon.*
———. *The Popcorn Book.*
———. *The Quicksand Book.*
Duvoisin, Roger. *Petunia.*
Fox, Mem. *Possum Magic.*
Hoban, Tana. *I Read Signs.*
———. *I Read Symbols.*
Johnston, Tony. *Amber on the Mountain.*
Lobel, Arnold. *Frog and Toad Together.*
———. *Mouse Soup.*
Marshall, James. *George and Martha Back in Town.*
Meddaugh, Susan. *Hog-Eye.*
Polacco, Patricia. *The Bee Tree.*
———. *Pink and Say.*
Sadler, Marilyn. *Alistair in Outer Space.*
Speed, Toby. *Hattie Baked a Wedding Cake.*
Stewart, Sarah. *The Library.*

Bolliger, Max. *The Lonely Prince.*
Briggs, Raymond. *Father Christmas.*
Brunhoff, Jean de. *The Story of Babar.*
Burningham, John. *Time to Get Out of the Bath, Shirley.*
Carle, Eric. *Walter the Baker.*
de Regniers, Beatrice Schenk. *May I Bring a Friend?*
Friedman, Aileen. *A Cloak for the Dreamer.*
Fritz, Jean. *The Great Adventure of Christopher Columbus.*
Garland, Sherry. *The Lotus Seed.*
Gerrard, Roy. *Sir Cedric.*
Goodall, John S. *Paddy's New Hat.*
Gregory, Valiska. *Through the Mickle Woods.*
Haugaard, Erik Christian. *Prince Boghole.*
Heine, Helme. *The Most Wonderful Egg in the World.*
Lobel, Arnold. *Uncle Elephant.*
Mahy, Margaret. *The Queen's Goat.*
Mendez, Phil. *The Black Snowman.*
Nesbit, E. *Melisande.*
Paxton, Tom. *Engelbert the Elephant.*
Price, Leontyne. *Aïda.*
Schwartz, Amy. *Her Majesty, Aunt Essie.*
Sendak, Maurice. *Where the Wild Things Are.*
Sis, Peter. *Follow the Dream.*
Steig, William. *Brave Irene.*
Tyler, Anne. *Tumble Tower.*
Yolen, Jane. *The Seeing Stick.*

SAFETY/DANGER
Agee, Jon. *The Return of Freddy LeGrand.*
Andrews, Jan. *Very First Time.*
Asch, Frank. *Skyfire.*
———. *Turtle Tale.*
Baker, Betty. *The Turkey Girl.*
Bang, Molly. *Delphine.*
Bodkin, Odds. *The Banshee Train.*
Brett, Jan. *Armadillo Rodeo.*
Brown, Ruth. *The Picnic.*
Browne, Anthony. *Bear Hunt.*
———. *Tunnel.*
Bunting, Eve. *How Many Days to America? A Thanksgiving Story.*
———. *The Mother's Day Mice.*
———. *Smoky Night.*
Burningham, John. *Come Away from the Water, Shirley.*
Calhoun, Mary. *Henry.*
Carle, Eric. *A House for Hermit Crab.*

———. *The Magic School Bus Lost in the Solar System.*
———. *The Magic School Bus on the Ocean Floor.*
Crews, Donald. *School Bus.*
dePaola, Tomie. *Oliver Button Is a Sissy.*
———. *The Art Lesson.*
Finchler, Judy. *Miss Malarkey Doesn't Live in Room 10.*
Goodall, John S. *Naughty Nancy Goes to School.*
Heide, Florence Parry. *The Shrinking of Treehorn.*
Henkes, Kevin. *Chrysanthemum.*
———. *Jessica.*
———. *Sheila Rae, the Brave.*
Hoffman, Mary. *Amazing Grace.*
Houston, Gloria. *My Great-Aunt Arizona.*
Hughes, Shirley. *The Big Alfie and Annie Rose Storybook.*
Isadora, Rachel. *Willaby.*
Jonas, Ann. *The Trek.*
Keller, Holly. *The New Boy.*
Kellogg, Steven. *The Mysterious Tadpole.*
Kroll, Steven. *The Tyrannosaurus Game.*
Kroll, Virginia L. *Masai and I.*
Lionni, Leo. *Matthew's Dream.*
McCully, Emily Arnold. *School.*
Meddaugh, Susan. *Hog-Eye.*
Mills, Lauren. *The Rag Coat.*
Noble, Trinka Hakes. *The Day Jimmy's Boa Ate the Wash.*
Rand, Gloria. *Prince William.*
Rathmann, Peggy. *Officer Buckle and Gloria.*
Rochelle, Belinda. *When Jo Louis Won the Title.*
Ryder, Joanne. *One Small Fish.*
Sadler, Marilyn. *Alistair's Elephant.*
Say, Allen. *The Bicycle Man.*
———. *Stranger in the Mirror.*
Schwartz, Amy. *Annabelle Swift, Kindergartner.*
———. *Bea and Mr. Jones.*
Steig, William. *The Amazing Bone.*
Stevenson, James. *The Night After Christmas.*
———. *That Dreadful Day.*
Ungerer, Tomi. *Crictor.*
Viorst, Judith. *Alexander and the Terrible, Horrible, No Good, Very Bad Day.*
Wells, Rosemary. *Timothy Goes to School.*
Wildsmith, Brian. *Goat's Trail.*
Yashima, Taro. *Crow Boy.*
SEASONS *See* **TIME—Specific seasons**
SECRETS
Ackerman, Karen. *The Tin Heart.*

Allard, Harry. *Miss Nelson Has a Field Day.*

———. *Miss Nelson Is Missing!*

Baylor, Byrd. *Your Own Best Secret Place.*

Baylor, Byrd, and Peter Parnall. *Your Own Best Place.*

Brown, Marc. *Arthur's April Fool.*

———. *Arthur's Valentine.*

Burningham, John. *Aldo.*

———. *Time to Get Out of the Bath, Shirley.*

Christiansen, Candace. *Calico and Tin Horns.*

Crews, Donald. *Shortcut.*

Fisher, Aileen. *Listen, Rabbit.*

Friedman, Ina R. *How My Parents Learned to Eat.*

Garland, Sherry. *The Lotus Seed.*

Gerstein, Mordicai. *William, Where are You?*

Heide, Florence Parry, and Judith Heide Gilliland. *The Day of Ahmed's Secret.*

Hoban, Lillian. *Arthur's Great Big Valentine.*

Hoban, Russell. *Emmet Otter's Jug-Band Christmas.*

Howard, Elizabeth Fitzgerald. *Papa Tells Chita a Story.*

Ichikawa, Satomi. *Nora's Castle.*

Innocenti, Roberto. *Rose Blanche.*

Jonas, Ann. *The Trek.*

Leedy, Loreen. *Tracks in the Sand.*

Lester, Alison. *Tessa Snaps Snakes.*

McCloskey, Robert. *One Morning in Maine.*

McCully, Emily Arnold. *Mirette on the High Wire.*

Mills, Lauren. *The Rag Coat.*

Oram, Hiawyn. *In the Attic.*

Polacco, Patricia. *Appelemando's Dreams.*

———. *Chicken Sunday.*

———. *Pink and Say.*

Rathmann, Peggy. *Officer Buckle and Gloria.*

Ringgold, Faith. *Aunt Harriet's Underground Railroad in the Sky.*

Ryder, Joanne. *The Goodbye Walk.*

Schertle, Alice. *Witch Hazel.*

Van Allsburg, Chris. *The Wretched Stone.*

SEEDS *See* **PLANTS—Seeds**

SELF-IDENTITY *See* **IDENTITY—Self-worth**

SENSES

Marshall, James. *George and Martha, One Fine Day.*

Ray, Deborah Kogan. *The Cloud.*

Rydell, Katy. *Wind Says Good Night.*

Ryder, Joanne. *Lizard in the Sun.*

———. *One Small Fish.*

———. *The Snail's Spell.*

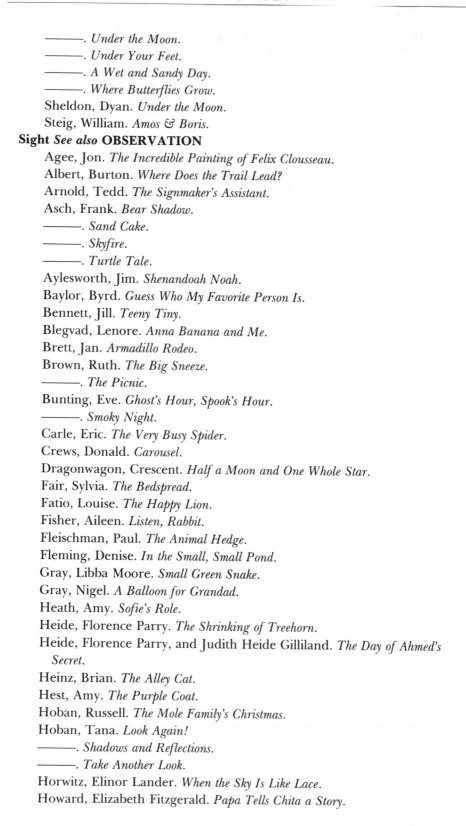

————. *Under the Moon.*

————. *Under Your Feet.*

————. *A Wet and Sandy Day.*

————. *Where Butterflies Grow.*

Sheldon, Dyan. *Under the Moon.*

Steig, William. *Amos & Boris.*

Sight *See also* **OBSERVATION**

Agee, Jon. *The Incredible Painting of Felix Clousseau.*

Albert, Burton. *Where Does the Trail Lead?*

Arnold, Tedd. *The Signmaker's Assistant.*

Asch, Frank. *Bear Shadow.*

————. *Sand Cake.*

————. *Skyfire.*

————. *Turtle Tale.*

Aylesworth, Jim. *Shenandoah Noah.*

Baylor, Byrd. *Guess Who My Favorite Person Is.*

Bennett, Jill. *Teeny Tiny.*

Blegvad, Lenore. *Anna Banana and Me.*

Brett, Jan. *Armadillo Rodeo.*

Brown, Ruth. *The Big Sneeze.*

————. *The Picnic.*

Bunting, Eve. *Ghost's Hour, Spook's Hour.*

————. *Smoky Night.*

Carle, Eric. *The Very Busy Spider.*

Crews, Donald. *Carousel.*

Dragonwagon, Crescent. *Half a Moon and One Whole Star.*

Fair, Sylvia. *The Bedspread.*

Fatio, Louise. *The Happy Lion.*

Fisher, Aileen. *Listen, Rabbit.*

Fleischman, Paul. *The Animal Hedge.*

Fleming, Denise. *In the Small, Small Pond.*

Gray, Libba Moore. *Small Green Snake.*

Gray, Nigel. *A Balloon for Grandad.*

Heath, Amy. *Sofie's Role.*

Heide, Florence Parry. *The Shrinking of Treehorn.*

Heide, Florence Parry, and Judith Heide Gilliland. *The Day of Ahmed's Secret.*

Heinz, Brian. *The Alley Cat.*

Hest, Amy. *The Purple Coat.*

Hoban, Russell. *The Mole Family's Christmas.*

Hoban, Tana. *Look Again!*

————. *Shadows and Reflections.*

————. *Take Another Look.*

Horwitz, Elinor Lander. *When the Sky Is Like Lace.*

Howard, Elizabeth Fitzgerald. *Papa Tells Chita a Story.*

Aylesworth, Jim. *McGraw's Emporium.*

Benjamin, Amanda. *Two's Company.*

Brown, Marc. *Arthur's TV Trouble.*

Carlstrom, Nancy White. *Baby-O.*

Daly, Niki. *Not So Fast, Songololo.*

de Regniers, Beatrice Schenk. *Waiting for Mama.*

Ets, Marie Hall, and Aurora Labastida. *Nine Days to Christmas.*

Florian, Douglas. *The City.*

Freeman, Don. *Corduroy.*

Goodall, John S. *The Story of a Main Street.*

Hall, Donald. *Ox-Cart Man.*

Hutchins, Pat. *You'll Soon Grow into Them, Titch.*

Kovalski, Maryann. *The Wheels on the Bus.*

Lester, Alison. *Clive Eats Alligators.*

Levitin, Sonia. *The Man Who Kept His Heart in a Bucket.*

Lobel, Anita. *On Market Street.*

McCloskey, Robert. *One Morning in Maine.*

Mendez, Phil. *The Black Snowman.*

Modell, Frank. *One Zillion Valentines.*

Polacco, Patricia. *Chicken Sunday.*

Potter, Beatrix. *The Tale of Peter Rabbit.*

Schroeder, Alan. *Carolina Shout!*

Titherington, Jeanne. *Sophy and Auntie Pearl.*

Williams, Vera B. *Something Special for Me.*

Wolff, Ferida. *The Woodcutter's Coat.*

Zion, Gene. *No Roses for Harry.*

SIGNS *See* **COMMUNICATIONS—Signs; WRITING—Signs**

SLAVERY

Ackerman, Karen. *The Tin Heart.*

Hopkinson, Deborah. *Sweet Clara and the Freedom Quilt.*

Mendez, Phil. *The Black Snowman.*

Ringgold, Faith. *Aunt Harriet's Underground Railroad in the Sky.*

———. *Dinner at Aunt Connie's House.*

Turner, Ann Warren. *Nettie's Trip South.*

Winter, Jeanette. *Follow the Drinking Gourd.*

SLEEPING *See also* **EVERYDAY EXPERIENCES—Time of day, bedtime; EVERYDAY EXPERIENCES—Time of day, nighttime**

Adoff, Arnold. *Hard to Be Six.*

Asch, Frank. *Mooncake.*

Bennett, Jill. *Teeny Tiny.*

Berger, Barbara. *Grandfather Twilight.*

Brown, Ruth. *The Big Sneeze.*

Burningham, John. *Hey! Get Off Our Train.*

Carlstrom, Nancy White. *Who Gets the Sun Out of Bed?*

Cohen, Caron Lee. *Whiffle Squeek.*

Dragonwagon, Crescent. *Half a Moon and One Whole Star.*

Freeman, Don. *Bearymore*.
Grifalconi, Ann. *Darkness and the Butterfly*.
Hutchins, Pat. *Good Night, Owl!*
————. *Where's the Baby?*
Inkpen, Mick. *Kipper*.
Kraus, Robert. *Milton the Early Riser*.
Lobel, Arnold. *Owl at Home*.
Luenn, Nancy. *Nessa's Fish*.
MacLachlan, Patricia. *Mama One, Mama Two*.
Minarik, Else Holmelund. *Little Bear's Visit*.
Murphy, Jill. *Peace at Last*.
Ormerod, Jan. *Moonlight*.
Pilkey, Dav. *When Cats Dream*.
Rice, Eve. *City Night*.
Rydell, Katy. *Wind Says Good Night*.
Ryder, Joanne. *The Night Flight*.
Shepperson, Rob. *The Sandman*.
Slobodkina, Esphyr. *Caps for Sale*.
Steig, William. *Gorky Rises*.
Twining, Edith. *Sandman*.
Vincent, Gabrielle. *Merry Christmas, Ernest and Celestine*.
Weiss, Nicki. *Where Does the Brown Bear Go?*
Wiesner, David. *Free Fall*.
Wildsmith, Brian. *Carousel*.
Wood, Audrey. *The Napping House*.
Zion, Gene. *The Plant Sitter*.

SNOW *See* **WEATHER—Snow**

SOUNDS *See* **SENSES**

SPACE *See also* **ASTRONOMY**

Asch, Frank. *Mooncake*.
Cole, Joanna. *The Magic School Bus Lost in the Solar System*.
Minarik, Else Holmelund. *Little Bear*.
Murphy, Jill. *What Next, Baby Bear!*
Sadler, Marilyn. *Alistair in Outer Space*.
Steig, William. *Gorky Rises*.

SPORTS *See also* **FISHING; MOUNTAIN CLIMBING**

Allard, Harry. *Miss Nelson Has a Field Day*.
Brown, Marc. *The True Francine*.
Browne, Anthony. *Bear Hunt*.
dePaola, Tomie. *Oliver Button Is a Sissy*.
Fox, Mem. *Koala Lou*.
Golenbock, Peter. *Teammates*.
Isadora, Rachel. *Max*.
Kroll, Steven. *Friday the 13th*.
Marshall, James. *George and Martha Back in Town*.

Rochelle, Belinda. *When Jo Louis Won the Title.*

Say, Allen. *El Chino.*

Teague, Mark. *The Field Beyond the Outfield.*

Van Allsburg, Chris. *The Wreck of the Zephyr.*

Welch, Willy. *Playing Right Field.*

STATUES

Blegvad, Lenore. *Anna Banana and Me.*

Browne, Anthony. *Tunnel.*

Coerr, Eleanor. *Sadako.*

Crews, Donald. *Bicycle Race.*

Hughes, Shirley. *The Big Alfie and Annie Rose Storybook.*

Leighton, Maxinne Rhea. *An Ellis Island Christmas.*

Levinson, Riki. *Watch the Stars Come Out.*

Ryder, Joanne. *The Night Flight.*

Tompert, Ann. *The Silver Whistle.*

STORIES

Minimal or no text *See also* OBSERVATION

Anno, Mitsumasa. *Anno's Alphabet.*

————. *Anno's Britain.*

————. *Anno's Italy.*

————. *Anno's Journey.*

————. *Anno's U.S.A.*

Asch, Frank, and Vladimir Vagin. *Here Comes the Cat! = Siuda idet kot!*

Azarian, Mary. *A Farmer's Alphabet.*

Baker, Jeannie. *Window.*

Baker, Keith. *Hide and Snake.*

————. *Who Is the Beast?*

Bang, Molly. *Delphine.*

————. *Yellow Ball.*

Barton, Byron. *Airport.*

Briggs, Raymond. *Father Christmas.*

————. *The Snowman.*

Brown, Craig McFarland. *The Patchwork Farmer.*

Carle, Eric. *Do You Want to Be My Friend?*

————. *1, 2, 3 to the Zoo.*

Crews, Donald. *Bicycle Race.*

————. *Flying.*

————. *Freight Train.*

————. *Harbor.*

————. *School Bus.*

————. *Truck.*

dePaola, Tomie. *The Knight and the Dragon.*

————. *Pancakes for Breakfast.*

————. *Sing, Pierrot, Sing.*

Dodds, Dayle Ann. *Wheel Away!*

Wood, Audrey. *The Napping House*.

Zemach, Harve. *The Judge: An Untrue Tale*.

Zolotow, Charlotte. *Do You Know What I'll Do?*

Zolotow, Charlotte. *Some Things Go Together*.

————. *This Quiet Lady*.

STORYTELLING

Ackerman, Karen. *Song and Dance Man*.

Arnold, Tedd. *No More Water in the Tub!*

Aylesworth, Jim. *Shenandoah Noah*.

Bang, Molly. *Dawn*.

Baylor, Byrd. *The Desert Is Theirs*.

Blegvad, Lenore. *Anna Banana and Me*.

Brown, Marc. *Arthur Babysits*.

Cazet, Denys. *I'm Not Sleepy*.

Coerr, Eleanor. *Sadako*.

Cohen, Barbara. *Gooseberries to Oranges*.

dePaola, Tomie. *The Popcorn Book*.

Flournoy, Valerie. *The Patchwork Quilt*.

Franklin, Kristine L. *The Old, Old Man and the Very Little Boy*.

Greenfield, Eloise. *Africa Dream*.

Gregory, Valiska. *Through the Mickle Woods*.

Grifalconi, Ann. *Osa's Pride*.

Griffith, Helen V. *Grandaddy's Place*.

Haley, Gail E. *Sea Tale*.

Hartley, Deborah. *Up North in Winter*.

Hathorn, Elizabeth. *Grandma's Shoes*.

Howard, Elizabeth Fitzgerald. *Aunt Flossie's Hats (And Crab Cakes Later)*.

————. *Papa Tells Chita a Story*.

Isadora, Rachel. *The Pirates of Bedford Street*.

Johnson, Angela. *Tell Me a Story, Mama*.

Kesey, Ken. *Little Tricker the Squirrel Meets Big Double the Bear*.

Ketteman, Helen. *The Year of No More Corn*.

Kroll, Steven. *The Tyrannosaurus Game*.

Kroll, Virginia L. *Africa Brothers and Sisters*.

Lester, Helen. *Me First*.

Levinson, Riki. *Watch the Stars Come Out*.

Lionni, Leo. *The Biggest House in the World*.

Lobel, Arnold. *Days with Frog and Toad*.

————. *Frog and Toad Are Friends*.

————. *Mouse Soup*.

————. *Mouse Tales*.

MacLachlan, Patricia. *Mama One, Mama Two*.

Marion, Jeff Daniel. *Hello, Crow*.

Marshall, James. *George and Martha, One Fine Day*.

Martin, Bill, and John Archambault. *Knots on a Counting Rope*.

Gerrard, Roy. *Sir Cedric.*
Goodall, John S. *The Story of a Castle.*
Haugaard, Erik Christian. *Prince Boghole.*
Ichikawa, Satomi. *Nora's Castle.*
Krahn, Fernando. *The Secret in the Dungeon.*
McCully, Emily Arnold. *The Amazing Felix.*
Paxton, Tom. *Engelbert the Elephant.*
Shecter, Ben. *Conrad's Castle.*
Steig, William. *Brave Irene.*
Tyler, Anne. *Tumble Tower.*

churches

Houston, Gloria. *The Year of the Perfect Christmas Tree.*
Hughes, Shirley. *The Big Alfie and Annie Rose Storybook.*
Tompert, Ann. *The Silver Whistle.*

houses and other dwellings *See also* **ROOMS**

Anno, Mitsumasa. *Anno's Counting Book.*
———. *Anno's Counting House.*
Arnold, Tedd. *No Jumping on the Bed!*
———. *No More Water in the Tub!*
Bedard, Michael. *Emily.*
Blos, Joan. *Old Henry.*
Briggs, Raymond. *Father Christmas.*
Brown, Marc. *Arthur's Halloween.*
Bunting, Eve. *Ghost's Hour, Spook's Hour.*
———. *Smoky Night.*
Burningham, John. *Hey! Get Off Our Train.*
Burton, Virginia Lee. *The Little House.*
Carrick, Carol. *The Foundling.*
Chetwin, Grace. *Box and Cox.*
Cole, Babette. *Hurray for Ethelyn.*
Conrad, Pam. *The Lost Sailor.*
Crews, Donald. *Bigmama's.*
dePaola, Tomie. *Nana Upstairs & Nana Downstairs.*
Dragonwagon, Crescent. *Home Place.*
Gerstein, Mordicai. *The Room.*
———. *William, Where are You?*
Hathorn, Elizabeth. *Way Home.*
Hill, Elizabeth Starr. *Evan's Corner.*
Hughes, Shirley. *Alfie Gets in First.*
———. *The Big Concrete Lorry: A Tale of Trotter Street.*
Hutchins, Pat. *Clocks and More Clocks.*
Johnson, Angela. *The Leaving Morning.*
Jonas, Ann. *The 13th Clue.*
———. *Where Can It Be?*
Joyce, William. *A Day with Wilbur Robinson.*

Kent, Jack. *There's No Such Thing as a Dragon.*
Khalsa, Dayal Kaur. *The Snow Cat.*
Krahn, Fernando. *Arthur's Adventure in the Abandoned House.*
Legge, David. *Bamboozled.*
Lionni, Leo. *The Biggest House in the World.*
Lobel, Arnold. *Ming Lo Moves the Mountain.*
———. *Owl at Home.*
Martin, Jacqueline Briggs. *Good Times on Grandfather Mountain.*
McDonald, Megan. *The Potato Man.*
McLerran, Alice. *I Want to Go Home.*
Murphy, Shirley Rousseau. *Tattie's River Journey.*
Mwenye Hadithi. *Lazy Lion.*
Paulsen, Gary. *Dogteam.*
Provensen, Alice, and Martin Provensen. *Shaker Lane.*
Ray, Mary Lyn. *Pianna.*
Rounds, Glen. *Sod Houses on the Great Plains.*
Rylant, Cynthia. *Miss Maggie.*
Small, David. *Paper John.*
Stevenson, James. *That Terrible Halloween Night.*
Thompson, Colin. *The Paper Bag Prince.*
Turner, Ann Warren. *Dakota Dugout.*
Van Allsburg, Chris. *The Garden of Abdul Gasazi.*
Waber, Bernard. *The House on East 88th Street.*
Wild, Margaret. *The Very Best of Friends.*
Williams, Linda. *The Little Old Lady Who Was Not Afraid of Anything.*
Williams, Vera B. *A Chair For My Mother.*
Wood, Audrey. *The Napping House.*
libraries
Cooney, Barbara. *Miss Rumphius.*
Day, Alexandra. *Frank and Ernest.*
dePaola, Tomie. *The Knight and the Dragon.*
McCully, Emily Arnold. *The Christmas Gift.*
Sadler, Marilyn. *Alistair in OuterSpace.*
Stewart, Sarah. *The Library.*
Zion, Gene. *The Plant Sitter.*
museums
Cohen, Miriam. *Lost in the Museum.*
Fair, Sylvia. *The Bedspread.*
Freeman, Don. *Norman the Doorman.*
Kellogg, Steven. *Prehistoric Pinkerton.*
Lionni, Leo. *Matthew's Dream.*
Zolotow, Charlotte. *My Grandson Lew.*
schools
Cole, Joanna. *The Magic School Bus Inside the Earth.*
———. *The Magic School Bus Inside the Human Body.*

————. *The Wall.*

Carle, Eric. *A House for Hermit Crab.*

Ernst, Lisa Campbell. *A Colorful Adventure of the Bee, Who Left Home One Monday Morning and What He Found Along the Way.*

Geisert, Arthur. *Pigs from A to Z.*

Gibbons, Gail. *Flying.*

Leaf, Margaret. *Eyes of the Dragon.*

Rey, H. A. *Curious George.*

Rylant, Cynthia. *An Angel for Solomon Singer.*

Seuss, Dr. *Horton Hatches the Egg.*

Spier, Peter. *Peter Spier's Circus!*

Vaughan, Marcia K., and Patricia Mullins. *The Sea-Breeze Hotel.*

Yolen, Jane. *Letting Swift River Go.*

Wellner, Frances Ward. *Matthew Wheelock's Wall.*

SUN *See* **ASTRONOMY**

SURPRISES

Alexander, Martha. *Even That Moose Won't Listen to Me.*

Allard, Harry. *Miss Nelson Has a Field Day.*

Arnold, Tedd. *Green Wilma.*

————. *The Signmaker's Assistant.*

Asch, Frank. *Just Like Daddy.*

————. *Moondance.*

Asch, Frank, and Vladimir Vagin. *Here Comes the Cat! = Siuda idet kot!*

Baker, Keith. *Who Is the Beast?*

Baylor, Byrd, and Peter Parnall. *Your Own Best Place.*

Birdseye, Tom. *Airmail to the Moon.*

Brett, Jan. *Berlioz the Bear.*

Brown, Craig McFarland. *The Patchwork Farmer.*

Brown, Marc. *Arthur Babysits.*

————. *Arthur's Halloween.*

————. *Arthur's Teacher Trouble.*

————. *Arthur's Thanksgiving.*

Brown, Ruth. *The Big Sneeze.*

————. *The Picnic.*

Browne, Anthony. *Changes.*

————. *Piggybook.*

Bunting, Eve. *The Valentine Bears.*

————. *The Wednesday Surprise.*

Charlip, Remy. *Fortunately.*

Christelow, Eileen. *Five Little Monkeys Jumping on the Bed.*

Cole, Joanna. *The Magic School Bus in the Time of the Dinosaurs.*

Dillon, Jana. *Jeb Scarecrow's Pumpkin Patch.*

Finchler, Judy. *Miss Malarkey Doesn't Live in Room 10.*

Fisher, Aileen. *Listen, Rabbit.*

Fleischman, Paul. *Time Train.*

Pinkney, Brian. *Max Found Two Sticks.*
Polacco, Patricia. *Meteor!*
———. *Rechenka's Eggs.*
Purdy, Carol. *Mrs. Merriwether's Musical Cat.*
Rathmann, Peggy. *Officer Buckle and Gloria.*
Ray, Deborah Kogan. *The Cloud.*
Ringgold, Faith. *Dinner at Aunt Connie's House.*
Rogers, Jean. *Runaway Mittens.*
Rosenberg, Liz. *Monster Mama.*
Roy, Ron. *Three Ducks Went Wandering.*
Rylant, Cynthia. *All I See.*
Sadler, Marilyn. *Alistair in Outer Space.*
———. *Alistair's Elephant.*
Say, Allen. *Stranger in the Mirror.*
———. *Tree of Cranes.*
Scamell, Ragnhild. *Solo Plus One.*
Sharmat, Marjorie Weinman. *The Best Valentine in the World.*
Small, David. *Imogene's Antlers.*
Soto, Gary. *Chato's Kitchen.*
Steig, William. *Doctor De Soto.*
———. *Gorky Rises.*
Titherington, Jeanne. *A Place for Ben.*
Van Allsburg, Chris. *Bad Day at Riverbend.*
———. *The Sweetest Fig.*
Vaughan, Marcia K., and Patricia Mullins. *The Sea-Breeze Hotel.*
Vincent, Gabrielle. *Merry Christmas, Ernest and Celestine.*
Waber, Bernard. *Ira Says Goodbye.*
Wahl, Jan. *My Cat Ginger.*
Weiss, Nicki. *Where Does the Brown Bear Go?*
Wild, Margaret. *Thank You, Santa.*
Wildsmith, Brian. *Give a Dog a Bone.*
Wood, Audrey. *The Napping House.*
Yolen, Jane. *The Seeing Stick.*

SURVIVAL

Agee, Jon. *The Return of Freddy LeGrand.*
Baker, Betty. *The Turkey Girl.*
Bodkin, Odds. *The Banshee Train.*
Browne, Anthony. *Bear Hunt.*
Cannon, Janell. *Stellaluna.*
Carle, Eric. *The Honeybee and the Robber.*
Chaffin, Lillie. *We Be Warm Till Springtime Comes.*
Conrad, Pam. *The Lost Sailor.*
Ernst, Lisa Campbell. *Zinnia and Dot.*
Fox, Mem. *Hattie and the Fox.*
Goodall, John S. *Naughty Nancy Goes to School.*

TEACHERS *See* **SCHOOL EXPERIENCES**
TEETH *See* **BODY—Parts of body, teeth**
TIME
    Across time *See also* **HISTORICAL PERIODS—Across time**

————. *Magic Beach.*
Lewin, Hugh. *Jafta—the Journey.*
Luenn, Nancy. *Nessa's Fish.*
Lyon, George Ella. *Together.*
Martin, Bill, and John Archambault. *Chicka Chicka Boom Boom.*
Martin, Rafe. *Will's Mammoth.*
McCloskey, Robert. *Time of Wonder.*
Ryder, Joanne. *Dancers in the Garden.*
————. *Lizard in the Sun.*
————. *Sea Elf.*
————. *White Bear, Ice Bear.*
————. *Winter Whale.*
Rylant, Cynthia. *Night in the Country.*
Schoenherr, John. *The Barn.*
Serfozo, Mary. *Rain Talk.*
Spier, Peter. *Peter Spier's Rain.*
Steig, William. *Gorky Rises.*
Tafuri, Nancy. *Have You See My Duckling?*
Tejima, Keizaburo. *Fox's Dream.*
————. *Owl Lake.*
————. *Swan Sky.*
Van Allsburg, Chris. *The Polar Express.*
Wiesner, David. *Hurricane.*
Williams, Sherley Anne. *Working Cotton.*

days of the week
Adoff, Arnold. *Hard to Be Six.*
Carle, Eric. *The Very Hungry Caterpillar.*
Clifton, Lucille. *Some of the Days of Everett Anderson.*
de Regniers, Beatrice Schenk. *May I Bring a Friend?*
Domanska, Janina. *Busy Monday Morning.*
Fair, Sylvia. *The Bedspread.*
Lewin, Hugh. *Jafta and the Wedding.*
Ward, Cindy. *Cookie's Week.*
Wood, Audrey. *Heckedy Peg.*
Yolen, Jane. *No Bath Tonight.*

months of the year
Bowen, Betsy. *Antler, Bear, Canoe: A Northwoods Alphabet Year.*
Carle, Eric. *A House for Hermit Crab.*
Ryder, Joanne. *The Bear on the Moon.*
Wild, Margaret. *Thank You, Santa.*

seasons
Anno, Mitsumasa. *Anno's Counting Book.*
Asch, Frank. *Mooncake.*
Bedard, Michael. *Emily.*
Blos, Joan. *Old Henry.*

Turner, Ann Warren. *Stars for Sarah.*

Twining, Edith. *Sandman.*

Weiss, Nicki. *Where Does the Brown Bear Go?*

Wiesner, David. *Tuesday.*

Wilhelm, Hans. *I'll Always Love You.*

Williams, Linda. *The Little Old Lady Who Was Not Afraid of Anything.*

Winter, Jeanette. *Follow the Drinking Gourd.*

Yolen, Jane. *Owl Moon.*

Specific seasons

spring

Dana, Katharine Floyd. *Over in the Meadow.*

Fisher, Aileen. *Listen, Rabbit.*

Johnston, Tony. *Amber on the Mountain.*

Lobel, Arnold. *Frog and Toad Are Friends.*

Lyon, George Ella. *Come a Tide.*

Ryder, Joanne. *When the Woods Hum.*

Steig, William. *The Amazing Bone.*

Tejima, Keizaburo. *Swan Sky.*

summer

Asch, Frank. *Sand Cake.*

Bahr, Mary. *The Memory Box.*

Brown, Marc. *Arthur's Family Vacation.*

Brown, Ruth. *The Big Sneeze.*

Chall, Marsha Wilson. *Up North at the Cabin.*

Crews, Donald. *Bigmama's.*

Griffith, Helen V. *Georgia Music.*

———. *Grandaddy's Place.*

McCloskey, Robert. *Time of Wonder.*

McCully, Emily Arnold. *Picnic.*

Minarik, Else Holmelund. *Little Bear's Friend.*

Ringgold, Faith. *Tar Beach.*

Ryder, Joanne. *The Goodbye Walk.*

———. *A Wet and Sandy Day.*

———. *When the Woods Hum.*

———. *Winter Whale.*

Rylant, Cynthia. *The Relatives Came.*

fall

Dillon, Jana. *Jeb Scarecrow's Pumpkin Patch.*

Hest, Amy. *The Purple Coat.*

Lionni, Leo. *Frederick.*

Lotz, Karen E. *Snowsong Whistling.*

Luenn, Nancy. *Nessa's Fish.*

Martin, Bill, and John Archambault. *The Ghost-Eye Tree.*

McCully, Emily Arnold. *School.*

McDonald, Megan. *The Great Pumpkin Switch.*

TOYS

    Hoban, Russell. *Bedtime for Frances.*

    Hoopes, Lyn Littlefield. *Wing-a-Ding.*

    Hutchins, Pat. *Tidy Titch.*

    Ichikawa, Satomi. *Nora's Castle.*

    Jonas, Ann. *The Quilt.*

    Le Guin, Ursula K. *A Ride on the Red Mare's Back.*

    Scott, Ann Herbert. *On Mother's Lap.*

    Twining, Edith. *Sandman.*

    Weiss, Nicki. *Where Does the Brown Bear Go?*

    Wildsmith, Brian. *Carousel.*

Balloons *See* **BALLOONS**

Bears

    Freeman, Don. *Corduroy.*

    ————. *A Pocket for Corduroy.*

    Hayes, Sarah. *This Is the Bear and the Scary Night.*

    Murphy, Jill. *What Next, Baby Bear!*

    Stevenson, James. *The Night After Christmas.*

    Twining, Edith. *Sandman.*

    Waber, Bernard. *Ira Sleeps Over.*

Bicycles *See Also* **TRANSPORTATION—Bicycles**

    Bang, Molly. *Delphine.*

Dolls

    Hutchins, Pat. *Changes, Changes.*

    Keller, Holly. *Geraldine's Blanket.*

    Mattingley, Christobel. *The Angel with a Mouth-Organ.*

    Minarik, Else Holmelund. *Little Bear's Friend.*

    Stevenson, James. *The Night After Christmas.*

    Zolotow, Charlotte. *William's Doll.*

Kites *See* **KITES**

Others

    Benjamin, Amanda. *Two's Company.*

    Conrad, Pam. *The Tub People.*

    Hoban, Russell. *A Bargain for Frances.*

    Keller, Holly. *Geraldine's Big Snow.*

    Lionni, Leo. *Alexander and the Wind-up Mouse.*

    Tafuri, Nancy. *The Ball Bounced.*

    Tompert, Ann. *The Silver Whistle.*

TRAILS

    Albert, Burton. *Where Does the Trail Lead?*

    Bang, Molly. *Delphine.*

    Harvey, Brett. *Cassie's Journey: Going West in the 1860's.*

TRAINS *See* **TRANSPORTATION—Trains**

TRANSFORMATION

    Agee, Jon. *The Incredible Painting of Felix Clousseau.*

    Bang, Molly. *Dawn.*

Cohen, Caron Lee. *Whiffle Squeek.*
Columbus, Christopher. *The Log of Christopher Columbus.*
Conrad, Pam. *The Lost Sailor.*
Cooney, Barbara. *Island Boy.*
Crews, Donald. *Harbor.*
———. *Sail Away.*
Fritz, Jean. *The Great Adventure of Christopher Columbus.*
Haley, Gail E. *Sea Tale.*
Jonas, Ann. *Aardvarks, Disembark!*
Leighton, Maxinne Rhea. *An Ellis Island Christmas.*
Lent, Blair. *Molasses Flood.*
Levinson, Riki. *Watch the Stars Come Out.*
Marzollo, Jean. *In 1492.*
McCloskey, Robert. *Burt Dow, Deep-Water Man.*
———. *One Morning in Maine.*
———. *Time of Wonder.*
McCully, Emily Arnold. *The Amazing Felix.*
McKissack, Patricia. *A Million Fish—More or Less.*
Nones, Eric Jon. *Caleb's Friend.*
Sendak, Maurice. *Where the Wild Things Are.*
Small, David. *Paper John.*
Smith, Barry. *The First Voyage of Christopher Columbus, 1492.*
Spier, Peter. *Father, May I Come?*
Steig, William. *Amos & Boris.*
Twining, Edith. *Sandman.*
Van Allsburg, Chris. *The Wreck of the Zephyr.*
———. *The Wretched Stone.*
Yolen, Jane. *Letting Swift River Go.*

Buses

Carlstrom, Nancy White. *Baby-O.*
Cole, Joanna. *The Magic School Bus in the Time of the Dinosaurs.*
———. *The Magic School Bus Inside the Earth.*
———. *The Magic School Bus Inside the Human Body.*
———. *The Magic School Bus Inside a Hurricane.*
———. *The Magic School Bus Lost in the Solar System.*
———. *The Magic School Bus on the Ocean Floor.*
Crews, Donald. *School Bus.*
Daly, Niki. *Not So Fast, Songololo.*
Dorros, Arthur. *Abuela.*
Hellen, Nancy. *The Bus Stop.*
Kovalski, Maryann. *The Wheels on the Bus.*
Lewin, Hugh. *Jafta—the Journey.*
Meddaugh, Susan. *Hog-Eye.*
Noble, Trinka Hakes. *The Day Jimmy's Boa Ate the Wash.*
Waggoner, Karen. *The Lemonade Babysitter.*

———. *Grandaddy's Stars.*

Hest, Amy. *The Purple Coat.*

Howard, Elizabeth Fitzgerald. *The Train to Lulu's.*

Lobel, Arnold. *Uncle Elephant.*

Ray, Mary Lyn. *Pianna.*

San Souci, Robert. *Kate Shelly: Bound for Legend.*

Stevenson, James. *Don't You Know There's a War On?*

Turner, Ann Warren. *Nettie's Trip South.*

Van Allsburg, Chris. *The Polar Express.*

Trucks

Burton, Virginia Lee. *The Little House.*

Crews, Donald. *Truck.*

Johnson, Angela. *The Leaving Morning.*

Rayner, Mary. *Garth Pig and the Ice-Cream Lady.*

Spier, Peter. *Peter Spier's Circus!*

Williams, Vera B. *A Chair For My Mother.*

Wagons

Brett, Jan. *Berlioz the Bear.*

Coerr, Eleanor. *The Josefina Story Quilt.*

Hall, Donald. *The Farm Summer 1942.*

Harvey, Brett. *Cassie's Journey: Going West in the 1860's.*

Lewin, Hugh. *Jafta—the Journey.*

Lydon, Kerry Raines. *A Birthday for Blue.*

Van Leeuwen, Jean. *Going West.*

Wildsmith, Brian. *The Lazy Bear.*

Others

Cox, David. *Bossyboots.*

Shaw, Nancy. *Sheep in a Jeep.*

Van Allsburg, Chris. *Bad Day at Riverbend.*

TRAVEL

Ackerman, Karen. *Araminta's Paintbox.*

Agee, Jon. *The Return of Freddy LeGrand.*

Anno, Mitsumasa. *Anno's Britain.*

———. *Anno's Italy.*

———. *Anno's Journey.*

———. *Anno's U.S.A.*

Babbitt, Natalie. *Nellie: A Cat on Her Own.*

Bang, Molly. *Yellow Ball.*

Barton, Byron. *Airport.*

Berger, Barbara. *The Donkey's Dream.*

Brown, Marc. *Arthur's Family Vacation.*

Brunhoff, Jean de. *The Story of Babar.*

Bunting, Eve. *How Many Days to America? A Thanksgiving Story.*

———. *The Wall.*

Burningham, John. *Hey! Get Off Our Train.*

Brown, Marc. *Arthur's Family Vacation.*
Chall, Marsha Wilson. *Up North at the Cabin.*
Crews, Donald. *Bigmama's.*
———. *Shortcut.*
Fleischman, Paul. *Time Train.*
Freeman, Don. *Bearymore.*
Garland, Michael. *My Cousin Katie.*
Griffith, Helen V. *Georgia Music.*
———. *Grandaddy's Place.*
———. *Grandaddy's Stars.*
Howard, Elizabeth Fitzgerald. *The Train to Lulu's.*
Krahn, Fernando. *The Secret in the Dungeon.*
McCloskey, Robert. *Time of Wonder.*
Minarik, Else Holmelund. *Little Bear's Friend.*
Robbins, Ken. *City/Country.*
Ryder, Joanne. *The Goodbye Walk.*
Rylant, Cynthia. *The Relatives Came.*
Seuss, Dr. *Horton Hatches the Egg.*
Shulevitz, Peter. *Dawn.*
Sis, Peter. *Komodo!*
Vaughan, Marcia K., and Patricia Mullins. *The Sea-Breeze Hotel.*
Zion, Gene. *The Plant Sitter.*

VEGETABLES *See* **GARDENS; PLANTS**

WAR *See also* **PEACE**
Ackerman, Karen. *The Tin Heart.*
Bunting, Eve. *The Wall.*
Coerr, Eleanor. *Sadako.*
Cohen, Barbara. *Gooseberries to Oranges.*
Friedman, Ina R. *How My Parents Learned to Eat.*
Garland, Sherry. *The Lotus Seed.*
Gerrard, Roy. *Sir Cedric.*
Hall, Donald. *The Farm Summer 1942.*
Houston, Gloria. *But No Candy.*
———. *The Year of the Perfect Christmas Tree.*
Howard, Elizabeth Fitzgerald. *Papa Tells Chita a Story.*
Innocenti, Roberto. *Rose Blanche.*
Lyon, George Ella. *Cecil's Story.*
Maruki, Toshi. *Hiroshima No Pika.*
Mattingley, Christobel. *The Angel with a Mouth-Organ.*
Mellecker, Judith. *Randolph's Dream.*
Morimoto, Junko. *My Hiroshima.*
Polacco, Patricia. *Pink and Say.*
Price, Leontyne. *Aïda.*
Say, Allen. *The Bicycle Man.*

Cooney, Barbara. *Hattie and the Wild Waves.*
——. *Island Boy.*
Crews, Donald. *Harbor.*
——. *Sail Away.*
Goodall, John S. *Naughty Nancy Goes to School.*
——. *Paddy to the Rescue.*
Haley, Gail E. *Sea Tale.*
Leedy, Loreen. *Tracks in the Sand.*
Leighton, Maxinne Rhea. *An Ellis Island Christmas.*
Lent, Blair. *John Tabor's Ride.*
Lester, Alison. *Magic Beach.*
Levinson, Riki. *Watch the Stars Come Out.*
Lionni, Leo. *Swimmy.*
Lobel, Arnold. *Uncle Elephant.*
Marshall, James. *George and Martha 'Round and 'Round.*
Marzollo, Jean. *In 1492.*
McCloskey, Robert. *Burt Dow, Deep-Water Man.*
——. *Time of Wonder.*
Ness, Evaline. *Sam, Bangs, & Moonshine.*
Nones, Eric Jon. *Caleb's Friend.*
Pryor, Bonnie. *Lottie's Dream.*
Rand, Gloria. *Prince William.*
Rey, H. A. *Curious George.*
Ryder, Joanne. *The Bear on the Moon.*
——. *A House by the Sea.*
——. *Sea Elf.*
——. *A Wet and Sandy Day.*
——. *Winter Whale.*
Shulevitz, Uri. *Rain Rain Rivers.*
Sis, Peter. *An Ocean World.*
Small, David. *Paper John.*
Smith, Barry. *The First Voyage of Christopher Columbus, 1492.*
Spier, Peter. *Father, May I Come?*
Steig, William. *Amos & Boris.*
Tafuri, Nancy. *Follow Me!*
Turkle, Brinton. *Do Not Open.*
Twining, Edith. *Sandman.*
Van Allsburg, Chris. *The Wreck of the Zephyr.*
——. *The Wretched Stone.*
Weller, Frances Ward. *Riptide.*
Zolotow, Charlotte. *The Storm Book.*

Ponds

Asch, Frank. *Bear Shadow.*
——. *Turtle Tale.*
Ets, Marie Hall. *Play with Me.*
Fleming, Denise. *In the Small, Small Pond.*

Johnston, Tony. *The Cowboy and the Black-eyed Pea.*
Ketteman, Helen. *The Year of No More Corn.*
Kroll, Steven. *The Tyrannosaurus Game.*
Lawson, Julie. *The Dragon's Pearl.*
Lyon, George Ella. *Come a Tide.*
MacLachlan, Patricia. *All the Places to Love.*
Marshall, James. *George and Martha 'Round and 'Round.*
Martin, Bill, and John Archambault. *Listen to the Rain.*
Murphy, Shirley Rousseau. *Tattie's River Journey.*
Mwenye Hadithi. *Lazy Lion.*
Rydell, Katy. *Wind Says Good Night.*
Ryder, Joanne. *A Wet and Sandy Day.*
Serfozo, Mary. *Rain Talk.*
Seuss, Dr. *The Cat in the Hat.*
Shulevitz, Uri. *Rain Rain Rivers.*
Spier, Peter. *Peter Spier's Rain.*
Wood, Audrey. *The Napping House.*
Yashima, Taro. *Umbrella.*
Zolotow, Charlotte. *The Storm Book.*

Rainbows

Asch, Frank. *Skyfire.*
Ehlert, Lois. *Planting a Rainbow.*
Ernst, Lisa Campbell. *A Colorful Adventure of the Bee, Who Left Home One Monday Morning and What He Found Along the Way.*
Martin, Bill, and John Archambault. *Listen to the Rain.*
Wood, Audrey. *The Napping House.*
Zolotow, Charlotte. *The Storm Book.*

Snow

Asch, Frank. *Mooncake.*
Briggs, Raymond. *Father Christmas.*
———. *The Snowman.*
dePaola, Tomie. *Jingle: The Christmas Clown.*
Hoban, Lillian. *Arthur's Great Big Valentine.*
Howard, Elizabeth Fitzgerald. *Chita's Christmas Tree.*
Keats, Ezra Jack. *The Snowy Day.*
Keller, Holly. *Geraldine's Big Snow.*
Khalsa, Dayal Kaur. *The Snow Cat.*
Krahn, Fernando. *The Mystery of the Giant Footprints.*
McCully, Emily Arnold. *First Snow.*
Mendez, Phil. *The Black Snowman.*
Neitzel, Shirley. *The Jacket I Wear in the Snow.*
Paulsen, Gary. *Dogteam.*
Rogers, Jean. *Runaway Mittens.*
Say, Allen. *Tree of Cranes.*
Steig, William. *Brave Irene.*
Stevenson, James. *The Night After Christmas.*

Kasza, Keiko. *A Mother for Choco.*

Keats, Ezra Jack. *Jennie's Hat.*

———. *Whistle for Willie.*

Keller, Holly. *Geraldine's Big Snow.*

Khalsa, Dayal Kaur. *Cowboy Dreams.*

———. *The Snow Cat.*

Lionni, Leo. *Alexander and the Wind-up Mouse.*

Lobel, Arnold. *Uncle Elephant.*

McCloskey, Robert. *One Morning in Maine.*

McKissack, Patricia. *Mirandy and Brother Wind.*

Minarik, Else Holmelund. *Little Bear.*

Moss, Thylias. *I Want to Be.*

Nesbit, E. *Melisande.*

Peet, Bill. *The Whingdingdilly.*

Pryor, Bonnie. *Lottie's Dream.*

Raskin, Ellen. *Nothing Ever Happens on My Block.*

Reddix, Valerie. *Dragon-Kite of the Autumn Moon.*

Ringgold, Faith. *Tar Beach.*

Rudolph, Marguerita. *How a Shirt Grew in the Field.*

Rylant, Cynthia. *An Angel for Solomon Singer.*

Say, Allen. *Stranger in the Mirror.*

———. *Tree of Cranes.*

Seuss, Dr. *The Cat in the Hat.*

Steig, William. *Sylvester and the Magic Pebble.*

Titherington, Jeanne. *A Place for Ben.*

Turkle, Brinton. *Do Not Open.*

Welch, Willy. *Playing Right Field.*

Wild, Margaret. *Thank You, Santa.*

Williams, Karen Lynn. *When Africa Was Home.*

Williams, Vera B. *A Chair For My Mother.*

———. *Something Special for Me.*

Wood, Audrey. *Heckedy Peg.*

Woodruff, Elvira. *The Wing Shop.*

Yashima, Taro. *Umbrella.*

Zolotow, Charlotte. *Someday.*

———. *William's Doll.*

WITCHES *See* **IMAGINATION—Imaginary creatures, witches)**

WORLD CULTURES/COUNTRIES

Africa

Franklin, Kristine L. *The Old, Old Man and the Very Little Boy.*

Greenfield, Eloise. *Africa Dream.*

Grifalconi, Ann. *Darkness and the Butterfly.*

———. *Osa's Pride.*

Kroll, Virginia L. *Africa Brothers and Sisters.*

Mwenye Hadithi. *Greedy Zebra.*

———. *Lazy Lion.*
Olaleye, Isaac O. *Bitter Bananas.*
Williams, Karen Lynn. *When Africa Was Home.*

Eastern
Feelings, Muriel. *Jambo Means Hello: Swahili Alphabet Book.*
———. *Mojo Means One: Swahili Counting Book.*
Kroll, Virginia L. *Masai and I.*

Northern
Gray, Nigel. *A Balloon for Grandad.*
Heide, Florence Parry, and Judith Heide Gilliland. *The Day of Ahmed's Secret.*
Price, Leontyne. *Aida.*

Southern
Daly, Niki. *Not So Fast, Songololo.*
Isadora, Rachel. *At the Crossroads.*
Lewin, Hugh. *Jafta.*
———. *Jafta and the Wedding.*
———. *Jafta—the Journey.*
———. *Jafta—the Town.*
———. *Jafta's Father.*
———. *Jafta's Mother.*

Western
French, Fiona. *Anancy and Mr. Dry-Bone.*
Grifalconi, Ann. *Flyaway Girl.*
Mendez, Phil. *The Black Snowman.*
Steig, William. *Amos & Boris.*

Asia
China
Lawson, Julie. *The Dragon's Pearl.*
Leaf, Margaret. *Eyes of the Dragon.*
Reddix, Valerie. *Dragon-Kite of the Autumn Moon.*
Yee, Paul. *Roses Sing on New Snow.*
Yolen, Jane. *The Seeing Stick.*

Japan
Coerr, Eleanor. *Sadako.*
Friedman, Ina R. *How My Parents Learned to Eat.*
Gomi, Taro. *Coco Can't Wait.*
Maruki, Toshi. *Hiroshima No Pika.*
Melmed, Laura. *The First Song Ever Sung.*
Morimoto, Junko. *My Hiroshima.*
Say, Allen. *The Bicycle Man.*
———. *Grandfather's Journey.*
———. *Tree of Cranes.*
Tsuchiya, Yukio. *Faithful Elephants.*
Wells, Ruth. *A to Zen: A Book of Japanese Culture.*
Yashima, Taro. *Crow Boy.*

Van Allsburg, Chris. *The Polar Express.*
Wild, Margaret. *Thank You, Santa.*
South America
Cherry, Lynne. *The Great Kapok Tree.*
WORLD REGIONS
Burningham, John. *Where's Julius?*
Desert
Alexander, Sue. *Nadia the Willful.*
Baylor, Byrd. *Amigo.*
———. *The Desert Is Theirs.*
———. *The Other Way to Listen.*
———. *We Walk in Sandy Places.*
Keats, Ezra Jack. *Clementina's Cactus.*
McLerran, Alice. *Roxaboxen.*
Mellecker, Judith. *Randolph's Dream.*
Forest
Bowen, Betsy. *Antler, Bear, Canoe: A Northwoods Alphabet Year.*
Brunhoff, Jean de. *The Story of Babar.*
Cannon, Janell. *Stellaluna.*
Hutchins, Pat. *Good Night, Owl!*
Kesey, Ken. *Little Tricker the Squirrel Meets Big Double the Bear.*
Kherdian, David. *The Cat's Midsummer Jamboree.*
Steig, William. *The Amazing Bone.*
———. *Caleb & Kate.*
Tejima, Keizaburo. *Fox's Dream.*
Yolen, Jane. *Owl Moon.*
Mountain
Bang, Molly. *Delphine.*
Bodkin, Odds. *The Banshee Train.*
Houston, Gloria. *The Year of the Perfect Christmas Tree.*
Johnston, Tony. *Amber on the Mountain.*
Jonas, Ann. *Aardvarks, Disembark!*
Krahn, Fernando. *The Mystery of the Giant Footprints.*
Lobel, Arnold. *Ming Lo Moves the Mountain.*
Martin, Jacqueline Briggs. *Good Times on Grandfather Mountain.*
Mills, Lauren. *The Rag Coat.*
Ray, Deborah Kogan. *The Cloud.*
Rylant, Cynthia. *The Relatives Came.*
———. *When I Was Young in the Mountains.*
Tejima, Keizaburo. *Owl Lake.*
Wildsmith, Brian. *Goat's Trail.*
Plain
Mwenye Hadithi. *Lazy Lion.*
Pryor, Bonnie. *Lottie's Dream.*
Turner, Ann Warren. *Dakota Dugout.*

Rain forest/Jungle

Baker, Jeannie. *Where the Forest Meets the Sea.*
Baker, Keith. *Who Is the Beast?*
Browne, Anthony. *Bear Hunt.*
Cazet, Denys. *I'm Not Sleepy.*
Cherry, Lynne. *The Great Kapok Tree: A Tale of the Amazon Rain Forest.*
Grifalconi, Ann. *Osa's Pride.*
Howard, Elizabeth Fitzgerald. *Papa Tells Chita a Story.*
Hutchins, Pat. *1 Hunter.*
Mwenye Hadithi. *Crafty Chameleon.*
———. *Greedy Zebra.*
Noll, Sally. *Watch Where You Go.*
Olaleye, Isaac O. *Bitter Bananas.*
Peet, Bill. *The Spooky Tail of Prewitt Peacock.*
Tafuri, Nancy. *Junglewalk.*

Seashore

Albert, Burton. *Where Does the Trail Lead?*
Andrews, Jan. *Very First Time.*
Asch, Frank. *Sand Cake.*
Bang, Molly. *Dawn.*
Burningham, John. *Come Away from the Water, Shirley.*
Conrad, Pam. *The Lost Sailor.*
Cooney, Barbara. *Hattie and the Wild Waves.*
———. *Island Boy.*
———. *Miss Rumphius.*
Goodall, John S. *Naughty Nancy Goes to School.*
Haley, Gail E. *Sea Tale.*
Leedy, Loreen. *Tracks in the Sand.*
Lent, Blair. *John Tabor's Ride.*
Lester, Alison. *Magic Beach.*
McCloskey, Robert. *One Morning in Maine.*
———. *Time of Wonder.*
Ness, Evaline. *Sam, Bangs, & Moonshine.*
Pryor, Bonnie. *Lottie's Dream.*
Rand, Gloria. *Prince William.*
Robbins, Ken. *City/Country.*
Ryder, Joanne. *A House by the Sea.*
———. *A Wet and Sandy Day.*
Small, David. *Paper John.*
Spier, Peter. *Father, May I Come?*
Steig, William. *Amos & Boris.*
Tafuri, Nancy. *Follow Me!*
Tresselt, Alvin R. *Hide and Seek Fog.*
Turkle, Brinton. *Do Not Open.*
Turner, Ann Warren. *Heron Street.*

Van Allsburg, Chris. *The Wreck of the Zephyr.*
Vaughan, Marcia K., and Patricia Mullins. *The Sea-Breeze Hotel.*
Weller, Frances Ward. *Riptide.*

WRITING
Diaries
Columbus, Christopher. *The Log of Christopher Columbus.*
Jonas, Ann. *The 13th Clue.*
Marshall, James. *George and Martha, One Fine Day.*
Sis, Peter. *Follow the Dream.*
Van Allsburg, Chris. *The Wretched Stone.*

Letters
Ahlberg, Janet. *The Jolly Postman.*
Baker, Keith. *The Dove's Letter.*
Bang, Molly. *Delphine.*
Bedard, Michael. *Emily.*
Blos, Joan. *Old Henry.*
Brown, Marc. *Arthur's Christmas.*
———. *Arthur's Family Vacation.*
Charlip, Remy. *Fortunately.*
Cole, Joanna. *The Magic School Bus Lost in the Solar System.*
———. *The Magic School Bus on the Ocean Floor.*
Freeman, Don. *Dandelion.*
Gregory, Valiska. *Through the Mickle Woods.*
Hoban, Russell. *The Mole Family's Christmas.*
Houston, Gloria. *But No Candy.*
Isadora, Rachel. *Willaby.*
Johnston, Tony. *Amber on the Mountain.*
Keats, Ezra Jack. *A Letter to Amy.*
———. *Louie.*
Lobel, Arnold. *Frog and Toad Are Friends.*
Mayer, Mercer. *There's an Alligator Under My Bed.*
Minarik, Else Holmelund. *Little Bear's Friend.*
Rathmann, Peggy. *Officer Buckle and Gloria.*
Ringgold, Faith. *Aunt Harriet's Underground Railroad in the Sky.*
Sharmat, Marjorie Weinman. *Gila Monsters Meet You at the Airport.*
Turner, Ann Warren. *Nettie's Trip South.*
Van Allsburg, Chris. *The Polar Express.*
Wild, Margaret. *Thank You, Santa.*
———. *The Very Best of Friends.*

Poems
Bedard, Michael. *Emily.*
Brown, Marc. *Arthur's Valentine.*
Bunting, Eve. *The Valentine Bears.*
Hoban, Lillian. *Arthur's Great Big Valentine.*
Isadora, Rachel. *Willaby.*

Picture Book Index

Abolafia, Yossi. *A Fish for Mrs. Gardenia*. New York: Greenwillow, 1988.

After a series of humorous, unexpected happenings, Mr. Bennett is able to show his friendship for Mrs. Gardenia by serving fish for dinner.

ANIMALS—Marine life, fishes
FISHING
FOOD AND EATING
FRIENDSHIP—Relationships
GOALS
HUMOR
LANGUAGE—Names
LOST AND FOUND
NEIGHBORHOODS AND COMMUNITIES—Specific, urban

Ackerman, Karen. *Araminta's Paintbox*. Betsy Lewin, illus. New York: Atheneum, 1990.

Araminta's paintbox slips out of the covered wagon during her family's move from Boston to California in 1847. After being lost and discovered several times, the box arrives in California and becomes Araminta's possession again.

CHANGES
GIFTS
GRAPHIC AND PERFORMING ARTS—Art and artists
HISTORICAL PERIODS—Nineteenth Century, pioneer/westward movement
LOST AND FOUND
MAPS
MOVING
STRUCTURES—Boxes and Containers
TRANSPORTATION
TRAVEL
UNITED STATES—Regions, West Coast

———. *The Banshee*. David Ray, illus. New York: Philomel, 1990.

When darkness comes to the simple village, the mysterious Banshee comes looking for a lonely soul to keep her company. Her search is in vain, for those in the village are enveloped in warm, caring relationships.

BEHAVIOR—Searching
EVERYDAY EXPERIENCES—Time of day, nighttime
IMAGINATION—Imaginary creatures
NEIGHBORHOODS AND COMMUNITIES—Specific, rural
TIME—Nighttime

————. *Song and Dance Man*. Stephen Gammell, illus. New York: Knopf, 1988.

A former vaudeville performer re-creates his song-and-dance act for his grand-children.

CLOTHING
ELDERLY
FAMILIES—Grandparents
GRAPHIC AND PERFORMING ARTS—Dance and dancers; Music and musicians
IDENTITY—Self-worth
MEMORIES
STORYTELLING
ROOMS—Attics
TIME—Across time

————. *The Tin Heart*. Michael Hays, illus. New York: Atheneum, 1990.

Two girls living on opposite sides of the Ohio River, which separated the North and South during the Civil War, have their friendship temporarily disrupted.

BEHAVIOR—Hiding
CLOTHING—Others
EMOTIONS—Sadness
FRIENDSHIP—Relationships
HISTORICAL PERIODS—Nineteenth Century, late
PERSONAL PROBLEMS—Running away; Others
SECRETS
SLAVERY
TRANSPORTATION—Boats
WAR
WATER AND BODIES OF WATER—Rivers

Adoff, Arnold. *Hard to Be Six*. Cheryl Hanna, illus. New York: Lothrop, 1991.

A six-year-old boy longs to do things that older, larger children are doing though he has many fun experiences, some because of his wonderful imagination. His grandmother's lesson helps him to be more patient with his lot in life.

BEHAVIOR—Patient; Pretending; Problem-solving
BODY—Shape and size
DEATH
EMOTIONS—Love
EVERYDAY EXPERIENCES—Time of day, daytime; Time of day, nighttime
FAMILIES—Grandparents; Parents; Siblings
IDENTITY—Self-worth
IMAGINATION
PARTIES
PLAY
READING
SLEEPING
TIME—Cycles, days of the week
UNITED STATES—Specific cultures, African American
WISHES

Agee, Jon. *The Incredible Painting of Felix Clousseau*. New York: Farrar, 1988.

Felix Clousseau's entry in the art contest, a painting of a duck, meets with ridicule from the judges, but when the duck magically becomes alive, Clousseau's work is in much demand. He meets with disaster, however, as the images in his paintings cause chaos in the lives of their owners. After one of his images wards off a jewel thief attempting to steal the king's crown, Clousseau is released from jail, proclaimed a hero, and allowed to return to his painting.

BEHAVIOR—Stealing
GRAPHIC AND PERFORMING ARTS—Art and artists
IDENTITY—Self-worth
MOVEMENT/SPEED
MAGIC
SENSES—Sight; Sound
STRUCTURES—Buildings, others
TRANSFORMATION

————. *The Return of Freddy LeGrand.* New York: Farrar, 1992.

The pioneer aviator, Freddy LeGrand, experiences much difficulty on his flights but is always rescued by his farm friends, Sophie and Albert.

ADVENTURES
BEHAVIOR—Ambitious/Persistent; Problem-solving
COMMUNICATION—Newspapers
CONSTRUCTION
EMOTIONS—Disappointment
FLYING—Aviation
FRIENDSHIP—Relationships
GOALS
HUMOR
NEIGHBORHOODS AND COMMUNITIES—Specific, rural
SAFETY/DANGER
SURVIVAL
TRANSPORTATION—Airplanes
TRAVEL
WORLD CULTURES/COUNTRIES—Europe, Northern

Ahlberg, Janet. *The Jolly Postman.* Janet and Allan Ahlberg, illus. Boston: Little, Brown, 1986.

Several well-known folklore motifs receive letters delivered by the postman.

IMAGINATION
OCCUPATIONS
WRITING—Letters

Albert, Burton. *Where Does the Trail Lead?* Brian Pinkney, illus. New York: Simon & Schuster, 1991.

A boy follows a path exploring Summertime Island and ends the day with a reunion with his family.

BEHAVIOR—Searching
EXPLORATION
FAMILIES—Family gatherings/Outings
ISLANDS
SAND
SENSES
TIME—Cycles, day and night
TRAILS

UNITED STATES—Specific cultures, African American
WORLD REGIONS—Seashore

Alexander, Martha. *Even That Moose Won't Listen to Me.* New York: Dial, 1988.

No one believes Rebecca when she tells them a moose is ruining the garden, and none of her solutions seem to work.

ANIMALS—Large animals, moose
BEHAVIOR—Destructive/Violent; Resourceful
CONSTRUCTION
DISASTERS
FAMILIES—Parents; Siblings
GARDENS
PLANTS
SCARECROWS
SURPRISES
TIME—Cycles, day and night

————. *When the New Baby Comes, I'm Moving Out.* New York: Dial, 1979.

Oliver is disturbed by the idea of a new baby in the family until his mother points out the benefits of being a big brother.

BEHAVIOR—Apprehensive; Patient
EMOTIONS—Anger; Happiness; Jealousy
FAMILIES—Babies and young siblings; Parents; Siblings
FAMILY PROBLEMS—New siblings
IDENTITY—Relationships
IMAGINATION
PERSONAL PROBLEMS—Fearing to try something new

Alexander, Sue. *Nadia the Willful.* Lloyd Bloom, illus. New York: Pantheon, 1983.

Nadia defies her father's orders by mentioning the name of her beloved brother who disappeared in the desert and never returned.

BEHAVIOR—Ambitious/Persistent; Courageous; Disobedient
DEATH
EMOTIONS—Sadness
FAMILIES—Parents; Siblings
IDENTITY—Geographic identity
MEMORIES
WORLD CULTURES/COUNTRIES—Middle East
WORLD REGIONS—Desert

Aliki. *The Two of Them.* New York: Greenwillow, 1979.

The special relationship of a girl and her grandfather from her birth to his death is described. When she is left alone, the girl remembers her grandfather by caring for his apple tree.

BEHAVIOR—Loyal; Sharing
BIOGRAPHY/LIFE STORIES
BIRTH
CHANGES
DEATH
ELDERLY
EMOTIONS—Happiness; Loneliness; Love; Sadness
FAMILIES—Grandparents

GIFTS
MEMORIES

Allard, Harry. *Miss Nelson Has a Field Day*. James Marshall, illus. Boston: Houghton Mifflin, 1985.

When Viola Swamp takes over as the football coach, the team begins to win. Only the audience will learn the true identity of Miss Swamp.

BEHAVIOR—Competitive; Disobedient; Tricking
FAMILIES—Twins
HUMOR
IDENTITY—Gender roles
OCCUPATIONS
SCHOOL EXPERIENCES
SECRETS
SPORTS
SURPRISES

———. *Miss Nelson Is Missing!* James Marshall, illus. Boston: Houghton Mifflin, 1977.

When Miss Nelson, a caring teacher, is replaced by a tyrant, the unruly students shape up and come to appreciate Miss Nelson. Both the students and Miss Nelson keep their secret.

BEHAVIOR—Apprehensive
BEHAVIOR—Bossy; Tricking
CHANGES
EMOTIONS—Sadness
HUMOR
LOST AND FOUND
MYSTERY
SCHOOL EXPERIENCES
SECRETS
WISHES

Allen, Pamela. *Mr. Archimedes' Bath*. New York: Lothrop, 1980.

As Mr. Archimedes bathes with his animal friends he discovers the famous principle of volume that carries his name.

ANIMALS—Personified
BEHAVIOR—Excited; Problem-solving
HEALTH—Bathing
LANGUAGE—Words
MATHEMATICS—Measurement, volume

Andrews, Jan. *Very First Time*. Ian Wallace, illus. New York: Atheneum, 1986.

Eva, a young Inuit girl, relates her first experience collecting mussels under a roof of ice when the tide is out and the seabed along the shore is exposed.

ANIMALS—Marine life, others
BEHAVIOR—Curious; Excited
EMOTIONS—Fear
FAMILIES—Parents
FOOD AND EATING
IDENTITY—Geographic identity

LANGUAGE—Words
LIGHT AND SHADOWS/REFLECTIONS
PERSONAL PROBLEMS—Getting lost
SAFETY/DANGER
TIME—Specific seasons, winter
TRANSPORTATION—Sleighs
WATER AND BODIES OF WATER—Oceans
WORLD CULTURES/COUNTRIES—North America, Canada
WORLD REGIONS—Seashore

Anno, Mitsumasa. *Anno's Alphabet*. New York: Crowell, 1975.

The three-dimensional painting of each letter which appears to be constructed of wood is misformed. On each page spread, the letter and a word that begins with it are also shown, along with borders full of images whose names also begin with the letter.
CONSTRUCTION
GAMES/PUZZLES/TRICKS
LANGUAGE—Alphabet
OBSERVATION
STORIES—Minimal or no text

————. *Anno's Britain*. London: Bodley Head, 1982.

Traveling through the British Isles, a lone traveler experiences its historical, geographical, and cultural elements.
IDENTITY—Geographic Identity
OBSERVATION
STORIES—Minimal or no text
TIME—Across time
TRANSPORTATION—Horses
TRAVEL
WORLD CULTURES/COUNTRIES—Europe, Northern

————. *Anno's Counting Book*. New York: Crowell, 1977.

A counting book (0 to 12) shows the growth of a village through a cycle of seasons. Several mathematical ideas are presented.
MATHEMATICS—Classification; Counting
OBSERVATION
STRUCTURES—Buildings, houses and other dwellings
TIME—Cycles, seasons

————. *Anno's Counting House*. New York: Philomel, 1982.

A counting book (1 to 10) presents many mathematical concepts while depicting children moving from one house into another.
CHANGES
MATHEMATICS—Classification; Counting; Numbers, shapes
MOVING
OBSERVATION
ROOMS
STRUCTURES—Buildings, houses and other dwellings

————. *Anno's Italy*. New York: Collins, 1980.

Traveling through Italy, a lone traveler experiences that country's historical, geographical, and cultural elements.

IDENTITY—Geographic identity
OBSERVATION
STORIES—Minimal or no text
TIME—Across time
TRANSPORTATION—Horses
TRAVEL
WORLD CULTURES/COUNTRIES—Europe, Southern

————. *Anno's Journey*. Cleveland: Collins-World, 1978.

A lone traveler tours Northern Europe and experiences the historical, geographical, and cultural elements of the area.

IDENTITY—Geographic identity
OBSERVATION
STORIES—Minimal or no text
TIME—Across time
TRANSPORTATION—Horses
TRAVEL
WORLD CULTURES/COUNTRIES—Europe, Northern

————. *Anno's U.S.A.* New York: Philomel, 1983.

A lone visitor experiences the diverse historical, geographical, and cultural elements of the United States as he travels across the country from west to east, arriving on the East Coast as Columbus's *Santa Maria* is sighted.

IDENTITY—Geographic identity
OBSERVATION
STORIES—Minimal or no text
TIME—Across time
TRANSPORTATION—Horses
TRAVEL
UNITED STATES—General

————. *The King's Flower*. New York: Collins, 1979.

A king who has to have everything bigger than anyone else discovers that bigger is not always better.

MATHEMATICS—Size
PLANTS—Flowers
ROYALTY
STRUCTURES—Buildings, castles/palaces

Arnold, Tedd. *Green Wilma*. New York: Dial, 1993.

Wilma awakes one day with a craving for flies. Her froglike behavior at school leads to much hilarity and a big surprise.

ADVENTURES
ANIMALS—Fantasy; Marine life, frogs
BEHAVIOR—Running away
DREAMS
EVERYDAY EXPERIENCES—Time of day, awakening for the day
FAMILIES—Parents
FLYING—Fantasy
FOOD AND EATING
MOVEMENT/SPEED
OCCUPATIONS
SCHOOL EXPERIENCES

STORIES—Predictable text
SURPRISES

————. *No Jumping on the Bed!* New York: Dial, 1987.

When Walter jumps on his bed, the floor cracks and he falls floor after floor through his apartment building, interrupting other residents' activities and taking them along.

BEHAVIOR—Destructive/Violent; Disobedient
DISASTERS
EVERYDAY EXPERIENCES—Time of day, bedtime
FAMILIES—Parents
FURNITURE—Beds
HUMOR
IMAGINATION—Imaginary worlds
MOVEMENT/SPEED
NEIGHBORHOODS AND COMMUNITIES—Specific, urban
ROOMS—Bedrooms
STORIES—Predictable text
STRUCTURES—Buildings, houses and other dwellings

————. *No More Water in the Tub!* New York: Dial, 1995.

After William fills the bathtub too full, he is swept out of the bathroom in a wave of water. He falls floor after floor through his apartment building, taking other residents with him and eventually becoming a hero.

BEHAVIOR—Destructive/Violent; Disobedient; Heroic
DISASTERS
EVERYDAY EXPERIENCES—Time of day, bedtime
FAMILIES—Parents; Siblings
FIRE
HEALTH—Bathing
HUMOR
IMAGINATION—Imaginary worlds
MOVEMENT/SPEED
NEIGHBORHOODS AND COMMUNITIES—Specific, urban
ROOMS—Bathrooms
STORIES—Predictable text
STORYTELLING
STRUCTURES—Buildings—houses and other dwellings

————. *The Signmaker's Assistant.* New York: Dial, 1992.

When the apprentice to the signmaker is left in charge, he creates his own signs and discovers how closely the townspeople adhere to them. Disaster follows.

BEHAVIOR—Destructive/Violent; Obedient; Tricking
DISASTERS
EMOTIONS—Anger
EVERYDAY EXPERIENCES—Time of day, daytime
GOALS
HUMOR
IDENTITY—Self-worth
NEIGHBORHOODS AND COMMUNITIES—Specific, urban
OBSERVATION
OCCUPATIONS

READING
SENSES—Sight
SURPRISES
WISHES
WRITING—Signs

Asch, Frank. *Bear Shadow*. Englewood Cliffs, NJ: Prentice-Hall, 1985.

Bear engages in many activities to get rid of his shadow.

ANIMALS—Large animals, bears; Personified
ASTRONOMY—Sun
BEHAVIOR—Ambitious/Persistent; Problem-solving; Resourceful
EMOTIONS—Fear
FISHING
LIGHT AND SHADOWS/REFLECTIONS
OBSERVATION
SENSES—Sight
TIME—Cycles, day and night
WATER AND BODIES OF WATER—Ponds

————. *Happy Birthday, Moon*. Englewood Cliffs, NJ: Prentice-Hall, 1992.

Bear thinks he is talking to the moon, but the voice he hears is his echo. Through these visits, Bear learns that the moon shares his birthday. He buys the moon a hat which fits perfectly, and the moon reciprocates.

ANIMALS—Large animals, bears; Personified
ASTRONOMY—Moon
BEHAVIOR—Searching; Sharing
BIRTHDAYS
CLOTHING—Hats
EMOTIONS—Love
EVERYDAY EXPERIENCES—Time of day, nighttime
FRIENDSHIP—Relationships
GIFTS
SENSES—Sound
SHOPPING/MARKETING

————. *Just Like Daddy*. Englewood Cliffs, NJ: Prentice-Hall, 1981.

A young bear identifies with his father, doing what he does, until it comes to fishing.

ANIMALS—Large animals, bears; Personified
BEHAVIOR—Imitating
FAMILIES—Parents
FISHING
IDENTITY—Gender roles
SURPRISES

————. *The Last Puppy*. Englewood Cliffs, NJ: Prentice-Hall, 1980.

The last puppy of the litter to be born finds that he is special because he is a boy's first puppy.

ANIMALS—Babies; Pets, dogs
BIRTH
MATHEMATICS—Numbers, ordinal

————. *Moon Bear*. New York: Scribner, 1978.

Bear feels responsible for the moon waning until he discovers that its phases are carried out independent of him.

ANIMALS—Hibernation; Large animals, bears; Personified
ASTRONOMY—Moon
BEHAVIOR—Apprehensive
CHANGES
EMOTIONS—Love; Sadness
FOOD AND EATING
FRIENDSHIP—Relationships
HEALTH—Health care
TIME—Nighttime

————. *Mooncake*. Englewood Cliffs, NJ: Prentice-Hall, 1983.

Bear builds a rocket to fulfill his wish to taste the moon.

ADVENTURES
ANIMALS—Hibernation; Large animals, bears; Personified
ASTRONOMY—Moon
BEHAVIOR—Problem-solving
CONSTRUCTION
FLYING—Fantasy
FOOD AND EATING
SLEEPING
SPACE
TIME—Cycles, seasons
WEATHER—Snow
WISHES

————. *Moondance*. New York: Scholastic, 1993.

Bear wishes to dance with the moon. His dream is fulfilled but not until he has first danced with the clouds and the rain.

ANIMALS—Large animals, bears; Personified
ASTRONOMY—Moon
BEHAVIOR—Ambitious/Persistent; Excited; Resourceful
EMOTIONS—Happiness
FRIENDSHIP—Relationships
GOALS
GRAPHIC AND PERFORMING ARTS—Dance and dancers
HUMOR
IDENTITY—Self-worth
IMAGINATION
LIGHT AND SHADOWS/REFLECTIONS
SURPRISES
TIME—Cycles, day and night
WEATHER—Clouds; Fog; Rain
WISHES

————. *Sand Cake*. New York: Parents' Magazine, 1978.

Papa Bear uses his imagination to create a sand cake, and in response, Baby Bear uses the same approach in eating it.

ANIMALS—Large animals, bears; Personified
BEHAVIOR—Pretending; Teasing
EMOTIONS—Happiness; Love
FAMILIES—Family gatherings/Outings; Parents
FOOD AND EATING
GAMES/PUZZLES/TRICKS
GRAPHIC AND PERFORMING ARTS—Art and artists
HUMOR
IMAGINATION
PLAY
SAND
SENSES—Sight
TIME—Specific seasons, summer
WATER AND BODIES OF WATER—Oceans
WORLD REGIONS—Seashore

————. *Skyfire*. Englewood Cliffs, NJ: Prentice-Hall, 1984.

Seeing a rainbow for the first time, Bear mistakes it for a skyfire.

ANIMALS—Large animals, bears; Personified
BEHAVIOR—Apprehensive
FIRE
SAFETY/DANGER
SENSES—Sight
TREASURES
WEATHER–Rainbows

————. *Turtle Tale*. New York: Dial, 1978.

A young turtle cannot decide whether to keep his head in or out until he gains the wisdom to cope.

ANIMALS—Small creatures, turtles/tortoises
APPLES
BEHAVIOR—Hiding; Problem solving; Wise
EMOTIONS—Sadness
ENEMIES
HEALTH—Illness and injury
IDENTITY—Self-worth
SAFETY/DANGER
SENSES—Sight; Smell and taste; Sound
WATER AND BODIES OF WATER—Ponds

Asch, Frank, and Vladimir Vagin. *Here Comes the Cat!=Siuda idet kot!* New York: Scholastic, 1988

A mouse, while riding different vehicles to avoid the cat, issues a warning over and over to other mice ("Here comes the cat!") only to discover that there is nothing to fear. The cat turns out to be benevolent and presents a large cheese to the mice. The text is in both English and Russian.

ANIMALS—Fantasy; Pets, cats; Small creatures, mice
EMOTIONS—Fear
ENEMIES
FRIENDSHIP—Relationships

GIFTS
LIGHT AND SHADOWS/REFLECTIONS
PEACE
STORIES—Minimal or no text
SURPRISES
WORLD CULTURES/COUNTRIES—Europe, Central/Eastern

Aylesworth, Jim. *Country Crossing*. Ted Rand, illus. New York: Atheneum, 1991.

On a country road in the summer, the occupants of an old car (representative of the early twentieth century) are signaled to stop for a train at a railroad crossing. The sounds of a country night and the passing of a train are vividly portrayed in the text and illustrations. The graphic code of size is used to relate the tremendous impact of the train as it speeds across the crossing.

HISTORICAL PERIODS—Twentieth Century, early
LIGHT AND SHADOWS/REFLECTIONS
MATHEMATICS—Size
MOVEMENT/SPEED
NEIGHBORHOODS AND COMMUNITIES—Specific, rural
OBSERVATION
SENSES—Sound
TIME—Nighttime
TRANSPORTATION—Cars; Trains

————. *The Folks in the Valley: A Pennsylvania Dutch ABC*. Stefano Vitale, illus. New York: HarperCollins, 1992.

This alphabet book focuses on the activities of rural people in a Pennsylvania Dutch settlement during the cycle of a day.

EVERYDAY EXPERIENCES—Time of day, daytime
FARMS
HISTORICAL PERIODS—Nineteenth Century, pioneer/westward movement
IDENTITY—Geographic identity
LANGUAGE—Alphabet
NEIGHBORHOODS AND COMMUNITIES—Specific, rural
OCCUPATIONS
STORIES—Predictable texts
TIME—Cycles, day and night
UNITED STATES—Regions, Northeast

————. *Hanna's Hog*. Glen Rounds, illus. New York: Atheneum, 1988.

Hanna Brodie teaches her thieving neighbor to leave her chickens and pet hog alone.

ANIMALS—Farm, pigs
BEHAVIOR—Lying; Stealing
EMOTIONS—Anger
FARMS
GOALS
HUMOR
IDENTITY—Gender roles
NEIGHBORHOODS AND COMMUNITIES—Specific, rural
OCCUPATIONS
SENSES—Sound
UNITED STATES—Regions, Appalachia

———. *McGraw's Emporium*. Mavis Smith, illus. New York: Holt, 1995.

A young boy searches for a special gift for a friend who is ill. After examining many items at a unique store, he finds an advertisement for free kittens, which turns out to be the perfect gift.

ANIMALS—Pets, cats
BEHAVIOR—Problem-solving
COMMUNICATION—Signs
FRIENDSHIP—Relationships
GIFTS
HEALTH—Illness and injury
IMAGINATION—Imaginary worlds
OCCUPATIONS
SHOPPING/MARKETING
STORIES—Predictable text
STRUCTURES—Buildings, stores

———. *Shenandoah Noah*. Glen Rounds, illus. New York: Holt, 1985.

In this tall tale, Shenandoah Noah gets rid of fleas contracted from his hounds by building a fire for bathwater. The smoke attracts a visitor, causing Noah to jump out of his tub and hide under a bearskin rug. Thus starts the rumor that he has turned into a talking bear.

ANIMALS—Pets, dogs
BEHAVIOR—Curious; Lazy; Problem-solving; Shy
EMOTIONS—Fear
FIRE
HEALTH—Bathing; Illness and injury
SENSES—Sight; Sound
STORYTELLING
UNITED STATES—Regions, Appalachia

Azarian, Mary. *A Farmer's Alphabet*. Boston: Godine, 1981.

Images of New England farm life in the past are presented through letters of the alphabet.

FARMS
LANGUAGE—Alphabet
STORIES—Minimal or no text

Babbitt, Natalie. *Nellie: A Cat on Her Own*. New York: Farrar, 1989.

After the death of her owner, a cat marionette believes that she will never dance again. Her friend, a real cat, helps her find a home in which she is content and has opportunities to dance with a gathering of friends.

ADVENTURES
ANIMALS—Personified; Pets, cats
ASTRONOMY—Moon
EMOTIONS—Happiness
GRAPHIC AND PERFORMING ARTS—Dance and dancers
IDENTITY—Self-worth
MAGIC
MOVING

PARTIES
PLANTS—Trees
PUPPETS
TIME—Nighttime
TRAVEL

Baer, Gene. *Thump, Thump, Rat-a-tat-tat*. Lois Ehlert, illus. New York: Harper & Row, 1989.

Through a rhythmic text and colorful graphic shapes, a band approaches and then disappears down the street. The viewer's perspective of the passing musicians is presented through the graphic code of size.

GRAPHIC AND PERFORMING ARTS—Music and musicians
MATHEMATICS—Classification; Shapes; Size
MOVEMENT/SPEED
OBSERVATION
PARADES
SENSES—Sound
STORIES—Predictable text

Bahr, Mary. *The Memory Box*. David Cunningham, illus. Morton Grove, IL: A. Whitman, 1992.

During a summer vacation, Zach and his grandparents collect memories of their experiences together as they face the grandfather's progressive illness, Alzheimer's disease.

BEHAVIOR—Forgetful
DISABILITIES
ELDERLY
EMOTIONS—Happiness; Sadness
FAMILIES—Grandparents
FAMILY PROBLEMS—Others
FISHING
GOALS
HEALTH—Illness and injury
IDENTITY—Relationships
MEMORIES
PERSONAL PROBLEMS—Getting lost
STRUCTURES—Boxes and containers
TIME—Specific seasons, summer
VACATIONS
WATER AND BODIES OF WATER—Lakes
WRITING—Others

Baker, Betty. *The Turkey Girl*. Harold Berson, illus. New York: Macmillan, 1983.

Tally, an orphan rejected by the villagers, lives with the turkeys on the edge of town until the king's son comes to hunt a ferocious wolf.

ANIMALS—Farm, turkeys; Large animals, wolves
BEHAVIOR—Courageous; Forgetful
CLOTHING
EMOTIONS—Loneliness
FAMILIES—Orphans
FRIENDSHIP—Relationships
GRAPHIC AND PERFORMING ARTS—Dance and dancers

NEIGHBORHOODS AND COMMUNITIES—Social gatherings
PARTIES
POVERTY
ROYALTY
SAFETY/DANGER
SURVIVAL
TIME—Specific seasons, winter

Baker, Jeannie. *Where the Forest Meets the Sea*. New York: Greenwillow, 1987.

On a camping trip, an Australian father shows his son the wonders of an ancient rain forest and ponders its future fate.

CAMPING
ECOLOGY/ENVIRONMENTAL PROBLEMS
IDENTITY—Geographical identity
IMAGINATION
TIME—Across time
VACATIONS
WORLD CULTURES/COUNTRIES—Australia and the Pacific Islands
WORLD REGIONS—Rain forest/Jungle

————. *Window*. New York: Greenwillow, 1991.

As a boy emerges into manhood he observes urban growth overtaking his wilderness environment.

CONSTRUCTION
ECOLOGY/ENVIRONMENTAL PROBLEMS
FAMILIES—Parents
GOALS
IDENTITY—Geographical identity
NEIGHBORHOODS AND COMMUNITIES—General
OBSERVATION
STORIES—Minimal or no text
TIME—Across time

Baker, Keith. *The Dove's Letter*. San Diego: Harcourt, 1988.

Attempting to deliver an unaddressed letter, a dove brings much happiness to the people who read it, each thinking it was written especially for them.

ANIMALS—Birds; Personified
BEHAVIOR—Responsible
EMOTIONS—Happiness; Love
FLYING—Fantasy
GOALS
IDENTITY—Self-worth
OCCUPATIONS
READING
SENSES—Sound
TIME—Daytime
WRITING—Letters

————. *Hide and Snake*. San Diego: Harcourt, 1991.

A brightly colored snake camouflaged among a group of familiar objects on each page spread invites observers to a game of hide and seek.

ANIMALS—Reptiles, snakes

BEHAVIOR—Hiding
GAMES/PUZZLES/TRICKS
MATHEMATICS—Classification
OBSERVATION
STORIES—Minimal or no text; Predictable text

———. *Who Is the Beast?* San Diego: Harcourt, 1990.

When the tiger realizes that the other animals in the jungle are afraid of him, he alleviates their fears by pointing out the features they have in common.

ANIMALS—Large animals, tigers; Small creatures
BEHAVIOR—Searching
BODY—Parts of body
EMOTIONS—Fear
OBSERVATION
SENSES—Sound
STORIES—Minimal or no text; Predictable text
SURPRISES
WORLD REGIONS—Rain forest/Jungle

Bang, Molly. *Dawn.* New York: Morrow, 1983.

A shipbuilder shares with his daughter the loneliness of losing his wife. Having pushed his wife to weave the sails for the boat he has under construction and then breaking his promise to not watch her work, he finds her transformed into her other state, that of a Canadian goose.

ANIMALS—Birds, wild geese
BEHAVIOR—Destructive/Violent; Greedy
EMOTIONS—Loneliness
FAMILIES—Husbands and wives; Parents
GOALS
HEALTH—Illness and injury
OCCUPATIONS
PERSONAL PROBLEMS—Breaking promises
STORYTELLING
TRANSFORMATION
TRANSPORTATION—Boats
WORLD REGIONS—Seashore

———. *Delphine.* New York: Morrow, 1988.

Delphine, unaffected by the risks she takes as she journeys from her mountaintop home to the post office, fears learning to ride the new bicycle she knows her grandmother has sent.

BEHAVIOR—Apprehensive; Courageous
EMOTIONS—Fear
FAMILIES—Grandparents
GIFTS
HUMOR
LANGUAGE—Names
MOUNTAIN CLIMBING
OBSERVATION
OCCUPATIONS
PERSONAL PROBLEMS—Fearing to try something new
SAFETY/DANGER

STORIES—Minimal or no text
TOYS—Bicycles
TRAILS
WORLD REGIONS—Mountain
WRITING—Letters

————. *The Paper Crane*. New York: Greenwillow, 1985.

The impoverished restaurant owner's business is restored when a mysterious elderly man pays for his meal by constructing an origami crane that comes alive and dances, drawing crowds of people.

ANIMALS—Birds
BEHAVIOR—Problem-solving; Sharing
ELDERLY
FOOD AND EATING
GIFTS
GRAPHIC AND PERFORMING ARTS—Art and artists; Dance and dancers; Music and
     musicians
MAGIC
MOVEMENT/SPEED
NEIGHBORHOODS AND COMMUNITIES—General
OCCUPATIONS
POVERTY
ROADS
SENSES—Sound
STRANGERS
TRANSFORMATION
UNITED STATES—Specific cultures, Asian American

————. *Ten, Nine, Eight*. New York: Greenwillow, 1983.

A father shares a bedtime counting game (10 to 1) with his young daughter.

EVERYDAY EXPERIENCES—Time of day, bedtime
FAMILIES—Parents
GAMES/PUZZLES/TRICKS
MATHEMATICS—Counting; Numbers
ROOMS—Bedrooms
UNITED STATES—Specific cultures, African American

————. *Yellow Ball*. Morrow, 1991.

A ball drifts away from a family on a beach, endures many experiences as it travels across the ocean, and is finally claimed by a child on another shore.

ADVENTURES
BALLOONS
COLORS
LANGUAGE—Words
LOST AND FOUND
MOVEMENT/SPEED
OBSERVATION
STORIES—Minimal or no text
TIME—Cycles, day and night
TRAVEL
WATER AND BODIES OF WATER—Oceans
WEATHER—Storms
WORLD CULTURES/COUNTRIES—Cross cultures

Barrett, Judi. *Animals Should Definitely Not Act Like People*. Ron Barrett, illus. New York: Atheneum, 1980.

Animals would be hampered in being themselves if they had to act like people.
ANIMALS—Fantasy
CLOTHING
HUMOR
OBSERVATION
STORIES—Predictable text

————. *Animals Should Definitely Not Wear Clothing*. Ron Barrett, illus. New York: Atheneum, 1970.

The text and illustrations relate how ridiculous it would be for animals to wear clothes.
ANIMALS—Fantasy
CLOTHING
HUMOR
IMAGINATION

————. *Cloudy with a Chance of Meatballs*. Ron Barrett, illus. New York: Atheneum, 1978.

In the town of Chewandswallow, the weather comes three times a day in the form of different foods at mealtime.
FOOD AND EATING
HUMOR
IMAGINATION—Imaginary worlds
WEATHER

Barton, Byron. *Airport*. New York: Crowell, 1982.

Taking an airplane trip—from arriving at the airport to becoming airborne—is described.
FLYING—Aviation
STORIES—Minimal or no text
TRANSPORTATION—Airplanes
TRAVEL

Bartone, Elisa. *Peppe the Lamplighter*. Ted Lewin, illus. New York: Lothrop, 1993.

Peppe's immigrant father thinks the job of a lamplighter in New York City's Little Italy is too lowly for his son until Peppe proves otherwise.
BEHAVIOR—Ambitious/Persistent; Responsible
EMOTIONS—Disappointment; Fear
ETHNIC CULTURES—Others
FAMILIES—Parents; Siblings
FAMILY PROBLEMS—Others
GOALS
HEALTH—Illness and injury
HISTORICAL PERIODS—Twentieth Century, early
IDENTITY—Self-worth
IMMIGRANTS/REFUGEES
LIGHT AND SHADOWS/REFLECTIONS
NEIGHBORHOODS AND COMMUNITIES—Specific, urban
OCCUPATIONS
POVERTY

TIME—Nighttime
UNITED STATES—Regions, Middle Atlantic

Baylor, Byrd. *Amigo*. Garth Williams, illus. New York: Macmillan, 1963.

A boy and a prairie dog carry out the same goal separately: To acquire each other as a pet.

ANIMALS—Pets, others; Small creatures, others
BEHAVIOR—Hiding; Patient; Searching
FAMILIES
FRIENDSHIP—Relationships
GOALS
POVERTY
UNITED STATES—Regions, Southwest; Specific cultures, Hispanic American
WORLD REGIONS—Desert

———. *The Desert Is Theirs*. Peter Parnall, illus. New York: Scribner, 1975.

This lyrical account of the ecological system of the desert includes people, animals, and plants.

ECOLOGY/ENVIRONMENTAL PROBLEMS
IDENTITY—Geographic identity
STORYTELLING
UNITED STATES—Regions, Southwest; Specific cultures, American Indian/Eskimo
WORLD REGIONS—Desert

———. *Guess Who My Favorite Person Is*. Robert Andrew Parker, illus. New York: Scribner, 1977.

A young girl and a man discuss their favorite things.

COLORS
DREAMS
FOOD AND EATING
FRIENDSHIP—Relationships
GAMES/PUZZLES/TRICKS
NEIGHBORHOODS AND COMMUNITIES—Specific, rural
SENSES—Sight; Smell and taste; Sound; Touch
UNITED STATES—Regions, Southwest

———. *Hawk, I'm Your Brother*. Peter Parnall, illus. New York: Scribner, 1976.

In pursuing his desire to fly, a boy develops a special kinship with a hawk.

ANIMALS—Birds
FAMILIES—Parents
GOALS
IDENTITY—Relationships
MOVEMENT/SPEED
UNITED STATES—Regions, Southwest; Specific cultures, American Indian/Eskimo
WEATHER—Wind
WISHES

———. *The Other Way to Listen*. Peter Parnall, illus. New York: Scribner, 1978.

With unhurried persistence and respect for nature, a boy begins to commune with the natural world.

BEHAVIOR—Patient; Searching
ELDERLY

EXPLORATION
IDENTITY—Relationships
PLANTS
ROCKS AND MINERALS
SENSES—Sound
UNITED STATES—Regions, Southwest
WISHES
WORLD REGIONS—Desert

————. *The Way to Start a Day*. Peter Parnall, illus. New York: Scribner, 1978.

People throughout time and in many cultures have celebrated the sunrise.

ASTRONOMY—Sun
BEHAVIOR—Sharing
EVERYDAY EXPERIENCES—Time of day, awakening for the day
GIFTS
GRAPHIC AND PERFORMING ARTS—Music and musicians
HISTORICAL PERIODS—Prehistoric
IDENTITY—Relationships
RELIGION
WORLD CULTURES/COUNTRIES—Cross cultures

————. *We Walk in Sandy Places*. Marilyn Schweitzer, illus. New York: Scribner, 1976.

The movements of small animals across the desert are observed in the sand.

ANIMALS—Small creatures
OBSERVATION
SAND
WORLD REGIONS—Desert

————. *Your Own Best Secret Place*. Peter Parnall, illus. New York: Scribner, 1979.

Claiming a hollow at the foot of a cottonwood tree as her secret place, the speaker discovers that it had been previously claimed by William Cottonwood and imagines how he felt about his special place.

EXPLORATION
IDENTITY—Geographic identity
PLANTS—Trees
SECRETS
UNITED STATES—Regions, Southwest
WRITING—Others

Baylor, Byrd, and Peter Parnall. *Your Own Best Place*. New York: Scribner, 1979.

The satisfaction of one's own secret place, wherever it may be, is portrayed.

BEHAVIOR—Sharing
IDENTITY—Geographic identity
INDIVIDUALITY
PLANTS—Trees
SECRETS
SURPRISES
UNITED STATES—Regions, Southwest
WRITING—Others

Bedard, Michael. *Emily*. Barbara Cooney, illus. New York: Doubleday, 1992.

> When the mysterious Emily invites a young girl's mother to play the piano at her home, the girl and the poet (Emily Dickinson) exchange special gifts.

BEHAVIOR—Curious; Hiding
CLOTHING—Dresses
EMOTIONS—Loneliness
GIFTS
GRAPHIC AND PERFORMING ARTS—Music and musicians
HISTORICAL PERIODS—Nineteenth Century, late
MYSTERY
NEIGHBORHOODS AND COMMUNITIES—Specific, urban
PLANTS—Flowers
ROOMS
SENSES—Sound
STRUCTURES—Buildings, houses and other dwellings
TIME—Cycles, seasons
WRITING—Letters; Poems

Benjamin, Amanda. *Two's Company*. New York: Viking, 1995.

> When Maddy's mother announces that she plans to remarry, Maddy fears that their close relationship will be affected. She seeks the advice of her best friend, a lizard named Adam Zurka, who suggests that they, too, marry.

BEHAVIOR—Apprehensive; Problem-solving; sharing
CHANGES
CLOTHING—Dresses
EMOTIONS—Jealousy; Love
FAMILIES—Family Gatherings/Outings; Marriage; Parents
IDENTITY—Relationships
IMAGINATION—Imaginary worlds
LANGUAGE—Names
SHOPPING/MARKETING
TOYS—Others

Bennett, Jill. *Teeny Tiny*. Tomie dePaola, illus. New York: Putnam, 1986.

> A teeny tiny woman discovers a bone in a churchyard. After she takes the bone home, she is awakened several times by a voice who demands that she return it.

BEHAVIOR—Apprehensive; Hiding
EMOTIONS—Fear
EVERYDAY EXPERIENCES—Time of day, nighttime
FOOD AND EATING
FURNITURE—Beds
IMAGINATION—Imaginary creatures, ghosts
SENSES—Sight; Sound
SLEEPING
STORIES—Predictable text

Berger, Barbara. *The Donkey's Dream*. New York: Philomel, 1985.

> The Nativity is told from the point of view of the donkey who carried Mary to Bethlehem.

ANIMALS—Farm, donkeys
DREAMS

HOLIDAYS AND CELEBRATIONS—Christmas
RELIGION
TRANSPORTATION
TRAVEL
WORLD CULTURES/COUNTRIES—Middle East

————. *Grandfather Twilight*. New York: Philomel, 1984.

Grandfather Twilight brings night to the world.
ASTRONOMY—Moon
EVERYDAY EXPERIENCES—Time of day, nighttime
IMAGINATION—Imaginary creatures, others
SLEEPING
TIME—Nighttime

Birdseye, Tom. *Airmail to the Moon*. Stephen Gammell, illus. New York: Holiday
   House, 1988.

When Ora Mae Cotton cannot find the tooth she left for the tooth fairy, she
accuses each member of her family of stealing it.
BEHAVIOR—Crying; Searching
BODY—Parts of Body, teeth
EMOTIONS—Anger; Embarrassment
FAMILIES—Parents; Siblings
FARMS
HUMOR
LANGUAGE—Names; Sayings and special language
LOST AND FOUND
NEIGHBORHOODS AND COMMUNITIES—Specific, rural
STORIES—Predictable text
SURPRISES

Blegvad, Lenore. *Anna Banana and Me*. Erik Blegvad, illus. New York: Atheneum,
   1985.

Anna Banana's fearless behavior helps her friend become more courageous.
ADVENTURES
BEHAVIOR—Apprehensive; Courageous; Pretending
CONSTRUCTION
EMOTIONS—Fear; Happiness
EXPLORATION
FRIENDSHIP—Relationships
IDENTITY—Gender roles; Self-worth
IMAGINATION—Imaginary creatures, monsters; Imaginary worlds
NEIGHBORHOODS AND COMMUNITIES—Specific, urban
SENSES—Sight; Sound; Touch
STATUES
STORYTELLING
WISHES

Blos, Joan. *Lottie's Circus*. Irene Trivas, illus. New York: Morrow, 1989.

Through her imagination, Lottie presents a circus in her backyard.
ANIMALS—Pets, cats
BEHAVIOR—Courageous
CIRCUS

GOALS
IMAGINATION
MAGIC
PLAY
WISHES

———. *Old Henry*. Stephen Gammell, illus. New York: Morrow, 1987.

When Henry fails to improve the old ramshackle house he has moved into, his neighbors try various means of encouraging him to do so. He rebels and moves away, but he misses his old neighbors and they miss him.

BEHAVIOR—Lazy
ECOLOGY/ENVIRONMENTAL PROBLEMS
EMOTIONS—Loneliness
GOALS
IDENTITY—Self-worth
INDIVIDUALITY
MEMORIES
MOVING
NEIGHBORHOODS AND COMMUNITIES—General
STRUCTURES—Buildings, houses and other dwellings
TIME—Cycles, seasons
WRITING—Letters

Bodkin, Odds. *The Banshee Train*. Ted Rose, illus. New York: Clarion, 1995.

A banshee saves a passenger train from disaster when a trestle collapses over a gorge in the mountains during the spring floods.

BEHAVIOR—Heroic; Problem-solving
EMOTIONS—Fear
HISTORICAL PERIODS—Twentieth Century, early
IMAGINATION—Imaginary creatures, others
MOVEMENT/SPEED
MYSTERY
OCCUPATIONS
SAFETY/DANGER
STRUCTURES—Bridges
SURVIVAL
TRANSPORTATION—Trains
UNITED STATES—Regions—Western mountain
WATER AND BODIES OF WATER—Floods
WEATHER—Fog; Storms
WORLD REGIONS—Mountain

Bohdal, Susi. *Bird Adalbert*. Boston: Picture Book Studio, 1983.

After Adalbert's wish to become a beautiful bird comes true, he is overcome with pride and mistreats the other birds. In response, they ignore him, leaving him lonely and ready to change his behavior.

BEHAVIOR—Boastful; Proud
EMOTIONS—Loneliness
FRIENDSHIP—Relationships
MAGIC
OBSERVATION
STORIES—Predictable text

TRANSFORMATION
WISHES

Bolliger, Max. *The Lonely Prince*. Jurg Obrist, illus. London: Methuen, 1981.

The sad young prince who has many possessions finds true happiness in friendship and sharing.

ANIMALS—Pets, others; Small creatures, rabbits
BEHAVIOR—Crying; Problem-solving; Sharing
EMOTIONS—Loneliness; Love; Sadness
FAMILIES—Parents
FRIENDSHIP—Relationships
ROYALTY
STRUCTURES—Buildings, castles/palaces
TRANSPORTATION—Hot-air Balloons
WISHES

Bottner, Barbara. *Hurricane Music*. Paul Yolowitz, illus. New York: Putnam, 1995.

When Aunt Margaret finds a clarinet in the basement, she uses it to explore the sounds of music in everything around her, including those of a hurricane.

BEHAVIOR—Imitating
EMOTIONS—Happiness; Sadness
FAMILIES—Husbands and wives; Other relatives
GRAPHIC AND PERFORMING ARTS—Music and musicians
HOBBIES
IMAGINATION
LOST AND FOUND
SENSES—Sound
WEATHER—Storms
WRITING—Signs

Bowen, Betsy. *Antler, Bear, Canoe: A Northwoods Alphabet Year*. Boston: Little, Brown, 1991.

Seasonal activities and northwoods concepts are presented within the structures of the alphabet.

ANIMALS—Large animals
IDENTITY—Geographical identity
LANGUAGE—Alphabet
TIME—Cycles, months of the year; Cycles, seasons
UNITED STATES—Regions, Midwest
WORLD REGIONS—Forest

Brett, Jan. *Armadillo Rodeo*. New York: Putnam, 1995.

In searching for adventure, Bo, an armadillo, mistakes a girl's red cowboy boots for another armadillo. In following the boots, he engages in many interesting events.

ADVENTURES
ANIMALS—Farm, horses; Personified; Small creatures, others
BEHAVIOR—Curious; Disobedient
CLOTHING—Shoes
COLORS
COWBOYS/COWGIRLS

GRAPHIC AND PERFORMING ARTS—Dance and dancers
LOST AND FOUND
NEIGHBORHOODS AND COMMUNITIES—Social gatherings
RANCHES
SAFETY/DANGER
SENSES—Sight
UNITED STATES—Regions, Southwest

————. *Berlioz the Bear*. New York: Putnam, 1991.

Worried about the strange noise in his double bass, Berlioz, the bear, is distracted and does not see a hole in the road. As a result, the wagonload of musicians on the way to play at the town ball are stuck and are in danger of missing their engagement. Surprisingly, the source of the noise in Berlioz's musical instrument solves the dilemma.

ANIMALS—Large animals, bears; Personified; Small creatures, insects
BEHAVIOR—Apprehensive; Problem-solving
GRAPHIC AND PERFORMING ARTS—Dance and dancers; Music and musicians
NEIGHBORHOODS AND COMMUNITIES—Social gatherings
SENSES—Sound
SURPRISES
TRANSPORTATION—Wagons

Briggs, Raymond. *Father Christmas*. New York: Coward, 1973.

Father Christmas, the British form of Santa Claus, grumbles about the perils of his winter holiday trip yet carries out his duties throughout the world.

BEHAVIOR—Apprehensive; Responsible
CLOTHING—Others
FLYING—Fantasy
HOLIDAYS AND CELEBRATIONS—Christmas
HUMOR
MOVEMENT/SPEED
NEIGHBORHOODS AND COMMUNITIES—General
ROYALTY
STORIES—Minimal or no text
STRUCTURES—Buildings, houses and other dwellings
TIME—Specific seasons, winter
TRANSPORTATION—Sleighs
WEATHER—Snow
WORLD CULTURES/COUNTRIES—Europe, Northern

————. *The Snowman*. New York: Random House, 1978.

In a small boy's dreams, a snowman comes to life and they have delightful experiences together.

ADVENTURES
CONSTRUCTION
DREAMS
EMOTIONS—Disappointment; Happiness
FLYING—Fantasy
FRIENDSHIP—Imaginary friends
PLAY
STORIES—Minimal or no text

TIME—Specific seasons, winter
WEATHER—Snow

Brown, Craig McFarland. *The Patchwork Farmer*. New York: Greenwillow, 1989.

Every time the farmer tears his overalls he patches them with scraps from his mending basket. By harvest time, his fields are ablaze with color and so are his overalls.

BEHAVIOR—Resourceful
CLOTHING—Others
COLORS
FARMS
IDENTITY—Gender roles
NEIGHBORHOODS AND COMMUNITIES—Specific, rural
OBSERVATION
OCCUPATIONS
PLANTS—Cycles
SEWING
STORIES—Minimal or no text
SURPRISES
TIME—Cycles, seasons

Brown, Marc. *Arthur Babysits*. Boston: Joy Street, 1992.

While babysitting with mischievous twins, Arthur cleverly uses storytelling to control them.

BABYSITTING
BEHAVIOR—Apprehensive; Disobedient; Mischievous; Problem-solving; Tricking
EVERYDAY EXPERIENCES—Time of day, bedtime
FAMILIES—Grandparents; Siblings; Twins
IDENTITY—Self-worth
IMAGINATION—Imaginary creatures, monsters
PLAY
STORYTELLING
SURPRISES

———. *Arthur's April Fool*. Boston: Little, Brown, 1983.

Arthur fears that he will be unable to concentrate on his tricks for the April Fool's Day Assembly after Binky Barnes, the school bully, threatens to pulverize him. Through his cleverness, Arthur is able to play a trick on Binky.

BEHAVIOR—Apprehensive; Bullying; Revengeful; Tricking
DREAMS
EMOTIONS—Fear
FRIENDSHIP—Relationships
GRAPHIC AND PERFORMING ARTS—Drama and actors
HOLIDAYS AND CELEBRATIONS—April Fool's Day
HUMOR
MAGIC
SCHOOL EXPERIENCES
SECRETS
WRITING—Others

————. *Arthur's Baby*. Boston: Joy Street, 1987.

Arthur is uneasy about a new baby in the family, but his apprehension dissolves once she arrives.

BABYSITTING
BEHAVIOR—Apprehensive
BIRTH
FAMILIES—Babies and young siblings; Parents; Siblings
FAMILY PROBLEMS—New Siblings
IDENTITY—Relationships

————. *Arthur's Chicken Pox*. Boston: Little, Brown, 1994.

Arthur fears that he will not be able to attend the circus because he has chicken pox, but in the end D. W. is the one who is unable to go.

BEHAVIOR—Competitive; Pretending; Teasing
CIRCUS
FAMILIES—Grandparents; Siblings
HEALTH—Illness and injury

————. *Arthur's Christmas*. Boston: Little, Brown, 1984.

Arthur gives careful consideration and time to Santa's gift. His combination of Santa's favorite foods is of concern to his sister, D. W.

ANIMALS—Personified
BEHAVIOR—Apprehensive; Searching
FAMILIES—Siblings
FOOD AND EATING
GIFTS
HOLIDAYS AND CELEBRATIONS—Christmas
WRITING—Letters

————. *Arthur's Eyes*. Boston: Little, Brown, 1979.

Arthur endures the teasing of his classmates when he gets glasses, but he soon wears them with pride.

BEHAVIOR—Problem-solving; Proud; Teasing
BODY—Parts of body, eyes
CHANGES
DISABILITIES
EMOTIONS—Embarrassment
FRIENDSHIP—Relationships
HEALTH—Health care
IDENTITY—Relationships
SCHOOL EXPERIENCES

————. *Arthur's Family Vacation*. Boston: Joy Street, 1993.

The summer family vacation without his friend, Buster, and with much rainy weather turns out to be more fun than Arthur had expected.

BEHAVIOR—Apprehensive
FAMILIES—Family gatherings/Outings; Siblings
FRIENDSHIP—Relationships
SCHOOL EXPERIENCES
TIME—Specific seasons, summer
TRAVEL

VACATIONS
WEATHER—Rain
WRITING—Letters

———. *Arthur's Halloween*. Boston: Little, Brown, 1982.

Arthur overcomes his fear of Halloween when he must rescue his little sister, D. W., from a spooky house during trick-or-treating. He learns that the occupant, Mrs. Tribble, is a friendly old lady.

ADVENTURES
BEHAVIOR—Courageous; Tricking
CLOTHING—Costumes
ELDERLY
EMOTIONS—Fear
FAMILIES—Siblings
FRIENDSHIP—Relationships
HOLIDAYS AND CELEBRATIONS—Halloween
HUMOR
IDENTITY—Self-worth
IMAGINATION—Imaginary creatures
NEIGHBORHOODS AND COMMUNITIES—Specific, urban
PARTIES
SCHOOL EXPERIENCES
STRUCTURES—Buildings, houses and other dwellings
SURPRISES
TIME—Nighttime

———. *Arthur's Teacher Trouble*. Boston: Atlantic Monthly, 1986.

Hard work in Mr. Ratburn's third grade pays off for Arthur when he wins the all-school spellathon.

BEHAVIOR—Ambitious/Persistent; Competitive
FAMILIES—Siblings
GOALS
IDENTITY—Self-worth
LANGUAGE—Words
OCCUPATIONS
SCHOOL EXPERIENCES
SURPRISES

———. *Arthur's Thanksgiving*. Boston: Little, Brown, 1983.

As director of the Thanksgiving play, Arthur has difficulty finding someone to play the part of the turkey.

ANIMALS—Farm, turkeys
BEHAVIOR—Courageous; Problem-solving
GRAPHIC AND PERFORMING ARTS—Drama and actors
HOLIDAYS AND CELEBRATIONS—Thanksgiving
SCHOOL EXPERIENCES
SURPRISES

———. *Arthur's Tooth*. Boston: Atlantic Monthly, 1985.

Arthur is the last in the class to lose a tooth.

BEHAVIOR—Apprehensive
BODY—Parts of Body, teeth
FRIENDSHIP—Relationships

HEALTH—Health care
SCHOOL EXPERIENCES

————. *Arthur's TV Trouble*. Boston: Little, Brown, 1995.

Arthur thinks the amazing Treat Timer advertised on television would be just the thing for his dog, Pal. He earns enough money to buy the gadget, but it frightens the dog.

ANIMALS—Personified; Pets, dogs
BEHAVIOR—Ambitious/Persistent
COMMUNICATION—Television
EMOTIONS—Disappointment
FAMILIES—Parents; Siblings
GOALS
HUMOR
IMAGINATION
INVENTIONS
MACHINES
MONEY
SHOPPING/MARKETING
TIME—Clocks and other time-telling methods

————. *Arthur's Valentine*. Boston: Little, Brown, 1980.

Arthur's school friends tease him about receiving valentine messages from a secret admirer. When he discovers that it is Francine, he plays a humorous trick on her.

BEHAVIOR—Teasing; Tricking
HOLIDAYS AND CELEBRATIONS—Valentine's
HUMOR
MYSTERY
SCHOOL EXPERIENCES
SECRETS
WRITING—Poems

————. *The Bionic Bunny Show*. Boston: Little, Brown, 1984.

As a television episode of "The Bionic Bunny Show" unfolds, the real-life process of developing a program is shown.

ANIMALS—Personified; Small creatures, rabbits
COMMUNICATION—Television
OCCUPATIONS

————. *The True Francine*. Boston: Little, Brown, 1981.

Francine is punished for Muffy's cheating, but eventually Muffy admits her guilt. Francine is allowed to play in the baseball game and becomes a hero.

BEHAVIOR—Heroic; Lying
FRIENDSHIP—Relationships
OCCUPATIONS
SCHOOL EXPERIENCES
SPORTS

Brown, Marcia. *All Butterflies: An ABC*. New York: Scribner, 1974.

Pairs of words, such as "All Butterflies," represents the sequence of the alphabet.

ANIMALS—Small creatures, butterflies/moths/caterpillars
LANGUAGE—Alphabet
STORIES—Predictable text

Brown, Ruth. *The Big Sneeze*. New York: Lothrop, 1985.

As a farmer dozes in the barn one hot afternoon, a lazy fly lands on his nose, causing him to sneeze. His hard sneeze sets off a chain of actions which leads to much havoc.

ANIMALS—Small creatures
BEHAVIOR—Destructive/Violent; Excited
BODY—Parts of body, noses
DISASTERS
FAMILIES—Husbands and wives
FARMS
HUMOR
MOVEMENT/SPEED
NEIGHBORHOODS AND COMMUNITIES—Specific, rural
OCCUPATIONS
SENSES—Sight; Sound; Touch
SLEEPING
STORIES—Predictable text
STRUCTURES—Buildings, barns
SURPRISES
TIME—Specific seasons, summer

————. *The Picnic*. New York: Dutton, 1993.

Several small creatures find their world invaded by picnickers and a dog. After the humans abandon their outing because of a rainstorm, the animals enjoy the food they left behind.

ANIMALS—Habitats; Pets, dogs; Small creatures
BEHAVIOR—Apprehensive; Hiding
EMOTIONS—Fear
EVERYDAY EXPERIENCES—Time of day, daytime
FAMILIES—Babies and young siblings; Family gatherings/Outings
FOOD AND EATING
OBSERVATION
SAFETY/DANGER
SENSES—Sight
SURPRISES
TIME—Daytime
WEATHER—Rain

Browne, Anthony. *Bear Hunt*. New York: Atheneum, 1980.

As Bear is pursued by hunters, he outwits them by drawing his way out of each situation.

ANIMALS—Large animals, bears; Personified
BEHAVIOR—Resourceful
FLYING—Fantasy
GRAPHIC AND PERFORMING ARTS—Art and artists
SAFETY/DANGER
SPORTS
SURVIVAL
WORLD REGIONS—Rain forest/Jungle

————. *Changes*. New York: Knopf, 1990.

Anticipating changes in their home after hearing his father's remarks, a boy imagines all kinds of fanciful transformations. However, he is surprised by the real-life change—a new baby.

BEHAVIOR—Apprehensive
CHANGES
FAMILIES—Babies and young siblings; Parents
IMAGINATION—Imaginary worlds
OBSERVATION
SURPRISES
TRANSFORMATION

————. *Piggybook*. New York: Knopf, 1986.

Mrs. Piggott overcomes her family's bigoted view of her role in the household.

ANIMALS—Farm, pigs; Personified
BEHAVIOR—Bossy; Sharing
EMOTIONS—Anger
FAMILY PROBLEMS—Others
GOALS
HUMOR
IDENTITY—Gender roles
IMAGINATION—Imaginary worlds
OBSERVATION
OCCUPATIONS
SURPRISES
TRANSFORMATION

————. *Tunnel*. New York: Knopf, 1989.

When her brother, who has taunted her about her fears, does not come out of the tunnel, the girl rescues him from his transformed state.

ADVENTURES
BEHAVIOR—Courageous; Heroic; Mischievous; Searching; Shy; Tricking
EMOTIONS—Fear; Love
FAMILIES—Siblings
IDENTITY—Gender roles
IMAGINATION—Imaginary worlds
INDIVIDUALITY
NEIGHBORHOODS AND COMMUNITIES—Specific, urban
OBSERVATION
SAFETY/DANGER
STATUES
STRUCTURES—Tunnels
TRANSFORMATION

Brunhoff, Jean de. *The Story of Babar*. New York: Random House, 1961.

Babar the elephant is orphaned in the forest, befriended in the city, and eventually finds true happiness in the forest when he marries and is crowned the king.

ADVENTURES
ANIMALS—Large animals, elephants; Personified
BEHAVIOR—Crying
CLOTHING

DEATH
ELDERLY
EMOTIONS—Happiness; Loneliness; Love; Sadness
ENEMIES
FAMILIES—Family gatherings/Outings
FLYING
FRIENDSHIP—Relationships
IMAGINATION—Imaginary worlds
NEIGHBORHOODS AND COMMUNITIES—Specific, rural; Specific, urban
PHOTOGRAPHY
ROYALTY
TRANSPORTATION—Cars, Hot-air Balloons
TRAVEL
WORLD REGIONS—Forest

Bunting, Eve. *Fly Away Home*. Ronald Himler, illus. New York: Clarion, 1991.

A homeless boy and his father hide in the airport. The boy desperately wishes for a home.

ANIMALS—Birds
BEHAVIOR—Hiding; Searching
DEATH
EMOTIONS—Anger; Sadness
FAMILIES—Parents
FAMILY PROBLEMS—Homelessness
IDENTITY—Relationships
OCCUPATIONS
POVERTY
STRUCTURES—Others
TRANSPORTATION—Airplanes
WISHES

———. *Ghost's Hour, Spook's Hour*. Donald Carrick, illus. New York: Clarion, 1987.

The boy and his dog discover satisfying explanations for their scary experiences at midnight.

ANIMALS—Pets, dogs
EMOTIONS—Fear; Love
FAMILIES—Parents
LIGHT AND SHADOWS/REFLECTIONS
SENSES—Sight; Sound; Touch
STRUCTURES—Buildings, houses and other dwellings
TIME—Nighttime

———. *How Many Days to America? A Thanksgiving Story*. Beth Peck, illus. New York: Clarion, 1988.

A family makes a dangerous journey by boat from the Caribbean to America, where they have reason to celebrate Thanksgiving as refugees.

BEHAVIOR—Courageous; Patient
EMOTIONS—Fear; Happiness
ENEMIES
FAMILIES

GOALS
HOLIDAYS AND CELEBRATIONS—Thanksgiving
IMMIGRANTS/REFUGEES
MOVING
SAFETY/DANGER
TRANSPORTATION—Boats
TRAVEL
WATER AND BODIES OF WATER—Oceans
WORLD CULTURES/COUNTRIES—Central America, Caribbean Islands

————. *The Man Who Could Call Down Owls*. Charles Mikolaycak, illus. New York: Macmillan, 1984.

When a stranger attempts to seize the owl man's power over the owls, he is driven away by them. Then the power is given to a young boy.

ANIMALS—Birds
BEHAVIOR—Destructive/Violent; Evil; Stealing
EMOTIONS—Jealousy
FRIENDSHIP—Relationships
MAGIC
STRANGERS
TIME—Specific seasons, winter
TRANSFORMATION

————. *The Mother's Day Mice*. Jan Brett, illus. New York: Clarion, 1986.

Three little mice search for presents to give their mother. The smallest mouse discovers that giving of oneself is a special gift.

ANIMALS—Personified; Pets, cats; Small creatures, mice
EMOTIONS—Love
FAMILIES—Parents; Siblings
GIFTS
GOALS
GRAPHIC AND PERFORMING ARTS—Music and musicians
MATHEMATICS—Size
SAFETY/DANGER

————. *Scary Scary Halloween*. Jan Brett, illus. New York: Clarion, 1986.

A mother cat and her three kittens are relieved when the monsters (trick-or-treaters) are gone at last.

ANIMALS—Pets, cats
BODY—Parts of body, eyes
HOLIDAYS AND CELEBRATIONS—Halloween
OBSERVATION
STORIES—Predictable text

————. *Smoky Night*. David Diaz, illus. San Diego: Harcourt, 1994.

A boy and his mother and cat survive an urban riot and are drawn into closer relationships with their neighbors of different cultures.

ANIMALS—Pets, cats
BEHAVIOR—Crying; Destructive/Violent; Sharing; Stealing
EMOTIONS—Anger; Fear

FAMILIES—Parents
FAMILY PROBLEMS—Homelessness
FIRE
FRIENDSHIP—Relationships
LOST AND FOUND
NEIGHBORHOODS AND COMMUNITIES—Specific, urban
OCCUPATIONS
SAFETY/DANGER
SENSES—Sight; Smell and taste; Sound
STRUCTURES—Buildings, houses and other dwellings
UNITED STATES—Cross cultural

———. *Someday a Tree*. Ronald Himler, illus. New York: Clarion, 1993.

Saddened by the poisoning of an old tree, a young girl's family and neighbors try to keep it alive, but their efforts are in vain. By planting the tree's acorns, the girl finds hope in looking forward to the seeds growing into trees.

BEHAVIOR—Problem-solving
ECOLOGY/ENVIRONMENTAL PROBLEMS
EMOTIONS—Sadness
NEIGHBORHOODS AND COMMUNITIES—Specific, rural
PLANTS—Cycles; Seeds; Trees

———. *A Turkey for Thanksgiving*. Diane de Groat, illus. New York: Clarion, 1991.

Mr. and Mrs. Moose invite a turkey to their Thanksgiving celebration. At first, the turkey fears he will be food for the feast rather than a guest.

ANIMALS—Farm, turkeys; Large animals, moose; Personified
BEHAVIOR—Searching
COMMUNICATION—Signs
EMOTIONS—Fear; Happiness
FOOD AND EATING
FRIENDSHIP—Relationships
FURNITURE—Chairs
HOLIDAYS AND CELEBRATIONS—Thanksgiving
HUMOR
LANGUAGE—Words
TIME—Specific seasons, winter

———. *The Valentine Bears*. Jan Brett, illus. New York: Clarion, 1983.

Because bears hibernate in the winter, Mr. and Mrs. Bear have not celebrated Valentine's Day. This year Mrs. Bear decides to wake up for the holiday. Both she and Mr. Bear receive Valentine surprises that represent their love for each other.

ANIMALS—Hibernation; Large animals, bears; Personified
EMOTIONS—Love
FOOD AND EATING
GIFTS
HOLIDAYS AND CELEBRATIONS—Valentine's
SENSES—Smell and taste
STRUCTURES—Caves
SURPRISES
TIME—Clocks and other time-telling methods; Specific seasons, winter
WRITING—Poems, Signs

————. *The Wall*. Ronald Himler, illus. New York: Clarion, 1990.

Visiting the Vietnam War Memorial in Washington, D.C., a boy and his father search for the name of the boy's grandfather, who was killed in the War. They pay homage to his honor.

BEHAVIOR—Crying; Proud; Searching
DEATH
EMOTIONS—Love; Sadness
FAMILIES—Family gatherings/Outings; Grandparents; Parents
HISTORICAL PERIODS—Twentieth Century, modern/contemporary
IDENTITY—Relationships
MEMORIES
SENSES—Touch
STRUCTURES—Others
TRAVEL
UNITED STATES—Regions, Middle Atlantic
WAR

————. *The Wednesday Surprise*. Donald Carrick, illus. New York: Clarion, 1989.

Anna and her grandmother have a special surprise for her father on his birthday: Anna has taught Grandma to read.

BEHAVIOR—Excited; Proud
BIRTHDAYS
ELDERLY
FAMILIES—Family gatherings/Outings; Grandparents; Parents
GIFTS
GOALS
READING
SURPRISES

Burningham, John. *Aldo*. New York: Crown, 1992.

A young child tells of her comfortable relationship with her imaginary friend, Aldo.

ANIMALS—Fantasy
BEHAVIOR—Shy
EMOTIONS—Fear
FRIENDSHIP—Imaginary friends
IDENTITY—Self-worth
SECRETS

————. *Come Away from the Water, Shirley*. New York: Crowell, 1977.

Shirley embarks on an exciting sea adventure in her imagination while back on the beach her parents give her warnings of real-life dangers.

ADVENTURES
BEHAVIOR—Courageous
EXPLORATION
FAMILIES—Parents
IMAGINATION—Imaginary worlds
PIRATES
SAFETY/DANGER
TRANSPORTATION—Boats

TREASURES
WATER AND BODIES OF WATER—Oceans
WORLD REGIONS—Seashore

———. *Granpa*. London: Cape, 1984.

A little girl and her grandfather share an easy relationship with many interesting moments.
COMMUNICATION
FAMILIES—Grandparents
IMAGINATION
LANGUAGE—Sayings and special language

———. *Hey! Get Off Our Train*. New York: Crown, 1989.

At bedtime, a young boy dreams of rescuing endangered animals while traveling on his toy train around the world.
ADVENTURES
ANIMALS—Endangered species
DREAMS
ECOLOGY/ENVIRONMENTAL PROBLEMS
EVERYDAY EXPERIENCES—Time of day, bedtime
IMAGINATION
ROOMS—Bedrooms
SLEEPING
STORIES—Predictable text
STRUCTURES—Buildings, houses and other dwellings
TIME—Cycles, day and night
TRANSPORTATION—Trains
TRAVEL

———. *John Patrick Norman McHennessy: The Boy Who Was Always Late*. New York: Crown, 1987.

A boy offers fanciful excuses for being late for school. When his disbelieving teacher encounters a far-out situation, his student has his turn at denying such an incident can happen.
BEHAVIOR—Disobedient
HUMOR
IMAGINATION
LANGUAGE—Names
OCCUPATIONS
SCHOOL EXPERIENCES
WRITING—Others

———. *Mr. Gumpy's Motor Car*. New York: Crowell, 1976.

Mr. Gumpy takes his human and animal friends for a ride in his old car, and they encounter a rainstorm.
ADVENTURES
ANIMALS—Personified
DISASTERS
EVERYDAY EXPERIENCES—Time of day, daytime
FRIENDSHIP—Relationships
STORIES—Predictable text

TRANSPORTATION—Cars
TRAVEL
WEATHER—Rain

————. *Mr. Gumpy's Outing*. New York: Holt, 1970.

Mr. Gumpy takes his human and animal friends for a boat ride. Even though he warns his passengers to not move about, they disobey, capsizing the boat. Being a true friend, Mr. Gumpy invites them home for tea.

ADVENTURES
ANIMALS—Personified
BEHAVIOR—Disobedient
DISASTERS
EMOTIONS—Happiness
EVERYDAY EXPERIENCES—Time of day, daytime
FRIENDSHIP—Relationships
MOVEMENT/SPEED
STORIES—Predictable text
TRANSPORTATION—Boats
TRAVEL

————. *Seasons*. London: Cape, 1969.

The cycle of seasons is portrayed through captioned illustrations.

TIME—Cycles, seasons

————. *Time to Get Out of the Bath, Shirley*. New York: Crowell, 1978.

Mother impatiently tidies up after Shirley when she takes a bath, not realizing that her daughter is engaged in imaginary adventures.

ADVENTURES
BEHAVIOR—Patient; Pretending
FAMILIES—Parents
HEALTH—Bathing
IMAGINATION—Imaginary worlds
OBSERVATION
ROOMS—Bathrooms
ROYALTY
SECRETS

————. *Where's Julius?* New York: Crown, 1986.

Julius creates bold adventures through his imagination while his parents maintain his real world.

ADVENTURES
FAMILIES—Parents
FOOD AND EATING
IMAGINATION
PLAY
WORLD REGIONS

————. *Would You Rather . . .* New York: Crowell, 1978.

The audience is given options for an imaginary world.

IMAGINATION—Imaginary worlds
INDIVIDUALITY

Burton, Virginia Lee. *The Little House*. Boston: Houghton Mifflin, 1942.

A little house in the country experiences the cycles of day and night and the seasons. When a city grows up around her, she becomes unhappy. The great-great-granddaughter of the man who built her discovers her hidden away in the city and moves her into the countryside.

BEHAVIOR—Responsible
CHANGES
CONSTRUCTION
ECOLOGY/ENVIRONMENTAL PROBLEMS
EMOTIONS—Sadness
IDENTITY—Geographic identity
LOST AND FOUND
MACHINES
MOVING
NEIGHBORHOODS AND COMMUNITIES—Specific, rural; Specific, urban
STRUCTURES—Buildings, houses and other dwellings
TIME—Across time; Cycles, day and night; Cycles, seasons
TRANSPORTATION—Trucks

————. *Mike Mulligan and His Steam Shovel*. Boston: Houghton Mifflin, 1939.

Mike Mulligan's steam shovel, Mary Ann, proves her worth in the face of techno-logical advancements and finds another job in the process.

BEHAVIOR—Ambitious/Persistent; Competitive; Problem-solving; Proud
CHANGES
CONSTRUCTION
EMOTIONS—Sadness
GOALS
IDENTITY—Self-worth
MACHINES
OCCUPATIONS
STRUCTURES—Buildings, others

Calhoun, Mary. *High-Wire Henry*. Erick Ingraham, illus. New York: Morrow, 1991.

When the family acquires a puppy, the cat, Henry, feels left out. Even though his tightrope walking was meant to impress the family, he eventually uses it to rescue the stranded puppy.

ADVENTURES
ANIMALS—Personified; Pets, cats; Pets, dogs
BEHAVIOR—Heroic; Problem-solving; Resourceful
EMOTIONS—Jealousy; Loneliness
FAMILIES
IDENTITY—Relationships; Self-worth
SAFETY/DANGER

Cannon, Janell. *Stellaluna*. San Diego: Harcourt, 1993.

Stellaluna, a baby bat, falls from her mother's clutches to a bird's nest, where she is raised with baby birds until she is reunited with her mother.

ANIMALS—Babies; Birds; Habitats, nests; Personified; Small creatures, others

BEHAVIOR—Imitating
LOST AND FOUND
SURVIVAL
TIME—Nighttime
WORLD REGIONS—Forest

Carle, Eric. *Do You Want to Be My Friend?* New York: Crowell, 1971.

In this wordless book, a mouse searches among many animals for a friend.

ANIMALS—Personified; Small creatures, mice
FRIENDSHIP—Relationships
IDENTITY—Relationships
OBSERVATION
STORIES—Minimal or no text

———. *The Honeybee and the Robber.* New York: Philomel, 1981.

The little honeybee saves the hive from an attacking bear.

ANIMALS—Large animals, bears; Small creatures, insects
BEHAVIOR—Heroic
PLANTS—Flowers
SURVIVAL

———. *A House for Hermit Crab.* Saxonville, MA: Picture Book Studio, 1987.

Throughout the months of the year, a hermit crab decorates his new shell by adding different sea creatures.

ANIMALS—Marine life, others
IDENTITY—Self-worth
MATHEMATICS—Measurement, mass; Size
MOVING
SAFETY/DANGER
STRUCTURES—Others
TIME—Cycles, months of the year
WATER AND BODIES OF WATER—Oceans

———. *The Mixed-Up Chameleon.* New York: Crowell, 1984.

A bored chameleon desiring to possess the qualities of other animals in the zoo finds that it is best to be oneself. The cutouts along the edges of the pages follow the progress of the story and show different animals and colors.

ANIMALS—Reptiles, lizards/chameleons; Zoo
BEHAVIOR—Bored
CHANGES
COLORS
ENEMIES
EXPLORATION
FOOD AND EATING
IDENTITY—Self-worth
IMAGINATION
WISHES

———. *1 2, 3 to the Zoo.* Cleveland: World, 1968.

In this counting book (1 to 10), one more zoo animal is presented as each train car is introduced.

ANIMALS—Zoo

MATHEMATICS—Counting
STORIES—Minimal or no text
TRANSPORTATION—Trains

————. *The Rooster Who Set Out to See the World*. New York: F. Watts, 1972.

In this counting book (1 to 5 and reversed), the rooster wishes to see the world and is joined one by one by other animals. However, when nighttime comes they decide that home is a better place.

ANIMALS—Farm, chickens
BEHAVIOR—Searching
DREAMS
EMOTIONS—Loneliness
MATHEMATICS—Counting
TIME—Cycles, day and night
TRAVEL
WISHES

————. *The Very Busy Spider*. New York: Philomel, 1984.

In this multisensory work, the spider persists in weaving a web even though the farm animals try to distract her.

ANIMALS—Farm; Habitats, webs; Small creatures, spiders
BEHAVIOR—Ambitious/Persistent
SENSES—Sight; Sound; Touch
STORIES—Predictable text
WEAVING

————. *The Very Hungry Caterpillar*. New York: Collins, 1979.

In a cumulative tale structured on the days of the week, a small hungry caterpillar gradually eats more and more until he is fat. Then he builds a cocoon for a home and finally emerges as a beautiful butterfly.

ANIMALS—Cycles; Eggs; Small creatures, butterflies/moths/caterpillars
CONSTRUCTION
FOOD AND EATING
HEALTH—Illness and injury
MATHEMATICS—Counting
OBSERVATION
STORIES—Predictable text
TIME—Cycles, days of the week
TRANSFORMATION

————. *The Very Quiet Cricket*. New York: Philomel, 1990.

The young cricket finally gets his wish to be able to create a sound. When he matures, a female cricket evokes from him a beautiful sound.

ANIMALS—Babies; Small creatures, insects
BIRTH
BODY—Parts of Body
IDENTITY—Gender roles
SENSES—Sound
STORIES—Predictable text
TIME—Cycles, day and night
WISHES

———. *Walter the Baker*. New York: Knopf, 1972; Simon & Schuster, 1995.

After the cat spills the milk, Walter, the baker, substitutes water in his pastries, much to the displeasure of the Duke. To be redeemed, the Duke tells the baker, he must create a roll through which the rising sun can shine three times. Hence, the pretzel is discovered.

ASTRONOMY—Sun
BEHAVIOR—Problem-solving
EMOTIONS—Anger
FOOD AND EATING
INVENTIONS
LANGUAGE—Words
OCCUPATIONS
RIDDLES
ROYALTY

Carlstrom, Nancy White. *Baby-O*. Sucie Stevenson, illus. Boston: Little, Brown, 1992.

Three generations of a West Indian family travel by bus with their wares to the local market.

FAMILIES—Babies and young siblings; Grandparents; Parents; Siblings
IDENTITY—Self-worth
NEIGHBORHOODS AND COMMUNITIES—Specific, rural
SHOPPING/MARKETING
STORIES—Predictable text
TRANSPORTATION—Buses
WORLD CULTURES/COUNTRIES—Central America, Caribbean Islands

———. *I'm Not Moving, Mama!* Thor Wickstrom, illus. New York: Macmillan, 1990.

A child mouse's many reasons for not wanting to move to a different home are countered by an insightful mother.

ANIMALS—Personified; Small creatures, mice
BEHAVIOR—Apprehensive; Patient; Wise
FAMILIES—Parents
MEMORIES
MOVING
NEIGHBORHOODS AND COMMUNITIES—General

———. *Jesse Bear, What Will You Wear?* Bruce Degen, illus. New York: Macmillan, 1986.

Jesse Bear engages in many daytime activities until it is bedtime.
ANIMALS—Personified
CLOTHING
EVERYDAY EXPERIENCES—Time of day, bedtime; Time of day, daytime
FAMILIES—Parents
STORIES—Predictable text
TIME—Cycles, day and night

———. *Who Gets the Sun Out of Bed?* David McPhail, illus. Boston: Little, Brown, 1992.

The sun refuses to get up until it is encouraged by a young boy.

ANIMALS—Pets, others
ASTRONOMY—Moon; Sun
BEHAVIOR—Lazy
FURNITURE—Beds
SLEEPING
TIME—Cycles, day and night

Carmine, Mary. *Daniel's Dinosaurs*. Martin Baynton, illus. New York: Scholastic, 1990.

Daniel, a young boy preoccupied with dinosaurs, finds marine life interesting when he visits an aquarium.

ANIMALS—Marine life; Marine life, aquariums
DINOSAURS
IMAGINATION

Carrick, Carol. *The Foundling*. Donald Carrick, illus. New York: Seabury, 1977.

Christopher slowly adjusts to his dog's death. At first, he rejects his parents' suggestion to find another dog, but then he finds an abandoned puppy.

ANIMALS—Pets, dogs
DEATH
DREAMS
EMOTIONS—Loneliness; Love; Sadness
FAMILIES—Adoption; Parents
IDENTITY—Relationships
MEMORIES
PERSONAL PROBLEMS—Fearing to try something new
STRUCTURES—Buildings, houses and other dwellings
WISHES

Castle, Caroline, and Peter Weevers. *Herbert Binns & the Flying Tricycle*. New York: Dial, 1987.

Herbert Binns, a clever mouse, rescues his invention, a flying tricycle, from sabotage by jealous acquaintances.

ANIMALS—Personified; Small creatures, mice
BEHAVIOR—Resourceful; Tricking
EMOTIONS—Jealousy
FLYING—Aviation
GOALS
IDENTITY—Self-worth
INVENTIONS
OCCUPATIONS
TRANSPORTATION—Bicycles

Cazet, Denys. *I'm Not Sleepy*. New York: Orchard, 1992.

Father tells Alex a bedtime story to prepare him for sleep, but he is interrupted several times before getting to the end of the story.

ANIMALS—Fantasy
EVERYDAY EXPERIENCES—Time of day, bedtime; Time of day, nighttime
FAMILIES—Parents
FLYING—Fantasy
IMAGINATION

ROOMS—Bedrooms
STORYTELLING
WORLD REGIONS—Rain forest/Jungle

Chaffin, Lillie. *We Be Warm Till Springtime Comes*. Lloyd Bloom, illus. New York: Macmillan, 1980.

A young Appalachian boy searches an old coal bank to find enough fuel to warm the house he shares with his mother and baby sister.

BEHAVIOR—Resourceful; Responsible
FAMILIES—Parents
IDENTITY—Self-worth
POVERTY
ROCKS AND MINERALS
SAFETY/DANGER
STRUCTURES—Buildings, cabins
SURVIVAL
TIME—Specific seasons, winter
UNITED STATES—Regions, Appalachia

Chall, Marsha Wilson. *Up North at the Cabin*. Steve Johnson, illus. New York: Lothrop, 1992.

A girl has many pleasurable experiences during her family's vacation at the cabin situated by a lake in the woods up north.

STRUCTURES—Buildings, cabins
TIME—Specific seasons, summer
UNITED STATES—Regions, Midwest
VACATIONS
WATER AND BODIES OF WATER—Lakes

Charlip, Remy. *Fortunately*. New York: Parents' Magazine, 1964.

Ned pursues an invitation to a surprise birthday party only to discover that it is for him.

BEHAVIOR—Ambitious/Persistent
BIRTHDAYS
LANGUAGE—Words
STORIES—Predictable text
SURPRISES
TRAVEL
WRITING—Letters

Cherry, Lynne. *The Great Kapok Tree: A Tale of the Amazon Train Forest*. San Diego: Harcourt, 1990.

A man ordered to cut down a tree in the Amazon rain forest falls asleep. One by one, animals living in the tree whisper words encouraging him to stop.

ANIMALS—Large animals; Small creatures
ECOLOGY/ENVIRONMENTAL PROBLEMS
MAPS
PLANTS—Trees
WORLD CULTURES/COUNTRIES—South America
WORLD REGIONS—Rain forest/Jungles

Chetwin, Grace. *Box and Cox*. David Small, illus. New York: Bradbury, 1990.

Mrs. Bouncer doubles her income by renting the same room to Mr. Box, who works nights, and Mr. Cox, who works days, until they both ask to marry her.

BEHAVIOR—Greedy; Tricking
HUMOR
MATHEMATICS—Size
MOVING
NEIGHBORHOODS AND COMMUNITIES—Specific, urban
OCCUPATIONS
ROOMS—Bedrooms
STRUCTURES—Buildings, houses and other dwellings
TIME—Cycles, day and night

Christelow, Eileen. *Five Little Monkeys Jumping on the Bed*. New York: Clarion, 1989.

At bedtime, five little monkeys jump on the bed, disobeying their mother and the doctor. One by one they fall off and get hurt, but they eventually settle down to sleep. Then, their mother has a turn.

ANIMALS—Small creatures, monkeys
BEHAVIOR—Disobedient
EVERYDAY EXPERIENCES—Time of day, bedtime
FAMILIES—Parents
FURNITURE—Beds
HEALTH—Health care; Illness and injury
HUMOR
MATHEMATICS—Counting
MOVEMENT/SPEED
OCCUPATIONS
SENSES—Sound
STORIES—Predictable text
SURPRISES

Christiansen, Candace. *Calico and Tin Horns*. Thomas Locker, illus. New York: Dial, 1992.

Based on a true incident that occurred in 1844, Hannah blows the dinner horn to warn her father and other Hudson River Valley farmers who have rebelled against the ruthless landlords and their lawmen.

ADVENTURES
BEHAVIOR—Courageous; Evil; Greedy; Hiding
ENEMIES
FAMILY PROBLEMS—Others
FARMS
HISTORICAL PERIODS—Nineteenth Century, early
NEIGHBORHOODS AND COMMUNITIES—Specific, rural
PEACE
SAFETY/DANGER
SECRETS
SEWING
UNITED STATES—Regions, Northeast

Chwast, Seymour. *The Twelve Circus Rings*. San Diego: Harcourt, 1993.

A counting book (from 1 to 12) patterned after "The Twelve Days of Christmas" presents circus images and performances and offer observational experiences and mathematical activities.

CIRCUS
GAMES/PUZZLES/TRICKS
MATHEMATICS—Classification; Counting; Numbers, ordinal
OBSERVATION

Cleaver, Elizabeth. *Petrouchka*. New York: Atheneum, 1988.

In this Russian ballet, Petrouchka, the ill-fated puppet, falls in love with a ballerina while performing at the fair.

BEHAVIOR—Destructive/Violent; Fighting/Quarreling
EMOTIONS—Jealousy; Love
FAIRS
GRAPHIC AND PERFORMING ARTS—Dance and dancers
MAGIC
PUPPETS
WORLD CULTURES/COUNTRIES—Europe, Central/Eastern

Clifton, Lucille. *Everett Anderson's Goodbye*. Ann Grifalconi, illus. New York: Holt, 1983.

Everett Anderson grieves after the death of his father, discovering that love never stops.

DEATH
EMOTIONS—Loneliness; Love; Sadness
FAMILIES—Parents

———. *Some of the Days of Everett Anderson*. Evaline Ness, illus. New York: Holt, 1970.

The everyday experiences of a young boy are described as the days of the week unfold.

EVERYDAY EXPERIENCES—Time of day, daytime; Time of day, nighttime
TIME—Cycles, days of the week

Coerr, Eleanor. *The Josefina Story Quilt*. Bruce Degen, illus. New York: Harper & Row, 1986.

Faith's father does not want to take her pet hen on the wagon train to California, but the hen proves valuable after all.

ANIMALS—Farm, chickens
BEHAVIOR—Crying; Hiding; Loyal
DEATH
DISASTERS
ENEMIES
FAMILIES—Parents
HISTORICAL PERIODS—Nineteenth Century, pioneer/westward movement
MOVING
QUILTS
TRANSPORTATION—Wagons

TRAVEL
UNITED STATES—Regions, West Coast

————. *Sadako*. Ed Young, illus. New York: Putnam, 1993.

Ten years after the bombing of Hiroshima, a young girl dying of leukemia attempts to fold a thousand paper cranes so that she can get well, as promised in an old legend.

ANIMALS—Birds
BEHAVIOR—Ambitious/Persistent; Courageous; Problem-solving
DEATH
DISASTERS
EMOTIONS—Fear; Love; Sadness
FAMILIES
FRIENDSHIP—Relationships
GOALS
GRAPHIC AND PERFORMING ARTS—Art and artists
HEALTH—Illness and injury
HISTORICAL PERIODS—Twentieth Century, World War II
HOLIDAYS AND CELEBRATIONS—Celebrations around the World
LUCK
MATHEMATICS—Counting
MOVEMENT/SPEED
NEIGHBORHOODS AND COMMUNITIES—Parks
PEACE
STATUES
STORYTELLING
WAR
WORLD CULTURES/COUNTRIES—Asia, Japan

Cohen, Barbara. *Gooseberries to Oranges*. Beverly Brodsky, illus. New York: Lothrop, 1992.

In the late 1800s, a girl from eastern Europe is reunited with her father in the United States after experiencing many hardships.

DEATH
EMOTIONS—Fear; Happiness; Loneliness; Sadness
ETHNIC CULTURES—Jewish
FAMILIES—Parents
FAMILY PROBLEMS—Separation
HEALTH—Illness and injury
HISTORICAL PERIODS—Nineteenth Century, late
IMMIGRANTS/REFUGEES
MEMORIES
MONEY
MOVING
PLANTS—Fruits
STORYTELLING
TRANSPORTATION—Boats
UNITED STATES—Regions, Middle Atlantic
WAR
WEATHER—Drought
WORLD CULTURES/COUNTRIES—Europe, Central/Eastern

Cohen, Caron Lee. *Whiffle Squeek*. Ted Rand, illus. New York: Dodd, Mead, 1987.

The seagoing cat experiences a narrow escape from the hungry monster.

ANIMALS—Marine life; Personified; Pets, cats
BEHAVIOR—Courageous; Destructive/Violent
DREAMS
ENEMIES
FISHING
IMAGINATION—Imaginary creatures, monsters
SAFETY/DANGER
SLEEPING
STORIES—Predictable text
TIME—Nighttime
TRANSPORTATION—Boats
WATER AND BODIES OF WATER—Oceans

Cohen, Miriam. *Lost in the Museum*. Lillian Hoban, illus. New York: Greenwillow, 1979.

In searching for the dinosaur on the first-grade field trip to a museum, Jim and some of his classmates disregard the teacher's directions to remain together and, as a result, become lost.

ANIMALS—Fantasy
BEHAVIOR—Apprehensive; Courageous; Crying; Disobedient; Searching; Teasing
DINOSAURS
EMOTIONS—Fear
OCCUPATIONS
PERSONAL PROBLEMS—Getting lost
SCHOOL EXPERIENCES
STRUCTURES—Buildings, museums

Cole, Babette. *Hurray for Ethelyn*. Boston: Little, Brown, 1991.

Jealous classmates try to sabotage Ethelyn's goal to become a brain surgeon by plotting to have her expelled from school. After their scheme is discovered, Ethelyn wins them over with her surgical expertise.

ANIMALS—Personified
BEHAVIOR—Destructive/Violent; Ridiculing
EMOTIONS—Jealousy
ENEMIES
FAMILIES—Siblings
FRIENDSHIP—Relationships
GOALS
OCCUPATIONS
ROOMS—Attics
SCHOOL EXPERIENCES
STRUCTURES—Buildings, houses and other dwellings

Cole, Joanna. *The Magic School Bus in the Time of the Dinosaurs*. Bruce Degen, illus. New York: Scholastic, 1994.

Ms. Frizzle's plans to take her class to a dinosaur dig are altered by a time machine.

ADVENTURES
ASTRONOMY
BEHAVIOR—Searching

DINOSAURS
EXPLORATION
HISTORICAL PERIODS—Prehistoric
MAGIC
OCCUPATIONS
SCHOOL EXPERIENCES
SURPRISES
TIME—Across time; Clocks and other time-telling methods
TRANSPORTATION—Buses
TRAVEL
WRITING—Other

————. *The Magic School Bus Inside the Earth*. Bruce Degen, illus. New York: Scholastic, 1987.

The magic school bus takes a class of children to explore the formation of the earth and rocks.

BEHAVIOR—Searching
EXPLORATION
GRAPHIC AND PERFORMING ARTS—Art and artists
LANGUAGE—Words
MAGIC
OCCUPATIONS
ROCKS AND MINERALS
SCHOOL EXPERIENCES
STRUCTURES—Buildings, schools; Caves
TRANSPORTATION—Buses
TRAVEL
WRITING—Others

————. *The Magic School Bus Inside the Human Body*. Bruce Degen, illus. New York: Scholastic, 1989.

When the magic school bus is mistakenly eaten by Arnold, Ms. Frizzle's class takes a field trip through his body.

BEHAVIOR—Searching
BODY
EXPLORATION
GRAPHIC AND PERFORMING ARTS—Art and artists
HEALTH—Illness and injury
LANGUAGE—Words
MAGIC
READING
SCHOOL EXPERIENCES
STRUCTURES—Buildings, schools
TRANSPORTATION—Buses
TRAVEL
WRITING—Others

————. *The Magic School Bus Inside a Hurricane*. Bruce Degen, illus. New York: Scholastic, 1995.

The magic school bus is transformed into a hot air balloon and then a weather plane as Ms. Frizzle's class experiences a hurricane firsthand.

ADVENTURES

EXPLORATION
FLYING
MAGIC
SAFETY/DANGER
SCHOOL EXPERIENCES
TRANSFORMATION
TRANSPORTATION—Airplanes; Buses; Hot-air balloons
TRAVEL
WEATHER—Rain; storms
WRITING—Other

————. *The Magic School Bus Lost in the Solar System.* Bruce Degen, illus. New York:
   Scholastic, 1990.

On a field trip, the magic school bus takes a class of children on an exploration of
space.

ASTRONOMY
BEHAVIOR—Searching
EXPLORATION
FLYING
GRAPHIC AND PERFORMING ARTS—Art and artists
MAGIC
OCCUPATIONS
READING
SCHOOL EXPERIENCES
SPACE
STRUCTURES—Buildings, schools
TRANSFORMATION
TRANSPORTATION—Buses
TRAVEL
WRITING—Letters; Others

————. *The Magic School Bus on the Ocean Floor.* Bruce Degen, illus. New York:
   Scholastic, 1992.

On a field trip, the magic school bus takes a class of children to explore the ocean
floor and its life.

ANIMALS—Marine life
BEHAVIOR—Searching
ECOLOGY/ENVIRONMENTAL PROBLEMS
EXPLORATION
GRAPHIC AND PERFORMING ARTS—Art and artists
HUMOR
MAGIC
OBSERVATION
OCCUPATIONS
READING
SCHOOL EXPERIENCES
STRUCTURES—Buildings, schools
TRANSPORTATION—Buses
TRAVEL
WATER AND BODIES OF WATER—Oceans
WRITING—Letters; Others

Columbus, Christopher. *The Log of Christopher Columbus*. Steve Lowe, adapt. Robert Sabuda, illus. New York: Philomel, 1992.

The high adventure of Columbus's first journey to the New World is told through an adaptation of his diary entries.

BEHAVIOR—Courageous
EXPLORATION
GOALS
HISTORICAL PERIODS—Exploration of the New World
TRANSPORTATION—Boats
TRAVEL
WATER AND BODIES OF WATER—Oceans
WRITING—Diaries

Conrad, Pam. *The Lost Sailor*. Richard Egielski, illus. New York: HarperCollins, 1992.

A sailor, marooned for years on a remote island, collapses in despair when he discovers that his hut is on fire. But the flame brings rescuers.

ADVENTURES
BEHAVIOR—Resourceful
BIOGRAPHY/LIFE STORIES
DISASTERS
FIRE
ISLANDS
LOST AND FOUND
OCCUPATIONS
PERSONAL PROBLEMS—Getting lost
SAFETY/DANGER
STRUCTURES—Buildings, houses and other dwellings
SURVIVAL
TIME—Across time
TRANSPORTATION—Boats
WATER AND BODIES OF WATER—Oceans
WEATHER—Storms
WORLD REGIONS—Seashore

————. *The Tub People*. Richard Egielski, illus. New York: Harper & Row, 1989.

The seven wooden toys, the tub people, fear that they have lost the Tub Child when he is swept down the drain.

EMOTIONS—Fear; Happiness; Sadness
LOST AND FOUND
MOUNTAIN CLIMBING
OCCUPATIONS
ROOMS—Bathrooms
TOYS—Others

Coomb, Patricia. *The Magic Pot*. New York: Lothrop, 1977.

Disguised as a magic pot, a demon brings riches and happiness to an elderly couple in poverty and outwits a greedy rich man.

BEHAVIOR—Greedy; Problem-solving
ELDERLY
FOOD AND EATING

GIFTS
IMAGINATION—Imaginary creatures, others
LANGUAGE—Sayings and special language
MAGIC
POVERTY
STRUCTURE—Boxes and containers
TREASURES

Cooney, Barbara. *Hattie and the Wild Waves*. New York: Viking, 1990.

Author/illustrator Barbara Cooney describes her mother's childhood and the events that led to the author's decision to become an artist.

BEHAVIOR—Ambitious/Persistent
BIOGRAPHY/LIFE STORIES
FAMILIES—Parents; Siblings
GRAPHIC AND PERFORMING ARTS—Art and artists
HISTORICAL PERIODS—Nineteenth Century, late
IDENTITY—Gender roles
NEIGHBORHOODS AND COMMUNITIES—Specific, urban
UNITED STATES—Regions, Northeast
WATER AND BODIES OF WATER—Oceans
WORLD REGIONS—Seashore

———. *Island Boy*. New York: Viking Kestrel, 1988.

Matthais spends his lifetime on an island, and succeeding generations find a fulfilling life there, too.

BIOGRAPHY/LIFE STORIES
DEATH
ELDERLY
FAMILIES—Grandparents; Parents
IDENTITY—Geographic identity
ISLANDS
MAPS
OCCUPATIONS
TIME—Across time
TRANSPORTATION—Boats
UNITED STATES—Regions, Northeast
WATER AND BODIES OF WATER—Oceans
WORLD REGIONS—Seashore

———. *Miss Rumphius*. New York: Viking, 1982.

In Alice's lifetime, she fulfills her dreams of going to faraway places and living by the sea, and then she satisfies her grandfather's admonition to make the world more beautiful.

BEHAVIOR—Responsible
BIOGRAPHY/LIFE STORIES
DREAMS
ECOLOGY/ENVIRONMENTAL PROBLEMS
ELDERLY
FAMILIES—Other relatives
GOALS
IDENTITY—Gender roles
OCCUPATIONS

PLANTS—Flowers
STRUCTURES—Buildings, libraries
TRAVEL
WORLD REGIONS—Seashore

Cox, David. *Bossyboots*. New York: Crown, 1987.

A girl uses her bossy behavior to subdue Flash Fred, one of the worst outlaws of the Australian bush. This setting is reminiscent of the American Wild West.
ADVENTURES
BEHAVIOR—Bossy; Courageous; Stealing
HUMOR
IDENTITY—Gender roles
SAFETY/DANGER
TRANSPORTATION—Others
WORLD CULTURES/COUNTRIES—Australia and the Pacific Islands

Crews, Donald. *Bicycle Race*. New York: Greenwillow, 1985.

The numbered positions of the twelve racers change as the bicycle race progresses.
BEHAVIOR—Competitive
COLORS
GOALS
IDENTITY—Self-worth
MATHEMATICS—Counting; Numbers
MOVEMENT/SPEED
OBSERVATION
SAFETY/DANGER
STATUES
STORIES—Minimal or no text
TRANSPORTATION—Bicycles

———. *Bigmama's*. New York: Greenwillow, 1991.

In the summer, a boy travels by train with his mother and siblings to his grandmother's farm to visit relatives.
FAMILIES—Family gatherings/Outings; Grandparents; Other relatives; Parents; Siblings
FARMS
NEIGHBORHOODS AND COMMUNITIES—Specific, rural
STRUCTURES—Buildings, houses and other dwellings
TIME—Nighttime; Specific seasons, summer
TRANSPORTATION—Trains
TRAVEL
UNITED STATES—Regions, South; Specific cultures, African American
VACATIONS

———. *Carousel*. New York: Greenwillow, 1982.

The carousel picks up speed and then slows to a stop, completing the ride.
CAROUSELS
FAIRS
MACHINES
MOVEMENT/SPEED
OBSERVATION
SENSES—Sight; Sound
TIME—Cycles

————. *Flying*. New York: Greenwillow, 1986.

An airplane flight is described from beginning to end.

FLYING—Aviation
MOVEMENT/SPEED
OBSERVATION
STORIES—Minimal or no text
TIME—Cycles, day and night
TRANSPORTATION—Airplanes
TRAVEL

————. *Freight Train*. New York: Greenwillow, 1979.

The journey of a freight train with cars of many colors is told through minimal text and illustrations.

COLORS
MOVEMENT/SPEED
OBSERVATION
STORIES—Minimal or no text
STRUCTURES—Tunnels
TRANSPORTATION—Trains

————. *Harbor*. New York: Greenwillow, 1982.

The harbor contains many different kinds of boats that are used for different purposes.

STORIES—Minimal or no text
TRANSPORTATION—Boats
WATER AND BODIES OF WATER—Harbors; Lakes; Oceans

————. *Parade*. New York: Greenwillow, 1983.

The sequence of events associated with a parade and its many elements are depicted.

GRAPHIC AND PERFORMING ARTS—Music and musicians
OCCUPATIONS
PARADES
TIME—Cycles
TRANSPORTATION
WRITING—Signs

————. *Sail Away*. New York: Greenwillow, 1995.

As a family takes a trip in a sailboat, they observe changes in the weather and movement from day to night.

CHANGES
FAMILIES—Family gatherings/Outings
MOVEMENT/SPEED
SENSES—Sound
STRUCTURES—Buildings, others
TIME—Day and night
TRANSPORTATION—Boats
WATER AND BODIES OF WATER—Harbors; Oceans
WEATHER—Storms; Wind

————. *School Bus*. New York: Greenwillow, 1984.

School buses take children to school, take them home again, and then complete their cycle by returning to their lot.
SCHOOL EXPERIENCES
STORIES—Minimal or no text
TIME—Cycles
TRANSPORTATION—Buses
TRAVEL

————. *Shortcut*. New York: Greenwillow, 1992.

The children take a shortcut home via the railroad tracks and encounter danger.
ADVENTURES
BEHAVIOR—Excited
EMOTIONS—Fear
FAMILIES—Grandparents
MOVEMENT/SPEED
OBSERVATION
SAFETY/DANGER
SECRETS
SENSES—Sound
TIME—Nighttime; Specific seasons, summer
TRANSPORTATION—Trains
UNITED STATES—Regions, South; Specific cultures, African American
VACATIONS

————. *Ten Black Dots*. New York: Greenwillow, 1986.

A counting book (1 to 10) depicts black dots as an integral part of common images.
CONSTRUCTION
MATHEMATICS—Counting; Shapes
OBSERVATION
STORIES—Predictable text

————. *Truck*. New York: Greenwillow, 1980.

The travel of a truck, with road signs along the way, are portrayed in a story without words.
COMMUNICATION—Signs
MOVEMENT/SPEED
OBSERVATION
STORIES—Minimal or no text
TRANSPORTATION—Trucks
TRAVEL
WRITING—Signs

Crowe, Robert. *Clyde Monster*. Kay Chorao, illus. New York: Dutton, 1976.

The young monster Clyde is afraid to go to bed in his cave because he fears that people may get him in the dark.
BEHAVIOR—Apprehensive
EMOTIONS—Fear
EVERYDAY EXPERIENCES—Time of day, bedtime
FAMILIES—Parents
IDENTITY—Relationships

IMAGINATION—Imaginary creatures, monsters
STRUCTURES—Caves

Cutler, Jane. *Darcy and Gran Don't Like Babies*. Susannah Ryan, illus. New York: Scholastic, 1993.

Gran, the only person who seems to understand why Darcy doesn't like the new baby, helps Darcy make a difficult adjustment.

BEHAVIOR—Problem-solving
EMOTIONS—Jealousy
EVERYDAY EXPERIENCES—Time of day, daytime
FAMILIES—Babies and young siblings; Grandparents; Parents
FAMILY PROBLEMS—New siblings
IDENTITY—Relationships
NEIGHBORHOODS AND COMMUNITIES—Parks
PLAY

Daly, Niki. *Not So Fast, Songololo*. New York: Atheneum, 1986.

A young black boy and his grandmother in South Africa embark on a special shopping trip to the city.

CLOTHING—Shoes
ELDERLY
EMOTIONS—Happiness
FAMILIES—Grandparents
LANGUAGE—Names
NEIGHBORHOODS AND COMMUNITIES—Specific, urban
SENSES—Sound
SHOPPING/MARKETING
TRANSPORTATION—Buses
WORLD CULTURES/COUNTRIES—Africa, Southern

Dana, Katharine Floyd. *Over in the Meadow*. David Carter, illus. New York: Scholastic, 1992.

Various meadow creatures portray the numbers one to ten in this traditional nursery rhyme first recorded by Olive Wadsworth.

ANIMALS—Babies; Small creatures
MATHEMATICS—Counting
OBSERVATION
STORIES—Predictable text
TIME—Specific seasons, spring

Day, Alexandra. *Frank and Ernest*. New York: Scholastic, 1988.

A personified elephant and bear assume the responsibility for running a diner and learn food language.

ADVENTURES
ANIMALS—Personified
BEHAVIOR—Cooperative; Responsible
FOOD AND EATING
IDENTITY—Self-worth
LANGUAGE—Sayings and special language

OCCUPATIONS
STRUCTURES—Buildings, libraries; others

de Regniers, Beatrice Schenk. *May I Bring a Friend?* Beni Montresor, illus. New York: Atheneum, 1964.

A boy receiving many invitations from the king and queen, one for each of the days of the week, politely asks to bring a friend each time.
ANIMALS—Zoo
FOOD AND EATING
FRIENDSHIP—Relationships
HOLIDAYS AND CELEBRATIONS—Halloween
MASKS
ROYALTY
STORIES—Predictable text
TIME—Cycles, days of the week

———. *Waiting for Mama.* Victoria de Larrea, illus. New York: Clarion, 1984.

While waiting patiently for her mother to finish her grocery shopping, Amy imagines the rest of her life.
BEHAVIOR—Bored; Obedient; Patient
FAMILIES—Parents
IDENTITY—Relationships
IMAGINATION
SHOPPING/MARKETING
STORIES—Predictable text
TIME—Across time

dePaola, Tomie. *The Art Lesson.* New York: Putnam, 1989.

Upon entering school, young Tommy, the aspiring artist, finds the school's rules restrictive. Finally, the art teacher promotes his individuality.
AESTHETIC APPRECIATION
BEHAVIOR—Ambitious/Persistent; Courageous; Problem-solving
BIOGRAPHY/LIFE STORIES
EMOTIONS—Disappointment; Happiness
FAMILIES—Grandparents; Other relatives; Parents
GOALS
GRAPHIC AND PERFORMING ARTS—Art and artists
HOBBIES
IDENTITY—Self-worth
INDIVIDUALITY
OCCUPATIONS
SCHOOL EXPERIENCES

———. *Charlie Needs a Cloak.* Englewood Cliffs, NJ: Prentice-Hall, 1974.

Charlie, a shepherd badly in need of a cloak, engages in the processes associated with creating a coat from sheep's wool.
ANIMALS—Farm, sheep
CLOTHING—Coats
HUMOR
OCCUPATION
SEWING

TIME—Cycles, seasons
WEAVING

————. *An Early American Christmas*. New York: Holiday House, 1987.

In the early 1880s, German immigrants bring their Christmas traditions to a New England village whose residents have previously shunned holiday celebrating.

APPLES
FAMILIES—Family gatherings/Outings
FOOD AND EATING
GRAPHIC AND PERFORMING ARTS—Art and artists; Music and musicians
HISTORICAL PERIODS—Nineteenth Century, late
HOLIDAYS AND CELEBRATIONS—Christmas
IMMIGRANTS/REFUGEES
LUCK
NEIGHBORHOODS AND COMMUNITIES—General
PARTIES
RELIGION
UNITED STATES—Regions, Northeast
WORLD CULTURES/COUNTRIES—Europe, Northern

————. *Jingle: The Christmas Clown*. New York: Putnam, 1992.

The little circus is forced to move on because recent disasters have caused the Italian village to be almost empty of inhabitants. Too tired to travel with the circus, the young animals cared for by the young clown, Jingle, remain in the village and give a memorable performance on Christmas Eve to the remaining residents, who are elderly.

ANIMALS—Babies
BEHAVIOR—Sharing
CIRCUS
COMMUNICATION—Signs
ELDERLY
EMOTIONS—Happiness; Sadness
GAMES/PUZZLES/TRICKS
GIFTS
HOLIDAYS AND CELEBRATIONS—Christmas
LANGUAGE—Words
SENSES—Sound
SEWING
TIME—Specific seasons, winter
TRAVEL
WEATHER—Snow
WORLD CULTURES/COUNTRIES—Europe, Southern

————. *The Knight and the Dragon*. New York: Putnam, 1980.

A librarian helps solve the dilemma of the inexperienced knight and dragon as they prepare to battle each other.

FOOD AND EATING
FRIENDSHIP—Relationships
IMAGINATION—Imaginary creatures, dragons
KNIGHTS
OCCUPATIONS
READING

STORIES—Minimal or no text
STRUCTURES—Buildings, libraries

————. *Nana Upstairs & Nana Downstairs*. New York: Putnam, 1973.

This intergenerational story tells of a young boy's loving relationship with his grandmother and great-grandmother and his experience with their deaths.
BEHAVIOR—Crying
DEATH
ELDERLY
EMOTIONS—Love; Sadness
FAMILIES—Grandparents
HEALTH—Health care
MEMORIES
ROOMS—Bedrooms
STRUCTURES—Buildings, houses and other dwellings

————. *Now One Foot, Now the Other*. New York: Putnam, 1981.

A young boy and his grandfather are close friends. The grandfather plays with the child and helps him learn to walk. Later, the boy assists his grandfather in learning to walk after a stroke.
DISABILITIES
ELDERLY
EMOTIONS—Fear; Loneliness; Love
FAMILIES—Grandparents
HEALTH—Health care; Illness and injury
IDENTITY—Relationships

————. *Oliver Button Is a Sissy*. New York: Harcourt, 1979.

Oliver Button's persistence in practicing dancing even though his peers label him a sissy turns him into a star.
BEHAVIOR—Ambitious/Persistent; Ridiculing
CLOTHING—Shoes
EMOTIONS—Disappointment
FAMILIES—Parents
GRAPHIC AND PERFORMING ARTS—Dance and dancers
IDENTITY—Gender roles
SCHOOL EXPERIENCES
SPORTS

————. *Pancakes for Breakfast*. New York: Harcourt, 1978.

An elderly woman's attempts to make pancakes for breakfast are thwarted by a lack of provisions and the hindrance of her cat. Her generous neighbors help fulfill her wish.
ANIMALS—Pets, cats
BEHAVIOR—Sharing
EMOTIONS—Disappointment
EVERYDAY EXPERIENCES—Time of day; awakening for the day
FOOD AND EATING
NEIGHBORHOODS AND COMMUNITIES—General
SENSES—Smell and taste
STORIES—Minimal or no text
TIME—Clocks and other time-telling methods
WISHES

———. *The Popcorn Book.* New York: Holiday House, 1978.

This concept book presents many facts about popcorn and the pleasure of eating it.

FOOD AND EATING
HUMOR
READING
STORYTELLING

———. *The Quicksand Book.* New York: Holiday House, 1977.

Discussions of quicksand composition and rescue procedures are presented while a rescue operation is carried out.

BEHAVIOR—Problem-solving
EMOTIONS—Fear
HUMOR
MATHEMATICS—Measurement, mass
READING
SAFETY/DANGER
SAND
WATER AND BODIES OF WATER—Rivers
WRITING—Others

———. *Sing, Pierrot, Sing.* San Diego: Harcourt, 1983.

Pierrot, the mime, finds consolation in children's friendship after his love for Columbine is thwarted.

CLOTHING—Costumes
EMOTIONS—Disappointment; Loneliness; Love
FRIENDSHIP—Relationships
GRAPHIC AND PERFORMING ARTS—Drama and actors
STORIES—Minimal or no text

———. *Watch Out for Chicken Feet in Your Soup.* Englewood Cliffs, NJ: Prentice-Hall, 1974.

Joey feels embarrassed to take his friend, Eugene, to visit his old-fashioned grandmother. When Eugene enjoys eating her cooking and wants to assist her in baking, Joey gains a new sense of appreciation for his grandmother.

BEHAVIOR—Sharing
EMOTIONS—Embarrassment; Love
FAMILIES—Grandparents
FOOD AND EATING
FRIENDSHIP—Relationships
IDENTITY—Relationships
UNITED STATES—Cross cultural

Dillon, Jana. *Jeb Scarecrow's Pumpkin Patch.* Boston: Houghton Mifflin, 1992.

When Jeb Scarecrow's pumpkin patch is threatened by crows, he devises an ingenious plan to save the pumpkins.

ANIMALS—Birds; Personified
BEHAVIOR—Ambitious/Persistent; Apprehensive; Boastful; Bullying; Destructive/Violent; Problem-solving; Tricking
EMOTIONS—Fear; Happiness
EVERYDAY EXPERIENCES—Time of day, nighttime
GOALS

HOLIDAYS AND CELEBRATIONS—Halloween
IDENTITY—Self-worth
PUMPKINS
SAFETY/DANGER
SCARECROWS
SURPRISES
TIME—Nighttime; Specific seasons, fall

DiSalvo-Ryan, DyAnne. *Uncle Willie and the Soup Kitchen*. New York: Morrow, 1991.

A boy becomes aware of people who are homeless and poor in his community. One day he helps his uncle prepare food in a soup kitchen for the needy.

BEHAVIOR—Responsible
EMOTIONS—Loneliness; Sadness
FAMILIES—Other relatives
FAMILY PROBLEMS—Homelessness
FOOD AND EATING—Soup
HEALTH—Health care
NEIGHBORHOODS AND COMMUNITIES—Social gatherings; Specific, urban
POVERTY

Dodds, Dayle Ann. *Wheel Away!* Thacher Hurd, illus. New York: Harper & Row, 1989.

The runaway wheel, depicted horizontally across the page spreads, causes much chaos as it moves through the community during the day. Its return trip at night is shown vertically across the pages until it is reunited with the boy.

ADVENTURES
LANGUAGE—Words
MACHINES—Wheels
MOVEMENT/SPEED
OBSERVATION
SENSES—Sound
STORIES—Minimal or no text; Predictable text
TIME—Cycles, day and night
TRANSPORTATION—Bicycles

Domanska, Janina. *Busy Monday Morning*. New York: Greenwillow, 1985.

A Polish folk song depicts father and child putting up the hay.

FAMILIES—Parents
FARMS
GRAPHIC AND PERFORMING ARTS—Music and musicians
OCCUPATIONS
PLANTS—Others
STORIES—Predictable text
TIME—Cycles, days of the week

Dorros, Arthur. *Abuela*. Elisa Kleven, illus. New York: Dutton, 1991.

A little girl imagines what it would be like to fly over New York City with her *abuela* (grandmother).

EMOTIONS—Happiness
FAMILIES—Grandparents

FLYING—Fantasy
IDENTITY—Relationships
IMAGINATION
NEIGHBORHOODS AND COMMUNITIES—Specific, urban
TRANSPORTATION—Buses
UNITED STATES—Regions, Northeast; Specific cultures, Hispanic American

Dragonwagon, Crescent. *Half a Moon and One Whole Star*. Jerry Pinkney, illus. New York: Macmillan, 1986.

A bedtime lullaby describes various nighttime activities near and far as Susan falls asleep.

ANIMALS
ASTRONOMY—Moon; Stars; Sun
DREAMS
EVERYDAY EXPERIENCES—Time of day, awakening for the day; Time of day, bedtime
FURNITURE—Beds
SENSES—Sight; Smell and taste; Sound
SLEEPING
STORIES—Predictable text
TIME—Nighttime

———. *Home Place*. Jerry Pinkney, illus. New York: Macmillan, 1990.

While walking through the woods, a family comes across the remains of an old homestead. The girl in the family imagines life there in earlier times. In the illustrations, the images of a black family and their farm life in the 1800s is depicted.

FAMILIES—Family gatherings/Outings
HISTORICAL PERIODS—Nineteenth Century, late
IMAGINATION
MEMORIES
NEIGHBORHOODS AND COMMUNITIES—Specific, rural
OBSERVATION
STRUCTURES—Buildings, houses and other dwellings
TIME—Across time
UNITED STATES—Cross cultural; Specific cultures, African American

Duke, Kate. *The Guinea Pig ABC*. New York: Dutton, 1983.

On each page a guinea pig demonstrates the action represented by a word beginning with that letter of the alphabet.

ANIMALS—Pets, others
LANGUAGE—Alphabet; Words
OBSERVATION
STORIES—Minimal or no text

———. *Guinea Pigs Far and Near*. New York: Dutton, 1984.

Images of guinea pigs enact the movement associated with prepositions.

ANIMALS—Small creatures, others
LANGUAGE—Words
MOVEMENT/SPEED
STORIES—Minimal or no text

Dunbar, Joyce. *Four Fierce Kittens*. Jakki Wood, illus. New York: Scholastic, 1991.

Four little kittens seek adventure and excitement on the farm.

ANIMALS—Farm; Pets, cats
BEHAVIOR—Searching
FARMS
INDIVIDUALITY
SENSES—Sound
STORIES—Predictable text

Dunrea, Oliver. *The Broody Hen*. New York: Doubleday, 1992.

The hen discovers that she can successfully hatch her chicks in a nest.

ANIMALS—Eggs; Farm, chickens; Habitats, nests
COLORS
FARMS
STORIES—Predictable text

———. *Deep Down Underground*. New York: Macmillan, 1989.

In this counting book (1 to 10), small animals move underground.

ANIMALS—Small creatures
MATHEMATICS—Counting
MOVEMENT/SPEED
STORIES—Predictable text
STRUCTURES—Tunnels

———. *The Painter Who Loved Chickens*. New York: Farrar, 1995.

A patron's appreciation of an artist's paintings of chickens provides him with the resources to purchase a farm where he can live with these creatures.

AESTHETIC APPRECIATION
ANIMALS—Farm, chickens
BEHAVIOR—Ambitious/Persistent; Problem-solving
FARMS
GRAPHIC AND PERFORMING ARTS—Art and artists
INDIVIDUALITY
OBSERVATION
WISHES

Duran, Cheli. *Hildilid's Night*. Arnold Lobel, illus. New York: Macmillan, 1971.

Night after night an old lady who hates the night tries to chase it away.

ASTRONOMY
BEHAVIOR—Impatient; Problem-solving
ELDERLY
EMOTIONS—Hate
HUMOR
MOVEMENT/SPEED
TIME—Cycles, day and night; Nighttime

Duvoisin, Roger. *Petunia*. New York: Knopf, 1950.

Petunia, the goose, learns from the many tragedies she causes others that wisdom does not come from carrying a book around but from reading it.

ANIMALS—Farm, geese; Personified
BEHAVIOR—Foolish; Pretending; Proud; Wise

DISASTERS
READING
SAFETY/DANGER
STRUCTURES—Boxes and containers

Ehlert, Lois. *Circus*. New York: HarperCollins, 1992.

Through the ringmaster's monologue, a circus performance is presented from beginning to end.

CIRCUS
MATHEMATICS—Shapes
MOVEMENT/SPEED
STORIES—Minimal or no text

————. *Color Farm*. New York: Lippincott, 1990.

Cutout shapes form the heads of different farm animals.

ANIMALS—Farm
COLORS
IMAGINATION
LANGUAGE—Words
MATHEMATICS—Shapes
OBSERVATION
SENSES—Touch

————. *Color Zoo*. New York: Lippincott, 1989.

Cutout shapes form a sequence of images representing different zoo animals.

ANIMALS—Zoo
COLORS
IMAGINATION
LANGUAGE—Words
MATHEMATICS—Shapes
OBSERVATION
SENSES—Touch

————. *Eating the Alphabet: Fruits and Vegetables from A to Z*. San Diego: Harcourt, 1989.

The alphabet serves as a structure to introduce both familiar and exotic fruits and vegetables.

FOOD AND EATING
GARDENS
LANGUAGE—Alphabet; Words
OBSERVATION
PLANTS—Fruits; Vegetables

————. *Feathers for Lunch*. San Diego: Harcourt, 1990.

A cat is unsuccessful in his attempts to catch a bird. The illustrations and text identify plants and birds and their songs.

ANIMALS—Birds; Pets, cats
BEHAVIOR—Tricking
BELLS

ENEMIES
LANGUAGE—Words
MATHEMATICS—Size
OBSERVATION
PLANTS
SENSES—Sound
STORIES—Predictable text

————. *Fish Eyes*. San Diego: Harcourt, 1990.

A little black fish invites readers to imagine what they might look like if they became fishes and to count the colorful fish with cutout eyes.

ANIMALS—Marine life, fishes
BODY—Parts of body, eyes
IMAGINATION
MATHEMATICS—Counting; Numbers, processes
OBSERVATION
SENSES—Touch
STORIES—Predictable text
WISHES

————. *Growing Vegetable Soup*. San Diego: Harcourt, 1987.

Father and child plant vegetables, tend to them as they grow, and then harvest them and make soup.

EVERYDAY EXPERIENCES—Time of day, daytime
FAMILIES—Parents
FOOD AND EATING—Soup
GARDENS
GOALS
LANGUAGE—Words
MATHEMATICS—Measurement, volume
PLANTS—Cycles; Seeds; Vegetables
STORIES—Minimal or no text
TIME—Cycles, seasons

————. *Planting a Rainbow*. San Diego: Harcourt, 1988.

Mother and child plant bulbs and seeds, watch them grow as plants, and pick their flowers all summer long.

COLORS
EVERYDAY EXPERIENCES—Time of day, daytime
FAMILIES—Parents
GARDENS
GOALS
LANGUAGE—Words
PLANTS—Cycles; Flowers; Seeds
STORIES—Minimal or no text
TIME—Cycles, seasons
WEATHER—Rainbows

————. *Red Leaf, Yellow Leaf*. San Diego: Harcourt, 1991.

The sprouting and growth of a maple tree is described by a child whose family buys a sapling at the garden center.

EVERYDAY EXPERIENCES—Time of day, daytime

FAMILIES—Parents
GOALS
LANGUAGE—Words
OBSERVATION
PLANTS—Trees
SENSES—Touch
STORIES—Minimal or no text
TIME—Cycles, seasons

Emberley, Barbara. *Drummer Hoff*. Ed Emberley, illus. Englewood Cliffs, NJ: Prentice-Hall, 1967.

In this cumulative tale, seven soldiers of increasingly higher rank build a cannon, but Drummer Hoff fires it off.

BEHAVIOR—Cooperative
CONSTRUCTION
IDENTITY—Relationships
LANGUAGE—Names
MACHINES
OCCUPATIONS
SENSES—Sound
STORIES—Predictable text

Ernst, Lisa Campbell. *A Colorful Adventure of the Bee, Who Left Home One Monday Morning and What He Found Along the Way*. Lee Ernst, illus. New York: Lothrop, 1986.

Leaving the hive, the bee encounters many colors in his exploration of the outside world.

ADVENTURES
ANIMALS—Small creatures, insects
COLORS
OBSERVATION
STORIES—Minimal or no text
STRUCTURES—Others
WEATHER—Rain; Rainbows

———. *Sam Johnson and the Blue Ribbon Quilt*. New York: Lothrop, 1983.

While mending the pigpen awning, Sam discovers that he enjoys sewing pieces of material together. His request to join his wife's quilting club is met with ridicule, so he and other men in the community form their own group.

AESTHETIC APPRECIATION
BEHAVIOR—Ambitious/Persistent; Competitive; Ridiculing
DISASTERS
EMOTIONS—Disappointment
FAIRS
FAMILIES—Husbands and wives
GOALS
GRAPHIC AND PERFORMING ARTS—Art and artists
HISTORICAL PERIODS—Twentieth Century, early
IDENTITY—Gender roles
INDIVIDUALITY
MAPS

NEIGHBORHOODS AND COMMUNITIES—Social gatherings; Specific, rural
QUILTS
SEWING
WEATHER—Storms

————. *When Bluebell Sang*. New York: Bradbury, 1989.

Bluebell, the singing cow, soon tires of her fame and longs to return to the farm.

ANIMALS—Farm, cows
BEHAVIOR—Tricking
EMOTIONS—Loneliness
FARMS
GRAPHIC AND PERFORMING ARTS—Music and musicians
HUMOR
IDENTITY—Self-worth
INDIVIDUALITY
TRAVEL

————. *Zinnia and Dot*. New York: Viking, 1992.

The hens, Zinnia and Dot, forgo their quarreling to protect the one remaining egg, which hatches and becomes their collective pride and joy.

ANIMALS—Eggs; Farm, chickens
BEHAVIOR—Boastful; Competitive; Destructive/Violent; Fighting/Quarreling; Sharing;
            Stealing
BIRTH
EMOTIONS—Love
ENEMIES
FAMILIES—Parents
FRIENDSHIP—Relationships
STRUCTURES—Buildings, others
SURVIVAL

Ets, Marie Hall. *Gilberto and the Wind*. New York: Viking, 1963.

The wind influences a young boy's life in many ways.

KITES
UNITED STATES—Specific cultures, Hispanic American
WEATHER—Wind

————. *Play with Me*. New York: Viking, 1955.

As a small girl waits quietly by the pond, each animal that she has tried to pursue as a playmate now approaches her.

BEHAVIOR—Problem-solving
OBSERVATION
PLAY
WATER AND BODIES OF WATER—Ponds

Ets, Marie Hall, and Aurora Labastida. *Nine Days to Christmas*. Marie Hall Ets, illus. New York: Viking, 1959.

A young girl in Mexico looks forward to selecting a pinata for her first Christmas party, a pasada.

BEHAVIOR—Excited
HOLIDAYS AND CELEBRATIONS—Christmas; Celebrations around the World

NEIGHBORHOODS AND COMMUNITIES—Social gatherings
PARTIES
SHOPPING/MARKETING
WORLD CULTURES/COUNTRIES—Central America, Mexico

Fair, Sylvia. *The Bedspread.* New York: Morrow, 1982.

Sitting at opposite ends of their bed, Maud and Amelia, elderly sisters, re-create through embroidery on the white bedspread their childhood home as each remembers it.

BEHAVIOR—Cooperative; Problem-solving
ELDERLY
EMOTIONS—Happiness
FAMILIES—Siblings
FURNITURE—Beds
IDENTITY—Self-worth
INDIVIDUALITY
MEMORIES
QUILTS
ROOMS—Bedrooms
SENSES—Sight
SEWING
STRUCTURES—Buildings, museums
TIME—Cycles, days of the week

Farber, Norma. *Return of the Shadows.* Andrea Baruffi, illus. New York: Harper-Collins, 1992.

Mimi's shadow challenges other shadows to run free. While they explore the world, they cast themselves from other images and encounter high noon. However, at nighttime they are glad to return to their original shapes.

ADVENTURES
BEHAVIOR—Running away
IMAGINATION—Imaginary worlds
LIGHT AND SHADOWS/REFLECTIONS
MOVEMENT/SPEED
OBSERVATION
TIME—Cycles, days and night
TRAVEL

Fatio, Louise. *The Happy Lion* New York: McGraw-Hill, 1954.

The zoo animal, Happy Lion, receives many friendly visits from people. When he leaves his cage after it is left unlocked and roams the streets, he receives much different responses.

ANIMALS—Large animals, lions; Zoo
BEHAVIOR—Apprehensive; Excited; Searching
EMOTIONS—Fear; Happiness
EXPLORATION
FRIENDSHIP—Relationships
LANGUAGE—Words
NEIGHBORHOODS AND COMMUNITIES—Specific, urban
OCCUPATIONS

SENSES—Sight; Sound
WORLD CULTURES/COUNTRIES—Europe, Northern
ZOOS

Feelings, Muriel. *Jambo Means Hello: Swahili Alphabet Book*. Tom Feelings, illus. New York: Dial, 1974.

The twenty-four letters of the Swahili language are associated with the East African culture.

LANGUAGE—Alphabet; Words
MAPS
WORLD CULTURES/COUNTRIES—Africa, Eastern

————. *Moja Means One: Swahili Counting Book*. Tom Feelings, illus. New York: Dial, 1971.

Swahili numbers 1 to 10 are related to different aspects of East African life.

LANGUAGE—Words
MAPS
MATHEMATICS—Counting
WORLD CULTURES/COUNTRIES—Africa, Eastern

Finchler, Judy. *Miss Malarkey Doesn't Live in Room 10*. Kevin O'Malley, illus. New York: Walker, 1995.

A boy in first grade imagines that his teacher's home is the classroom. When she moves into his apartment building, he discovers that she has a life away from school.

BEHAVIOR—Excited
CHANGES
HUMOR
IDENTITY—Relationships
IMAGINATION
INDIVIDUALITY
MOVING
NEIGHBORHOODS AND COMMUNITIES—Specific, urban
OCCUPATIONS
PARTIES
SCHOOL EXPERIENCES
SURPRISES

Fisher, Aileen. *Listen, Rabbit*. Symeon Shimin, illus. New York: Crowell, 1964.

Wanting a pet, a boy seeks out a rabbit and finds in the springtime that she has given him a surprise.

ANIMALS—Babies; Small creatures, rabbits
BEHAVIOR—Excited; Searching
EMOTIONS—Happiness
IDENTITY—Relationships
MOVEMENT/SPEED
SECRETS
SENSES—Sight; Sound
SURPRISES
TIME—Specific seasons, spring

Fisher, Leonard Everett. *Boxes! Boxes!* New York: Viking, 1984.

Boxes can be different sizes and shapes and can be used by a child for different purposes.
MATHEMATICS—Shapes; Size
STORIES—Minimal or no text
STRUCTURES—Boxes and containers

Fleischman, Paul. *The Animal Hedge*. Lydia Dabcovich, illus. New York: Dutton, 1983.

A drought causes a farmer to sell his farm and the animals that he prizes. To cope with his tragedy, he shapes his hedge to reflect his past life and foretell the future.
ANIMALS—Farm
BEHAVIOR—Resourceful
EMOTIONS—Disappointment; Happiness; Loneliness; Sadness
FAMILIES—Parents
FARMS
IMAGINATION
MEMORIES
NEIGHBORHOODS AND COMMUNITIES—Specific, rural
OCCUPATIONS
PLANTS—Others
POVERTY
SENSES—Sight
WEATHER—Drought

————. *Rondo in C*. Janet Wentworth, illus. New York: Harper & Row, 1988.

Beethoven's "Rondo in C" played by a girl in a piano recital evokes memories for members of the audience.
COMMUNICATION
GRAPHIC AND PERFORMING ARTS—Music and musicians
INDIVIDUALITY
MEMORIES
SENSES—Sound
STORIES—Predictable text

————. *Shadow Play*. Eric Beddows, illus. New York: Harper & Row, 1990.

Two children attend a shadow play performance of "Beauty and the Beast" performed by Monsieur Le Grand and his Family of Shadow at the fair.
FAIRS
GRAPHIC AND PERFORMING ARTS—Drama and actors
PUPPETS
STORIES—Minimal or no text

————. *Time Train*. Claire Ewart, illus. New York: HarperCollins, 1991.

A class on a trip experiences prehistoric times firsthand when they board the Rocky Mountain Unlimited.
ADVENTURES
DINOSAURS
HISTORICAL PERIODS—Prehistoric
MAGIC
SURPRISES

TIME—Across Time
TRANSPORTATION—Trains
TRAVEL
UNITED STATES—General
VACATIONS

Fleischman, Sid. *The Scarebird*. Peter Sis, illus. New York: Greenwillow, 1988.

In his isolation, Lonesome John plays his harmonica and seeks companionship by dressing a scarecrow. When a homeless boy drifts into his life, the elderly farmer gradually transfers the clothing and his feelings to the boy, developing a new friendship.

CLOTHING
CONSTRUCTION
ELDERLY
EMOTIONS—Loneliness
FARMS
FRIENDSHIP—Relationships
GAMES/PUZZLES/TRICKS
GRAPHIC AND PERFORMING ARTS—Music and musicians
IMAGINATION
NEIGHBORHOODS AND COMMUNITIES—Specific, rural
SCARECROWS

Fleming, Denise. *Barnyard Banter*. New York: Holt, 1994.

Different farm animals and their sounds are introduced in rollicking rhyme as a barnyard search is conducted for a missing goose.

ANIMALS—Farm
BEHAVIOR—Searching
FARMS
LOST AND FOUND
OBSERVATION
SENSES—Sound
STORIES—Predictable text

———. *In the Small, Small Pond*. New York: Holt, 1993.

A frog describes life in and near a pond throughout the year.

ANIMALS—Small creatures
LANGUAGE—Words
MOVEMENT/SPEED
OBSERVATION
SENSES—Sight; Sound
STORIES—Predictable text
TIME—Cycles, seasons
WATER AND BODIES OF WATER—Ponds

———. *In the Tall, Tall Grass*. New York: Holt, 1991.

A young child follows a caterpillar as it moves through the grass, encountering many small creatures and their rhythmic, rhyming sounds and movements.

ANIMALS—Birds; Small creatures
EVERYDAY EXPERIENCES—Time of day, daytime; Time of day, nighttime
LANGUAGE—Words
SENSES—Sound

STORIES—Minimal or no text
TIME—Cycles, day and night

Florian, Douglas. *The City*. New York: Crowell, 1982.

In this wordless story, a woman with a red bag can be observed passing through city scenes.

NEIGHBORHOODS AND COMMUNITIES—Specific, urban
OBSERVATION
SHOPPING/MARKETING
STORIES—Minimal or no text

Flournoy, Valerie. *The Patchwork Quilt*. Jerry Pinkney, illus. New York: Dial, 1985.

When Grandmother becomes ill, Tanya and her mother help complete the quilt she has started. The quilt is made of fabric pieces representing family experiences from the past.

BEHAVIOR—Ambitious/Persistent; Patient; Problem-solving
ELDERLY
FAMILIES—Grandparents; Parents
GIFTS
HEALTH—Illness and injury
MEMORIES
QUILTS
STORYTELLING
SURPRISE
TIME—Cycles, seasons
UNITED STATES—Specific cultures, African American

———. *Tanya's Reunion*. Jerry Pinkney, illus. New York: Dial, 1995.

At first Tanya is lonely and bored while visiting the Virginia farm where Grandma spent her childhood. When Grandma shares her memories, Tanya begins to appreciate these surroundings and anticipates the upcoming reunion.

BEHAVIOR—Bored
EMOTIONS—Disappointment
EVERYDAY EXPERIENCES
FAMILIES—Family gatherings/Outings; Grandparents; Other relatives
FARMS
MEMORIES
NEIGHBORHOODS AND COMMUNITIES—Specific, rural
TRAVEL
UNITED STATES—Regions, South; Specific cultures, African American

Fort, Patrick. *Redbird*. New York: Orchard, 1988.

The flight of Redbird, the airplane, is told in braille and through raised images.

KITES
LANGUAGE—Sayings and special language
SAFETY/DANGER
SENSES—Touch
TRANSPORTATION—Airplanes
WEATHER—Storms

Fox, Mem. *Hattie and the Fox.* Patricia Mullins, illus. New York: Bradbury, 1987.

Even though Hattie, the big black hen, has warned the other animals of danger numerous times, they ignore it. They are surprised when they are attacked by a fox.

ANIMALS—Farm, chickens; Large animals, foxes
BEHAVIOR—Courageous
EMOTIONS—Fear
ENEMIES
FARMS
NEIGHBORHOODS AND COMMUNITIES—Specific, rural
SAFETY/DANGER
STORIES—Predictable text
SURPRISES
SURVIVAL

————. *Koala Lou.* Pamela Lofts, illus. San Diego: Harcourt, 1988.

A young koala bear misses her mother's reminders that she loves her as new siblings occupy her mother's time. One day Koala Lou devises a plan to get her mother's attention.

ANIMALS—Personified; Small creatures, others
BEHAVIOR—Competitive; Courageous
EMOTIONS—Jealousy; Loneliness; Love; Sadness
FAMILIES—Babies and young siblings; Parents
FAMILY PROBLEMS—New siblings
GOALS
SPORTS
WORLD CULTURES/COUNTRIES—Australia and the Pacific Islands

————. *Possum Magic.* Julie Vivas, illus. Nashville: Abingdon, 1987.

Australian possums search for magic that will change the invisible one into a visible form.

ANIMALS—Personified; Small creatures, others
BEHAVIOR—Searching; Tricking
MAGIC
READING
TRANSFORMATION
TRAVEL
WORLD CULTURES/COUNTRIES—Australia and the Pacific Islands

————. *Shoes from Grandpa.* Patricia Mullins, illus. New York: Orchard, 1990.

Starting with the new shoes her grandpa gave her, other members of the family contribute to Jessie's wardrobe. After receiving many articles of clothing, she finds that she is missing an important item—jeans, which her grandpa buys for her.

CLOTHING
EMOTIONS—Happiness
FAMILIES—Grandparents; Other relatives; Parents; Siblings
GIFTS
STORIES—Predictable text
WISHES

———. *Wilfrid Gordon McDonald Partridge*. Julie Vivas, illus. Brooklyn, NY: Kane/Miller, 1985.

In a young boy's search for the meaning of memory, he finds a way to restore meaning to an elderly woman's life.

BEHAVIOR—Searching
DISABILITIES
ELDERLY
FRIENDSHIP—Relationships
GIFTS
GOALS
HEALTH—Health care; Illness and injury
LANGUAGE—Names
LOST AND FOUND
MEMORIES
NEIGHBORHOODS AND COMMUNITIES

Franklin, Kristine L. *The Old, Old Man and the Very Little Boy*. Terea D. Shaffer, illus. New York: Atheneum, 1992.

A small boy listens to an old man's stories in an African village. When the boy becomes elderly, he too comes to understand that all grow old but remain a child inside.

BEHAVIOR—Sharing; Wise
BIOGRAPHY/LIFE STORIES
ELDERLY
MEMORIES
STORYTELLING
TIME—Across time
WORLD CULTURES/COUNTRIES—Africa

Freeman, Don. *Bearymore*. New York: Viking, 1976.

The circus bear has difficulty hibernating because he must think of a new act for the upcoming circus season. Unexpectedly, he finds an act that is popular with the audience.

ANIMALS—Hibernation
ANIMALS—Large animals, bears
CIRCUS
DREAMS
MACHINES—Wheels
SLEEPING
TIME—Specific seasons, winter
VACATIONS

———. *Corduroy*. New York: Viking, 1968.

A toy bear in a department store finally gets his wish for a friend.

BEHAVIOR—Searching
CLOTHING—Buttons
EMOTIONS—Sadness
FRIENDSHIP—Relationships
LOST AND FOUND
SHOPPING/MARKETING
STRUCTURES—Buildings, stores

TOYS—Bears
WISHES

———. *Dandelion*. New York: Viking, 1964.

Dandelion disregards the type of party—"come as you are"—as stated in the invitation. When he arrives at the party dressed up, his hostess does not recognize him and turns him away. He learns that it is best to be oneself.

ANIMALS—Large animals, lions; Personified
BEHAVIOR—Excited; Resourceful
CHANGES
CLOTHING
EMOTIONS—Disappointment; Happiness
FRIENDSHIP—Relationships
IDENTITY—Self-worth
PARTIES
WEATHER—Storms
WRITING—Letters

———. *Mop Top*. New York: Viking, 1955.

A young boy is reluctant to have a haircut.

BEHAVIOR—Apprehensive; Hiding
BIRTHDAYS
BODY—Parts of the body, hair
MONEY
OCCUPATIONS
PERSONAL PROBLEMS—Fearing to try something new
PLAY

———. *Norman the Doorman*. New York: Viking, 1959.

When the mouse, Norman, the doorman, wins the museum's art contest with his wire sculpture, he asks that his prize be a tour of the museum's upstairs.

ANIMALS—Small creatures, mice
GRAPHIC AND PERFORMING ARTS—Art and artists
STRUCTURES—Buildings, museums

———. *A Pocket for Corduroy*. New York: Viking, 1978.

Corduroy, a toy bear, searches for a pocket in a laundromat.

ADVENTURES
BEHAVIOR—Searching
CLOTHING—Pockets
FRIENDSHIP—Relationships
LOST AND FOUND
PERSONAL PROBLEMS—Getting lost
STRUCTURES—Buildings, others
TOYS—Bears
WISHES

Freeman, Lydia. *Pet of the Met*. New York: Viking, 1953.

Something magical happens during a performance of Mozart's *The Magic Flute*. The mouse prompter and his cat enemy become enchanted and dance on stage together.

ANIMALS—Personified; Pets, cats; Small creatures, mice
ENEMIES
GRAPHIC AND PERFORMING ARTS—Dance and dancers; Music and musicians
MAGIC
SURPRISES

French, Fiona. *Anancy and Mr. Dry-Bone*. Boston: Little, Brown, 1991.

Poor Anancy's trickery wins Miss Louise away from marrying the very rich Mr. Dry Bones.

BEHAVIOR—Resourceful; Tricking
EMOTIONS—Happiness
FAMILIES—Husbands and wives
FRIENDSHIP—Relationships
GOALS
MAGIC
POVERTY
WORLD CULTURES/COUNTRIES—Africa, Western Central America, Caribbean Islands

Friedman, Aileen. *A Cloak for the Dreamer*. Kim Howard, illus. New York: Scholastic, 1994.

Misha, the tailor's youngest son, does not follow in the footsteps of his father and two older brothers. Instead, he dreams of traveling around the world.

BEHAVIOR—Competitive; Problem-solving
CLOTHING—Coats
COLORS
DREAMS
EMOTIONS—Love; Sadness
FAMILIES—Parents; Siblings
FAMILY PROBLEMS—Separation
GOALS
IDENTITY—Self-worth
INDIVIDUALITY
MAPS
MATHEMATICS—Shapes
OCCUPATIONS
ROYALTY
SEWING
TRAVEL

Friedman, Ina R. *How My Parents Learned to Eat*. Allen Say, illus. Boston: Houghton Mifflin, 1984.

While courting after World War II, an American sailor and a Japanese girl learn each other's way of eating.

BEHAVIOR—Cooperative
FAMILIES—Marriage; Parents
FOOD AND EATING
HISTORICAL PERIODS—Twentieth Century, World War II
SECRETS
WAR
WORLD CULTURES/COUNTRIES—Asia, Japan; Cross cultures

Fritz, Jean. *The Great Adventure of Christopher Columbus*. Tomie dePaola, illus. New
York: Putnam & Grosset, 1992.

The story of Columbus's first journey to the New World is accompanied by pop-
up and pull-the-tab illustrations.
BEHAVIOR—Courageous
EXPLORATION
GOALS
HISTORICAL PERIODS—Exploration of the New World
ROYALTY
TRANSPORTATION—Boats
TRAVEL
WORLD CULTURES/COUNTRIES—Europe, Northern

Gág, Wanda. *Millions of Cats*. New York: Coward-McCann, 1928.

Searching for a cat as a pet, an elderly couple finds themselves with "millions and
billions and trillions of cats." When they ask the multitude to decide who is the
prettiest among them, the cats engage in much quarreling. As a result, the couple
is left with a frightened kitten who makes a splendid pet.
ANIMALS—Pets, cats
BEHAVIOR—Fighting/Quarreling; Searching
ELDERLY
EMOTIONS—Fear; Loneliness; Love
FAMILIES—Husbands and wives
MATHEMATICS—Numbers, ideas
STORIES—Predictable text
TRAVEL

Gage, Wilson. *Cully Cully and the Bear*. James Stevenson, illus. New York: Greenwillow, 1983.

When Cully Cully, the hunter, decides he needs a new bearskin on which to lie, he
goes into the forest and meets a bear. A humorous episode follows in which Cully
Cully and the bear chase each other.
ANIMALS—Large animals, bears
HUMOR
MOVEMENT/SPEED

Gantos, Jack. *Rotten Ralph*. Nicole Rubel, illus. Boston: Houghton Mifflin, 1976.

Rotten Ralph, a bad cat, is left to live at a circus where he finds life difficult and
much different from living with Sara and her family.
ANIMALS—Pets, cats
BEHAVIOR—Destructive/Violent; Ridiculing
CIRCUS
EMOTIONS—Anger
HUMOR

Gardner, Beau. *What Is It? A Spin-About Book*. New York: Putnam, 1989.

Shapes can be manipulated to form four different images on each page.
GAMES/PUZZLES/TRICKS

IMAGINATION
LANGUAGE—Words
MATHEMATICS—Shapes
MOVEMENT/SPEED
OBSERVATION
SENSES—Touch
TRANSFORMATION

Garland, Michael. *Dinner at Magritte's*. New York: Dutton, 1995.

The boy, Pierre, encounters many unusual experiences as he spends the day with surrealist artists, René Magritte and Salvador Dali.

ADVENTURES
AESTHETIC APPRECIATION
BEHAVIOR—Bored; Excited
GRAPHIC AND PERFORMING ARTS—Art and artists
IDENTITY—Relationships
INDIVIDUALITY
MYSTERY
OBSERVATION
SURPRISES

————. *My Cousin Katie*. New York: Crowell, 1989.

Katie's cousin anticipates her visit on the farm with its many elements, but she particularly looks forward to seeing Katie.

EMOTIONS—Happiness
FAMILIES—Other relatives
FARMS
NEIGHBORHOODS AND COMMUNITIES—Specific, rural
TRAVEL
VACATIONS

Garland, Sherry. *The Lotus Seed*. Tatsuro Kiuchi, illus. San Diego: Harcourt, 1993.

A Vietnamese girl plucks a lotus seed from the Imperial Garden the day the emperor abdicates. She carries it through many hardships until years later her grandson loses the seed. When it sprouts in the earth, the grandmother gives her grandchildren seeds to remember their heritage.

BEHAVIOR—Ambitious/Persistent; Crying
BIOGRAPHY/LIFE STORIES
DISASTERS
EMOTIONS—Happiness; Sadness
FAMILIES—Grandparents
IDENTITY—Geographic identity
IMMIGRANTS/REFUGEES
LOST AND FOUND
LUCK
MEMORIES
MOVING
NEIGHBORHOODS AND COMMUNITIES—Specific, urban
PLANTS—Flowers; Seeds
ROYALTY

SAFETY/DANGER
SECRETS
SURPRISES
TRAVEL
WAR
WORLD CULTURES/COUNTRIES—Asia, others

Gauch, Patricia Lee. *Tanya and Emily in a Dance for Two*. Satomi Ichikawa, illus. New York: Philomel, 1994.

From their emerging friendship, Tanya, the smallest dancer, and Emily, the most talented one, learn more about dance.

ANIMALS—Zoo
BEHAVIOR—Ambitious/Persistent; Imitating
FRIENDSHIP—Relationships
GRAPHIC AND PERFORMING ARTS—Dance and dancers
INDIVIDUALITY
LANGUAGE—Words
SURPRISES

Geisert, Arthur. *Pigs from A to Z*. Boston: Houghton Mifflin, 1986.

Seven pigs build a tree house in a setting with hidden letters.

ANIMALS—Farms, pigs; Personified
BEHAVIOR—Hiding
CONSTRUCTION
GAMES/PUZZLES/TRICKS
LANGUAGE—Alphabet
MATHEMATICS—Numbers, ideas
OBSERVATION
PLANTS—Trees
STORIES—Minimal or no text
STRUCTURES—Others

———. *Pigs from 1 to 10*. Boston: Houghton Mifflin, 1992.

The audience can observe ten pigs in their quest for a lost, fabled place, but they can also search for the numerals 0 through 9 hidden on each page spread.

ADVENTURES
ANIMALS—Farm, pigs; Personified
BEHAVIOR—Searching
CONSTRUCTION
GAMES/PUZZLES/TRICKS
IMAGINATION—Imaginary worlds
MATHEMATICS—Counting
OBSERVATION
STORIES—Minimal or no text
TRAVEL

Gerrard, Roy. *Sir Cedric*. New York: Farrar, 1984.

Sir Cedric, the Good, looking for adventure, saves the kingdom from the evil Black Ned and wins the hand of the princess.

ADVENTURES
BEHAVIOR—Courageous; Evil; Revengeful
BODY—Shape and size

FAMILIES—Marriage
HUMOR
IDENTITY—Gender roles
KNIGHTS
ROYALTY
STRUCTURES—Buildings, castles/palaces
TRANSPORTATION—Horses
WAR

Gershator, Phillis. *Rata-pata-scata-fata*. Holly Meade, illus. Boston: Little, Brown, 1994.

The dreamy boy, Junjun, living in the Caribbean, discovers magic words that seem to make wishes come true.

BEHAVIOR—Pretending
FAMILIES—Parents
IMAGINATION—Imaginary worlds
ISLANDS
LANGUAGE—Sayings and special language
MAGIC
UNITED STATES—Specific cultures, Hispanic American
WEATHER—Rain
WISHES
WORLD CULTURES/COUNTRIES—Central America, Caribbean Islands

———. *Sambalena Show-Off*. Leonard Jenkins, illus. New York: Simon & Schuster, 1995.

Inspired by a Caribbean folk song, the author tells the story of a boy who sets a pot on top of his head to show off, only to have it slip down over his head.

BEHAVIOR—Boastful; Lazy; Problem-solving
BODY—Parts of body
CHANGES
CLOTHING—Hats
EMOTIONS—Embarrassment
FAMILIES—Grandparents; Parents
GRAPHIC AND PERFORMING ARTS—Dance and dancers; Music and musicians
PARTIES
PERSONAL PROBLEMS—Other
STRUCTURES—Boxes and containers
WORLD CULTURES/COUNTRIES—Central America, Caribbean Islands

Gerstein, Mordicai. *Roll Over!* New York: Crown, 1984.

One by one nine animals fall out of bed as a child commands, "Roll over!"

ANIMALS—Personified
EVERYDAY EXPERIENCES—Time of day, bedtime
FURNITURE—Beds
GAMES/PUZZLES/TRICKS
MATHEMATICS—Numbers, processes
OBSERVATION
ROOMS—Bedrooms
STORIES—Predictable text
SURPRISES
TIME—Cycles, day and night

————. *The Room*. New York: Harper & Row, 1984.

Years pass as various occupants move in and out of the room, and now it is available for rent again.

MEMORIES
MOVING
NEIGHBORHOODS AND COMMUNITIES—Specific, urban
OBSERVATION
ROOMS
STRUCTURES—Buildings, houses and other dwellings
TIME—Across time

————. *William, Where are You?* New York: Crown, 1985.

William hides in a most unlikely place at bedtime and causes his parents to go on an extensive search.

BEHAVIOR—Hiding; Searching
EVERYDAY EXPERIENCES—Time of day, bedtime
FAMILIES—Parents
OBSERVATION
SECRETS
STORIES—Minimal or no text
STRUCTURES—Buildings, houses and other dwellings
SURPRISES
TIME—Nighttime

Gibbons, Gail. *Flying*. New York: Holiday House, 1986.

Flying has been a timeless interest of humans. Types of aviation from early to modern times is presented.

ADVENTURES
FLYING—Aviation
STRUCTURES—Others
TRANSPORTATION—Airplanes; Hot-air balloons

Giganti, Paul. *How Many Snails? A Counting Book*. Donald Crews, illus. New York: Greenwillow, 1988.

A child counts and classifies familiar images.

EVERYDAY EXPERIENCES—Time of day, daytime; Time of day, nighttime
MATHEMATICS—Classification; Counting
OBSERVATION

Ginsburg, Mirra. *Across the Stream*. Nancy Tafuri, illus. New York: Greenwillow, 1982.

The duck and duckling rescue the hen and her chicks from their bad dream of their enemy, the fox.

ANIMALS—Farm, chickens; Farm, ducks
DREAMS
EMOTIONS—Fear
ENEMIES
SAFETY/DANGER
STORIES—Minimal or no text
WATER AND BODIES OF WATER—Rivers

————. *Good Morning, Chick.* Byron Barton, illus. New York: Greenwillow, 1980.

The chick hatches from the shell. While attempting to crow like the rooster, the chick does not look where he is going and falls into a puddle. He is rescued by his mother.

ANIMALS—Farm, chickens
BIRTH
FARMS
SAFETY/DANGER
SENSES—Sound
STORIES—Minimal or no text
TIME—Daytime

Glass, Andrew. *Jackson Makes His Move.* New York: F. Warne, 1982.

In searching for fulfillment through his painting, Jackson, the raccoon, discovers that he needs to focus on emotions and learns to express himself through color and movement.

ANIMALS—Personified
BEHAVIOR—Searching
GRAPHIC AND PERFORMING ARTS—Art and artists
INDIVIDUALITY
MOVING

Golenbock, Peter. *Teammates.* Paul Bacon, illus. San Diego: Harcourt, 1990.

This real-life story tells of Pee Wee Reese's efforts to ease racial tensions during Jackie Robinson's early baseball career.

BEHAVIOR—Courageous; Problem-solving
BIOGRAPHIES/LIFE STORIES
EMOTIONS—Anger
IDENTITY—Relationships
SPORTS
UNITED STATES—Cross cultural; Specific cultures, African American

Gomi, Taro. *Coco Can't Wait.* New York: Morrow, 1984.

Coco and her grandmother carefully plan their next meeting so they do not miss each other or collide on the way.

EMOTIONS—Disappointment; Happiness
FAMILIES—Grandparents
GOALS
HUMOR
MOVEMENT/SPEED
STORIES—Minimal or no text
TRANSPORTATION
TRAVEL
WORLD CULTURES/COUNTRIES—Asia, Japan

Goodall, John S. *The Adventures of Paddy Pork.* New York: Harcourt, 1968.

Paddy Pork finds home inviting after running away to the circus.

ANIMALS—Farm, pigs; Large animals, wolves; Personified
BEHAVIOR—Destructive/Violent; Disobedient; Evil; Running Away
CIRCUS
EMOTIONS—Disappointment; Sadness

ENEMIES
FAMILIES—Parents
GAMES/PUZZLES/TRICKS
STORIES—Minimal or no text

————. *An Edwardian Christmas.* New York: Atheneum, 1978.

In this story without a text, Christmas is celebrated in an English country home at the beginning of the twentieth century.

HISTORICAL PERIODS—Nineteenth Century, late
HOLIDAYS AND CELEBRATIONS—Christmas
STORIES—Minimal or no text
WORLD CULTURES/COUNTRIES—Europe, Northern

————. *Naughty Nancy Goes to School.* New York: Atheneum, 1985.

Nancy's classroom distractions are forgiven when she saves a schoolmate on the beach during a school outing.

ANIMALS—Personified; Small creatures, mice
BEHAVIOR—Courageous; Disobedient
IDENTITY—Gender roles; Self-worth
OBSERVATION
OCCUPATIONS
SAFETY/DANGER
SCHOOL EXPERIENCES
STORIES—Minimal or no text
SURVIVAL
TRAVEL
WATER AND BODIES OF WATER—Oceans
WORLD REGIONS—Seashore

————. *Paddy to the Rescue.* New York: Atheneum, 1985.

When Paddy Pork responds to cries for help, he becomes involved in apprehending a jewel thief.

ADVENTURES
ANIMALS—Personified
BEHAVIOR—Stealing
FRIENDSHIP—Relationships
JEWELS/JEWELRY
OBSERVATION
STORIES—Minimal or no text
WATER AND BODIES OF WATER—Oceans

————. *Paddy's New Hat.* New York: Atheneum, 1980.

Chasing his new hat which is carried by the wind into the police station, Paddy is mistakenly recruited for the police force. As a policeman, he encounters many adventures that eventually make him a hero.

ANIMALS—Farms, pigs; Personified
BEHAVIOR—Courageous; Heroic
CLOTHING—Hats
OCCUPATIONS
ROYALTY
STORIES—Minimal or no text
WEATHER—Wind

————. *Shrewbettina's Birthday*. New York: Harcourt, 1971.

The gentleman who retrieves Shrewbettina's purse from a thief helps her give a grand birthday party for herself.

ANIMALS—Personified
BEHAVIOR—Heroic; Stealing
BIRTHDAYS
STORIES—Minimal or no text

————. *The Story of a Castle*. New York: McElderry, 1986.

Through a wordless picture book with full and half pages, the history of an English castle from its construction in the late 1100s to its public opening in 1970 is illustrated.

CHANGES
STORIES—Minimal or no text
STRUCTURES—Buildings, castles/palaces
TIME—Across time
WORLD CULTURES/COUNTRIES—Europe, Northern

————. *The Story of a Farm*. New York: McElderry, 1989.

Through alternating half- and full-page illustrations, this wordless book depicts the history of an English farm from the early Middle Ages to the years after World War II.

CHANGES
FARMS
STORIES—Minimal or no text
TIME—Across time
WORLD CULTURES/COUNTRIES—Europe, Northern

————. *The Story of a Main Street*. New York: Macmillan, 1987.

In another wordless book, alternating half- and full-page spreads depict the changes on an English main street from medieval times to the present.

CHANGES
NEIGHBORHOODS AND COMMUNITIES—Specific, urban
OBSERVATION
SHOPPING/MARKETING
STORIES—Minimal or no text
STRUCTURES—Buildings, others
TIME—Across time
WORLD CULTURES/COUNTRIES—Europe, Northern

————. *The Story of an English Village*. New York: Atheneum, 1979.

Through alternating half- and full-page illustrations and without text, the development of an English village, seen from the same vantage point, is traced from a simple clearing during medieval times to a congested urban area in contemporary times.

CHANGES
NEIGHBORHOODS AND COMMUNITIES—General
STORIES—Minimal or no text
TIME—Across time
WORLD CULTURES/COUNTRIES—Europe, Northern

Gould, Deborah Lee. *Grandpa's Slide Show*. Cheryl Harness, illus. New York: Lothrop, 1987.

> After Grandpa dies, his family continues to view his slides as a way of coping with their grief.

DEATH
EMOTIONS—Sadness
FAMILIES—Family gatherings/Outings; Grandparents
IDENTITY—Relationships
MEMORIES
PHOTOGRAPHY

Graham, Thomas. *Mr. Bear's Chair*. New York: Dutton, 1987.

> As a surprise for Mrs. Bear, her husband constructs a chair to replace her broken one.

ANIMALS—Large animals, bears; Personified
CONSTRUCTION
FAMILIES—Husbands and wives
FURNITURE—Chairs
GIFTS
GOALS
SENSES—Sound
STORIES—Minimal or no text
SURPRISES

Gray, Libba Moore. *Small Green Snake*. Holly Meade, illus. New York: Orchard, 1994.

> A young snake strays from his family because he hears some curious sounds. A gardener discovers him and traps him in a glass jar.

ANIMALS—Personified; Reptiles, snakes
BEHAVIOR—Curious; Disobedient
ENEMIES
FAMILIES—Parents
GARDENS
LANGUAGE—Sayings and special language
MOVEMENT/SPEED
PERSONAL PROBLEMS—Breaking promises
SAFETY/DANGER
SENSES—Sight; Sound
STRUCTURES—Boxes and containers
SURPRISES

Gray, Nigel. *A Balloon for Grandad*. Jane Ray, illus. New York: Orchard, 1988.

> Saddened by the loss of his balloon, a boy imagines that it is traveling to visit his grandfather in Egypt.

BALLOONS
EMOTIONS—Happiness; Love; Sadness
FAMILIES—Grandparents; Parents
FLYING
IMAGINATION
LOST AND FOUND
SENSES—Sight

TRAVEL
WORLD CULTURES/COUNTRIES—Africa, Northern

Greenfield, Eloise. *Africa Dream*. Carole Byard, illus. New York: John Day, 1977.

An African American child moves across time and space in her dreams to experience her African heritage.

BEHAVIOR—Searching
DREAMS
EMOTIONS—Loneliness
FAMILIES—Other relatives
IDENTITY—Geographic identity; Relationships
STORYTELLING
TIME—Across time
TRAVEL
WORLD CULTURES/COUNTRIES—Africa

———. *Grandpa's Face*. Floyd Cooper, illus. New York: Philomel, 1988.

Tamika is afraid that someday her grandfather will confront her with the mean face he makes when he is rehearsing for a play, but he assures her that his love is unconditional.

EMOTIONS—Anger; Fear; Love
FAMILIES—Grandparents
FOOD AND EATING
GRAPHIC AND PERFORMING ARTS—Drama and actors
UNITED STATES—Specific cultures, African American

———. *She Comes Bringing Me That Little Baby Girl*. John Steptoe, illus. Philadelphia: Lippincott, 1974.

As he realizes the importance of the older brother's role, a young boy's disappointment and jealousy over a new baby sister turns into pride and a sense of responsibility.

BEHAVIOR—Apprehensive; Proud; Responsible; Sharing
EMOTIONS—Jealousy
FAMILIES—Babies and new siblings; Parents
FAMILY PROBLEMS—New siblings

Gregory, Valiska. *Through the Mickle Woods*. Boston: Little, Brown, 1992.

When the queen dies, the boy Michael persuades the king to make a journey to the mickle woods to listen to the bear's stories, which will help him overcome his grief.

ANIMALS—Large animals, bears; Personified
DEATH
EMOTIONS—Sadness
HISTORICAL PERIODS—Medieval/Renaissance
JEWELS/JEWELRY
ROYALTY
STORYTELLING
TIME—Nighttime
TRAVEL
WORLD CULTURES/COUNTRIES—Europe, Northern
WRITING—Letters

Grifalconi, Ann. *Darkness and the Butterfly*. Boston: Little, Brown, 1987.

> Osa is courageous and curious during the day but fearful at night. The Wise Woman shows her that the small butterfly is pursued by the darkness but flies on. Osa finds the light of her courage will help her cope with nighttime.

> ANIMALS—Small Creatures, butterflies/moths/caterpillars
> BEHAVIOR—Apprehensive; Courageous; Curious; Wise
> DREAMS
> EMOTIONS—Fear
> EVERYDAY EXPERIENCES—Time of day, nighttime
> FAMILIES—Parents
> FLYING—Fantasy
> IMAGINATION—Imaginary creatures
> LOST AND FOUND
> MATHEMATICS—Size
> SLEEPING
> TIME—Cycles, day and night
> WORLD CULTURES/COUNTRIES—Africa

———. *Flyaway Girl*. Boston: Little, Brown, 1992.

> As an African mother prepares for the New Year's celebration, she teaches her daughter, assisted by ancestral spirits, about the responsibilities of womanhood.

> BEHAVIOR—Obedient; Responsible
> FAMILIES—Parents
> GOALS
> HOLIDAYS AND CELEBRATIONS—New Year
> IDENTITY—Gender role
> IMAGINATION
> MAGIC
> MASKS
> SENSES—Smell and taste; Sound
> TIME—Daytime
> WORLD CULTURES/COUNTRIES—Africa, Western

———. *Osa's Pride*. Boston: Little, Brown, 1990.

> Grandmother helps Osa see the foolishness of her pride by sharing the story cloth with her.

> BEHAVIOR—Boastful; Proud
> EMOTIONS—Sadness
> FAMILIES—Grandparents
> FAMILY PROBLEMS—Separation
> GOALS
> GRAPHIC AND PERFORMING ARTS—Art and artists
> IDENTITY—Relationships
> PLAY
> SEWING
> STORYTELLING
> WORLD CULTURES/COUNTRIES—Africa
> WORLD REGIONS—Rain forest/Jungle

Griffith, Helen V. *Georgia Music*. James Stevenson, illus. New York: Greenwillow, 1986.

> A girl is able to make her ill grandfather laugh when she re-creates on the har-

monica the Georgia summer sounds they had experienced during her visit to his farm the previous summer.

ELDERLY
EMOTIONS—Happiness; Loneliness; Sadness
FAMILIES—Grandparents
FARMS
GOALS
GRAPHIC AND PERFORMING ARTS—Music and musicians
HEALTH—Illness and injury
IDENTITY—Self-worth
MEMORIES
NEIGHBORHOODS AND COMMUNITIES—Specific, rural
SENSES—Sound
TIME—Cycles, day and night; Specific seasons, summer
TRANSPORTATION—Trains
TRAVEL
UNITED STATES—Regions, South
VACATIONS

————. *Grandaddy's Place*. James Stevenson, illus. New York: Greenwillow, 1987.

A girl from the city learns to appreciate the farm when she spends a summer vacation with her grandfather.

ANIMALS—Farm
ELDERLY
EMOTIONS—Fear; Happiness
FAMILIES—Grandparents
FARMS
FISHING
NEIGHBORHOODS AND COMMUNITIES—Specific, rural
SENSES—Sound
STORYTELLING
TIME—Cycles, day and night; Specific seasons, summer
TRANSPORTATION—Trains
TRAVEL
UNITED STATES—Regions, South
VACATION

————. *Grandaddy's Stars*. James Stevenson, illus. New York: Greenwillow, 1995.

Janetta makes a list of important things for Grandaddy to see when he comes to Boston for a visit, but she fears he will be bored by them.

ASTRONOMY—Stars
BEHAVIOR—Apprehensive; Excited; Sharing
EMOTIONS—Love
EVERYDAY EXPERIENCES
FAMILIES—Grandparents; Parents
HUMOR
IDENTITY—Relationships
NEIGHBORHOODS AND COMMUNITIES—Specific, urban
TRANSPORTATION—Trains
TRAVEL
UNITED STATES—Regions, Northeast
VACATIONS
WRITING—Others

Grindley, Sally. *Knock, Knock! Who's There?* Anthony Browne, illus. New York:
    Knopf, 1985.

    A young girl plays a repetitive game at bedtime with her father.
    EMOTIONS—Happiness
    EVERYDAY EXPERIENCES—Time of day, bedtime
    FAMILIES—Parents
    GAMES/PUZZLES/TRICKS
    IMAGINATION
    OBSERVATION
    ROOMS—Bedrooms
    SENSES—Sound
    STORIES—Predictable text

Grossman, Bill. *Donna O'Neeshuck Was Chased by Some Cows.* Sue Truesdell, illus.
    New York: Harper & Row, 1988.

    After being chased by many different types of animals, Donna O'Neeshuck dis-
    covers that they are seeking her irresistible pats on the head.
    ANIMALS
    IDENTITY—Self-worth
    MOVEMENT/SPEED
    SENSES—Touch
    TRANSPORTATION

Haley, Gail E. *Sea Tale.* New York, Dutton, 1990.

    A young sailor's love for a mermaid is preserved in a ring created from a golden
    strand of her hair. When he returns home from his seafaring journey, he is
    reminded of his promise to a mysterious elderly woman that he must bring back to
    her a lock of his sweetheart's hair.
    DREAMS
    EMOTIONS—Love
    GIFTS
    GOALS
    IMAGINATION—Imaginary creatures, others; Imaginary world
    JEWELS
    LOST AND FOUND
    OCCUPATIONS
    STORYTELLING
    TRANSPORTATION—Boats
    TRAVEL
    WATER AND BODIES OF WATER—Oceans
    WORLD REGIONS—Seashore

Hall, Donald. *The Farm Summer 1942.* Barry Moser, illus. New York: Dial, 1994.

    A young boy visits his grandparents' farm in 1942 while his mother is involved in a
    war project and his father is serving in the military.
    FAMILIES—Grandparents; Parents
    FAMILY PROBLEMS—Separation
    FARMS
    HISTORICAL PERIODS—Twentieth Century, World War II

TRANSPORTATION—Airplanes; Wagons
TRAVEL
UNITED STATES—Regions, Northeast
WAR

————. *I Am the Dog, I Am the Cat.* Barry Moser, illus. New York: Dila, 1994.

In a dialogue between a cat and a dog, both explain its own point of view. The conversation ends with a brief physical encounter.

ANIMALS—Pets, cats; Pets, dogs
EVERYDAY EXPERIENCES
HUMOR
IDENTITY—Relationships; Self-worth
INDIVIDUALITY
OBSERVATION

————. *Ox-Cart Man.* Barbara Cooney, illus. New York: Viking, 1979.

A year in the life of an early nineteenth-century New England farm family is described.

BEHAVIOR—Resourceful
FAMILIES
FARMS
HISTORICAL PERIODS—Nineteenth Century, early
SHOPPING/MARKETING
TIME—Cycles, seasons
TRAVEL
UNITED STATES—Regions, Northeast

Hartley, Deborah. *Up North in Winter.* Lydia Dabcovich, illus. New York: Dutton, 1986.

Because times are hard, a man takes a job in a town farther away from home. On a visit to his family during the bitter winter, he encounters a frozen fox who gives him a surprise.

ANIMALS—Large animals, foxes
FAMILIES—Grandparents
FAMILY PROBLEMS—Separation
HISTORICAL PERIODS—Twentieth Century, early
OCCUPATIONS
STORYTELLING
SURPRISES
SURVIVAL
TIME—Specific seasons, winter
TRAVEL
UNITED STATES—Regions, Midwest

Harvey, Brett. *Cassie's Journey: Going West in the 1860's.* Deborah Kogan Ray, illus. New York: Holiday House, 1988.

Cassie shares her family's experiences as they travel by covered wagon to California in the 1860s.

BEHAVIOR—Apprehensive
CAMPING
EMOTIONS—Loneliness

FAMILIES—Parents
FRIENDSHIP—Relationships
GOALS
HISTORICAL PERIODS—Nineteenth Century—pioneer westward movement
MAPS
MOVING
SAFETY/DANGER
SURVIVAL
TRAILS
TRANSPORTATION—Wagons
TRAVEL
UNITED STATES—Regions, Midwest; Regions, Western Mountain

Haseley, Dennis. *The Old Banjo*. Stephen Gammell, illus. New York: Macmillan, 1983.

Musical instruments abandoned on a farm bring enchantment to a farmer and his son worn with poverty and hard work.

BEHAVIOR—Searching
FAMILIES—Parents
FARMS
GRAPHIC AND PERFORMING ARTS—Music and musicians
MAGIC
MEMORIES
OCCUPATIONS
POVERTY
ROOMS—Attics
WISHES

Hathorn, Elizabeth. *Grandma's Shoes*. Elivia, illus. Boston: Little, Brown, 1994.

A young girl grieving after her grandmother's death wears the older woman's shoes and creates a fantasy with her.

BEHAVIOR—Crying; Problem-solving; Searching; Sharing
CLOTHING—Shoes
DEATH
EMOTIONS—Sadness
FAMILIES—Grandparents
FLYING—Fantasy
GOALS
IMAGINATION
LANGUAGE—Sayings and special language
MEMORIES
ROOMS—Bedrooms
STORYTELLING
TRANSFORMATION
TREASURES

————. *Way Home*. Gregory Rogers, illus. New York: Crown, 1994.

A homeless boy rescues a stray cat and takes it to his home which is at the end of an alley.

ANIMALS—Pets, cats
BEHAVIOR—Courageous; Destructive/Violent; Heroic; Pretending; Sharing
EMOTIONS—Fear; Love

ENEMIES
FOOD AND EATING
FRIENDSHIP—Relationships
IDENTITY—Geographic identity
LANGUAGE—Names
LOST AND FOUND
NEIGHBORHOODS AND COMMUNITIES—Specific, urban
POVERTY
ROOMS
SAFETY/DANGER
STRANGERS
STRUCTURES—Buildings, houses and other dwellings
SURPRISES
SURVIVAL
TIME—Nighttime
TRANSPORTATION—Cars

Haugaard, Erik Christian. *Prince Boghole*. Julie Downing, illus. New York: Macmillan, 1987.

An Irish king offers his daughter to the prince who will bring the fairest fowl.
ANIMALS—Birds
BEHAVIOR—Competitive
EMOTIONS—Love
FAMILIES—Parents
GOALS
GRAPHIC AND PERFORMING ARTS—Music and musicians
MATHEMATICS—Numbers, ideas
ROYALTY
STRUCTURES—Buildings, castles/palaces
WORLD CULTURES/COUNTRIES—Europe, Northern

Hayes, Sarah. *The Grumpalump*. Barbara Firth, illus. New York: Clarion, 1990.

In this cumulative story, each animal gets the same grumpy response from the mysterious lump until the gnu arrives on the scene.
ANIMALS—Personified
FLYING—Aviation
MATHEMATICS—Measurement, mass
OBSERVATION
STORIES—Predictable text
SURPRISES
TRANSPORTATION—Hot-air balloons

————. *This Is the Bear and the Scary Night*. Helen Craig, illus. Boston: Joy Street, 1992.

When a stuffed bear is accidentally left in the park, it has many adventures but is happy to be reclaimed the next morning.
BEHAVIOR—Apprehensive; Forgetful; Patient
EMOTIONS—Fear
ENEMIES
LOST AND FOUND
NEIGHBORHOODS AND COMMUNITIES—Parks
STORIES—Predictable text

TIME—Nighttime
TOYS—Bears

Heath, Amy. *Sofie's Role*. Sheila Hamanaka, illus. New York: Four Winds, 1992.

Sophie, an African American girl, helps her parents for the first time in their bakery on the day before Christmas.

BEHAVIOR—Apprehensive; Excited; Proud; Responsible
EMOTIONS—Happiness
FAMILIES—Parents
FOOD AND EATING
HOLIDAYS AND CELEBRATIONS—Christmas
IDENTITY—Self-worth
NEIGHBORHOODS AND COMMUNITIES—Specific, urban
OCCUPATIONS
SENSES—Sight; Sound
UNITED STATES—Specific cultures, African American

Heide, Florence Parry. *The Shrinking of Treehorn*. Edward Gorey, illus. New York: Holiday House, 1971.

Treehorn spends an unhappy day shrinking with little support from parents and school personnel. He is rescued from his dilemma by playing a game discovered under his bed.

BODY—Shape and size
CHANGES
FAMILIES—Parents
GAMES/PUZZLES/TRICKS
HUMOR
MAGIC
SCHOOL EXPERIENCES
SENSES—Sight

Heide, Florence Parry, and Judith Heide Gilliland. *The Day of Ahmed's Secret*. Ted Lewin, illus. New York: Lothrop, 1990.

Ahmed, an Egyptian boy, prizes the secret he will share with his family: knowing how to write his name.

BEHAVIOR—Excited
FAMILIES—Parents
LANGUAGE—Names
NEIGHBORHOODS AND COMMUNITIES—Specific, urban
OCCUPATIONS
SECRETS
SENSES—Sight; Sound
WORLD CULTURES/COUNTRIES—Africa, Northern
WRITING—Others

Heine, Helme. *The Most Wonderful Egg in the World*. New York: Atheneum, 1983.

When the quarreling hens ask the king to determine which of them is the most beautiful, he counters with another test: "Who can lay the most unusual egg?" All three comply with a spectacular egg-laying feat, so the king makes all of them princesses.

ANIMALS—Eggs; Farm, chickens

BEHAVIOR—Competitive; Problem-solving
FRIENDSHIP—Relationships
GOALS
INDIVIDUALITY
ROYALTY

Heinz, Brian. *The Alley Cat*. David Christiana, illus. New York: Delacorte, 1993.

A male alley cat prowls the dangerous city streets at night to find food for his mate and kittens.

ANIMALS—Babies; Pets, cats
BEHAVIOR—Competitive; Courageous; Fighting/Quarreling; Searching; Sharing
ENEMIES
FOOD AND EATING
NEIGHBORHOODS AND COMMUNITIES—Specific, urban
SAFETY/DANGER
SENSES—Sight; Sound
STORIES—Predictable text
SURVIVAL
TIME—Nighttime

Hellen, Nancy. *The Bus Stop*. New York: Orchard, 1988.

Pages in decreasing widths and cutouts portray the growing number of people congregating at the bus stop.

EVERYDAY EXPERIENCES—Time of day, daytime
MATHEMATICS—Numbers, ordinal
NEIGHBORHOODS AND COMMUNITIES—Specific, rural
OBSERVATION
STORIES—Minimal or no text; Predictable text
TRANSPORTATION—Buses
TRAVEL

Hendershot, Judith. *In Coal Country*. Thomas B. Allen, illus. New York: Knopf, 1987.

A coal miner's daughter tells of life throughout the year in a mining village during the 1930s.

FAMILIES—Parents
HISTORICAL PERIODS—Twentieth Century, early
IDENTITY—Relationships
MEMORIES
NEIGHBORHOODS AND COMMUNITIES—Specific, rural
OBSERVATION
OCCUPATIONS
TIME—Cycles, seasons
UNITED STATES—Regions, Appalachia

Henkes, Kevin. *The Biggest Boy*. Nancy Tafuri, illus. New York: Greenwillow, 1995.

A young boy fantasizes with his parents about being the biggest boy in the world.

ASTRONOMY
BEHAVIOR—Pretending
BODY—Shape and size

CLOTHING
DREAMS
EVERYDAY EXPERIENCES—Time of day, bedtime
FAMILIES—Babies and young siblings; Parents
IDENTITY—Self-worth
IMAGINATION—Imaginary worlds
OBSERVATION
PLAY
TRANSFORMATION

————. *Chester's Way.* New York: Greenwillow, 1988.

Chester and Wilson learn that acquiring a new friend, Lilly, expands their horizons and makes their life more enjoyable.

ANIMALS—Personified; Small creatures, mice
BEHAVIOR—Boastful; Courageous; Sharing
CHANGES
CLOTHING—Costumes
EVERYDAY EXPERIENCES—Time of day, daytime
FRIENDSHIP—Relationships
HUMOR
IDENTITY—Gender roles; Self-worth
MOVING
NEIGHBORHOODS AND COMMUNITIES—General
SURPRISES

————. *Chrysanthemum.* New York: Greenwillow, 1991.

When Chrysanthemum starts school, her classmates make fun of her name until their music teacher enlightens them.

ANIMALS—Personified; Small creatures, mice
BEHAVIOR—Ridiculing
DREAMS
EMOTIONS—Disappointment
FAMILIES—Parents
IDENTITY—Self-worth
LANGUAGE—Names
OCCUPATIONS
PLANTS—Flowers
SCHOOL EXPERIENCES

————. *Jessica.* New York: Greenwillow, 1989.

Ruthie insists on taking her imaginary friend Jessica to kindergarten, but she soon discovers that she does not need her there.

EMOTIONS—Loneliness
FAMILIES—Parents
FRIENDSHIP—Imaginary friends; Relationships
PLAY
SCHOOL EXPERIENCES

————. *Julius, the Baby of the World.* New York: Greenwillow, 1990.

Lilly changes her mind about how disgusting her new baby brother is when her cousin comes to visit and shares the same opinion of the baby.

ANIMALS—Personified; Small creatures, mice
BEHAVIOR—Competitive; Disobedient

EMOTIONS—Jealousy
FAMILIES—Babies and young siblings; Other relatives; Parents
FAMILY PROBLEMS—New siblings
HUMOR
IDENTITY—Relationships

————. *Owen*. New York: Greenwillow, 1993.

When none of the neighbor's suggestions for giving up a security blanket work with Owen, his mother finds a way. She converts his blanket into handkerchiefs he can take to school.

ANIMALS—Personified
BEHAVIOR—Problem-solving
CLOTHING—Others
FAMILIES—Parents
PERSONAL PROBLEMS—Giving up security objects
PLAY
SEWING

————. *Sheila Rae, the Brave*. New York: Greenwillow, 1987.

When Sheila Rae, who is usually brave, is overwhelmed with being lost, her younger sister rescues her.

ADVENTURES
ANIMALS—Personified; Small creatures, mice
BEHAVIOR—Boastful; Courageous; Crying; Heroic; Problem-solving
CHANGES
EMOTIONS—Fear
FAMILIES—Siblings
IDENTITY—Self-worth
OBSERVATION
PERSONAL PROBLEMS—Getting lost
SCHOOL EXPERIENCES

Herriot, James. *Blossom Comes Home*. Ruth Brown, illus. New York: St. Martin's, 1988.

A farmer tries to send his old cow to market, but she returns on her own accord. He decides she deserves to stay on the farm.

ANIMALS—Farm, cows
EMOTIONS—Love
FARMS
NEIGHBORHOODS AND COMMUNITIES—Specific, rural
OCCUPATIONS
SURPRISES
SURVIVAL
WORLD CULTURES/COUNTRIES—Europe, Northern

————. *Bonny's Big Day*. Ruth Brown, illus. New York: St. Martin's, 1987.

Despite her size, a retired cart horse wins first prize in the local pet show.

ANIMALS—Farm, horses; Pets, others
FARMS
NEIGHBORHOODS AND COMMUNITIES—Social gatherings
OCCUPATIONS
WORLD CULTURES/COUNTRIES—Europe, Northern

————. *The Christmas Day Kitten*. Ruth Brown, illus. New York: St. Martin's, 1986.

A stray cat brings her kitten to a caring woman on Christmas Day and then dies.

ANIMALS—Pets, cats
GIFTS
HOLIDAYS AND CELEBRATIONS—Christmas
NEIGHBORHOODS AND COMMUNITIES—Specific, rural
OCCUPATIONS
SURVIVAL
WORLD CULTURES/COUNTRIES—Europe, Northern

Hest, Amy. *The Purple Coat*. New York: Four Winds, 1986.

Each fall Gabrielle's mother takes her to her grandfather's tailor shop to be fitted for a new coat, which is always navy blue. When Gabrielle begs her grandfather to sew a purple coat for her this year, he devises an ingenious solution.

BEHAVIOR—Apprehensive; Problem-solving
BODY—Shape and size
CLOTHING—Coats; Dresses
COLORS
FAMILIES—Family gatherings/Outings; Grandparents; Parents
FOOD AND EATING
INDIVIDUALITY
MATHEMATICS—Measurement, length
MEMORIES
NEIGHBORHOODS AND COMMUNITIES—Specific, urban
OCCUPATIONS
PERSONAL PROBLEMS—Fearing to try something new
SENSES—Sight; Smell and taste; Sound
STRUCTURES—Buildings, others
TIME—Specific seasons, fall
TRANSPORTATION—Trains
TRAVEL
WISHES

Hill, Elizabeth Starr. *Evan's Corner*. Nancy Grossman, illus. New York: Holt, 1967.

Evan wishes for a space of his own. After his mother gives him his own corner, Evan begins to realize that helping others brings him happiness.

BEHAVIOR—Sharing
EMOTIONS—Loneliness
FAMILIES—Parents; Siblings
IDENTITY—Geographic identity; Self-worth
NEIGHBORHOODS AND COMMUNITIES—Specific, urban
ROOMS—Others
STRUCTURES—Buildings, houses and other dwellings
UNITED STATES—Specific cultures, African American
WISHES

Hoban, Lillian. *Arthur's Great Big Valentine*. New York: Harper & Row, 1989.

Arthur creates a very special valentine in the snow to regain Norman's friendship.

ANIMALS—Personified; Small creatures, monkeys
BEHAVIOR—Fighting/Quarreling
EMOTIONS—Anger

FAMILIES—Siblings
FRIENDSHIP—Relationships
GIFTS
GRAPHIC AND PERFORMING ARTS—Art and artists
HOLIDAYS AND CELEBRATIONS—Valentine's
PARTIES
PLAY
SECRETS
TIME—Specific seasons, winter
WEATHER—Snow
WRITING—Poems

Hoban, Russell. *A Baby Sister for Frances.* Lillian Hoban, illus. New York: Harper & Row, 1964.

From Frances's perspective, her position in the family is threatened by the arrival of a baby sister. When she runs away to resolve her problem, she discovers that her parents miss her and that her family is incomplete without her.

ANIMALS—Personified
EMOTIONS—Jealousy
FAMILIES—Babies and young siblings; Parents
FAMILY PROBLEMS—New siblings
FOOD AND EATING
IDENTITY—Self-worth
IMAGINATION—Imaginary worlds
PERSONAL PROBLEMS—Running away

————. *A Bargain for Frances.* Lillian Hoban, illus. New York: Harper & Row, 1970.

When Frances decides to teach Thelma a lesson about friendship, Thelma's trickery backfires.

ANIMALS—Personified
BEHAVIOR—Sharing; Tricking
FRIENDSHIP—Relationships
MEMORIES
PLAY
TOYS—Others

————. *A Birthday for Frances.* Lillian Hoban, illus. New York: Harper & Row, 1968.

Frances is jealous of the attention her sister is receiving over her upcoming birthday. Finally, the spirit of the event prompts her to buy her a sister a present which is given with some reluctance.

BEHAVIOR—Selfish
BIRTHDAYS
EMOTIONS—Jealousy
FAMILIES—Babies and young siblings
FRIENDSHIP—Imaginary friends
GIFTS
PARTIES
WISHES

————. *Bedtime for Frances*. Garth Williams, illus. New York: Harper, 1960.

Going to sleep is difficult for Frances because the objects and sounds in her room appear frightfully different at night.

EMOTIONS—Fear
EVERYDAY EXPERIENCES—Time of day, bedtime
FAMILIES—Parents
IMAGINATION—Imaginary creatures
LANGUAGE—Alphabet
ROOMS—Bedrooms
SENSES—Sound
TOYS

————. *Best Friends for Frances*. Lillian Hoban, illus. New York: Harper & Row, 1969.

Frances resolves her friendship problems by convincing Albert of the benefits he can gain from her friendship and by learning to appreciate the companionship of her younger sister, Gloria.

FAMILIES—Babies and young siblings; Family gatherings/Outings
FOOD AND EATING
FRIENDSHIP—Relationships
IDENTITY—Gender roles
PLAY

————. *Emmet Otter's Jug-Band Christmas*. Lillian Hoban, illus. New York: Parents' Magazine, 1971.

Ma Otter and her son, Emmet, try to win the talent show so they can surprise each other with Christmas presents. They discover that their talent as musicians is in demand and their poverty is eased.

ANIMALS—Personified; Small creatures, others
BEHAVIOR—Ambitious/Persistent
FAMILIES—Parents
GIFTS
GRAPHICS AND PERFORMING ARTS—Music and musicians
HOLIDAYS AND CELEBRATIONS—Christmas
POVERTY
SECRETS
SURPRISES

————. *The Mole Family's Christmas*. Lillian Hoban, illus. New York: Parents' Magazine, 1969.

The nearsighted mole family ask Santa for a telescope so they can view the stars.

ANIMALS—Personified; Small creatures, others
ASTRONOMY—Stars
BEHAVIOR—Curious; Problem-solving
BODY—Parts of body, eyes
ENEMIES
FAMILIES—Family gatherings/Outings
GIFTS
HOLIDAYS AND CELEBRATIONS—Christmas
SENSES—Sight

TIME—Nighttime
WISHES
WRITING—Letters

Hoban, Tana. *A, B, See!* New York: Greenwillow, 1982.

Photograms of common objects representing each letter of the alphabet are presented. At the bottom of each page, the position of the featured letter is shown in the alphabet's sequence.

LANGUAGE—Alphabet
OBSERVATION
STORIES—Minimal or no text

———. *All About Where.* New York: Greenwillow, 1991.

Photographs on pages of increasing breadth depict the fifteen prepositions listed on the outer margins.

EVERYDAY EXPERIENCES—Time of day, daytime
LANGUAGE—Words
OBSERVATION
STORIES—Minimal or no text

———. *Big Ones, Little Ones.* New York: Greenwillow, 1976.

Photographs without text portray various animals and their young.

ANIMALS (general); Babies
MATHEMATICS—Size
OBSERVATION
STORIES—Minimal or no text

———. *Circles, Triangles, and Squares.* New York: Macmillan, 1974.

Through photographs without text, geometric concepts of circles, triangles, and squares are depicted in everyday images.

MATHEMATICS—Shapes
OBSERVATION
STORIES—Minimal or no text

———. *Count and See.* New York: Macmillan, 1972.

Numbers (1 through 15, 20, 30, 40, 50, and 100) are introduced through photographs with images to count.

MATHEMATICS—Counting
OBSERVATION
STORIES—Minimal or no text

———. *Dig, Drill, Dump, Fill.* New York: Greenwillow, 1975.

Black and white photographs show the heavy machines used in construction.

CONSTRUCTION
MACHINES
STORIES—Minimal or no text

———. *Exactly the Opposite.* New York: Greenwillow, 1990.

Colored photographs of images in the outdoors portray pairs of opposites.

LANGUAGE—Sayings and special language

OBSERVATION
STORIES—Minimal or no text

———. *I Read Signs.* New York: Greenwillow, 1983.

Colored photographs depict common traffic signs and signals.
COMMUNICATION—Signs
OBSERVATION
READING
SAFETY/DANGER
STORIES—Minimal or no text
TRANSPORTATION

———. *I Read Symbols.* New York: Greenwillow, 1983.

International traffic signs and signals are presented through colored photographs.
COMMUNICATION—Signs
READING
STORIES—Minimal or no text
TRANSPORTATION

———. *Is It Red? Is It Yellow? Is It Blue? An Adventure in Color.* New York: Greenwillow, 1978.

Color, shape, and size concepts can be explored through colored photographs.
COLORS
MATHEMATICS—Shapes; Size
OBSERVATION
STORIES—Minimal or no text

———. *Look Again!* New York: Macmillan, 1971.

Visual clues to well-known images are provided through cutouts.
OBSERVATION
SENSES—Sight

———. *Of Colors and Things.* New York: Greenwillow, 1989.

Items are grouped on pages by color with one usually being slightly different than the others.
COLORS
MATHEMATICS—Classification
OBSERVATION
STORIES—Minimal or no text

———. *Over, Under & Through, and Other Spatial Concepts.* New York: Macmillan, 1973.

Spatial concepts represented by prepositions are depicted in photographs.
LANGUAGE—Words
OBSERVATION

———. *Push, Pull, Empty, Fill: A Book of Opposites.* New York: Macmillan, 1972.

Pairs of opposites are illustrated in photographs.
LANGUAGES—Words
OBSERVATION

———. *Shadows and Reflections*. New York: Greenwillow, 1990.

Colored photographs portray shadows and reflections associated with different images.

LIGHT AND SHADOWS/REFLECTIONS
OBSERVATION
SENSES—Sight
STORIES—Minimal or no text

———. *Shapes and Things*. New York: Macmillan, 1970.

Shapes that can be seen in common objects appear in color photographs.

MATHEMATICS—Shapes
OBSERVATION

———. *Shapes, Shapes, Shapes*. New York: Greenwillow, 1986.

Shapes found in familiar objects are featured in colored photographs.

MATHEMATICS—Shapes
OBSERVATION
STORIES—Minimal or no text

———. *Take Another Look*. New York: Greenwillow, 1981.

Cutouts provide visual clues of images in the photographs.

OBSERVATION
SENSES—Sight

———. *26 Letters and 99 Cents*. New York: Greenwillow, 1987.

Colored photographs present the alphabet, counting, and coin systems.

LANGUAGE—Alphabet
MATHEMATICS—Counting
MONEY
STORIES—Minimal or no text

Hoffman, Mary. *Amazing Grace*. Caroline Binch, illus. New York: Dial, 1991.

Grace wants to play the part of Peter Pan in the school production, but some of her classmates tell her that her wish is impossible because she is black and a girl.

BEHAVIOR—Ambitious/Persistent; Competitive
FAMILIES—Grandparents; Parents
GOALS
GRAPHIC AND PERFORMING ARTS—Drama and actors
IDENTITY—Gender roles; Relationships; Self-worth
PLAY
SCHOOL EXPERIENCES
UNITED STATES—Specific cultures; African American

Hoopes, Lyn Littlefield. *Wing-a-Ding*. Stephen Gammell, illus. Boston: Joy Street, 1990.

One by one Jack's friends and neighbors offer suggestions for getting his toy wing-a-ding out of the tree, but none are successful until the group starts to sing.

BEHAVIOR—Problem-solving
EVERYDAY EXPERIENCES—Time of day, daytime
GRAPHIC AND PERFORMING ARTS—Music and musicians
IMAGINATION

NEIGHBORHOODS AND COMMUNITIES
PLANTS—Trees
PLAY
STORIES—Predictable text
TOYS

Hopkinson, Deborah. *Sweet Clara and the Freedom Quilt.* James Ransome, illus. New York: Knopf, 1993.

Sweet Clara, a young slave in the South, dreams of freedom and being united with her mother. Through making a quilt depicting the route to freedom, she fulfills her goal and also assists others to freedom.

BEHAVIOR—Apprehensive; Courageous; Resourceful; Sharing
EMOTIONS—Love; Sadness
FAMILY PROBLEMS—Separation
GOALS
HISTORICAL PERIODS—Nineteenth Century, early
IDENTITY—Relationships
MEMORIES
PERSONAL PROBLEMS—Running away
QUILTS
SAFETY/DANGER
SEWING
SLAVERY
TRAVEL
UNITED STATES—Regions, South; Specific cultures, African American
WISHES

Horwitz, Elinor Lander. *When the Sky Is Like Lace.* Barbara Cooney, illus. Philadelphia: Lippincott, 1975.

On a "bimulous" night when the sky is like lace, strange and splendid happenings occur.

EVERYDAY EXPERIENCES—Time of day, nighttime
FOOD AND EATING
GIFTS
GRAPHIC AND PERFORMING ARTS—Music and musicians
MAGIC
SENSES—Sight; Smell and taste; Sound; Touch
WEATHER—Clouds

Houghton, Eric. *The Backwards Watch.* Simone Abel, illus. New York: Orchard, 1992.

When Sally winds her grandfather's watch backwards, they are transposed back in time to his youth. Sally finds him to be a delightful playmate and discovers that he also received adult disapproval for getting dirty and untidy.

ADVENTURES
BEHAVIOR—Impatient
CONSTRUCTION
EMOTIONS—Love
FAMILIES—Grandparents
IDENTITY—Self-worth
MEMORIES

PLAY
TIME—Across time; Clocks and other time-telling methods
TRANSFORMATION

Houston, Gloria. *But No Candy*. Lloyd Bloom, illus. New York: Philomel, 1992.

By the end of World War II, Lee discovers that her priorities have changed. Eating chocolate is not as important as having the war over and her soldier uncle home.

BEHAVIOR—Hiding
CHANGES
FAMILIES—Family gatherings/Outings; Other relatives; Parents
FOOD AND EATING
HISTORICAL PERIODS—Twentieth Century, World War II
LANGUAGE—Sayings and special language
STRUCTURES—Buildings, stores
WAR
WISHES
WRITING—Letters

———. *My Great-Aunt Arizona*. Susan Condie Lamb, illus. New York: Harper-Collins, 1992.

As a teacher in Appalachia, Arizona Houston Hughes influences several generations of schoolchildren.

BEHAVIOR—Responsible
BIOGRAPHY/LIFE STORIES
EMOTIONS—Love
FAMILIES—Other relatives
FRIENDSHIP—Relationships
GAMES/PUZZLES/TRICKS
GOALS
HISTORICAL PERIODS—Nineteenth Century, late; Twentieth Century, early
HOLIDAYS AND CELEBRATIONS—Christmas
IMAGINATION
LANGUAGE—Names
MEMORIES
NEIGHBORHOODS AND COMMUNITIES—Specific, rural
OCCUPATIONS
SCHOOL EXPERIENCES
STRUCTURES—Buildings, schools
TRAVEL
UNITED STATES—Regions, Appalachia

———. *The Year of the Perfect Christmas Tree*. Barbara Cooney, illus. New York: Dial, 1988.

Even though Papa has left to become a soldier in World War I, Ruthie and her mother fulfill the family's obligation to supply the Christmas tree for the village celebration.

BEHAVIOR—Courageous; Responsible
CLOTHING
EMOTIONS—Happiness; Sadness
FAMILIES—Parents

FAMILY PROBLEMS—Separation
GIFTS
GOALS
HISTORICAL PERIODS—Twentieth Century, early
HOLIDAYS AND CELEBRATIONS—Christmas
MEMORIES
NEIGHBORHOODS AND COMMUNITIES—Specific, rural
PLANTS—Trees
STRUCTURES—Buildings, cabins; Buildings, churches
SURPRISES
TIME—Cycles, seasons
UNITED STATES—Regions, Appalachia
WAR
WORLD REGIONS—Mountains

Howard, Elizabeth Fitzgerald. *Aunt Flossie's Hats (And Crab Cakes Later)*. James Ransome, illus. New York: Clarion, 1991.

Two young African American girls look forward to their Sunday afternoon visits with Great-Aunt Flossie, who shares with them her collection of hats and the experiences associated with them.

CLOTHING—Hats
ELDERLY
EMOTIONS—Happiness
FAMILIES—Other relatives
FOOD AND EATING
HISTORICAL PERIODS—Twentieth Century, early
IDENTIFY—Relationships
MEMORIES
NEIGHBORHOODS AND COMMUNITIES—Specific, urban
PLAY
STORYTELLING
UNITED STATES—Regions, Middle Atlantic; Specific cultures, African American

———. *Chita's Christmas Tree*. Floyd Cooper, illus. New York: Bradbury, 1989.

Chita, a young African American girl living in Baltimore at the turn of the century, celebrates Christmas by traveling with her father into the woods to select a special tree for their family gathering.

ANIMALS—Farm horses
EMOTIONS—Happiness; Love
FAMILIES—Family gatherings/Outings; Other relatives; Parents
FOOD AND EATING—Cookies
GIFTS
HISTORICAL PERIODS—Twentieth Century, early
HOLIDAYS AND CELEBRATIONS—Christmas
NEIGHBORHOODS AND COMMUNITIES—Specific, urban
OCCUPATIONS
PLANTS—Trees
TIME—Specific seasons, winter
TRANSPORTATION
UNITED STATES—Regions, Middle Atlantic; Specific cultures, African American
WEATHER—Snow

————. *Papa Tells Chita a Story.* Floyd Cooper, illus. New York: Simon & Schuster, 1995.

Chita, a young African-American girl, enjoys her father's stories of experiences in the Spanish-American War.

BEHAVIOR—Ambitious/persistent; Courageous; Heroic; Problem-solving; Sharing; Tricking
EVERYDAY EXPERIENCES—Time of day, bedtime
FAMILIES—Parents
HISTORICAL PERIODS—Nineteenth Century, late
IMAGINATION
LANGUAGE—Names
MEMORIES
OCCUPATIONS
SAFETY/DANGER
SECRETS
SENSES—Sight; Sound
STORYTELLING
SURVIVAL
UNITED STATES—Specific cultures, African American
WAR
WORLD CULTURES/COUNTRIES—Central America, Caribbean Islands
WORLD REGIONS—Rainforest/Jungle

————. *The Train to Lulu's.* Robert Casilla, illus. New York: Bradbury, 1988.

Two young African American sisters travel alone by train from Boston to Baltimore to visit their great aunt for the summer.

BEHAVIOR—Apprehensive; Excited
EMOTIONS—Happiness
FAMILIES—Other relatives; Siblings
HISTORICAL PERIODS—Twentieth Century, early
MAPS
MATHEMATICS—Measurement, length
OCCUPATIONS
PERSONAL PROBLEMS—Fearing to try something new
TRANSPORTATION—Trains
TRAVEL
UNITED STATES—Regions, Middle Atlantic; Specific cultures, African American
VACATIONS

Hughes, Shirley. *Alfie Gets in First.* New York: Lothrop, 1982.

Racing ahead from shopping, Alfie closes the door of his house, locking out his mother and little sister. He cannot reach the lock but is rescued by the neighbors.

BEHAVIOR—Problem-solving
EMOTIONS—Sadness
FAMILIES—Parents; Siblings
FAMILY PROBLEMS—Separation
MATHEMATICS—Numbers, ordinal
NEIGHBORHOODS AND COMMUNITIES—Specific, urban
STRUCTURES—Buildings, houses and other dwellings

————. *Alfie Gives a Hand.* New York: Lothrop, 1983.

In being helpful at a birthday party, Alfie gives up his security blanket temporarily.

BEHAVIOR—Apprehensive; Courageous; Problem-solving; Rude; Shy
BIRTHDAYS
FRIENDSHIP—Relationships
GIFTS
PARTIES
PERSONAL PROBLEMS—Giving up security objects
WRITING—Others

————. *The Big Alfie and Annie Rose Storybook.* New York: Lothrop, 1989.

Young Alfie and his baby sister have many childhood experiences.

BEHAVIOR—Hiding
BIRTHDAYS
CLOTHING—Hats; Others
EMOTIONS—Jealousy
EVERYDAY EXPERIENCES—Time of day, awakening for the day; Time of day, bedtime
FAMILIES—Babies and Young Siblings; Grandparents; Parents
FOOD AND EATING
GAMES/PUZZLES/TRICKS
LANGUAGE—Sayings and special language
MEMORIES
NEIGHBORHOODS AND COMMUNITIES—Parks; Social gatherings
PLAY
SCHOOL EXPERIENCES
STATUES
STRUCTURES—Buildings, churches

————. *The Big Concrete Lorry: A Tale of Trotter Street.* New York: Lothrop, 1990.

Rather than moving, the Patterson family decides to build an addition onto their house. When the cement mixer arrives on the wrong day, the family and their neighbors move rapidly to solve the problem.

BEHAVIOR—Excited
CONSTRUCTION
FAMILIES—Parents; Siblings
GOALS
MACHINES
MOVEMENT/SPEED
MOVING
NEIGHBORHOODS AND COMMUNITIES—Specific, urban
PLAY
ROOMS
STRUCTURES—Buildings, houses and other dwellings
SURPRISES
WISHES

Hunt, Jonathan. *Illuminations.* New York: Bradbury, 1989.

In this alphabet book, concepts associated with medieval life are presented for each letter of the alphabet.

GRAPHIC AND PERFORMING ARTS, Art and artists
HISTORICAL PERIODS—Medieval/Renaissance
LANGUAGE—Alphabet

Hutchins, Pat. *Changes, Changes.* New York: Macmillan, 1971.

Two wooden dolls build structures which they use in their exciting adventures.

ADVENTURES
BEHAVIOR—Pretending
CHANGES
CONSTRUCTION
IMAGINATION
MATHEMATICS—Shapes
STORIES—Minimal or no text
TOYS—Dolls

————. *Clocks and More Clocks.* New York: Macmillan, 1970.

As time passes, Mr. Higgins notes the differences in the settings of the clocks in the rooms throughout his house. He checks on their correctness by way of his pocket watch.

BEHAVIOR—Problem-solving
HUMOR
MOVEMENT/SPEED
OCCUPATIONS
STRUCTURES—Buildings, houses and other dwellings
TIME—Clocks and other time-telling methods

————. *The Doorbell Rang.* New York: Greenwillow, 1986.

As more and more children arrive, Victoria and Sam realize that they will get fewer and fewer of the cookies their mother has baked. Then, their grandmother arrives with a solution.

BEHAVIOR—Problem-solving; Sharing
FAMILIES—Grandparents; Parents
FOOD AND EATING—Cookies
FRIENDSHIP—Relationships
MATHEMATICS—Measurement, mass; Numbers, processes
STORIES—Predictable text
SURPRISES

————. *Good Night, Owl!* New York: Macmillan, 1972.

After being kept awake during the day by the noises of the different birds in the forest, the owl awakens them while they are asleep at night.

ANIMALS—Birds
BEHAVIOR—Revengeful
EVERYDAY EXPERIENCES—Time of day, bedtime
SENSES—Sound
SLEEPING
STORIES—Predictable text
TIME—Cycles, day and night
WORLD REGIONS—Forests

————. *1 Hunter.* New York: Greenwillow, 1982.

In this counting book (1 to 10), the hunter stalks through the jungle, observed by a progressively larger group of animals. When he realizes that he is being watched, he flees and the numerals move backward from 10 to 1.

ADVENTURES
ANIMALS
BEHAVIOR—Searching
CHANGES
EMOTIONS—Fear
ENEMIES
MATHEMATICS—Counting
MOVEMENT/SPEED
OBSERVATION
SURPRISES
WORLD REGIONS—Rain forest/Jungle

————. *Rosie's Walk.* New York: Macmillan, 1968.

Rosie, the hen, unaware that the fox is after her, leads him into a series of disasters.

ANIMALS—Farm, chickens; Large animals, foxes
BEHAVIOR—Evil
DISASTERS
ENEMIES
HUMOR
LANGUAGE—Words
LUCK
OBSERVATION
SAFETY/DANGER
STORIES—Minimal or no text
SURVIVAL

————. *Tidy Titch.* New York: Greenwillow, 1991.

Titch's tidy room changes when he accepts the cast-off toys from his brother's and sister's room-cleaning projects.

CHANGES
EVERYDAY EXPERIENCES—Time of day, daytime
FAMILIES—Siblings
HUMOR
ROOMS—Bedrooms
TOYS

————. *The Very Worst Monster.* New York: Greenwillow, 1985.

The new baby's parents and grandparents declare that he is the worst monster, ignoring his older sister's abilities, to her chagrin. Hazel meets this challenge by proving that she is the worst monster and her brother is the worst baby monster.

BEHAVIOR—Competitive; Destructive/Violent
EMOTIONS—Jealousy
FAMILIES—Babies and young siblings; Grandparents; Parents
FAMILY PROBLEMS—New siblings
IDENTITY—Self-worth
IMAGINATION—Imaginary creatures, monsters

————. *What Game Shall We Play?* New York: Greenwillow, 1990.

The owl answers the animals' question, "What game shall we play?"

ANIMALS—Birds
BEHAVIOR—Problem-solving
GAMES/PUZZLES/TRICKS
LANGUAGE—Sayings and special language
STORIES—Predictable text

————. *Where's the Baby?* New York: Greenwillow, 1988.

Hazel Monster and her grandma and ma search for missing Baby Monster by following his messy trail.

BEHAVIOR—Destructive/Violent; Searching
EMOTIONS—Anger; Jealousy
FAMILIES—Babies and young siblings; Grandparents; Parents
IMAGINATION—Imaginary creatures, monsters
PERSONAL PROBLEMS—Getting lost
SLEEPING
SURPRISES

————. *The Wind Blew.* New York: Macmillan, 1974.

The wind snatches objects from many different people.

MOVEMENT/SPEED
PARADES
STORIES—Predictable text
WEATHER—Wind

————. *You'll Soon Grow into Them, Titch.* New York: Greenwillow, 1983.

Titch gives his outgrown clothing to his new baby brother, just as his brother and sister have handed down their clothing to him.

BEHAVIOR—Sharing
CLOTHING
EVERYDAY EXPERIENCES—Time of day, daytime
FAMILIES—Babies and young siblings; Siblings
SHOPPING/MARKETING

Ichikawa, Satomi. *Nora's Castle.* New York: Philomel, 1986.

Nora explores an abandoned castle and decides to have a party for its inhabitants.

ADVENTURES
IMAGINATION—Imaginary worlds
PARTIES
ROOMS—Attics
SECRETS
STRUCTURES—Buildings, castles/palaces
TIME—Cycles, day and night
TOYS
TRANSPORTATION—Bicycles

Inkpen, Mick. *Kipper.* Boston: Little, Brown, 1992.

A dog investigates the ways other animals sleep but decides to return to his old ways.

ANIMALS—Pets, dogs

BEHAVIOR—Imitating; Searching
IDENTITY—Relationships
PERSONAL PROBLEMS—Giving up security objects
SLEEPING

Innocenti, Roberto. *Rose Blanche*. Mankato, MN: Creative Education, 1985.

A young German girl in World War II stumbles onto a concentration camp and strives to help its victims.

BEHAVIOR—Destructive/Violent; Sharing
DEATH
EMOTIONS—Sadness
ENEMIES
FOOD AND EATING
FRIENDSHIP—Relationships
HISTORICAL PERIODS—Twentieth Century, World War II
NEIGHBORHOODS AND COMMUNITIES—Specific, urban
SECRETS
TIME—Cycles, seasons
WAR
WORLD CULTURES/COUNTRIES—Europe, Northern

Isaacs, Anne. *Swamp Angel*. Paul O. Zelinsky, illus. New York: Dutton, 1994.

This tall tale tells of an enormous woman, Angelica Longrider, also known as Swamp Angel, and her heroic feats, which include her victory over the bear, Thundering Tarnation.

ADVENTURES
ANIMALS—Large animals, bears
ASTRONOMY
BEHAVIOR—Ambitious/Persistent; Competitive; Courageous; Fighting/Quarreling; Heroic; Problem-solving
BODY—Shape and size
ENEMIES
HUMOR
IDENTITY—Gender roles; Geographic identity; Self-worth
IMAGINATION
INDIVIDUALITY
LANGUAGE—Names
NEIGHBORHOODS AND COMMUNITIES—Specific, rural
TRAVEL
UNITED STATES—Regions, Appalachia

Isadora, Rachel. *At the Crossroads*. New York: Greenwillow, 1991.

With excitement, black children in South Africa welcome home their fathers, who have been away for many months working in the mines.

BEHAVIOR—Excited; Patient
EMOTIONS—Happiness; Loneliness; Love
FAMILIES—Parents
FAMILY PROBLEMS—Separation
GRAPHIC AND PERFORMING ARTS—Dance and dancers; Music and musicians
NEIGHBORHOODS AND COMMUNITIES
OCCUPATIONS
POVERTY

ROADS
TIME—Cycles, day and night
WORLD CULTURES/COUNTRIES—Africa, Southern

————. *Ben's Trumpet*. New York: Greenwillow, 1979.

Ben, a young boy in the 1920s longing to be a musician, plays an imaginary horn until a trumpet player from a neighborhood night club discovers his goal.

BEHAVIOR—Pretending; Ridiculing; Sharing
GOALS
GRAPHIC AND PERFORMING ARTS—Music and musicians
HISTORICAL PERIODS—Twentieth Century, early
IMAGINATION—Imaginary objects
NEIGHBORHOODS AND COMMUNITIES—Specific, urban

————. *Max*. New York: Macmillan, 1976.

Attending his sister's dance class offers Max a new way to warm up for his Saturday baseball game.

BEHAVIOR—Apprehensive
FAMILIES—Siblings
GRAPHIC AND PERFORMING ARTS—Dance and dancers
IDENTITY—Gender roles
SPORTS

————. *Opening Night*. New York: Greenwillow, 1984.

A young ballerina experiences the excitement of the opening night at the ballet.

CLOTHING—Costumes
GRAPHIC AND PERFORMING ARTS—Dance and dancers

————. *The Pirates of Bedford Street*. New York: Greenwillow, 1988.

Through his drawing, Joey relives tories.

ELDERLY
FAMILIES—Parents
GRAPHIC AND PERFORMING ARTS—Art and artists
IMAGINATION—Imaginary worlds
NEIGHBORHOODS AND COMMUNITIES—Specific, urban
PIRATES
STORYTELLING

————. *Willaby*. New York: Macmillan, 1977.

Willaby, a first grader, is occupied with drawing at all times and everywhere. When her teacher becomes ill, Willaby's drawing keeps her from completing the get-well card, but her teacher appreciates the get-well picture.

BEHAVIOR—Apprehensive; Forgetful
GRAPHIC AND PERFORMING ARTS—Art and artists
HEALTH—Illness and injury
IDENTITY—Self-worth
INDIVIDUALITY
OCCUPATIONS
SCHOOL EXPERIENCES
UNITED STATES—Specific cultures, African-American
WRITING—Letters; Poems

James, Betsy. *Mary Ann*. New York: Dutton, 1994.

Amy learns that change can bring sadness and happiness. After her friend Mary
Ann moves away, she acquires a praying mantis and loses it, too, after it lays eggs.
When her human friend leaves, Amy in her loneliness wishes for hundreds and
hundreds of Mary Anns. Her wish comes true in another sense when the praying
mantis's eggs hatch.

ANIMALS—Eggs; Small creatures, insects
EMOTIONS—Happiness; Sadness
FRIENDSHIP—Relationships
LANGUAGE—Names
MATHEMATICS—Numbers, ideas
MOVING
STRUCTURES—Boxes and containers
SURPRISES
WISHES

Johnson, Angela. *The Leaving Morning*. David Soman, illus. New York: Orchard,
1992.

On the morning of their move, the children say goodbye to their neighborhood
and receive support from their parents.

EMOTIONS—Love; Sadness
FAMILIES—Parents; Siblings
MOVING
NEIGHBORHOODS AND COMMUNITIES—Specific, urban
OCCUPATIONS
STRUCTURES—Buildings, houses and other dwellings
TRANSPORTATION—Trucks

———. *Tell Me a Story, Mama*. David Soman, illus. New York: Orchard, 1988.

A young girl recalls with her mother her mother's childhood experiences.

EMOTIONS—Love
FAMILIES—Other relatives; Parents
IDENTITY—Relationships
MEMORIES
NEIGHBORHOODS AND COMMUNITIES—General
STORYTELLING
UNITED STATES—Specific cultures, African American

———. *When I Am Old With You*. David Soman, illus. New York: Orchard, 1990.

A young African American imagines what it would be like if he and his grandfather could be old at the same time.

ELDERLY
EMOTIONS—Love
FAMILIES—Grandparents
GOALS
IDENTITY—Relationships
IMAGINATION
TIME—Across time
UNITED STATES—Specific culture, African American

Johnston, Tony. *Amber on the Mountain*. Robert Duncan, illus. New York: Dial, 1994.

Amber finds she is not isolated on her mountain farm when she can exchange letters with her friend, Anna, who has taught her to read.

BEHAVIOR—Ambitious/Persistent; Problem-solving; Shy
CONSTRUCTION
EMOTIONS—Happiness; Loneliness; Sadness
FAMILIES—Grandparents
FARMS
FRIENDSHIP—Relationships
GIFTS
GOALS
GRAPHIC AND PERFORMING ARTS—Dancing and dancers
NEIGHBORHOODS AND COMMUNITIES—Specific, rural
READING
ROADS
TIME—Specific seasons, spring; Specific seasons, winter
TRAVEL
UNITED STATES—Regions, Appalachia
WORLD REGIONS—Mountain
WRITING—Letters

————. *The Cowboy and the Black-eyed Pea*. Warren Ludwig, illus. New York: Putnam, 1992.

Farethee Well, a daughter of a prosperous Texas rancher, resolves her problem of finding a genuine cowboy for a husband.

ANIMALS—Farm, cows
BEHAVIOR—Boastful; Pretending; Problem-solving; Searching; Tricking
COWBOYS/COWGIRLS
FAMILIES—Marriage; Parents
HUMOR
LUCK
PLANTS—Seeds
RANCHES
SENSES—Touch
SURPRISES
TRANSPORTATION—Horses
UNITED STATES—Regions, Southwest
WEATHER—Rain; Storms

————. *Farmer Mack Measures His Pig*. Megan Lloyd, illus. New York: Harper & Row, 1986.

In the process of measuring his fat pig, Farmer Mack encounters many wild experiences.

ANIMALS—Farm, pigs
BEHAVIOR—Competitive; Running away; Searching
FARMS
GRAPHIC AND PERFORMING ARTS—Music and musicians
HUMOR
LOST AND FOUND
MATHEMATICS—Measurement, length; Size

———. *Pages of Music.* Tomie dePaola, illus. New York: Putnam, 1988.

As a child visiting the poor island of Sardinia, Paola is enthralled by the music piped by the shepherds. He grows up to become an accomplished composer and conductor. One Christmas he returns with his orchestra, presenting a concert to thank the islanders for their kindnesses during his youth. The audience hears their folk melodies played during the concert.

BEHAVIOR—Ambitious/Persistent; Sharing
BIOGRAPHY/LIFE STORIES
EMOTIONS—Happiness
FAMILIES—Parents
FOOD AND EATING
GIFTS
GOALS
GRAPHIC AND PERFORMING ARTS—Art and artists; Music and musicians
HOLIDAYS AND CELEBRATIONS—Christmas
ISLANDS
MEMORIES
OCCUPATIONS
POVERTY
SURPRISES
TRAVEL
WORLD CULTURES/COUNTRIES—Europe, Southern

———. *The Quilt Story.* New York: Putnam, 1985.

A quilt sewn by a pioneer woman for her daughter is found in an attic generations later, and then history repeats itself.

CHANGES
EMOTIONS—Loneliness
FAMILIES—Parents
HISTORICAL PERIODS—Nineteenth Century, pioneer/westward movement
MOVING
QUILTS
ROOMS—Attics
SEWING
STRUCTURES—Buildings, cabins
TIME—Across time
TRAVEL

———. *Yonder.* Lloyd Bloom, illus. New York: Dial, 1988.

Changes on the farm occur as it is passed from one generation to the next.

BIOGRAPHY/LIFE STORIES
CHANGES
FAMILIES—Grandparents; Parents
FARMS
HISTORICAL PERIODS—Nineteenth Century, pioneer/westward movement
LANGUAGE—Words
OCCUPATIONS
PLANTS—Trees
STORIES—Predictable text
TIME—Cycles, seasons
TIME—Across time

Jonas, Ann. *Aardvarks, Disembark!* New York: Greenwillow, 1990.

When the flood is over, Noah calls the animals out of the ark in alphabetical order, only to discover there are many he cannot identify—extinct and endangered species.

ANIMALS—Endangered species
LANGUAGE—Alphabet; Words
OBSERVATION
PARADES
RELIGION
STORIES—Minimal or no text
TIME—Cycles, day and night
TRANSPORTATION—Boats
WATER AND BODIES OF WATER—Floods
WORLD REGIONS—Mountain

————. *Color Dance.* New York: Greenwillow, 1989.

Three dancers representing the primary colors mix their scarves to make secondary colors. They are joined by a fourth dancer representing white, gray, and black to create more colors.

CLOTHING
COLORS
GRAPHIC AND PERFORMING ARTS—Dance and dancers
LANGUAGE—Words
MOVEMENT/SPEED
OBSERVATION
STORIES—Minimal or no text

————. *The Quilt.* New York: Greenwillow, 1984.

A new patchwork quilt is the source of memories and adventures at bedtime for a small girl.

ADVENTURES
BEHAVIOR—Hiding; Searching
DREAMS
EVERYDAY EXPERIENCES—Time of day, bedtime
FAMILIES—Parents
IMAGINATION—Imaginary worlds
LOST AND FOUND
MEMORIES
QUILTS
SEWING
STRUCTURES—Tunnels
TIME—Cycles, day and night
TOYS

————. *Round Trip.* New York: Greenwillow, 1983.

A round trip that starts in the country at the beginning of a day involves traveling to the city and returning home at night.

NEIGHBORHOODS AND COMMUNITIES—Specific, rural; Specific, urban
OBSERVATION
TIME—Cycles, day and night
TRAVEL

———. *The 13th Clue.* New York: Greenwillow, 1992.

A girl follows thirteen clues guiding her to a surprise birthday party.

BEHAVIOR—Searching; Tricking
BIRTHDAYS
EXPLORATION
GAMES/PUZZLES/TRICKS
LIGHT AND SHADOWS/REFLECTIONS
MATHEMATICS—Numbers, ordinal
MYSTERY
PARTIES
STORIES—Minimal or no text
STRUCTURES—Buildings, houses and other dwellings
SURPRISES
WRITING—Diaries

———. *The Trek.* New York: Greenwillow, 1985.

A child's imagination allows her to see all sorts of wild animals on the way to school.

ADVENTURES
ANIMALS—Fantasy
GAMES/PUZZLES/TRICKS
IMAGINATION
NEIGHBORHOODS AND COMMUNITIES—Specific, urban
OBSERVATION
SCHOOL EXPERIENCES
SECRETS
STORIES—Minimal or no text

———. *Where Can It Be?* New York: Greenwillow, 1986.

By opening the flaps, the audience can accompany the child searching the house for the special blanket which is missing.

BEHAVIOR—Forgetful; Searching
LOST AND FOUND
STRUCTURES—Buildings, houses and other dwellings

Joyce, William. *A Day with Wilbur Robinson. New York: Harper & Row, 1990.*

While spending a day at Wilbur Robinson's house, a friend encounters bizarre people and experiences.

ADVENTURES
BEHAVIOR—Searching
BODY—Parts of body, teeth
FAMILIES
FRIENDSHIP—Relationships
HUMOR
IMAGINATION—Imaginary worlds
OBSERVATION
SENSES—Sound
STRUCTURES—Buildings, houses and other buildings

————. *George Shrinks*. New York: Harper & Row, 1985.

Left with doing home chores and caring for his baby brother while his parents are away, and coping with his sudden shrunken size, George has an unexpected, interesting day.

ADVENTURES
ANIMALS—Pets, cats
BEHAVIOR—Apprehensive; Courageous; Responsible
BODY—Shape and size
CHANGES
DREAMS
ENEMIES
EVERYDAY EXPERIENCES—Time of day, daytime
FAMILIES—Babies and young siblings; Parents
FAMILY PROBLEMS—Separation
FLYING—Fantasy
GAMES/PUZZLES/TRICKS
HUMOR
IMAGINATION—Imaginary worlds
ROOMS—Bedrooms
SAFETY/DANGER
SENSES—Sight
WRITING—Others

Kasza, Keiko. *A Mother for Choco*. New York: Putnam, 1992.

The lonely young bird, Choco, searches for a mother. He finds love with Mrs. Bear, even though she does not have any physical characteristics in common with a bird.

ANIMALS—Birds; Large animals, bears; Personified
BEHAVIOR—Searching
EMOTIONS—Happiness; Loneliness
FAMILIES—Adoption; Parents
IDENTITY—Relationships
WISHES

Keats, Ezra Jack. *Clementina's Cactus*. New York: Viking, 1982.

The child, Clementina, is surprised when she discovers flowers on a prickly cactus.

PLANTS—Flowers; Others
STORIES—Minimal or no text
SURPRISES
WORLD REGIONS—Desert

————. *Dreams*. New York: Macmillan, 1974.

While everyone is sleeping during the night, a small boy watches his paper mouse come alive and rescue a cat from a dog.

ANIMALS—Small creatures, mice
DREAMS
EVERYDAY EXPERIENCES—Time of day, bedtime
GRAPHIC AND PERFORMING ARTS—Art and artists

IMAGINATION—Imaginary worlds
LIGHT AND SHADOWS/REFLECTIONS
NEIGHBORHOODS AND COMMUNITIES—Specific, urban
SAFETY/DANGER
TIME—Nighttime

————. *Goggles.* New York: Macmillan, 1969.

Peter and Archie outsmart the older neighborhood boys who try to bully them out of their newfound treasure: goggles.

ANIMALS—Pets, dogs
BEHAVIOR—Bullying; Fighting/Quarreling; Hiding; Problem-solving
CLOTHING—Others
EMOTIONS—Fear
ENEMIES
FRIENDSHIP—Relationships
NEIGHBORHOODS AND COMMUNITIES—Specific, urban
SAFETY/DANGER
STRUCTURES—Tunnels
TREASURES

————. *Hi, Cat!* New York: Macmillan, 1970.

Archie's day is turned upside down by a new cat he meets.

ANIMALS—Pets, cats; Pets, dogs
BEHAVIOR—Destructive/Violent
CLOTHING—Costumes
EVERYDAY EXPERIENCES—Time of day, daytime
FRIENDSHIP—Relationships
LIGHT AND SHADOWS/REFLECTIONS
MOVEMENT
NEIGHBORHOODS AND COMMUNITIES—Specific, urban
SURPRISES
UNITED STATES—Specific cultures, African American

————. *Jennie's Hat.* New York: Harper & Row, 1966.

Birds transform Jenny's hat into a marvelous creation.

ANIMALS—Birds
CLOTHING—Hats
EMOTIONS—Disappointment
GIFTS
TRANSFORMATION
WISHES

————. *A Letter to Amy.* New York: Harper & Row, 1968.

Peter runs into difficulty when he mails a birthday party invitation to Amy.

BIRTHDAYS
COMMUNICATION
FRIENDSHIP—Relationships
IDENTITY—Gender roles
MOVEMENT/SPEED
NEIGHBORHOODS AND COMMUNITIES—Specific, urban
PARTIES
SURPRISES

WEATHER—Storms
WRITING—Letters

———. *Louie.* New York: Greenwillow, 1975.

Shy Louie befriends a puppet.

BEHAVIOR—Excited; Pretending; Ridiculing; Sharing; Shy
CONSTRUCTION
DREAMS
GIFTS
GRAPHIC AND PERFORMING ARTS—Art and artists; Drama and Actors
IDENTITY—Relationships
IMAGINATION—Imaginary objects: imaginary worlds
PUPPETS
WRITING—Letters

———. *Pet Show!* New York: Macmillan, 1972.

Even though he cannot find his cat, Archie succeeds in entering an exhibit in the neighborhood pet show and wins the prize.

ANIMALS—Pets, others
BEHAVIOR—Competitive; Problem-solving; Searching
FRIENDSHIP—Relationships
NEIGHBORHOODS AND COMMUNITIES—Social gatherings; Specific, urban

———. *Peter's Chair.* New York: Harper & Row, 1967.

Peter resents his parents giving his belongings to his baby sister. After he runs away with his dog, he discovers several things that make giving up old possessions acceptable.

ANIMALS—Pets, dogs
EMOTIONS—Jealousy
FAMILIES—Babies and young siblings; Parents
FAMILY PROBLEMS—New siblings
FURNITURE—Chairs
PERSONAL PROBLEMS—Running away

———. *The Snowy Day.* New York: Viking, 1962.

A young boy explores the pleasures of snow.

DREAMS
EMOTIONS—Disappointment
EVERYDAY EXPERIENCES—Time of day, daytime
EXPLORATION
NEIGHBORHOODS AND COMMUNITIES—Specific, urban
PLAY
TIME—Specific seasons, winter
UNITED STATES—Specific cultures, African American
WEATHER—Snow

———. *The Trip.* New York: Greenwillow, 1978.

Louie, the new kid on the block, creates a magical box that takes him back to his old neighborhood where his friends are trick-or-treating. In reality children in the new neighborhood are at his door ready to take him Halloweening.

BEHAVIOR—Pretending; Resourceful

CLOTHING—Costumes
CONSTRUCTION
EMOTIONS—Loneliness
FLYING—Fantasy
FRIENDSHIP—Relationships
GRAPHIC AND PERFORMING ARTS—Art and artists
HOLIDAYS AND CELEBRATIONS—Halloween
IDENTITY—Geographic identity
IMAGINATION—Imaginary objects; Imaginary worlds
MAGIC
MOVING
NEIGHBORHOODS AND COMMUNITIES—Specific, urban
SENSES—Sight; Sound
STRUCTURES—Boxes and containers
SURPRISES

————. *Whistle for Willie*. New York: Viking, 1964.

After much effort, Willie learns to whistle.

ANIMALS—Pets, dogs
BEHAVIOR—Ambitious/Persistent; Pretending
FAMILIES—Parents
GOALS
GRAPHIC AND PERFORMING ARTS—Music and musicians
NEIGHBORHOODS AND COMMUNITIES—Specific, urban
SENSES—Sound
STRUCTURES—Boxes and containers
WISHES

Keller, Holly. *Furry*. New York: Greenwillow, 1992.

Laura searches for a pet that will not aggravate her allergies, but it is her younger
brother who finds the perfect solution.

ANIMALS—Pets, others; Reptiles, lizards/chameleons; Small creatures
BEHAVIOR—Crying; Problem-solving
FAMILIES—Siblings
HEALTH—Illness and injury
LANGUAGE—Names

————. *Geraldine's Big Snow*. New York: Greenwillow, 1988.

Geraldine anxiously awaits the snow so she can use her new sled.

ANIMALS—Personified
FAMILIES—Parents
NEIGHBORHOODS AND COMMUNITIES—General
PLAY
TIME—Specific seasons, winter
TOYS—Others
WEATHER—Snow
WISHES

————. *Geraldine's Blanket*. New York: Greenwillow, 1984.

Geraldine finds a way to overcome the need for a security blanket.

ANIMALS—Personified
BEHAVIOR—Problem-solving

FAMILIES—Parents
GIFTS
PERSONAL PROBLEMS—Giving up security objects
SEWING
TOYS—Dolls

————. *Horace.* New York: Greenwillow, 1991.

Horace, an adopted child, searches for a family that looks like him.
ANIMALS—Personified
BEHAVIOR—Searching
EMOTIONS—Loneliness; Love
FAMILIES—Adoption
IDENTITY—Self-worth
NEIGHBORHOODS AND COMMUNITIES—Parks

————. *The New Boy.* New York: Greenwillow, 1991.

Milton, the new boy at school, tries to behave in a way that will gain him friends.
ANIMALS—Personified
BEHAVIOR—Crying; Destructive/Violent
CHANGES
EMOTIONS—Loneliness
FRIENDSHIP—Relationships
IDENTITY—Self-worth
MOVING
SCHOOL EXPERIENCES

Kellogg, Steven. *The Mysterious Tadpole.* New York: Dial, 1977.

For his birthday, Louis receives a tadpole which grows into an extraordinarily huge pet.
ANIMALS—Eggs; Marine life, frogs; Pets, others
BIRTHDAYS
CHANGES
EXPLORATION
GIFTS
IMAGINATION—Imaginary creatures
LANGUAGE—Names
MYSTERY
NEIGHBORHOODS AND COMMUNITIES—General
SCHOOL EXPERIENCES
SURPRISES

————. *Pinkerton, Behave!* New York: Dial, 1979.

Pinkerton, the puppy, does not respond to commands even when taken to obedience school. When his young mistress mixes signals, he rescues the family.
ANIMALS—Babies; Pets, dogs
BEHAVIOR—Destructive/Violent; Disobedient; Stealing; Tricking
DREAMS
EMOTIONS—Love
HUMOR
OBSERVATION
OCCUPATIONS
SAFETY/DANGER

————. *Prehistoric Pinkerton.* New York: Dial, 1987.

Pinkerton, the Great Dane puppy, causes chaos while teething.

ANIMALS—Pets, dogs; Prehistoric
BODY—Parts of body, teeth
DINOSAURS
HUMOR
IDENTITY—Relationships
STRUCTURES—Buildings, museums

————. *A Rose for Pinkerton.* New York: Dial, 1981.

At first Rose the cat makes a questionable companion for the lonely Pinkerton.

ANIMALS—Pets, cats; Pets, dogs
EMOTIONS—Fear; Loneliness
FAIRS
FRIENDSHIP—Relationships
HUMOR
IDENTITY—Relationships

Kent, Jack. *Silly Goose.* Englewood Cliffs, NJ: Prentice-Hall, 1983.

The arrogant fox repeatedly tells the goose she is dumb, yet she saves him from several dangerous situations.

ANIMALS—Farm, geese; Large animals, foxes
BEHAVIOR—Boastful; Responsible; Ridiculing
SAFETY/DANGER

————. *Socks for Supper.* New York: Parents' Magazine, 1978.

A poor couple is tired of having nothing to eat but turnips, so they trade socks for cheese and milk.

CLOTHING—Others
FAMILIES—Husbands and wives
FOOD AND EATING
GIFTS
POVERTY

————. *There's No Such Thing as a Dragon.* New York: Golden, 1975.

Billy Bixbee's mother does not readily admit that dragons exist. When the dragon grows to an immense size, Billy explains this phenomenon as a means of getting attention.

BEHAVIOR—Searching
FAMILIES—Parents
FOOD AND EATING
IDENTITY—Relationships
IMAGINATION—Imaginary creatures, dragons
MATHEMATICS—Size
MOVEMENT/SPEED
ROOMS—Bedrooms
SENSES—Sight; Smell and taste
STRUCTURES—Buildings, houses and other dwellings

Kesey, Ken. *Little Tricker the Squirrel Meets Big Double the Bear.* Barry Moser, illus. New York: Viking, 1990.

The vicious bear, Big Double, terrorizes the animals of the forest, but Little Tricker the squirrel gets revenge.

ANIMALS—Hibernation; Large animals, bears; Small creatures, squirrels
BEHAVIOR—Bullying; Destructive/Violent; Lazy; Revengeful; Tricking
MOVEMENT/SPEED
STORYTELLING
UNITED STATES—Regions, Midwest
WORLD REGIONS—Forests

Ketteman, Helen. *The Year of No More Corn.* Robert Andrew Parker, illus. New York: Orchard, 1993.

Grandfather tells Beanie a tall tale about the year of the corn crop failure and how he made corn trees grow from whittled corn kernels.

ANIMALS—Birds
BEHAVIOR—Bored; Problem-solving
FAMILIES—Grandparents
FARMS
FOOD AND EATING
GRAPHIC AND PERFORMING ARTS—Art and artists
HISTORICAL PERIODS—Twentieth Century, early
IMAGINATION
NEIGHBORHOODS AND COMMUNITIES—Specific, rural
PLANTS—Seeds; Trees
SENSES—Smell and taste
STORYTELLING
UNITED STATES—Regions, Midwest
WATER AND BODIES OF WATER—Floods
WEATHER—Drought; Rain; Sunshine; Wind

Khalsa, Dayal Kaur. *Cowboy Dreams.* New York: Clarkson N. Potter, 1990.

As a city child, a girl creates an imaginary world to satisfy her wish to be a cowgirl riding her horse on the range.

ANIMALS—Farm, horses
BEHAVIOR—Courageous; Pretending
CAROUSELS
CONSTRUCTION
COWBOYS/COWGIRLS
GRAPHIC AND PERFORMING ARTS—Music and musicians
HUMOR
IDENTITY—Geographic identity
IMAGINATION—Imaginary worlds
MEMORIES
OBSERVATION
PLAY
UNITED STATES—Regions, Southwest
WISHES

———. *The Snow Cat.* New York: Clarkson N. Potter, 1992.

Elsie wishes for a cat because she is lonely in her house at the edge of the woods. When her wish comes true, she and the snow cat establish a lasting relationship.

ANIMALS—Pets, cats
BEHAVIOR—Disobedient
CHANGES
EMOTIONS—Loneliness
IMAGINATION—Imaginary creatures, others
NEIGHBORHOODS AND COMMUNITIES—Specific, rural
PLAY
SENSES—Sight; Sound
STRUCTURES—Buildings, houses and other dwellings
TIME—Specific seasons, winter
WATER AND BODIES OF WATER—Ponds
WEATHER—Snow
WISHES

Kherdian, David. *The Cat's Midsummer Jamboree.* Nonny Hogrogian, illus. New York: Philomel, 1990.

A traveling cat who loves to sing and strum his mandolin gathers a group of musicians (seven animals) to create a jamboree.

ANIMALS—Personified; Pets, cats
GRAPHIC AND PERFORMING ARTS—Music and musicians
PARTIES
PLANTS—Trees
STORIES—Predictable text
TRAVEL
WORLD REGIONS—Forest

Kimmel, Eric A. *Hershel and the Hanukkah Goblins.* Trina Schart Hyman, illus. New York: Holiday House, 1989.

Because of his courage, Hershel outwits the goblins who are preventing the villagers from celebrating Hanukkah.

BEHAVIOR—Courageous; Problem-solving; Tricking
EMOTIONS—Fear; Sadness
ETHNIC CULTURES—Jewish
GAMES/PUZZLES/TRICKS
HOLIDAYS AND CELEBRATIONS—Hanukkah
IMAGINATION–Imaginary creatures, others
LIGHT AND SHADOWS/REFLECTIONS
MAGIC
MATHEMATICS—Numbers, ordinal
NEIGHBORHOODS AND COMMUNITIES—General
TIME—Nighttime

King-Smith, Dick. *Farmer Bungle Forgets.* Martin Honeysett, illus. New York: Atheneum, 1987.

Farmer Bungle has a difficult time remembering things, including his name.

BEHAVIOR—Forgetful
FAMILIES—Husbands and wives

FARMS
HUMOR
LANGUAGE—Names
NEIGHBORHOODS AND COMMUNITIES—Specific, rural
OCCUPATIONS

Kitchens, Bert. *Animal Alphabet.* New York: Dial, 1984.

In this alphabet book, each animal is arranged in an interesting way around the letter that begins its name.

ANIMALS—Zoo
LANGUAGE—Alphabet
OBSERVATION
STORIES—Minimal or no text

————. *Animal Numbers.* New York: Dial, 1987.

For each number (1 through 10, 15, 25, 50, 75, and 100) in this counting book, images representing each quantitative idea are arranged around the numeral in an interesting way.

ANIMALS
MATHEMATICS—Counting
OBSERVATION
STORIES—Minimal or no text

Koralek, Jenny. *The Cobweb Curtain: A Christmas Story.* Pauline Baynes, illus. New York: H. Holt, 1989.

A spider spins a web that protects the Christ Child and his family.

ANIMALS—Habitats, webs; Small creatures, spiders
BEHAVIOR—Hiding
HOLIDAYS AND CELEBRATIONS—Christmas
STRUCTURES—Caves

Kovalski, Maryann. *The Wheels on the Bus.* Boston: Joy Street, 1987.

Tired of waiting for a bus, a grandmother and her grandchildren become preoccupied with singing and miss the bus.

BEHAVIOR—Patient; Problem-solving
FAMILIES—Grandparents
GRAPHIC AND PERFORMING ARTS—Music and musicians
MOVEMENT/SPEED
NEIGHBORHOODS AND COMMUNITIES—Specific, urban
SENSES—Sound
SHOPPING/MARKETING
STORIES—Predictable text
TRANSPORTATION—Buses
TRAVEL

Krahn, Fernando. *Arthur's Adventure in the Abandoned House.* New York: Dutton, 1981.

Arthur overcomes danger as he explores an abandoned house.

ADVENTURES
BEHAVIOR—Problem-solving

ENEMIES
SAFETY/DANGER
STORIES—Minimal or no text
STRUCTURES—Buildings, houses and other dwellings
WRITING—Others

————. *The Mystery of the Giant Footprints.* New York: Dutton, 1977.

When parents search for their children who have followed giant footprints in the snow, they find delightful creatures.

BEHAVIOR—Searching
HUMOR
IMAGINATION
MYSTERY
SAFETY/DANGER
STORIES—Minimal or no text
WEATHER—Snow
WORLD REGIONS—Mountain

————. *The Secret in the Dungeon.* New York: Clarion, 1983.

A child falls into a dungeon with a dragon while on a family outing to an ancient castle.

ADVENTURES
BEHAVIOR—Curious
EXPLORATION
FAMILIES—Family gatherings/Outings
IMAGINATION—Imaginary creatures, dragons
PERSONAL PROBLEMS—Getting lost
ROOMS—Others
STORIES—Minimal or no text
STRUCTURES—Buildings, castles/palaces
VACATIONS

Kraus, Robert. *Leo the Late Bloomer.* Jose Aruego, illus. New York: Windmill, 1971.

Under the anxious and trusting care of his parents, Leo finally grows a great deal.

ANIMALS—Large animals, tigers; Personified
BEHAVIOR—Apprehensive; Patient
FAMILIES—Parents
IDENTITY—Self-worth

————. *Milton the Early Riser.* Jose and Ariane Aruego, illus. New York: Simon & Schuster, 1987.

Waking early, Milton, the panda, tries to involve others in his activities, but they keep sleeping. When the other animals do awaken, Milton has worn himself out and has gone to sleep.

ANIMALS—Large animals, bears; Personified
EVERYDAY EXPERIENCES—Time of day, awakening for the day
PLAY
SLEEPING

————. *Owliver.* Jose Aruego and Ariane Dewey, illus. New York: Windmill, 1974.

The young owl chooses his own vocation despite much encouragement from his parents to choose other occupations.

ANIMALS—Birds; Personified
EXPLORATION
FAMILIES—Parents
GRAPHIC AND PERFORMING ARTS—Drama and actors
IDENTITY—Self-worth
INDIVIDUALITY
OCCUPATIONS
SURPRISES

———. *Whose Mouse are You?* Jose Aruego, illus. New York: Macmillan, 1970.

A lonely mouse finds his family members and gains a new sibling.

ANIMALS—Personified; Small creatures, mice
BEHAVIOR—Problem-solving
EMOTIONS—Loneliness; Love
FAMILIES—Babies and young siblings; Parents; Siblings
FAMILY PROBLEMS—Separation
IDENTITY—Relationships
LANGUAGE—Sayings and special language
STORIES—Predictable text

Kroll, Steven. *Friday the 13th.* Dick Gackenbach, illus. New York: Holiday House, 1981.

The unfortunate Harold has a change of fortune on Friday the 13th.

BEHAVIOR—Apprehensive; Heroic; Ridiculing
EMOTIONS—Embarrassment
EVERYDAY EXPERIENCES—Time of day, daytime
FAMILIES—Siblings
IDENTITY—Self-worth
LUCK
SPORTS

———. *One Tough Turkey: A Thanksgiving Story.* John Wallner, illus. New York: Holiday House, 1982.

In this fanciful version of the first Thanksgiving, the turkeys hunted by the Pilgrims outwit them, so they have to be content with squash for their holiday meal.

ANIMALS—Farm, turkeys
BEHAVIOR—Tricking
FOOD AND EATING
HISTORICAL PERIODS—Colonial
HOLIDAYS AND CELEBRATIONS—Thanksgiving
HUMOR
WRITING—Signs

———. *The Tyrannosaurus Game.* Tomie dePaola, illus. New York: Holiday House, 1976.

Many children participate in telling this add-on story about a tyrannosaurus.

ADVENTURES
BEHAVIOR—Bored
DINOSAURS
GAMES/PUZZLES/TRICKS

IMAGINATION
SCHOOL EXPERIENCES
STORYTELLING
WEATHER—Rain

Kroll, Virginia L. *Africa Brothers and Sisters*. Vanessa French, illus. New York: Four
Winds, 1993.

Together, Jesse and his father explore their African heritage and connect it to
their lives.
BEHAVIOR—Curious; Searching
FAMILIES—Parents
GAMES/PUZZLES/TRICKS
IDENTITY—Geographic identity
MAPS
STORYTELLING
UNITED STATES—Specific cultures, African American
WORLD CULTURES/COUNTRIES—Africa; Cross cultures

————. *Masai and I*. Nancy Carpenter, illus. New York: Four Winds, 1992.

In studying East Africa in school, an African American girl compares and con-
trasts aspects of her life with those of a contemporary in an African culture. As a
result, she develops a kinship with the East African culture.
IDENTITY—Relationships
IMAGINATION
NEIGHBORHOODS AND COMMUNITIES—General
SCHOOL EXPERIENCES
UNITED STATES—Specific cultures, African American
WORLD CULTURES/COUNTRIES—Africa, Eastern; Cross cultures

Kuskin, Karla. *The Philharmonic Gets Dressed*. Marc Simont, illus. New York: Harper & Row, 1982.

Musicians in the philharmonic orchestra demonstrate many different ways of
dressing and bathing as they get ready for a performance.
CLOTHING
GRAPHIC AND PERFORMING ARTS—Music and musicians
HEALTH—Bathing

Lawson, Julie. *The Dragon's Pearl*. Paul Morin, illus. New York: Clarion, 1993.

A poor boy finds a magic pearl which causes everything it touches to multiply.
When he swallows it, he is transformed into a river dragon who brings water to the
region.
BEHAVIOR—Ambitious/Persistent; Crying; Destructive/Violent; Excited; Greedy; Prob-
lem-solving; Sharing
EMOTIONS—Sadness
FAMILIES—Parents
GRAPHIC AND PERFORMING ARTS—Music and musicians
IMAGINATION—Imaginary creatures, dragons
JEWELS/JEWELRY

LANGUAGE—Sayings and special language
LUCK
MAGIC
MATHEMATICS—Measurement, volume; Size
MONEY
PLANTS—Others
POVERTY
SAFETY/DANGER
SENSES—Sound
TRANSFORMATION
WATER AND BODIES OF WATER—Rivers
WEATHER—Drought; Rain
WORLD CULTURES/COUNTRIES—Asia, China

Leaf, Margaret. *Eyes of the Dragon.* Ed Young, illus. New York: Lothrop, 1987.

Chinese villagers learn too late why the artist commissioned to paint a dragon on the wall surrounding the village is reluctant to give it eyes.

ANIMALS—Fantasy
BEHAVIOR—Bossy; Proud
BODY—Parts of body, eyes
EMOTIONS—Fear
GRAPHIC AND PERFORMING ARTS—Art and artists
IMAGINATION—Imaginary creatures, dragons
NEIGHBORHOODS AND COMMUNITIES—General
OCCUPATIONS
SAFETY/DANGER
STRUCTURES—Others
TRANSFORMATION
WORLD CULTURES/COUNTRIES—Asia, China

Leedy, Loreen. *Tracks in the Sand.* New York: Doubleday, 1993.

The cycle of the sea turtle begins with it emerging from the ocean to lay its eggs in the sand. After the young hatch, they return to the sea, only to return to lay their eggs on the seashore.

ANIMALS—Cycles; Eggs; Marine life, others; Small creatures, turtles/tortoises
BIRTH
SAND
SECRETS
TIME—Nighttime
WATER AND BODIES OF WATER—Oceans
WORLD REGIONS—Seashore

Legge, David. *Bamboozled.* New York: Scholastic, 1994.

Sensing that something seems odd on her weekly visit to her grandfather's house, a girl tries to discover what it is.

BEHAVIOR—Searching
CLOTHING—Others
EMOTIONS—Love
FAMILIES—Grandparents
GAMES/PUZZLES/TRICKS
HUMOR

IMAGINATION—Imaginary worlds
OBSERVATION
STRUCTURES—Buildings, houses and other dwellings

Le Guin, Ursula K. *A Ride on the Red Mare's Back.* Julie Downing, illus. New York: Orchard, 1992.

With the assistance of her wooden horse, a brave girl travels to the mountains to rescue her brother, who has been kidnapped by the trolls.

BEHAVIOR—Destructive/Violent; Evil; Heroic; Problem-solving; Searching
FAMILIES—Siblings
IMAGINATION—Imaginary creatures, others
MAGIC
SAFETY/DANGER
TOYS
TRAVEL

Leighton, Maxinne Rhea. *An Ellis Island Christmas.* Dennis Nolan, illus. New York: Viking, 1992.

A young immigrant girl journeys to America from Poland. On Christmas Eve she is reunited with her father on Ellis Island.

BEHAVIOR—Courageous
EMOTIONS—Happiness; Loneliness; Sadness
FAMILIES—Parents
FAMILY PROBLEMS—Separation
HISTORICAL PERIODS—Nineteenth Century, late
HOLIDAYS AND CELEBRATIONS—Christmas
IMMIGRANTS/REFUGEES
MEMORIES
MOVING
SAFETY/DANGER
STATUES
TRANSPORTATION—Boats
TRAVEL
UNITED STATES—Regions, Northeast
WATER AND BODIES OF WATER—Oceans

Lent, Blair. *John Tabor's Ride.* Boston: Little, Brown, 1966.

A shipwrecked John Tabor is carried by a whale through many experiences at sea and finally onto the streets of Nantucket.

ADVENTURES
ANIMALS—Marine life, whales
IMAGINATION—Imaginary creatures, others
TRAVEL
WATER AND BODIES OF WATER—Oceans
WORLD REGIONS—Seashore

———. *Molasses Flood.* Boston: Houghton Mifflin, 1992.

The author's tall tale is an elaborated version of a story told to him as a child by his mother. Based on a real event in Boston, the story tells of a huge tank of molasses which exploded during a warming period one January. A boy, Charley Owen

Muldoon, announces the coming flood to the town as he rides his house on a slow-moving sea of sweet-tasting molasses.

BEHAVIOR—Excited; Responsible
CHANGES
DISASTERS
FAMILIES—Parents
FOOD AND EATING
IMAGINATION—Imaginary worlds
MATHEMATICS—Measurement, volume
MOVEMENT/SPEED
NEIGHBORHOODS AND COMMUNITIES—Specific, urban
SENSES—Sight; Smell and taste; Sound
STRUCTURES—Buildings, others
SURPRISES
TIME—Specific seasons, winter
TRANSPORTATION—Boats
UNITED STATES—Regions, Northeast
WATER AND BODIES OF WATER—Harbors

Lester, Alison. *Clive Eats Alligators.* Boston: Houghton Mifflin, 1986.

The preferences of seven children are presented as they go through the day.

ANIMALS—Pets, others
EVERYDAY EXPERIENCES—Time of day, daytime
FOOD AND EATING
GAMES/PUZZLES/TRICKS
IDENTITY—Self-worth
INDIVIDUALITY
MATHEMATICS—Classification
PLAY
SHOPPING/MARKETING
STORIES—Predictable text
TIME—Cycles, day and night

———. *The Journey Home.* Boston: Houghton Mifflin, 1991.

Two Australian children who have fallen through a hole to the North Pole meet several famous characters on their way home.

ADVENTURES
FAMILIES—Siblings
GOALS
IMAGINATION—Imaginary creatures, others; Imaginary worlds
LANGUAGE—Names
MATHEMATICS—Measurement, length
PLAY
TRAVEL
WORLD CULTURES/COUNTRIES—Australia and the Pacific Islands; Polar regions

———. *Magic Beach.* Boston: Joy Street, 1992.

Children at the beach fantasize about what could happen there.

EMOTIONS—Happiness
GAMES/PUZZLES/TRICKS
IMAGINATION
OBSERVATION

PLAY
STORIES—Predictable text
TIME—Cycles, day and night
WATER AND BODIES OF WATER—Oceans
WORLD REGIONS—Seashore

————. *Tessa Snaps Snakes*. Boston: Houghton Mifflin, 1991.

The seven children in *Clive Eats Alligators* return in this sequel presenting more preferences.

EMOTIONS—Fear
EVERYDAY EXPERIENCES
GAMES/PUZZLES/TRICKS
IDENTITY—Self-worth
INDIVIDUALITY
MATHEMATICS—Classification
MONEY
PLAY
SECRETS
STORIES—Predictable text

Lester, Helen. *Me First*. Lynn Munsinger, illus. Boston: Houghton Mifflin, 1992

Pinkerton, the pig who must always be first at all costs, learns a lesson from a witch: There can be satisfaction in being last.

ANIMALS—Farm, pigs; Personified
BEHAVIOR—Greedy; Rude; Tricking
FOOD AND EATING
IMAGINATION—Imaginary creatures, witches; Imaginary worlds
LANGUAGE—Sayings and special language
STORYTELLING

Levinson, Riki. *Watch the Stars Come Out*. Diane Goode, illus. New York: Dutton, 1985.

A grandmother tells her granddaughter about her ocean voyage to America as an immigrant child.

ASTRONOMY—Stars
EMOTIONS—Happiness; Sadness
FAMILIES—Grandparents; Parents; Siblings
FAMILY PROBLEMS—Separation
HEALTH—Illness and injury
HISTORICAL PERIODS—Nineteenth Century, late
IMMIGRANTS/REFUGEES
MEMORIES
MOVING
SAFETY/DANGER
STATUES
STORYTELLING
TRANSPORTATION—Boats
TRAVEL
UNITED STATES—Regions, Northeast
WATER AND BODIES OF WATER—Oceans

Levitin, Sonia. *The Man Who Kept His Heart in a Bucket.* Jerry Pinkney, illus. New York: Dial, 1991.

Jack keeps his heart safe in a bucket so that it will not be broken again. One day a young maiden snatches it and refuses to give it back until Jack finds the answers to her riddle. In the process, he finds the meaning of love.

BEHAVIOR—Searching
BODY—Parts of body
COLORS
EMOTIONS—Love; Sadness
FRIENDSHIP—Relationships
LANGUAGE—Words
LOST AND FOUND
MAGIC
MATHEMATICS—Numbers, ideas
OCCUPATIONS
RIDDLES
SHOPPING/MARKETING
TRANSFORMATION

Lewin, Hugh. *Jafta.* Lisa Kopper, illus. Minneapolis: Carolrhoda, 1983.

Jafta associates his feelings with the movement of animals.

ANIMALS
IDENTITY—Self-worth
MOVEMENT/SPEED
WORLD CULTURES/COUNTRIES—Africa, Southern

———. *Jafta and the Wedding.* Lisa Kopper, illus. Minneapolis: Carolrhoda, 1983.

A young South African boy, Jafta, tells of the week his sister's wedding was celebrated.

FAMILIES—Family gatherings/Outings; Husbands and wives; Marriage; Siblings
HOLIDAYS AND CELEBRATIONS—Celebrations around the World
TIME—Cycles, days of the week
WORLD CULTURES/COUNTRIES—Africa, Southern

———. *Jafta—the Journey.* Lisa Kopper, illus. Minneapolis: Carolrhoda, 1984.

Jafta travels with his mother to the city where his father works.

BEHAVIOR—Excited
FAMILIES—Parents
FAMILY PROBLEMS—Separation
NEIGHBORHOODS AND COMMUNITIES—Specific, urban
TIME—Cycles, day and night
TRANSPORTATION—Buses; Wagons
WORLD CULTURES/COUNTRIES—Africa, Southern

———. *Jafta—the Town.* Lisa Kopper, illus. Minneapolis: Carolrhoda, 1984.

Jafta is taken for the first time to a bustling city to visit his father, who is working there, and to attend his uncle's funeral.

BEHAVIOR—Crying
DEATH
EMOTIONS—Sadness
FAMILIES—Other relatives; Parents

FAMILY PROBLEMS—Separation
NEIGHBORHOODS AND COMMUNITIES—Specific, urban
WORLD CULTURES/COUNTRIES—Africa, Southern

————. *Jafta's Father*. Lisa Kopper, illus. Minneapolis: Carolrhoda, 1983.

A lonely young South African boy describes the good times he had with his father before he went away to work.
EMOTIONS—Loneliness; Sadness
FAMILIES—Parents
FAMILY PROBLEMS—Separation
MEMORIES
TIME—Cycles, seasons
WORLD CULTURES/COUNTRIES—Africa, Southern

————. *Jafta's Mother*. Lisa Kopper, illus. Minneapolis: Carolrhoda, 1983.

Jafta describes the role his mother plays in making his life secure.
EMOTIONS—Love
FAMILIES—Parents
WORLD CULTURES/COUNTRIES—Africa, Southern

Lionni, Leo. *Alexander and the Wind-up Mouse*. New York: Pantheon, 1969.

Alexander, the mouse, wants to be like his friend Willy, the toy mouse, until he realizes that the toy is going to be discarded.
ANIMALS—Small creatures, mice
IDENTITY—Self-worth
MACHINES
MAGIC
ROCKS AND MINERALS
TOYS—Others
TRANSFORMATION
WISHES

————. *The Biggest House in the World*. New York: Pantheon, 1968.

In this modern fable, the theme "biggest is not always best" is developed. Through a story, a wise father snail tells his son, who aspires to have a large shell, that it is not practical in view of their need for mobility.
ANIMALS—Small creatures, others
BEHAVIOR—Wise
MATHEMATICS—Measurement, mass; Size
MOVEMENT/SPEED
STORYTELLING
STRUCTURES—Buildings, houses and other dwellings

————. *Cornelius: A Fable*. New York: Pantheon, 1983.

Cornelius, a crocodile, shares the knowledge he has gained through his ability to walk upright.
ANIMALS—Marine life, crocodiles
BEHAVIOR—Sharing
EMOTIONS—Disappointment; Sadness
IDENTITY—Self-worth
INDIVIDUALITY

————. *Fish Is Fish.* New York: Pantheon, 1970.

After his friend, the frog, leaves the pond, the fish decides he must also leave to explore the world. His exploration leads to disastrous results and an awareness of his habitat's value.

ANIMALS—Cycles; Habitats; Marine life, fishes; Marine life, frogs
CHANGES
EXPLORATION
IMAGINATION—Imaginary worlds
MATHEMATICS—Classification
TRANSFORMATION
WATER AND BODIES OF WATER—Ponds

————. *Frederick.* New York: Pantheon, 1967.

Frederick, the field mouse, does not help his fellow mice gather food for the winter because he is preoccupied with other ideas. When the food runs out, his ideas rescue the family.

AESTHETIC APPRECIATION
ANIMALS—Personified; Small creatures, mice
BEHAVIOR—Heroic; Lazy; Resourceful; Sharing
COLORS
FOOD AND EATING
LANGUAGE—Words
SENSES—Sight; Touch
SURVIVAL
TIME—Specific seasons, fall; Specific seasons, winter
WRITING—Poems

————. *Geraldine, the Music Mouse.* New York: Pantheon, 1979.

After the cheese mouse is eaten to satisfy the mice's hunger Geraldine, the mouse, finds that its flute melodies are a part of her.

ANIMALS—Personified; Small creatures, mice
FOOD AND EATING
GRAPHIC AND PERFORMING ARTS—Music and musicians
SENSES—Sound

————. *Inch by Inch.* New York: I. Obolensky, 1960.

An inch worm saves himself from being eaten by the nightingale and also proves that some things cannot be measured.

ANIMALS—Birds; Small creatures, others
EXPLORATION
GRAPHIC AND PERFORMING ARTS—Music and musicians
MATHEMATICS—Measurement, length
SURVIVAL

————. *Little Blue and Little Yellow.* New York: McDowell, Obolensky, 1959.

The relationship of Little Blue and Little Yellow creates something new: green.

CHANGES
COLORS
FAMILIES—Parents
FRIENDSHIP—Relationships
IDENTITY—Relationships

———. *Matthew's Dream*. New York: Knopf, 1991.

After the mouse child, Matthew, visits a museum, he decides he wants to become a painter. He sets his goal and achieves it through hard work.

ANIMALS—Fantasy; Small creatures, mice
BEHAVIOR—Ambitious/Persistent
BIOGRAPHY/LIFE STORIES
DREAMS
EMOTIONS—Love
GOALS
GRAPHIC AND PERFORMING ARTS—Art and artists
IDENTITY—Self-worth
OCCUPATIONS
ROOMS—Attics
SCHOOL EXPERIENCES
SENSES—Sight
STRUCTURES—Buildings, museums

———. *Six Crows: A Fable*. New York: Knopf, 1988.

An owl negotiates a compromise between a farmer and the crows over the rights to a wheat crop.

ANIMALS—Birds
BEHAVIOR—Apprehensive; Cooperative; Problem-solving; Wise
FARMS
KITES
LANGUAGE—Words
OCCUPATIONS
PEACE
PLANTS
SCARECROWS

———. *Swimmy*. New York: Pantheon, 1963.

With the cooperation of other fish, Swimmy, the small black fish, carries out his plan to live safely among their enemies in the ocean.

ANIMALS—Marine life, fishes
BEHAVIOR—Cooperative; Problem-solving
ENEMIES
SAFETY/DANGER
SURVIVAL
WATER AND BODIES OF WATER—Oceans

Lobel, Anita. *Alison's Zinnia*. New York: Greenwillow, 1990.

Girls giving gifts of flowers are presented in an alphabetical sequence based on their names and the names of the flowers.

GIFTS
LANGUAGE—Alphabet; Names
OBSERVATION
PLANTS—Flowers
STORIES—Predictable text

————. *On Market Street.* Arnold Lobel, illus. New York: Mulberry, 1989.

On a shopping spree, a child buys presents from A to Z for a friend.

LANGUAGE—Alphabet
MATHEMATICS—Classification
OBSERVATION
SHOPPING/MARKETING

Lobel, Arnold. *Days with Frog and Toad.* New York: Harper & Row, 1979.

In these four short stories, Frog and Toad share many experiences—flying kites, telling scary stories, and celebrating birthdays. Although they are friends, they find that sometimes it is good to be alone.

ANIMALS—Marine life, frogs; Personified; Small creatures, others
BEHAVIOR—Ambitious/Persistent; Resourceful
BIRTHDAYS
CLOTHING—Hats
EMOTIONS—Fear
FRIENDSHIP—Relationships
GIFTS
KITES
STORYTELLING

————. *Frog and Toad Are Friends.* New York: Harper & Row, 1970.

Frog is a true friend. He helps Toad wake up in the spring, look for a lost button, and sends him a letter when he discovers Toad never receives mail.

ANIMALS—Marine life, frogs; Personified
CLOTHING—Buttons
HEALTH—Illness and injury
LOST AND FOUND
SEWING
STORYTELLING
TIME—Specific seasons, Spring
WRITING—Letters

————. *Frog and Toad Together.* New York: Harper & Row, 1972.

Frog and Toad do many things together, including planting a garden, eating cookies, and reading a book.

ANIMALS—Marine life, frogs; Personified
FOOD AND EATING
FRIENDSHIP—Relationships
GARDENS
READING
WRITING—Others

————. *Ming Lo Moves the Mountain.* New York: Greenwillow, 1982.

Ming Lo and his wife seek a way to move the mountain from their home.

BEHAVIOR—Problem-solving; Wise
CONSTRUCTION
FAMILIES—Husbands and wives
GRAPHIC AND PERFORMING ARTS—Dance and dancers

HUMOR
MOVING
STRUCTURES—Buildings, houses and other dwellings
WORLD REGIONS—Mountain

———. *Mouse Soup*. New York: Harper & Row, 1977.

A mouse outwits a weasel who is planning to make mouse soup out of him.

ANIMALS—Small creatures, mice
BEHAVIOR—Tricking
FOOD AND EATING—Soup
READING
SAFETY/DANGER
STORYTELLING
SURPRISES
SURVIVAL

———. *Mouse Tales*. New York: Harper & Row, 1972.

At bedtime, the father mouse tells a story about each of his seven sons.

ANIMALS—Personified; Small creatures, mice
EVERYDAY EXPERIENCES—Time of day, bedtime
FAMILIES—Parents
STORYTELLING

———. *On the Day Peter Stuyvesant Sailed into Town*. New York: Harper & Row, 1971.

The new governor, Peter Stuyvesant, finds New Amsterdam in a disgraceful disarray and proceeds with a strong hand to correct the situation.

BEHAVIOR—Ambitious/Persistent; Bossy; Impatient; Problem-solving
DISABILITIES
DREAMS
ECOLOGY/ENVIRONMENTAL PROBLEMS
EMOTIONS—Anger
HISTORICAL PERIODS—Colonial
NEIGHBORHOODS AND COMMUNITIES—General
UNITED STATES—Regions, Northeast

———. *Owl at Home*. New York: Harper & Row, 1975.

Owl is visited by winter, frightened by two bumps in his bed, and followed by the moon.

ANIMALS—Birds; Personified
ASTRONOMY—Moon
BEHAVIOR—Crying; Sharing
EMOTIONS—Sadness
FOOD AND EATING
SLEEPING
STRUCTURES—Buildings, houses and other dwellings
TIME—Nighttime; Specific seasons, Winter

———. *The Rose in My Garden*. Anita Lobel, illus. New York: Greenwillow, 1984.

In this cumulative story, different kinds of flowers are added to those giving shade to a sleeping bee until the bee is awakened by a cat chasing a mouse.

ANIMALS—Pets, cats; Small creatures, insects
BEHAVIOR—Destructive/Violent
GARDENS
HEALTH—Illness and injury
PLANTS—Flowers
STORIES—Predictable text

————. *A Treeful of Pigs.* Anita Lobel, illus. New York: Greenwillow, 1979.

After the farmer's wife uses drastic means to get her lazy husband to work, he agrees to always keep his promises.

ANIMALS—Farm, pigs
BEHAVIOR—Lazy; Tricking
FAMILIES—Husbands and wives
FARMS
OCCUPATIONS
PERSONAL PROBLEMS—Breaking promises

————. *Uncle Elephant.* New York: Harper & Row, 1981.

When the young elephant's parents are lost at sea, his elderly uncle provides many interesting experiences for him until his parents are rescued.

ANIMALS—Large animals, elephants; Personified
BEHAVIOR—Crying
CLOTHING
ELDERLY
EMOTIONS—Love; Sadness
ENEMIES
FAMILIES—Orphans; Other relatives; Parents
FAMILY PROBLEMS—Separation
GARDENS
IMAGINATION
LOST AND FOUND
MAGIC
MATHEMATICS—Counting
ROYALTY
SENSES—Sound
TRANSPORTATION—Trains
TRAVEL
WATER AND BODIES OF WATER—Oceans
WISHES
WRITING—Others

Locker, Thomas. *Where the River Begins.* New York: Dial, 1984.

Two boys and their grandfather go on a camping trip to find the source of the nearby river.

ADVENTURES
CAMPING
EXPLORATION
FAMILIES—Family gatherings/Outings; Grandparents
WATER AND BODIES OF WATER—Rivers

Lotz, Karen E. *Snowsong Whistling*. Elisa Kleven, illus. New York: Dutton, 1993.

Rhymes describe everyday activities that signal the end of autumn and the beginning of winter.

CHANGES
EMOTIONS—Happiness
EVERYDAY EXPERIENCES—Time of day, daytime
NEIGHBORHOODS AND COMMUNITIES—Specific, rural
OBSERVATION
SENSES—Sight; Smell and taste; Sound
STORIES—Predictable text
TIME—Specific seasons, fall; Specific seasons, winter

Luenn, Nancy. *Nessa's Fish*. Neil Waldman, illus. New York: Atheneum, 1990.

On an inland fishing expedition, an Eskimo girl, Nessa, and her grandmother catch many fish to take back to the people in their camp. When her grandmother becomes ill on the return trip, Nessa protects her and the fish from wild animals until help arrives.

ANIMALS—Large animals; Large animals, bears; Large animals, foxes; Large animals, wolves; Marine life, fishes
BEHAVIOR—Courageous; Problem-solving; Responsible
ELDERLY
FAMILIES—Grandparents
FISHING
FOOD AND EATING
GRAPHIC AND PERFORMING ARTS—Music and musicians
HEALTH—Illness and injury
SAFETY/DANGER
SLEEPING
SURVIVAL
TIME—Cycles, day and night; Specific seasons, fall
UNITED STATES—Specific cultures, American Indian/Eskimo
WATER AND BODIES OF WATER—Lakes
WORLD CULTURES/COUNTRIES—Polar regions

Lydon, Kerry Raines. *A Birthday for Blue*. Michael Hays, illus. Niles, IL: A. Whitman, 1989.

The boy, Blue, celebrates his seventh birthday as he travels west with his family in a wagon along the Cumberland Road.

BIRTHDAYS
ECOLOGY/ENVIRONMENTAL PROBLEMS
GIFTS
HISTORICAL PERIODS—Nineteenth Century, pioneer/westward movement
PLANTS—Trees
TRANSPORTATION—Wagons
TRAVEL

Lyon, George Ella. *Cecil's Story*. Peter Catalanotto, illus. New York: Orchard, 1991.

Through his imagination and in his dreams, a boy envisions his father becoming a soldier in the Civil War and the consequences for his family.

CHANGES
DREAMS

EMOTIONS—Fear
FAMILIES—Parents
FAMILY PROBLEMS—Separation
FARMS
HISTORICAL PERIODS—Nineteenth Century, late
IMAGINATION
MOVEMENT/SPEED
NEIGHBORHOODS AND COMMUNITIES—Specific, rural
STRUCTURES—Buildings, cabins
WAR

————. *Come a Tide*. Stephen Gammell, illus. New York: Orchard, 1990.

The people of a rural mountain community are caught up in a spring flood.
BEHAVIOR—Excited
FAMILIES—Grandparents; Parents
FAMILY PROBLEMS—Others
MATHEMATICS—Measurement, volume
MOVING
NEIGHBORHOODS AND COMMUNITIES—Specific, rural
SURVIVAL
TIME—Across time; Specific seasons, spring
UNITED STATES—Regions, Appalachia
WATER AND BODIES OF WATER—Floods
WEATHER—Rain

————. *Together*. Vera Rosenberry, illus. New York: Orchard, 1989.

Two friends list many things they can do together.
FLYING—Fantasy
FRIENDSHIP—Relationships
IMAGINATION
STORIES—Predictable text
TIME—Cycles, day and night

————. *Who Came Down That Road?* Peter Catalanotto, illus. New York: Orchard, 1992.

Moving back through succeeding times to a prehistoric era, a child and his mother consider who might have used the old road.
CHANGES
FAMILIES—Parents
IMAGINATION
MYSTERY
ROADS
TIME—Across time
TRAVEL

MacDonald, Suse. *Alphabatics*. New York: Bradbury, 1986.

The letters of the alphabet are transformed into familiar images.
LANGUAGE–Alphabet
OBSERVATION
TRANSFORMATION

MacDonald, Suse, and Bill Oakes. *Numblers*. New York: Dial, 1988.

> In this counting book (1 to 10), each number is transformed into a familiar image with its parts matching the numerical concept.
> MATHEMATICS—Counting; Numbers, ideas
> OBSERVATION
> SENSES—Sight
> TRANSFORMATION

MacLachlan, Patricia. *All the Places to Love*. Mike Wimmer, illus. New York: HarperCollins, 1994.

> A young boy is a member of a family that promotes individual identity by sharing places on the farm special to each one.
> BABYSITTING
> BEHAVIOR—Responsible
> BIRTH
> BIRTHDAYS
> EMOTIONS—Love
> FAMILIES—Babies and young siblings; Grandparents; Parents
> FARMS
> IDENTITY—Geographic identity; Relationships
> LANGUAGE—Names
> NEIGHBORHOODS AND COMMUNITIES—Specific, rural
> SENSES—Sight; Sound
> STRUCTURES—Buildings, barns
> WEATHER—Rain

———. *Mama One, Mama Two*. Ruth Lercher Bornstein, illus. New York: Harper & Row, 1982.

> A young girl learns to relate to her foster mother (Mama Two) until her own mother (Mama One) is well enough to care for her again.
> BEHAVIOR—Apprehensive; Crying
> EMOTIONS—Loneliness; Love; Sadness
> FAMILIES—Parents
> FAMILY PROBLEMS—Separation
> HEALTH—Illness and injury
> IDENTITY—Relationships
> OCCUPATIONS
> SLEEPING
> STORYTELLING

———. *Through Grandpa's Eyes*. Deborah Ray, illus. New York: Harper & Row, 1980.

> From his blind grandfather, a young boy learns to use the senses other than sight to know about the world.
> DISABILITIES
> FAMILIES—Grandparents
> SENSES—Smell and taste; Sound; Touch

Mahy, Margaret. *The Queen's Goat*. Emma Chichester Clark, illus. New York: Dial, 1991.

> Determined to be a part of the pet parade, the young queen and her runaway goat end up participating in the event and winning an unexpected prize.

ANIMALS—Farm, Goats; Pets, others
BEHAVIOR—Competitive; Problem-solving; Running away
CLOTHING
FAIRS
HUMOR
PARADES
ROYALTY

Marion, Jeff Daniel. *Hello, Crow.* Leslie Bowman, illus. New York: Orchard, 1992.

An elderly man observes a crow and is reminded of a crow's antics in his youth.

ANIMALS—Birds
BEHAVIOR—Hiding
CIRCUS
ELDERLY
FAMILIES—Grandparents
FARMS
LOST AND FOUND
MEMORIES
MYSTERY
SENSES—Sound
STORYTELLING
SURPRISES
TIME—Across time
TREASURES

Marshall, James. *George and Martha.* Boston: Houghton Mifflin, 1972.

Through honesty and caring, George and Martha's friendship stays intact and is strengthened: They discover that both dislike split pea soup. Martha supports George when he loses his favorite tooth.

ANIMALS—Large animals, hippopotami; Personified
BEHAVIOR—Crying; Tricking
BODY—Parts of body, teeth
EMOTIONS—Happiness
FLYING—Aviation
FOOD AND EATING
FRIENDSHIP—Relationships
HEALTH—Bathing
HUMOR
OCCUPATIONS
TRANSPORTATION—Hot-air balloons

———. *George and Martha Back in Town.* Boston: Houghton Mifflin, 1984.

The friends, George and Martha, deal with several problems, such as snooping, fear of dining, and dealing with a new job.

ANIMALS—Large animals, hippopotami; Personified
BEHAVIOR—Apprehensive; Courageous; Curious; Disobedient; Sharing; Tricking
EMOTIONS—Fear; Loneliness
FOOD AND EATING
FRIENDSHIP—Relationships
OCCUPATIONS
READING
SPORTS

STRUCTURES—Boxes and containers
SURPRISES

———. *George and Martha, One Fine Day*. Boston: Houghton Mifflin, 1978.

Five short stories tell of George and Martha's experiences, including tightrope walking, storytelling, and spying.

ADVENTURES
ANIMALS—Large animals, hippopotami; Personified
BEHAVIOR—Apprehensive; Curious; Hiding; Tricking
EMOTIONS—Fear
FRIENDSHIP—Relationships
GAMES/PUZZLES/TRICKS
HOBBIES
HUMOR
SAFETY/DANGER
SENSES
STORYTELLING
STRUCTURES—Tunnels
WRITING—Diaries

———. *George and Martha 'Round and 'Round*. Boston: Houghton Mifflin, 1988.

Five short stories about two hippopotami friends address several aspects of getting along.

ADVENTURES
ANIMALS—Large animals, hippopotami; Personified
BEHAVIOR—Fighting/Quarreling; Loyal; Mischievous; Sharing; Tricking
EMOTIONS—Anger; Fear; Happiness
FRIENDSHIP—Relationships
GIFTS
GRAPHIC AND PERFORMING ARTS—Art and artists
HUMOR
IMAGINATION
ROOMS—Attics
WATER AND BODIES OF WATER—Oceans
WEATHER—Rain

———. *George and Martha, Tons of Fun*. Boston: Houghton Mifflin, 1980.

George and Martha remain friends through a series of positive and negative experiences.

ANIMALS—Large animals, hippopotami; Personified
BIRTHDAYS
EMOTIONS—Anger
FOOD AND EATING
FRIENDSHIP—Relationships
GAMES/PUZZLES/TRICKS
GIFTS
GRAPHIC AND PERFORMING ARTS—Music and musicians
HEALTH—Health care
HOBBIES
HUMOR
PERSONAL PROBLEMS—Breaking promises

Martin, Bill. *Brown Bear, Brown Bear, What Do You See?* Eric Carle, illus. New York: Holt, 1983.

Animals are depicted in different colors in this rhythmic chant.
ANIMALS
COLORS
SENSES—Sight
STORIES—Predictable text

———. *Polar Bear, Polar Bear, What Do You Hear?* Eric Carle, illus. New York: Holt, 1991.

In this rhythmic chant, zoo animals make their particular sounds and the book's audience is invited to reproduce these sounds for the zookeeper.
ANIMALS—Zoo
OCCUPATIONS
SENSES—Sound
STORIES—Predictable text

Martin, Bill, and John Archambault. *Barn Dance!* Ted Rand, illus. New York: Holt, 1986.

Unable to sleep on a night with a full moon, a farm boy is lured to an unusual barn dance.
ANIMALS—Farm
ASTRONOMY—Moon
FARMS
GRAPHIC AND PERFORMING ARTS—Dance and dancers; Music and musicians
SCARECROWS
SENSES—Sound
TIME—Nighttime

———. *Chicka Chicka Boom Boom.* Lois Ehlert, illus. New York: Simon & Schuster, 1989.

The letters of the alphabet race each other up the coconut tree in this rhyming chant.
ADVENTURES
BEHAVIOR—Competitive; Excited
LANGUAGE—Alphabet
MOVEMENT/SPEED
PLANTS—Trees
STORIES—Predictable text
TIME—Cycles, day and night

———. *The Ghost-Eye Tree.* Ted Rand, illus. New York: Holt, 1985.

On an errand one dark autumn night, a brother and sister pretend not to be afraid. Their imaginations win out, and they become terrified of the Ghost-Eye Tree.
BEHAVIOR—Pretending; Ridiculing
CLOTHING—Hats
EMOTIONS—Fear
FAMILIES—Siblings
IMAGINATION

NEIGHBORHOODS AND COMMUNITIES—Specific, rural
PLANTS—Trees
SENSES—Sound
TIME—Nighttime; Specific seasons, fall

———. *Knots on a Counting Rope.* Ted Rand, illus. New York: Holt, 1987.

To represent the passage of time and his grandson's courage despite his blindness, the grandfather ties knots on a rope as he tells of the child's life.
ADVENTURES
BEHAVIOR—Courageous; Searching
BIRTH
DISABILITIES
EMOTIONS—Happiness; Love
FAMILIES—Family gatherings/Outings; Grandparents; Parents
GOALS
IDENTITY—Self-worth
LANGUAGE—Names
MEMORIES
MOVEMENT/SPEED
SENSES—Sight; Sound; Touch
STORYTELLING
TIME—Clocks and other time-telling methods
UNITED STATES—Specific cultures, American Indian/Eskimo

———. *Listen to the Rain.* James Endicott, illus. New York: Holt, 1988.

Rain is described from the first light sprinkles to the pounding downpour and the resulting rainbow.
OBSERVATION
SENSES—Sound
STORIES—Predictable text
WEATHER—Rain; Rainbows

Martin, Jacqueline Briggs. *Good Times on Grandfather Mountain.* Susan Gaber, illus. New York: Orchard, 1992.

A mountain man whittles away every problem that comes his way.
ANIMALS—Farm
BEHAVIOR—Lazy; Resourceful; Running Away
EMOTIONS—Happiness
FARMS
GRAPHIC AND PERFORMING ARTS—Art and artists; Music and musicians
NEIGHBORHOODS AND COMMUNITIES—Specific, rural
OCCUPATIONS
PARTIES
STRUCTURES—Buildings, houses and other dwellings
WEATHER—Storms
WORLD REGIONS—Mountain

Martin, Rafe. *Will's Mammoth.* Stephen Gammell, illus. New York: Putnam, 1989.

Will spends a wintry day with the woolly mammoths despite the fact that his parents say they no longer exist.
ANIMALS—Fantasy; Prehistoric
FAMILIES—Parents

IMAGINATION—Imaginary creatures; Imaginary worlds
PLAY
STORIES—Minimal or no text
TIME—Across time; Cycles, day and night; Specific seasons, winter

Maruki, Toshi. *Hiroshima No Pika*. New York: Lothrop, 1980.

A young girl and her family experience the devastation of the bombing of Hiroshima in 1945.

BEHAVIOR—Crying
DEATH
DISASTERS
FAMILIES—Parents
FAMILY PROBLEMS—Homelessness
FIRE
HEALTH—Illness and injury
HISTORICAL PERIODS—Twentieth Century, World War II
LIGHT AND SHADOWS/REFLECTIONS
MEMORIES
NEIGHBORHOODS AND COMMUNITIES—Specific, urban
SAFETY/DANGER
SURVIVAL
WAR
WORLD CULTURES/COUNTRIES—Asia, Japan

Marzollo, Jean. *In 1492*. Steve Bjorkman, illus. New York: Scholastic, 1991.

The common rhyme "In fourteen hundred ninety-two, Columbus sailed the ocean blue" is expanded and illustrated.

BEHAVIOR—Courageous
EXPLORATION
GOALS
HISTORICAL PERIODS—Exploration of the New World
STORIES—Predictable text
TRANSPORTATION—Boats
TRAVEL
WATER AND BODIES OF WATER—Oceans

Mattingley, Christobel. *The Angel with a Mouth-Organ*. Astra Lacis, illus. New York: Holiday House, 1986.

As the glass angel ornament is placed on the Christmas tree, a mother is reminded of its special significance in her life. She tells her children about her own childhood in a war-torn country and the hope this ornament gave to her family.

BEHAVIOR—Destructive/Violent
DEATH
EMOTIONS—Fear; Sadness
ENEMIES
FAMILIES—Parents
FAMILY PROBLEMS—Separation
GOALS
GRAPHIC AND PERFORMING ARTS—Music and musicians
HEALTH—Illness and injury
HISTORICAL PERIODS—Twentieth Century, World War II
HOLIDAYS AND CELEBRATIONS—Christmas

MEMORIES
MOVING
SAFETY/DANGER
STORYTELLING
TOYS—Dolls
TRAVEL
WAR
WORLD CULTURES/COUNTRIES—Europe, Northern

Mayer, Mercer. *A Boy, a Dog, and a Frog.* New York: Dial, 1967.

The frog joins the boy and his dog in the bathtub after the boy unsuccessfully tries to catch him in an outdoor pond.

ADVENTURES
ANIMALS—Marine life, frogs; Pets, dogs
EMOTIONS—Disappointment
EVERYDAY EXPERIENCES—Time of day, daytime
HEALTH—Bathing
HUMOR
NEIGHBORHOODS AND COMMUNITIES—Specific, rural
OBSERVATION
STORIES—Minimal or no text

———. *Frog Goes to Dinner.* New York: Dial, 1974.

Frog hides in the boy's pocket as the family goes to a restaurant. When they arrive, Frog emerges to cause a great deal of chaos.

ANIMALS—Marine life, frogs; Pets, others
BEHAVIOR—Destructive/Violent; Hiding; Mischievous
EMOTIONS—Anger; Embarrassment
FAMILIES—Family gatherings/Outings
FOOD AND EATING
GRAPHIC AND PERFORMING ARTS—Music and musicians
HUMOR
STORIES—Minimal or no text

———. *There's an Alligator Under My Bed.* New York: Dial, 1987.

The boy goes to bed cautiously because there is an alligator under his bed . . . until he locks the alligator in the garage.

ANIMALS—Fantasy; Marine life—Alligators
BEHAVIOR—Hiding; Tricking
EMOTIONS—Fear
EVERYDAY EXPERIENCES—Time of day, bedtime
FAMILIES—Parents
FOOD AND EATING
FURNITURE—Beds
IMAGINATION—Imaginary creatures
ROOMS—Bedrooms
WRITING—Letters

Mayer, Mercer, and Marianna Mayer. *One Frog Too Many.* New York: Dial, 1975.

A boy's pet frog resents the new little frog given to the boy for his birthday. His attempts to rid the family of the new pet lead to humorous incidents.

ANIMALS—Marine life, frogs; Personified; Pets, others
BEHAVIOR—Bullying; Searching

BIRTHDAYS
FAMILY PROBLEMS—New siblings
GIFTS
HUMOR
STORIES—Minimal or no text

McBratney, Sam. *Guess How Much I Love You*. Anita Jeram, illus. Cambridge, Mass.: Candlewick, 1995.

Little Nutbrown Hare and his father try to surpass each other in describing their love for the other.

ANIMALS—Personified; Small creatures, rabbits
ASTRONOMY—Moon
BEHAVIOR—Competitive
EMOTIONS—Happiness; Love
EVERYDAY EXPERIENCES—Time of day, bedtime
FAMILIES—Parents
GAMES/PUZZLES/TRICKS
IDENTITY—Relationships
IMAGINATION
LANGUAGE—Sayings and special language
MATHEMATICS—Measurement

McCloskey, Robert. *Blueberries for Sal*. New York: Viking, 1948.

While picking blueberries, both a small girl and a bear cub lose their mothers and at one point find each other's mother.

ADVENTURES
ANIMALS—Large animals, bears
BEHAVIOR—Searching
FAMILIES—Parents
IDENTITY—Relationships
LOST AND FOUND
PLANTS—Fruits
SAFETY/DANGER
SENSES—Sound

———. *Burt Dow, Deep-Water Man*. New York: Viking, 1963.

Burt has an extraordinary fishing experience. He catches a whale, takes refuge from a storm in its stomach, and decorates the tails of a school of whales with striped Band-Aids.

ANIMALS—Marine life, whales
ELDERLY
FISHING
OCCUPATIONS
SENSES—Sight; Sound
TRANSPORTATION—Boats
WATER AND BODIES OF WATER—Oceans
WEATHER—Storms

———. *Make Way for Ducklings*. New York: Viking, 1941.

With the help of friends, the mallard pair and their ducklings return to the Boston Public Garden.

ANIMALS—Farm, ducks
BEHAVIOR—Searching

CONSTRUCTION
MOVEMENT/SPEED
NEIGHBORHOODS AND COMMUNITIES—Parks; Specific, urban
OCCUPATIONS
SAFETY/DANGER
TRAVEL
UNITED STATES—Regions, Northeast

————. *One Morning in Maine*. New York: Viking, 1952.

The young girl, Sal, has a special day, losing her tooth and taking a trip to the grocery store on the mainland.

ANIMALS
EVERYDAY EXPERIENCES—Time of day, daytime
BODY—Parts of body, teeth
ISLANDS
SAFETY/DANGER
SECRETS
SHOPPING/MARKETING
TRANSPORTATION—Boats
TRAVEL
UNITED STATES—Regions, Northeast
WEATHER—Sunshine
WISHES
WORLD REGIONS—Seashore

————. *Time of Wonder*. New York: Viking, 1957.

The family has many summertime experiences on an island in the sea.

CHANGES
FAMILIES—Parents
ISLANDS
MOVING
NEIGHBORHOODS AND COMMUNITIES—General
OCCUPATIONS
TIME—Cycles, day and night; Specific seasons, summer
TRANSPORTATION—Boats
VACATIONS
WATER AND BODIES OF WATER—Oceans
WEATHER—Storms
WORLD REGIONS—Seashore

McCully, Emily Arnold. *The Amazing Felix*. New York: Putnam, 1993.

Preoccupied with learning magical tricks, Felix fails to practice the piano despite his pianist father's orders before he left on tour. When Father arranges for his family to be reunited in an English castle, Felix's ability rescues other children trapped in the dungeon. From this feat, his father is able to accept Felix's lack of interest in practicing the piano.

ADVENTURES
BEHAVIOR—Ambitious/Persistent; Courageous; Disobedient; Heroic
EMOTIONS—Fear
FAMILIES—Family gatherings/Outings; Parents; Siblings
GAMES/PUZZLES/TRICKS
GRAPHIC AND PERFORMING ARTS—Music and musicians

HISTORICAL PERIODS—Twentieth Century, early
HOBBIES
IDENTITY—Self-worth
LOST AND FOUND
MAGIC
MONEY
PERSONAL PROBLEMS—Breaking promises; Getting lost
STRUCTURES—Buildings, castles/palaces
TRANSPORTATION—Boats
TRAVEL

———. *The Christmas Gift*. New York: Harper & Row, 1988.

When a young mouse's new Christmas toy breaks, her grandfather restores her happiness with a toy train from his childhood.

ANIMALS—Personified; Small creatures, mice
BEHAVIOR—Crying
EMOTIONS—Disappointment; Happiness
FAMILIES—Family gatherings/Outings; Grandparents
GIFTS
HOLIDAYS AND CELEBRATIONS—Christmas
STORIES—Minimal or no text
STRUCTURES—Buildings, houses and other dwellings
TIME—Specific seasons, winter

———. *First Snow*. New York: Harper & Row, 1985.

A timid young mouse learns the pleasure of sledding.

ANIMALS—Personified; Small creatures, mice
BEHAVIOR—Boastful; Shy
EMOTIONS—Fear; Happiness
FAMILIES—Family gatherings/Outings
PERSONAL PROBLEMS—Fearing to try something new
STORIES—Minimal or no text
TIME—Specific seasons, winter
WEATHER—Snow

———. *Mirette on the High Wire*. New York: Putnam, 1992.

Mirette learns to walk the tightwire from a famous artist who no longer performs because of fear. She helps him return to the wire, and the two perform together.

BEHAVIOR—Courageous; Curious
CIRCUS
EMOTIONS—Fear
FRIENDSHIP—Relationships
HISTORICAL PERIODS—Twentieth Century, early
MATHEMATICS—Measurement, length
NEIGHBORHOODS AND COMMUNITIES—Specific, urban
OCCUPATIONS
PERSONAL PROBLEMS—Others
SAFETY/DANGER
SECRETS
WORLD CULTURES/COUNTRIES—Europe, Northern

————. *Picnic*. New York: Harper & Row, 1984.

On the way to a family picnic, a young mouse is separated from her family.

ANIMALS—Personified; Small creatures, mice
FAMILIES—Family gatherings/Outings
FOOD AND EATING
PERSONAL PROBLEMS—Getting lost
STORIES—Minimal or no text
TIME—Specific seasons, summer

————. *School*. New York: Harper & Row, 1987.

A curious little mouse journeys to school to explore it.

ADVENTURES
ANIMALS—Personified; Small creatures, mice
EXPLORATION
SCHOOL EXPERIENCES
STORIES—Minimal or no text
TIME—Specific seasons, fall

McDonald, Megan. *The Great Pumpkin Switch*. Ted Lewin, illus. New York: Orchard, 1992.

In grandfather's story from his childhood, he and his friend, Otto, accidentally sever the vine of his sister's large pumpkin. They replace it without her knowing the difference.

BEHAVIOR—Lying; Problem-solving; Resourceful
FAMILIES—Grandparents; Parents; Siblings
FRIENDSHIP—Relationships
HISTORICAL PERIODS—Twentieth Century, early
MATHEMATICS—Measurement, mass
MEMORIES
MONEY
OCCUPATIONS
PUMPKINS
STORYTELLING
TIME—Specific seasons, fall

————. *The Potato Man*. Ted Lewin, illus. New York: Orchard, 1991.

Grandpa relates his childhood experiences with a disabled huckster of fruits and vegetables. He tells how negative feelings and responses turned to positives through kindness.

BEHAVIOR—Responsible; Stealing; Teasing
DISABILITIES
FAMILIES—Grandparents
FOOD AND EATING
FRIENDSHIP—Relationships
GIFTS
HISTORICAL PERIODS—Twentieth Century, early
HOLIDAYS AND CELEBRATIONS—Christmas
MEMORIES
NEIGHBORHOODS AND COMMUNITIES—Specific, urban
OCCUPATIONS
STORYTELLING

STRUCTURES—Buildings, houses and other dwellings
TRANSPORTATION—Horses

McKissack, Patricia. *A Million Fish—More or Less*. Dena Schutzer, illus. New York: Knopf, 1992.

From his fishing experience, a boy tells a tall tale, as others do in Bayou Clapateaux.

ANIMALS—Marine life, fishes
BEHAVIOR—Boastful; Tricking
EVERYDAY EXPERIENCES—Time of day, daytime
FISHING
IMAGINATION
MATHEMATICS—Numbers, ideas; Numbers, processes
MEMORIES
STORYTELLING
TRANSPORTATION—Boats
UNITED STATES—Regions, South; Specific cultures, African American
WATER AND BODIES OF WATER—Lakes

————. *Mirandy and Brother Wind*. Jerry Pinkney, illus. New York: Knopf, 1988.

Knowing whoever catches Brother Wind can make him do their bidding, Mirandy catches him to be her partner in the Junior Cakewalk. When Ezel is betrayed by his partner, Mirandy presents her wish to Brother Wind, and she and Ezel win the dance contest.

BEHAVIOR—Competitive
EMOTIONS—Happiness
FRIENDSHIP—Relationships
GOALS
GRAPHIC AND PERFORMING ARTS—Dance and dancers
IMAGINATION—Imaginary creatures
MAGIC
NEIGHBORHOODS AND COMMUNITIES—Social gatherings
PARTIES
STORYTELLING
UNITED STATES—Specific cultures, African American
WEATHER—Wind
WISHES

McLerran, Alice. *I Want to Go Home*. Jill Kastner, illus. New York: Tambourine, 1992.

Marta's mother gives her a cat to help her adjust to a new home.

ANIMALS—Pets, cats
BEHAVIOR—Responsible
EMOTIONS—Loneliness; Sadness
FAMILIES—Parents
GIFTS
IDENTITY—Relationships
LOST AND FOUND
MOVING
STRUCTURES—Buildings, houses and other dwellings

————. *Roxaboxen*. Barbara Cooney, illus. New York: Lothrop, 1991.

A group of children transforms an unused lot into an imaginary town for their play.

BEHAVIOR—Pretending; Resourceful
CHANGES
CONSTRUCTION
FRIENDSHIP—Relationships
IMAGINATION—Imaginary worlds
MEMORIES
NEIGHBORHOODS AND COMMUNITIES—Specific, rural
PLAY
ROCKS AND MINERALS
STRUCTURES—Boxes and containers
TIME—Across time
TRANSFORMATION
UNITED STATES—Regions, Southwest
WORLD REGIONS—Desert

McNulty, Faith. *The Lady and the Spider*. Bob Marstall, illus. New York: Harper & Row, 1986.

After a woman picks a head of lettuce in which a spider lives, she returns it to its garden habitat.

ANIMALS—Habitats; Small creatures, spiders
ECOLOGY/ENVIRONMENTAL PROBLEMS
GARDENS
PLANTS—Vegetables

McPhail, David. *Pig Pig Rides*. New York: Dutton, 1982.

Pig Pig tells his mother of his intended adventures for the day. Out of love for him, she cautions him to be careful and to return by dark.

ADVENTURES
ANIMALS—Farm, pigs; Personified
BEHAVIOR—Boastful; Pretending
EMOTIONS—Love
FAMILIES—Parents
IMAGINATION
TRANSPORTATION

Meddaugh, Susan. *Hog-Eye*. Boston: Houghton Mifflin, 1995.

Through her ability to read and the power of the Hog-Eye, a young pig escapes her kidnapper, the wolf, who plans to eat her.

ANIMALS—Farm, pigs; Large animals, wolves; Personified
BEHAVIOR—Boastful; Courageous; Evil; Problem-solving; Tricking
COMMUNICATION—Signs
FAMILIES—Siblings
FAMILY PROBLEMS—Separation
FOOD AND EATING—Soup
HEALTH—Illness and injury
HUMOR
IDENTITY—Self-worth

PLANTS—Others; Vegetables
READING
SAFETY/DANGER
SCHOOL EXPERIENCES
STORYTELLING
SURPRISES
SURVIVAL
TRANSPORTATION—Buses

————. *Martha Speaks*. Boston: Houghton Mifflin, 1992.

After the alphabet soup she ate went to her head rather than to her stomach, Martha, the family dog, finally learns how and when to use her newfound ability.

ANIMALS—Personified; Pets, dogs
BEHAVIOR—Problem-solving; Stealing
COMMUNICATION—Telephones
EMOTIONS—Anger; Disappointment; Embarrassment
FOOD AND EATING—Soup
HUMOR
IDENTITY—Self-worth
LANGUAGE—Alphabet
MAGIC SURPRISES

Mellecker, Judith. *Randolph's Dream*. Robert Andrew Parker, illus. New York: Knopf, 1991.

An English boy lonely for his soldier father during World War II dreams of saving his life.

BEHAVIOR—Problem-solving
DREAMS
EMOTIONS—Loneliness
FAMILIES—Parents
FAMILY PROBLEMS—Separation
FLYING—Fantasy
HISTORICAL PERIODS—Twentieth Century, World War II
SAFETY/DANGER
SURVIVAL
WAR
WORLD REGIONS—Desert

Melmed, Laura. *The First Song Ever Sung*. Ed Young, illus. New York: Lothrop, 1993.

A series of characters respond to a little boy's question, "What was the first song ever sung?"

BEHAVIOR—Curious
EMOTIONS—Love
GRAPHIC AND PERFORMING ARTS—Music and musicians
IDENTITY—Relationships
IMAGINATION
STORIES—Predictable text
STORYTELLING
WORLD CULTURES/COUNTRIES—Asia, Japan

Mendez, Phil. *The Black Snowman*. Carole Byard, illus. New York: Scholastic, 1989.

A boy finds dignity in his African American heritage through involvement with a black snowman and a magical *kente*, a colorful cloth brought from Africa long ago.

BEHAVIOR—Courageous; Heroic; Proud; Resourceful; Teasing
CLOTHING—Others
COLORS
DREAMS
EMOTIONS—Anger; Sadness
FAMILIES—Parents; Siblings
FIRE
HOLIDAYS AND CELEBRATIONS—Christmas; Kwanzaa
IDENTITY—Relationships; Self-worth
IMAGINATION—Imaginary creatures; Imaginary objects
MAGIC
MEMORIES
POVERTY
ROYALTY
SHOPPING/MARKETING
SLAVERY
STORYTELLING
TIME—Across time; Specific seasons, winter
TRANSFORMATION
UNITED STATES—Specific cultures, African American
WEATHER—Snow
WORLD CULTURES/COUNTRIES—Africa, Western

Miles, Miska. *Annie and the Old One*. Peter Parnall, illus. Boston: Little, Brown, 1971.

A Navajo girl learns the meaning of death and carries on the family traditions through her weaving.

DEATH
EMOTIONS—Sadness
FAMILIES—Grandparents; Parents
GRAPHIC AND PERFORMING ARTS—Art and artists
IDENTITY—Relationships
UNITED STATES—Regions, Southwest; Specific cultures, American Indian/Eskimo
WEAVING

Miller, Margaret. *Whose Hat?* New York: Greenwillow, 1988.

The hats worn by people in different occupations are presented in color photographs. Additional pictures show children wearing the hats and role-playing the occupation.

CLOTHING—Hats
GRAPHIC AND PERFORMING ARTS—Drama and actors
LANGUAGE—Words
OCCUPATIONS
PLAY

Mills, Lauren. *The Rag Coat*. Boston: Little, Brown, 1991.

Minna is deeply hurt when the other children at school make fun of her new patchwork coat. After she shares the children's stories associated with the patches, they also develop an appreciation for the special coat.

BEHAVIOR—Resourceful; Sharing
CLOTHING—Coats
DEATH
EMOTIONS—Disappointment; Sadness
FAMILIES—Parents
GIFTS
GOALS
HEALTH—Illness and injury
IDENTITY—Self-worth
MEMORIES
NEIGHBORHOODS AND COMMUNITIES—Specific, rural
OCCUPATIONS
POVERTY
QUILTS
SCHOOL EXPERIENCES
SECRETS
SEWING
STRUCTURES—Buildings, cabins
UNITED STATES—Regions, Appalachia
WORLD REGIONS—Mountain

Minarik, Else Holmelund. *A Kiss for Little Bear*. Maurice Sendak, illus. New York: Harper & Row, 1968.

Many animals pass along Grandmother's kiss for Little Bear with a happy consequence.

ANIMALS—Large animals, Bears; Personified; Small creatures
BEHAVIOR—Sharing
EMOTIONS—Happiness; Love
FAMILIES—Grandparents; Marriage
GIFTS
GRAPHIC AND PERFORMING ARTS—Arts and artists

———. *Little Bear*. Maurice Sendak, illus. New York: Harper, 1957.

Four experiences—common and uncommon—of Little Bear are told.

ADVENTURES
ANIMALS—Large animals, bears; Personified
ASTRONOMY—Moon
BEHAVIOR—Teasing
BIRTHDAYS
CLOTHING
EMOTIONS—Love
FAMILIES—Parents
FLYING—Fantasy
IMAGINATION
SPACE
WISHES

———. *Little Bear's Friend*. Maurice Sendak, illus. New York: Harper, 1960.

Little Bear and his friends have fun playing with a girl who is camping with her family for the summer. When she leaves to go back to school, Little Bear is consoled by the idea of writing to her.

ANIMALS—Birds; Large animals, bears; Personified
EMOTIONS—Sadness
FAMILIES—Family gatherings/Outings
FRIENDSHIP—Relationships
GIFTS
HEALTH—Illness and injury
LOST AND FOUND
PARTIES
PLANTS—Trees
PLAY
TIME—Specific seasons, summer
TOYS—Dolls
VACATIONS
WRITING—Letters

———. *Little Bear's Visit.* Maurice Sendak, illus. New York: Harper, 1961.

Little Bear's visit to his grandparents is filled with many experiences, particularly storytelling.

ANIMALS—Birds; Large animals, bears; Personified
FAMILIES—Grandparents; Parents
IMAGINATION—Imaginary creatures, others
SLEEPING
STORYTELLING

Mitchell, Rita Phillips. *Hue Boy.* Caroline Binch, illus. New York: Dial, 1993.

Hue Boy, small for his age, is disappointed because none of the suggestions for making him grow seem to work. Then, one day his father's ship comes in, and Hue Boy walks tall beside his father, not feeling small at all.

BEHAVIOR—Teasing
BODY—Shape and size
EMOTIONS—Disappointment
FAMILIES—Parents
FAMILY PROBLEMS—Separation
IDENTITY—Self-worth
MATHEMATICS—Measurement, length
NEIGHBORHOODS AND COMMUNITIES—Specific, rural
PERSONAL PROBLEMS—Others
WORLD CULTURES/COUNTRIES—Central America, Caribbean Islands

Moss, Lloyd. *Zin! Zin! Zin! A Violin.* Marjorie Priceman, illus. New York: Simon & Schuster, 1995.

One by one, instruments are added to a musical group until an orchestra evolves. Instruments are identified and collective nouns are introduced for musical groups, comprising one to ten members.

AESTHETIC APPRECIATION
GRAPHIC AND PERFORMING ARTS—Music and musicians
LANGUAGE—Words
MATHEMATICS—Counting; Numbers, ideas
STORIES—Predictable text

Modell, Frank. *One Zillion Valentines.* New York: Greenwillow, 1981.

Marvin shows Milton how to make valentines. They make more than enough for all the neighbors, so they buy each other a present from the sale of the extras.

BEHAVIOR—Resourceful
COMMUNICATION—Signs
FOOD AND EATING
FRIENDSHIP—Relationships
GRAPHIC AND PERFORMING ARTS—Arts and artists
HOLIDAYS AND CELEBRATIONS—Valentine's
MATHEMATICS—Numbers, ideas
MONEY
NEIGHBORHOODS AND COMMUNITIES—Specific, Urban
SHOPPING/MARKETING

Mora, Pat. *A Birthday Basket for Tia.* Cecily Lang, illus. New York: Macmillan, 1992.

Cecilia gathers items that represent special experiences for her Great-Aunt Tia's ninetieth birthday.

ANIMALS—Pets, cats
BEHAVIOR—Sharing
BIRTHDAYS
ELDERLY
EMOTIONS—Happiness
FAMILIES—Other relatives
GIFTS
IDENTITY—Relationships
INDIVIDUALITY
LANGUAGE—Words
MEMORIES
PARTIES
STRUCTURES—Boxes and containers
SURPRISES
UNITED STATES—Specific cultures, Hispanic American

Morimoto, Junko. *My Hiroshima.* New York: Viking, 1990.

The author tells of her memories of the bombing of her community, Hiroshima.

BIOGRAPHY/LIFE STORIES
CHANGES
DEATH
DISASTERS
EMOTIONS—Sadness
HISTORICAL PERIODS—Twentieth Century, World War II
IDENTITY—Geographic identity
MEMORIES
NEIGHBORHOODS AND COMMUNITIES—Specific, urban
OBSERVATION
SAFETY/DANGER
SURVIVAL
WAR
WORLD CULTURES/COUNTRIES—Asia, Japan

Moss, Thylias. *I Want to Be.* Jerry Pinkney, illus. New York: Dial, 1993.

After much exploration, a girl discovers the kind of person she wishes to be.

BEHAVIOR—Searching

GRAPHIC AND PERFORMING ARTS—Dance and dancers; Music and musicians
IDENTITY—Self-worth
IMAGINATION
INDIVIDUALITY
MATHEMATICS—Size
MOVEMENT/SPEED
OCCUPATIONS
PLAY
SENSES—Sight; Smell and taste; Sound; Touch
WISHES

Munari, Bruno. *ABC*. Cleveland: World, 1960.

Each letter of the alphabet is accompanied by illustrations of images that begin with that letter.

LANGUAGE—Alphabet

————. *Bruno Munari's Zoo*. Cleveland: World, 1963.

Animals are depicted in brightly colored illustrations and with clever descriptions.

ANIMALS—Zoo

————. *The Circus in the Mist*. New York: World, 1969.

The mood is bright at the circus even though the town is surrounded by a fog.

CIRCUS
EMOTIONS—Happiness
NEIGHBORHOODS AND COMMUNITIES—Specific, urban
SENSES—Sight; Sound
WEATHER—Fog

Murphy, Jill. *All in One Piece*. New York: Putnam, 1987.

The young elephant's parents prepare to go out for the evening to a dinner dance.

ANIMALS—Large animals, elephants; Personified
BABYSITTING
CLOTHING
FAMILIES—Grandparents; Husband and wives; Parents
PARTIES
SURPRISES

————. *Peace at Last*. New York: Dial, 1980.

In the search for a quiet night of sleep, Mr. Bear experiences many sounds.

ANIMALS—Large animals, bears; Personified
EVERYDAY EXPERIENCES—Time of day, bedtime; Time of day, nighttime
FAMILY PROBLEMS—Others
SENSES—Sound
SLEEPING

————. *What Next, Baby Bear!* New York: Dial, 1984.

Baby Bear prepares for and takes a rocket trip to the moon while his mother draws his bath before bedtime.

ADVENTURES
ANIMALS—Large animals, bears; Personified
ASTRONOMY—Moon

BEHAVIOR—Pretending
CONSTRUCTION
EVERYDAY EXPERIENCES—Time of day, bedtime
FAMILIES—Parents
FLYING—Fantasy
HEALTH—Bathing
IDENTITY—Geographic identity
IMAGINATION—Imaginary worlds
SPACE
STRUCTURES—Boxes and containers
TIME—Nighttime
TOYS—Bears
TRAVEL

Murphy, Shirley Rousseau. *Tattie's River Journey.* Tomie dePaola, illus. New York: Dial, 1983.

Even though Tattie's house is swept away in the flood, she has a wonderful travel adventure, giving shelter to animals and people. When the flood recedes, her house is resting on a bridge, which makes a unique setting for a grand life.

ADVENTURES
EMOTIONS—Happiness
FARMS
MATHEMATICS—Measurement, volume
NEIGHBORHOODS AND COMMUNITIES—Specific, rural
STRUCTURES—Bridges; Buildings, houses and other dwellings
TRAVEL
WATER AND BODIES OF WATER—Floods; Rivers
WEATHER—Rain

Mwenye Hadithi. *Crafty Chameleon.* Adrienne Kennaway, illus. Boston: Little, Brown, 1987.

Tired of being bullied by the leopard and the crocodile, the clever chameleon uses his transformation ability to rid himself of their harassment.

ANIMALS—Marine life—crocodiles; Reptiles—Lizards/Chameleons
BEHAVIOR—Tricking
EMOTIONS—Anger; Fear
ENEMIES
TRANSFORMATION
WORLD REGIONS—Rain forest/Jungle

———. *Greedy Zebra.* Adrienne Kennaway, illus. Boston: Little, Brown, 1984.

The tale explains how the animals of the world acquired their particular coats and how the zebra, with his greedy appetite, came to have his coat of stripes.

ANIMALS—Large animals, others
BEHAVIOR—Greedy
COLORS
FOOD AND EATING
MATHEMATICS—Measurement, length
WORLD CULTURES/COUNTRIES—Africa
WORLD REGIONS—Rain forest/Jungle

————. *Lazy Lion*. Adrienne Kennaway, illus. Boston: Little, Brown, 1990.

Different animals respond to the Lazy Lion's order to build a house for him before the rain arrives. Because they could not please him, to this day he wanders the African plains without a house.

ANIMALS—Large animals, lions
BEHAVIOR—Bossy; Lazy; Searching
CONSTRUCTION
STRUCTURES—Buildings, houses and other dwellings
WEATHER—Rain
WORLD CULTURES/COUNTRIES—Africa
WORLD REGIONS—Plain

————. *Tricky Tortoise*. Adrienne Kennaway. Boston: Little, Brown, 1988.

Angered when Elephant steps on him, Tortoise and his brother prove that small creatures can be clever.

ANIMALS—Large animals, elephants; Small creatures, turtles/tortoises
BEHAVIOR—Tricking
EMOTIONS—Anger
GAMES/PUZZLES/TRICKS
MATHEMATICS—Size

Netizel, Shirley. *The Dress I'll Wear to the Party*. Nancy Winslow Parker, illus. New York: Greenwillow, 1992.

The story of a girl dressing up in her mother's things to go to a party is told in cumulative verse and a rebus.

BEHAVIOR—Pretending
CLOTHING
EMOTIONS—Anger
FAMILIES—Parents
IMAGINATION
JEWELS
LANGUAGE—Sayings and special language
OBSERVATION
PARTIES
STORIES—Predictable text

————. *The Jacket I Wear in the Snow*. Nancy Winslow Parker, illus. New York: Greenwillow, 1989.

In cumulative rhyme, a young girl lists the clothes she puts on to go outside in the winter.

BEHAVIOR—Crying
CLOTHING
FAMILIES—Parents
FOOD AND EATING
LANGUAGE—Words
OBSERVATION
PLAY
TIME—Cycles; Specific seasons, winter
WEATHER—Snow

Nesbit, E. *Melisande.* P. J. Lynch, illus. San Diego: Harcourt, 1989.

Princess Melisande seeks a way to overcome the baldness inflicted on her by an evil fairy's curse. Without thinking about the consequences, she wishes for golden hair a yard long that grows an inch each day and twice as fast when cut.

BEHAVIOR—Evil
BODY—Parts of body, hair
EMOTIONS—Anger; Sadness
FAMILIES—Family gatherings/Outings
IMAGINATION—Imaginary creatures, others
MAGIC
MATHEMATICS—Measurement, length
ROYALTY
WISHES

Ness, Evaline. *Sam, Bangs, & Moonshine.* New York: Holt, 1966.

A young girl learns the difference between the imaginary and the real worlds after she pulls her friend and cat from danger.

ANIMALS—Personified; Pets, cats; Pets, others
BEHAVIOR—Lying; Obedient; Searching; Sharing
CHANGES
DREAMS
FAMILIES—Parents
FRIENDSHIP—Relationships
HEALTH—Illness and injury
IMAGINATION—Imaginary creatures, others
ISLANDS
LANGUAGE—Words
LOST AND FOUND
NEIGHBORHOODS AND COMMUNITIES—General
OCCUPATIONS
PLAY
SAFETY/DANGER
STORYTELLING
WATER AND BODIES OF WATER—Oceans
WEATHER
WORLD REGIONS—Seashore

Nikola-Lisa, W. *Night Is Coming.* Jamichael Henterly, ills. New York: Dutton, 1991.

The sights and sounds of approaching nightfall in the country are described.

FAMILIES—Grandparents
NEIGHBORHOODS AND COMMUNITIES—Specific, rural
SENSES—Sight; Sound
TIME—Nighttime

Noble, Trinka Hakes. *The Day Jimmy's Boa Ate the Wash.* Steven Kellogg, illus. New York: Dial, 1980.

A field trip to a farm turns into chaos due in part to the presence of Jimmy's boa constrictor.

ANIMALS—Reptiles, snakes
BEHAVIOR—Destructive/Violent
DISASTERS

FARMS
HUMOR
SCHOOL EXPERIENCES
TRANSPORTATION—Buses

————. *Jimmy's Boa Bounces Back*. Steven Kellogg, illus. New York: Dial, 1984.

The garden party is wrecked by the havoc caused by Maggie's mother when she arrives wearing a boa-constrictor scarf.

ANIMALS—Reptiles, snakes
BEHAVIOR—Destructive/Violent
CLOTHING
HUMOR
IMAGINATION
MOVEMENT/SPEED
OBSERVATION
PARTIES

————. *Meanwhile Back at the Ranch*. Tony Ross, illus. New York: Dial, 1987.

A rancher goes to town looking for excitement. Meanwhile, his wife experiences it in abundance at home on the ranch.

BEHAVIOR—Bored; Searching
FAMILIES—Husbands and wives
HUMOR
IDENTITY—Gender roles
MONEY
NEIGHBORHOODS AND COMMUNITIES—Specific, rural
OCCUPATIONS
RANCHES
SURPRISES
TRAVEL
UNITED STATES—Regions, West Coast

Noll, Sally. *Watch Where You Go*. New York: Greenwillow, 1990.

A dragonfly warns a small mouse of potential dangers as it scurries home.

ADVENTURES
ANIMALS—Personified; Small creatures, insects; Small creatures, mice
EMOTIONS—Fear
ENEMIES
GOALS
MOVEMENT/SPEED
OBSERVATION
SAFETY/DANGER
STORIES—Minimal or no text
SURPRISES
SURVIVAL
TRAVEL
WORLD REGIONS—Rain forest/Jungle

Nones, Eric Jon. *Caleb's Friend*. New York: Farrar, 1993.

Caleb is angry when he discovers that the other fishermen intend to make his friend—part boy, part fish—a spectacle at a freak show.

FRIENDSHIP—Relationships

GIFTS
IMAGINATION—Imaginary creatures, others
OCCUPATIONS
SAFETY/DANGER
SURVIVAL
TRANSPORTATION—Boats
WATER AND BODIES OF WATER—Harbors
WEATHER—Storms

Norman, Howard A. *The Owl-Scatterer*. Michael McCurdy, illus. Boston: Atlantic
    Monthly, 1986.

When a Canadian village is invaded with owls, an elderly man who lives apart
from the community uses his ability to disburse them.

ANIMALS—Birds
BEHAVIOR—Problem-solving
ELDERLY
SENSES—Sound
STRUCTURES—Buildings, cabins
WATER AND BODIES OF WATER—Lakes
WORLD CULTURES/COUNTRIES—North America, Canada

Norman, Philip Ross. *A Mammoth Imagination*. Boston: Little, Brown, 1992.

Little Bonbon, a wild boa, has a wonderful imagination that provides remarkable
adventures.

ADVENTURES
ANIMALS—Personified; Prehistoric
BEHAVIOR—Curious; Pretending; Searching
IDENTITY—Self-worth
IMAGINATION—Imaginary creatures, monsters
PLAY

Numeroff, Laura Joffe. *If You Give a Mouse a Cookie*. Felicia Bond, illus. New York:
    Harper & Row, 1985.

A boy speculates on the future course of action that will be required if he gives a
mouse a cookie.

ANIMALS—Small creatures, mice
BEHAVIOR—Responsible
EVERYDAY EXPERIENCES—Time of day, daytime
FOOD AND EATING—Cookies
GIFTS
STORIES—Predictable text
TIME—Cycles

Oberman, Sheldon. *The Always Prayer Shawl*. Ted Lewin, illus. Honesdale, PA:
    Boyds Mills, 1994.

A prayer shawl in a Russian Jewish family is passed from grandfather to grandson
over several generations. All are named Adam, suggesting that some things do not
change.

BIOGRAPHY/LIFE STORIES

CHANGES
CLOTHING—Others
ELDERLY
EMOTIONS—Love
ETHNIC CULTURES—Jewish
FAMILIES—Grandparents
IDENTITY—Relationships
IMMIGRANTS/REFUGEES
LANGUAGE—Names
MOVING
SEWING
TIME—Across time
TRAVEL

Olaleye, Isaac O. *Bitter Bananas.* Ed Young, illus. Honesdale, PA: Boyd Mills, 1994.

The boy, Yusuf, living in a long ago African village, finds a solution to the problem of baboons stealing his palm sap.

ANIMALS—Large animals, other
BEHAVIOR—Ambitious/Persistent; Problem-solving; Stealing; Tricking
EMOTIONS—Anger
ENEMIES
FOOD AND EATING
LANGUAGE—Sayings and special language
SENSES—Sound
SURPRISES
WORLD CULTURES/COUNTRIES—Africa
WORLD REGIONS—Rain forest/Jungle

Oppenheim, Joanne. *You Can't Catch Me!* Andrew Shachat, illus. Boston: Houghton Mifflin, 1986.

A black fly has a fatal encounter after he pesters other animals and boasts that they cannot catch him.

ANIMALS—Small creatures, insects; Small creatures, turtles/tortoise
BEHAVIOR—Boastful; Mischievous
DEATH
EMOTIONS—Anger
MATHEMATICS—Size
STORIES—Predictable text

Oram, Hiawyn. *In the Attic.* Satoshi Kitamura, illus. New York: Holt, 1985.

Out of boredom, a boy climbs into the attic and finds an intriguing fantasy world.

BEHAVIOR—Bored
IMAGINATION—Imaginary worlds
OBSERVATION
PLAY
ROOMS—Attics
SECRETS

Ormerod, Jan. *Moonlight.* New York: Lothrop, 1982.

In the process of helping their child fall asleep at bedtime, the parents also become sleepy.

ASTRONOMY—Moon
EVERYDAY EXPERIENCES—Time of day, bedtime
FAMILIES—Parents
SLEEPING
STORIES—Minimal or no text
TIME—Nighttime

————. *Sunshine.* New York: Lothrop, 1981.

A small girl, awakened by the sun, arouses her parents and is part of their preparation for leaving the house for daytime activity.

ASTRONOMY—Sun
EVERYDAY EXPERIENCES—Time of day, awakening for the day
FAMILIES—Parents
STORIES—Minimal or no text
TIME—Daytime
WEATHER—Sunshine

Over in the Meadow. Ezra Jack Keats, illus. New York: Four Winds, 1971.

A traditional counting-verse story (1 to 10) describes the activities of different animals and their young.

ANIMALS—Babies; Habitats
MATHEMATICS—Counting
STORIES—Predictable text

Owens, Mary Beth. *A Caribou Alphabet.* Brunswick, ME: Dog Ear, 1988.

This alphabet book describes the life and characteristics of the caribou.

ANIMALS—Large animals, deer
IDENTITY—Geographic identity
LANGUAGE—Alphabet
STORIES—Predictable text
WORLD CULTURES/COUNTRIES—North America (not United States)

Paulsen, Gary. *Dogteam.* Ruth Wright Paulsen, illus. New York: Delacorte, 1993.

The experience of taking sled dogs on a night run is described in a lyrical manner.

ANIMALS—Large animals, wolves; Pets, dogs
MOVEMENT/SPEED
SENSES—Sight; Sound
STRUCTURES—Buildings, houses and other dwellings
TIME—Nighttime; Specific seasons, winter
TRANSPORTATION—Sleighs
TRAVEL
WEATHER—Snow

Paxton, Tom. *Engelbert the Elephant.* Steven Kellogg, illus. New York: Morrow, 1990.

By chance Engelbert, the elephant, receives an invitation to the queen's ball. He proves to be a delightful guest.

ANIMALS—Large animals, elephants; Personified
DISASTERS

GRAPHIC AND PERFORMING ARTS—Dance and dancers
PARTIES
ROYALTY
STRUCTURES—Buildings, castles/palaces
WRITING—Others

Peet, Bill. *Cowardly Clyde*. Boston: Houghton Mifflin, 1979.

Clyde, a cowardly warhorse, creates a new image for himself by rescuing his knight.

ADVENTURES
ANIMALS—Farm, horses
BEHAVIOR—Apprehensive; Boastful; Courageous; Fighting/Quarreling; Heroic; Loyal;
         Pretending; Proud
EMOTIONS—Fear
IDENTITY—Self-worth
IMAGINATION—Imaginary creatures, monsters
KNIGHTS
MOVEMENT/SPEED
NEIGHBORHOODS AND COMMUNITIES—Specific, rural
SAFETY/DANGER
SURPRISES

———. *The Spooky Tail of Prewitt Peacock*. Boston: Houghton Mifflin, 1972.

Because Prewitt's scraggly tail changes in appearance to a frightening green-eyed monster, the other peacocks want either the tail or Prewitt to go. When his tail frightens their enemy, the tiger, Prewitt's position in the group is greatly elevated.

ANIMALS—Birds; Large animals, tigers
BEHAVIOR—Bullying; Destructive/Violent; Evil; Proud
DREAMS
EMOTIONS—Fear; Sadness
ENEMIES
IDENTITY—Relationships; Self-worth
MOVEMENT/SPEED
SURPRISES
SURVIVAL
WORLD REGIONS—Rain forest/Jungle

———. *The Whingdingdilly*. Boston: Houghton Mifflin, 1970.

Discontented with his lot in life, Scamp wishes for more attention. When a witch turns him into a whingdingdilly, a creature that is a compilation of parts from many animals, he finds that a dog's life with a caring young master is joyful.

ANIMALS—Farm, horses; Pets, dogs
BODY—Parts of body
EMOTIONS—Fear; Happiness; Sadness
FARMS
IDENTITY—Self-worth
IMAGINATION—Imaginary creatures, witches; Imaginary creatures, others
LANGUAGE—Sayings and special language
MAGIC
OCCUPATIONS
SENSES—Sight
SURPRISES

TRANSFORMATION
WISHES

Phillips, Mildred. *The Sign in Mendel's Window*. Margot Zemach, illus. New York: Macmillan, 1985.

Mendel, the butcher, is rescued from his tenant's false accusation by the townspeople and his clever wife.

BEHAVIOR—Excited; Loyal; Problem-solving; Stealing
FAMILIES—Husbands and wives
FRIENDSHIP—Relationships
MONEY
NEIGHBORHOODS AND COMMUNITIES—General
OCCUPATIONS
POVERTY
SENSES—Sound
STRANGERS
STRUCTURES—Buildings, stores

Pilkey, Dav. *The Hallo-Weiner*. New York: Blue Sky, 1995.

Oscar, the dachshund puppy, endures teasing from other dogs because of his size and shape. On one Halloween he rescues the others from danger, thus winning their acceptance.

ANIMALS—Personified; Pets, dogs
BEHAVIOR—Courageous; Heroic; Sharing; Teasing
BODY—Shape and size
CHANGES
CLOTHING—Costumes
EMOTIONS—Embarrassment; Fear
FAMILIES—Parents
HOLIDAYS AND CELEBRATIONS—Halloween
HUMOR
IDENTITY—Self-worth
LANGUAGE—Names
PERSONAL PROBLEMS—Name-calling
TIME—Nighttime

———. *When Cats Dream*. New York: Orchard, 1992.

While sleeping, cats' dreams take them into imaginary worlds.

ANIMALS—Pets, cats
BEHAVIOR—Courageous
DREAMS
IMAGINATION—Imaginary worlds
OBSERVATION
SLEEPING

Pinkney, Brian. *Max Found Two Sticks*. New York: Simon & Schuster, 1994.

When two twigs fall out of a tree, Max picks them up and uses them to imitate the rhythms he hears around him.

BEHAVIOR—Imitating
GAMES/PUZZLES/TRICKS
GRAPHIC AND PERFORMING ARTS—Music and musicians

HOBBIES
IDENTITY—Self-worth
IMAGINATION
INDIVIDUALITY
NEIGHBORHOODS AND COMMUNITIES—Specific, urban
OBSERVATION
PARADES
SENSES—Sound
SURPRISES

Polacco, Patricia. *Appelemando's Dreams.* New York: Philomel, 1991.

Even though Appelemando's friends recognize his special gift of sharing his dreams in color, the villagers do not see his worth until his visual message helps them rescue the lost children.

BEHAVIOR—Heroic; Lying
DREAMS
EMOTIONS—Sadness
FRIENDSHIP—Relationships
GRAPHIC AND PERFORMING ARTS—Art and artists
IDENTITY—Self-worth
LOST AND FOUND
NEIGHBORHOODS AND COMMUNITIES—Specific, urban
SECRETS
SENSES—Sight
SURVIVAL

————. *The Bee Tree.* New York: Philomel, 1993.

Mary Ellen's grandfather compares the reading process to chasing a bee to its hive in a tree and tasting its sweet honey.

ADVENTURES
ANIMALS—Small creatures, insects
BEHAVIOR—Bored; Searching; Sharing
FAMILIES—Grandparents
FOOD AND EATING
GAMES/PUZZLES/TRICKS
GOALS
IDENTITY—Relationships
MOVEMENT/SPEED
NEIGHBORHOODS AND COMMUNITIES—Social gatherings
PLANTS—Trees
READING
SENSES—Smell and taste
STRUCTURES—Boxes and containers

————. *Chicken Sunday.* New York: Philomel, 1992.

The children work to fulfill Miss Eula's wish for an Easter hat by decorating and selling eggs with Eastern European designs in an elderly Russian immigrant's shop. To their surprise, the shopkeeper gives them the hat for bringing back cherished memories.

ANIMALS—Eggs
BEHAVIOR—Resourceful; Sharing
CLOTHING—Hats
ELDERLY

EMOTIONS—Happiness; Sadness
ETHNIC CULTURES—Jewish
FAMILIES—Family gatherings/Outings; Grandparents
FOOD AND EATING
FRIENDSHIP—Relationships
GIFTS
GOALS
GRAPHIC AND PERFORMING ARTS—Art and artists; Music and musicians
HOLIDAYS AND CELEBRATIONS—Easter
IMMIGRANTS/REFUGEES
MEMORIES
NEIGHBORHOODS AND COMMUNITIES—Specific, urban
RELIGION
SECRETS
SHOPPING/MARKETING
UNITED STATES—Cross cultural; Specific cultures, African American

––––––. *The Keeping Quilt.* New York: Simon & Schuster, 1988.

A quilt, constructed from clothing worn by members of a Russian Jewish family as they immigrated to America, becomes a symbol of continuity for four generations.

BEHAVIOR—Cooperative
ELDERLY
EMOTIONS—Happiness; Love
ETHNIC CULTURES—Jewish
FAMILIES—Babies and young siblings; Family gatherings/Outings; Grandparents; Marriage
IDENTITY—Geographic identity
IMMIGRANTS/REFUGEES
MEMORIES
PARTIES
QUILTS
RELIGION
TIME—Across time
TRAVEL
WORLD CULTURES/COUNTRIES—Europe, Central/Eastern

––––––. *Meteor!* New York: Dodd, Mead, 1987.

A falling meteor in a rural community creates much excitement and celebration.

ASTRONOMY—Other
BEHAVIOR—Excited
COMMUNICATION—Telephones
EMOTIONS—Happiness
FAMILIES—Grandparents
MACHINES
MEMORIES
NEIGHBORHOODS AND COMMUNITIES—Social gatherings; Specific, rural
PARADES
ROCKS AND MINERALS
SAFETY/DANGER
STORYTELLING
SURPRISES
TIME—Nighttime

TRANSPORTATION—Hot-air balloons
UNITED STATES—Regions, Midwest

———. *Mrs. Katz and Tush.* New York: Bantam, 1992.

A young African American boy initiates a lasting friendship with a lonely Jewish widow when he gives her a runt kitten. In their emerging friendship, Mrs. Katz shares her Jewish heritage with the boy, Larnel, and she becomes part of his family.

ANIMALS—Pets, cats
BODY—Parts of the body
DEATH
ELDERLY
EMOTIONS—Happiness; Love
ETHNIC CULTURES—Jewish
FAMILIES—Grandparents
FRIENDSHIP—Relationships
GIFTS
IDENTITY—Relationships
IMMIGRANTS/REFUGEES
LANGUAGE—Names
MEMORIES
NEIGHBORHOODS AND COMMUNITIES—Specific, urban
RELIGION
STORYTELLING
UNITED STATES—Cross cultural; Specific cultures, African American

———. *Pink and Say.* New York: Philomel, 1994.

Sheldon Russell Curtis's experiences as a young Union deserter in the Civil War are retold through several generations of his family. They recall especially his relationship with Pinkus Aylee, a black Union soldier.

BEHAVIOR—Courageous; Crying; Destructive/Violent; Evil
DEATH
EMOTIONS—Fear; Love
ENEMIES
FAMILIES—Parents
FAMILY PROBLEMS—Separation
FRIENDSHIP—Relationships
HEALTH—Illness and injury
HISTORICAL PERIODS—Nineteenth Century, late
IDENTITY—Relationships
MEMORIES
PERSONAL PROBLEMS—Running away
POVERTY
READING
SAFETY/DANGER
SECRETS
STORYTELLING
STRUCTURES—Buildings, cabins
SURVIVAL
TIME—Across time
UNITED STATES—Cross cultural
WAR

————. *Rechenka's Eggs.* New York: Philomel, 1988.

The injured goose, Rechenka, taken in by an elderly grandmother, or Babushka, accidentally overturns the woman's basket of decorated eggs which she had planned to sell at the Easter festival. Rechenka lays brilliantly designed eggs to replace the broken ones. When Rechenka returns to a flock, she leaves Babushka an egg that will hatch into a companion.

ANIMALS—Eggs; Farm, chickens
BEHAVIOR—Destructive/Violent
BIRTH
DISASTERS
ELDERLY
EMOTIONS—Disappointment; Happiness
FOOD AND EATING
FRIENDSHIP—Relationships
GIFTS
GRAPHIC AND PERFORMING ARTS—Art and artists
HEALTH—Illness and injury
HOLIDAYS AND CELEBRATIONS—Easter
LANGUAGE—Names
MAGIC
NEIGHBORHOODS AND COMMUNITIES—Social gatherings
SURPRISES
TIME—Cycles, seasons
WORLD CULTURES/COUNTRIES—Europe, Central/Eastern

————. *Thunder Cake.* New York: Philomel, 1990.

As a thunderstorm approaches, a Russian grandmother, or Babushka, helps her young granddaughter overcome her fear of thunder and lightning. The two work quickly to gather ingredients and bake a cake before the storm arrives.

ANIMALS—Farm
BEHAVIOR—Resourceful
ELDERLY
EMOTIONS—Fear; Love
FAMILIES—Grandparents
FOOD AND EATING
GOALS
IMMIGRANTS/REFUGEES
MATHEMATICS—Counting; Measurement, volume
MEMORIES
SAFETY/DANGER
SENSES—Sound
STORYTELLING
TIME—Clocks and other time-telling methods
WEATHER—Storms
WRITING—Other

Pomerantz, Charlotte. *Flap Your Wings and Try.* Nancy Tafuri, illus. New York: Greenwillow, 1989.

The family encourages the young bird to fly, and in turn, he encourages others to try.

ANIMALS—Birds

FAMILIES
IDENTITY—Self-worth
MOVEMENT/SPEED
PERSONAL PROBLEMS—Fearing to try something new

————. *One Duck, Another Duck.* Jose Aruego and Ariane Dewey, illus. New York: Greenwillow, 1984.

Danny practices counting (1 to 10) ducks at first and then finds other images to count.

ANIMALS—Farm, ducks; Personified
FAMILIES—Grandparents
MATHEMATICS—Counting; Numbers, processes
WATER AND BODIES OF WATER—Ponds

Potter, Beatrix. *The Tale of Peter Rabbit.* London: F. Warne, 1903.

Peter Rabbit disobeys his mother and gets into much mischief and difficulty in Mr. McGregor's garden.

ANIMALS—Personified; Small creatures, rabbits
BEHAVIOR—Crying; Disobedient; Hiding
CLOTHING
EMOTIONS—Fear
FOOD AND EATING
GARDENS
HEALTH—Illness and injury
PLANTS—Vegetables
SAFETY/DANGER
SCARECROWS
SHOPPING/MARKETING

Price, Leontyne. *Aïda.* Leo Dillon and Diane Dillon, illus. San Diego: Harcourt, 1990.

From Verdi's opera, the well-known opera singer retells the tragic love story of an Ethiopian princess forced into slavery and an Egyptian general.

BEHAVIOR—Loyal; Tricking
EMOTIONS—Love
FAMILIES—Parents
FRIENDSHIP—Relationships
GRAPHIC AND PERFORMING ARTS—Music and musicians
IDENTITY—Geographic identity
ROYALTY
WAR
WORLD CULTURES/COUNTRIES—Africa, Northern

Provensen, Alice. *The Glorious Flight: Across the Channel with Louis Bleriot, July 25, 1909.* New York: Viking, 1983.

In the early 1900s, Louis Bleriot's interest in flying leads him to invent an airplane that will distinguish him as an aviator.

ADVENTURES
BIOGRAPHY/LIFE STORIES
CONSTRUCTION
FLYING—Aviation

GOALS
HISTORICAL PERIODS—Twentieth Century, early
INVENTIONS
SAFETY/DANGER
TRANSPORTATION—Airplanes
TRAVEL
WORLD CULTURES/COUNTRIES—Europe, Northern

Provensen, Alice, and Martin Provensen. *Shaker Lane*. New York: Viking Kestrel, 1987.

The residents of Shaker Lane must move when a reservoir is built on their property.

CHANGES
MAPS
MEMORIES
MOVING
NEIGHBORHOODS AND COMMUNITIES—General
STRUCTURES—Buildings, houses and other dwellings
UNITED STATES—Regions, Middle Atlantic
WATER AND BODIES OF WATER—Lakes

Pryor, Bonnie. *Lottie's Dream*. Mark Graham, illus. New York: Simon & Schuster, 1992.

As an elderly person, Lottie, who was a child during the westward movement and a woman on the plains, realizes her dream of living by the sea.

ADVENTURES
BEHAVIOR—Courageous
BIOGRAPHY/LIFE STORIES
ELDERLY
EMOTIONS—Happiness
FAMILIES—Grandparents
FARMS
HISTORICAL PERIODS—Nineteenth Century, pioneer/westward movement
IDENTITY—Relationships
INDIVIDUALITY
TRAVEL
UNITED STATES—Regions, Midwest
WATER AND BODIES OF WATER—Oceans
WISHES
WORLD REGIONS—Plain; Seashore

Purdy, Carol. *Mrs. Merriwether's Musical Cat*. Petra Mathers, illus. New York: Putnam, 1994.

The presence of the stray cat taken in by the piano teacher, Mrs. Merriwether, transforms her students into serious performers.

AESTHETIC APPRECIATION
ANIMALS—Pets, cats
BEHAVIOR—Patient
GRAPHIC AND PERFORMING ARTS—Music and musicians
HUMOR
INDIVIDUALITY

LOST AND FOUND
NEIGHBORHOODS AND COMMUNITIES—Specific, urban
OCCUPATIONS
SURPRISES
TIME—Daytime
TRANSFORMATION

Radin, Ruth Yaffe. *A Winter Place*. Mattie Lou O'Kelley, illus. Boston: Little, Brown, 1982.

A family carries their skates through villages, farms, and forests on a winter outing to a frozen lake up in the hills.
ADVENTURES
FAMILIES—Family gatherings/Outings
GRAPHIC AND PERFORMING ARTS—Art and artists
HISTORICAL PERIODS—Nineteenth Century, late
NEIGHBORHOODS AND COMMUNITIES—Specific, rural
TIME—Specific seasons, winter
TRAVEL
WATER AND BODIES OF WATER—Lakes

Rand, Gloria. *Prince William*. Ted Rand, illus. New York: Holt, 1992.

When an oil spill devastates their Alaskan seashore, an entire community works to recover the wildlife. A young girl rescues a baby seal that is in peril and names him Prince William.
ANIMALS—Babies; Marine life, others
BEHAVIOR—Problem-solving
CHANGES
DEATH
DISASTERS
ECOLOGY/ENVIRONMENTAL PROBLEMS
FRIENDSHIP—Relationships
HEALTH—Illness and injury
IDENTITY—Geographic identity
NEIGHBORHOODS AND COMMUNITIES—Specific, rural
SCHOOL EXPERIENCES
SENSES–Sight; Touch
UNITED STATES—Regions, Alaska
WATER AND BODIES OF WATER—Oceans
WORLD REGIONS—Seashore

Raschka, Christopher. *Yo! Yes?* New York: Orchard, 1993.

Two boys, one black and one white, begin a conversation that leads to friendship.
BEHAVIOR—Apprehensive; Excited
EMOTIONS—Happiness
FRIENDSHIP—Relationships
STORIES—Minimal or no text
UNITED STATES—Cross cultural

Raskin, Ellen. *Nothing Ever Happens on My Block*. New York: Atheneum, 1966.

While wishing for interesting incidents on his block, Chester misses the real excitement that is occurring.

ADVENTURES
BEHAVIOR—Bored
HUMOR
NEIGHBORHOODS AND COMMUNITIES—Specific, urban
OBSERVATION
WISHES

Rathmann, Peggy. *Officer Buckle and Gloria*. New York: Putnam, 1995.

Officer Buckle learns about the advantages of teamwork when Gloria, the police dog, joins him in teaching children about safety.

ANIMALS—Pets, dogs
BEHAVIOR—Imitating
COMMUNICATION—Televisions
EMOTIONS—Embarrassment
FRIENDSHIP—Relationship
GRAPHIC AND PERFORMING ARTS—Drama and actors
HUMOR
IDENTITY—Relationships; Self-worth
OCCUPATIONS
SAFETY/DANGER
SCHOOL EXPERIENCES
SECRETS
SURPRISES
WRITING—Letters

Ray, Deborah Kogan. *The Cloud*. New York: Harper & Row, 1984.

After hiking up and down the mountain looking for a cloud with her mother, a young girl unexpectedly finds one.

BEHAVIOR—Searching
CAMPING
EMOTIONS—Disappointment; Fear; Happiness
MOUNTAIN CLIMBING
OBSERVATION
SENSES
SURPRISES
WEATHER—Clouds; Fog
WORLD REGIONS—Mountain

Ray, Mary Lyn. *Pianna*. Bobbie Henba, illus. San Diego: Harcourt, 1994.

For eighty years Anna lives in the same house, playing the same piano.

BEHAVIOR—Ambitious/Persistent
BIOGRAPHY/LIFE STORIES
ELDERLY
GRAPHIC AND PERFORMING ARTS—Music and musicians
INDIVIDUALITY
LANGUAGE—Names
MEMORIES
NEIGHBORHOODS AND COMMUNITIES—Specific, rural
STRUCTURES—Buildings, houses and other dwellings
TIME—Across time
TRANSPORTATION—Trains
UNITED STATES—Regions, Northeast

Rayner, Mary. *Garth Pig and the Ice-Cream Lady.* New York: Atheneum, 1977.

Garth Pig is kidnapped by Mrs. Wolf, the driver of the ice cream truck, as he tries to buy ice cream for his family.

ANIMALS—Farm, pigs; Large animals, wolves; Personified
BEHAVIOR—Evil
FAMILIES—Parents; Siblings
FAMILY PROBLEMS—Separation
FOOD AND EATING
MOVEMENT/SPEED
PLAY
SAFETY/DANGER
TRANSPORTATION—Bicycles; Trucks

————. *Mr. and Mrs. Pig's Evening Out.* New York: Atheneum, 1976.

Through their resourcefulness, the piglets rescue themselves from their evil baby-sitter.

ANIMALS—Farm, pigs; Large animals, wolves; Personified
BABYSITTING
BEHAVIOR—Evil; Resourceful
FAMILIES—Husbands and wives; Parents; Siblings
SAFETY/DANGER

Reddix, Valerie. *Dragon Kite of the Autumn Moon.* Jean and Mou-Sien Tseng, illus. New York: Lothrop, 1991.

Following a holiday custom in Formosa, each year Grandfather has made a kite for his grandson to fly to carry their misfortune away. Because his grandfather is too ill to make a kite this year, the boy flies the special dragon kite given to him at his birth and creates much magic.

BEHAVIOR—Problem-solving; Sharing
ELDERLY
EMOTIONS—Disappointment; Love; Sadness
FAMILIES—Grandparents
GRAPHIC AND PERFORMING ARTS—Arts and artists
HEALTH—Illness and injury
IMAGINATION—Imaginary creatures, dragons
KITES
LIGHT AND SHADOWS/REFLECTIONS
MAGIC
TIME—Nighttime
TRANSFORMATION
WISHES
WORLD CULTURES/COUNTRIES—Asia, China

Reiss, John. *Colors.* Englewood Cliffs, NJ: Bradbury, 1969.

Eight color concepts are represented by animal, food, insect, and flower images.
COLORS
LANGUAGE—Words

————. *Numbers.* Scarsdale, NY: Bradbury, 1971.

Bright illustrations present counting experiences (1 to 20, groups of 10, 20, and 100, and 1000).
MATHEMATICS—Counting

Renberg, Dalia Hardof. *Hello, Clouds.* Alona Frankel, illus. New York: Harper & Row, 1985.

A small child observes the clouds and imagines amazing adventures, including riding a horse over the rainbow, playing tag, and painting faces on sheep clouds.
IMAGINATION
OBSERVATION
WEATHER—Clouds

Rey, H. A. *Curious George.* Boston: Houghton Mifflin, 1941.

Curious George, a small monkey, has many adventures and eventually ends up in a zoo.
ADVENTURES
ANIMALS—Small creatures, monkeys; Zoo
BALLOONS
BEHAVIOR—Curious
COMMUNICATION—Telephones
OCCUPATIONS
STRUCTURES—Others
TRAVEL
WATER AND BODIES OF WATER—Oceans

Rice, Eve. *City Night.* Peter Sis, illus. New York: Greenwillow, 1987.

The many sights and sounds of a city are portrayed in this lyrical account.
LANGUAGE—Words
NEIGHBORHOODS AND COMMUNITIES—Specific, urban
SENSES—Sight; Sound
SLEEPING
STORIES—Predictable text
TIME—Nighttime

———. *Goodnight, Goodnight.* New York: Greenwillow, 1980.

The greeting "Goodnight" is extended to others by residents of the city and also to the little cat by its mother.
ANIMALS—Pets, cats
NEIGHBORHOODS AND COMMUNITIES—Specific, urban
PLAY
SENSES—Sound
TIME—Nighttime

———. *Peter's Pockets.* Nancy Winslow Parker, illus. New York: Greenwillow, 1989.

Peter, the young boy, has no pockets in his new pants to put his treasures. His mother solves this problem in an interesting, colorful way.
BEHAVIOR—Problem-solving; Resourceful
CLOTHING—Pockets
EMOTIONS—Happiness
EXPLORATION
FAMILIES—Other relatives; Parents
SENSES—Sight; Sound
SEWING
TREASURES
WATER AND BODIES OF WATER—Ponds

————. *Sam Who Never Forgets.* New York: Greenwillow, 1977.

Sam, the zookeeper, not only remembers to feed the animals but also provides each animal with a food that is particularly enjoyed.

ANIMALS—Zoo
BEHAVIOR—Forgetful
COLORS
EMOTIONS—Love; Sadness
FOOD AND EATING
IDENTITY—Relationships
OCCUPATIONS
ZOOS

Ringgold, Faith. *Aunt Harriet's Underground Railroad in the Sky.* New York: Crown, 1992.

One hundred years after Harriet Tubman's first flight to freedom, Cassie Louise Lightfoot enters a fantasy world in which she travels the underground railroad to freedom in Canada.

BEHAVIOR—Hiding; Running away
BIOGRAPHY/LIFE STORIES
FAMILIES—Siblings
FAMILY PROBLEMS—Separation
FLYING—Fantasy
GOALS
HISTORICAL PERIODS—Nineteenth Century, early
IDENTITY—Relationships
IMAGINATION—Imaginary worlds
LOST AND FOUND
MAPS
QUILTS
SAFETY/DANGER
SECRETS
SLAVERY
SURVIVAL
TIME—Across time
TRAVEL
UNITED STATES—Specific cultures, African American
WRITING—Letters

————. *Dinner at Aunt Connie's House.* New York: Hyperion, 1993.

Melody's summer outing with her family at Aunt Connie's house is further enhanced by becoming acquainted with an adopted cousin and discovering twelve talking portraits of famous African American women in the attic. These portraits share their accomplishments with the children and join them at Aunt Connie's table for dinner.

BEHAVIOR—Curious; Sharing
BIOGRAPHY/LIFE STORIES
FAMILIES—Adoption; Family gatherings/Outings
FOOD AND EATING
GRAPHIC AND PERFORMING ARTS—Art and artists
IDENTITY—Gender roles
PLAY

QUILTS
ROOMS—Attics
SLAVERY
SURPRISES
TIME—Across time
TRANSFORMATION
UNITED STATES—Specific cultures, African American

————. *Tar Beach.* New York: Crown, 1991.

Based on a story quilt, a young African American dreams of flying to claim a better life for her family.

ADVENTURES
BEHAVIOR—Pretending; Searching
CONSTRUCTION
EMOTIONS—Happiness
FAMILIES—Parents; Siblings
FLYING—Fantasy
GRAPHIC AND PERFORMING ARTS—Art and artists
HISTORICAL PERIODS—Twentieth Century, early
IDENTITY—Self-worth
IMAGINATION—Imaginary worlds
NEIGHBORHOODS AND COMMUNITIES—Social gatherings; Specific, urban
OCCUPATIONS
POVERTY
QUILTS
STORYTELLING
STRUCTURES—Bridges
TIME—Nighttime; Specific seasons, summer
UNITED STATES—Regions, Northeast; Specific cultures, African American
WISHES

Robbins, Ken. *City/Country.* New York: Viking Kestrel, 1985.

A child describes a trip from the city to the country and to the seashore.

NEIGHBORHOODS AND COMMUNITIES—Specific, rural; Specific, urban
STORIES—Minimal or no text
STORYTELLING
STRUCTURES—Buildings, others
TRAVEL
VACATIONS
WORLD REGIONS—Seashore

Rochelle, Belinda. *When Jo Louis Won the Title.* Larry Johnson, illus. Boston: Houghton Mifflin, 1994.

An African-American girl finds her name embarrassing until her grandfather explains the reason for it.

BEHAVIOR—Apprehensive
EMOTIONS—Embarrassment
FAMILIES—Grandparents
FRIENDSHIP—Relationships
IDENTITY—Self-worth
LANGUAGE—Names
MEMORIES

MOVING
NEIGHBORHOODS AND COMMUNITIES—Specific, urban
SCHOOL EXPERIENCES
SPORTS
STORYTELLING
TIME—Across time
UNITED STATES—Regions, Northeast; Specific cultures, African American

Rogers, Jean. *Runaway Mittens*. Rie Munoz, illus. New York: Greenwillow, 1988.

Pica is always searching for his misplaced mittens, retrieving them from many different places. However, one day he decides to leave them where he finds them—in the box with Pin and her newborn puppies.

ANIMALS—Babies; Pets, dogs
BEHAVIOR—Forgetful; Searching
CLOTHING—Mittens
EVERYDAY EXPERIENCES—Time of day, daytime
FAMILIES—Grandparents
LOST AND FOUND
SEWING
STRUCTURES—Boxes and containers
SURPRISES
TIME—Specific seasons, winter
UNITED STATES—Regions, Alaska; Specific cultures, American Indian/Eskimo
WEATHER—Snow

Rosen, Michael. *We're Going on a Bear Hunt*. Helen Oxenbury, illus. New York: McElderry, 1989.

Members of a family think they are unafraid until they encounter many obstacles on their bear hunt.

ANIMALS—Large animals, bears; Pets, dogs
BEHAVIOR—Courageous; Searching
EMOTIONS—Family gatherings/Outings
FURNITURE—Beds
MOVEMENT/SPEED
SENSES—Sound
STORIES—Predictable text
STRUCTURES—Caves
SURVIVAL
TRAVEL

Rosenberg, Liz. *Monster Mama*. Stephen Gammell, illus. New York: Philomel, 1993.

Even though Patrick Edward's mother is an unusual person, she is loving and loyal to him and helps him cope with bullies.

BEHAVIOR—Bullying; Destructive/Violent; Loyal; Proud; Rude; Sharing
EMOTIONS—Love
FAMILIES—Parents
FOOD AND EATING
FRIENDSHIP—Relationships
IDENTITY—Relationships
IMAGINATION—Imaginary creatures, monsters
INDIVIDUALITY

LANGUAGE—Sayings and special language
MAGIC
MOVEMENT/SPEED
PERSONAL PROBLEMS—Name-calling
SAFETY/DANGER
SENSES—Sight
STRUCTURES—Caves
SURPRISES

Rounds, Glen. *Cowboys*. New York: Holiday House, 1991.

Based on his memories as a child living on a Montana ranch, the author describes everyday activities in the life of a cowboy.

ANIMALS—Farm, horses
COWBOYS/COWGIRLS
IDENTITY—Geographic identity
MEMORIES
OCCUPATIONS
RANCHES
SAFETY/DANGER
TRANSPORTATION—Horses
UNITED STATES—Regions, Western Mountain

———. *Sod Houses on the Great Plains*. New York: Holiday House, 1995.

Pioneers found that sod houses had both advantages and disadvantages.

BEHAVIOR—Resourceful
CONSTRUCTION
HISTORICAL PERIODS—Nineteenth Century, pioneer/westward movement
STRUCTURES—Buildings, houses and other dwellings

Roy, Ron. *Three Ducks Went Wandering*. Paul Galdone, illus. New York: Seabury, 1979.

As the ducklings wander from the farmyard, they encounter many dangers from other animals.

ADVENTURES
ANIMALS—Farm, ducks; Personified
DISABILITIES
ENEMIES
LUCK
SAFETY/DANGER
SURPRISES

Rudolph, Marguerita. *How a Shirt Grew in the Field*. Erika Weihs, illus. New York: Clarion, 1992.

In this story, originally published over one hundred years ago, a young Ukrainian boy, Vasya, observes the cycle of growing flax and the processes of transforming the grain into linen and the linen into an embroidered shirt for him.

BEHAVIOR—Patient
CLOTHING—Others
EMOTIONS—Happiness
FAMILIES—Parents; Siblings
HISTORICAL PERIODS—Nineteenth Century, late

NEIGHBORHOODS AND COMMUNITIES—Specific, rural
PLANTS—Cycles
SEWING
TIME—Cycles, seasons
WEAVING
WISHES
WORLD/CONTINENTS—Cultures/Countries—Europe—Central/Eastern

Rydell, Katy. *Wind Says Good Night*. David Jorgensen, illus. Boston: Houghton Mifflin, 1994.

In this cumulative story, the actions of the wind curtails the influences of the night, weather, and animals that are distracting the young child from falling asleep.

ANIMALS—Small creatures
COLORS
EVERYDAY EXPERIENCES—Time of day, bedtime
GRAPHIC AND PERFORMING ARTS—Music and musicians
ROOMS—Bedrooms
SENSES
SLEEPING
STORIES—Predictable text
TIME—Nighttime
WEATHER—Clouds; Rain; Wind

Ryder, Joanne. *The Bear on the Moon*. Carol Lacey, illus. New York: Morrow, 1991.

In the beginning of time, a polar bear created the Arctic lands by digging snow and ice on the moon and throwing it to earth. Young bears observing the moon today believe she continues the practice.

ANIMALS—Fantasy; Large animals, bears
ASTRONOMY—Moon
BEHAVIOR—Curious
IMAGINATION—Imaginary worlds
TIME—Cycles, months of the year
TRANSFORMATION
WATER AND BODIES OF WATER—Oceans
WORLD CULTURES/COUNTRIES—Polar regions

———. *Catching the Wind*. Michael Rothman, illus. New York: Morrow, 1989.

Readers are invited to imagine that for one day they are a Canadian goose flying south with the rest of the flock.

ANIMALS—Birds, wild geese; Cycles
FLYING—Fantasy
OBSERVATION
SENSES—Sight; Sound
TIME—Specific seasons, fall
TRANSFORMATION

———. *Chipmunk Song*. Lynne Cherry, illus. New York: Dutton, 1987.

A child reduced to the size of a chipmunk describes what it is like living as this small creature.

ANIMALS—Cycles; Small creatures, others

IMAGINATION
OBSERVATION
SENSES—Sight; Sound; Touch
STRUCTURES—Tunnels
TIME—Cycles, seasons
TRANSFORMATION

————. *Dancers in the Garden.* Judith Lopez, illus. San Francisco: Sierra Club, 1992.

A tiny hummingbird in San Francisco's Golden Gate Park dances his way through the day meeting a female hummingbird along the way.

ANIMALS—Birds; Habitats, nests
MOVEMENT/SPEED
NEIGHBORHOODS AND COMMUNITIES—Parks
OBSERVATION
TIME—Cycles, day and night

————. *Fireflies.* Don Bolognese, illus. New York: Harper & Row, 1977.

The life cycle of a firefly is described.

ANIMALS—Cycles; Habitats; Small creatures, Insects

————. *The Goodbye Walk.* Deborah Haeffele, illus. New York: Lodestar, 1993.

A young girl describes her thoughts and feelings as she takes one last walk before leaving a special summer vacation spot.

MEMORIES
OBSERVATION
SECRETS
TIME—Specific seasons, summer
VACATIONS

————. *Hello, Tree!* Michael Hays, illus. New York: Lodestar, 1991.

A young girl describes many ways you can associate with a tree, especially if you consider it a special friend.

CHANGES
EVERYDAY EXPERIENCES—Time of day, daytime
FRIENDSHIP—Relationships
IDENTITY—Relationships
NEIGHBORHOODS AND COMMUNITIES—General
OBSERVATION
PLANTS—Cycles; Trees
TIME—Cycles, seasons

————. *A House by the Sea.* Melissa Sweet, illus. New York: Morrow, 1994.

A lyrical text portrays children's play experiences, real and imagined, at the seashore.

ANIMALS—Marine life
IMAGINATION
PLAY
SAND
STORIES—Predictable text
WATER AND BODIES OF WATER—Oceans
WORLD REGIONS—Seashore

————. *Lizard in the Sun.* Michael Rothman, illus. New York: Morrow, 1990.

A lizard's characteristics are described by a child who spends a day as an American chameleon.

ANIMALS—Reptiles, lizards/chameleons
COLORS
IMAGINATION
OBSERVATION
SENSES
TIME—Cycles, day and night
TRANSFORMATION

————. *Mockingbird Morning.* Dennis Nolan, illus. New York: Four Winds, 1989.

The reader accompanies a young girl on a walk to explore nature in the early morning.

ANIMALS—Birds; Habitats; Small creatures
IMAGINATION
OBSERVATION
SENSES—Sight; Sound
TIME—Daytime

————. *My Father's Hands.* Mark Graham, illus. New York: Morrow, 1994.

A child's father helps her discover and appreciate small creatures in his garden.

ANIMALS—Small creatures
BODY—Parts of body
ECOLOGY/ENVIRONMENTAL PROBLEMS
EVERYDAY EXPERIENCES—Time of day, daytime
FAMILIES—Parents
GARDENS
IDENTITY—Relationships
SAFETY/DANGER
TREASURES

————. *The Night Flight.* Amy Schwartz, illus. New York: Four Winds, 1985.

Anna plays in the park one day. That night she dreams of flying to the park and finding it transformed into a jungle paradise.

ANIMALS—Fantasy; Large animals; Marine life, fishes
DREAMS
FAMILIES—Parents
FLYING—Fantasy
NEIGHBORHOODS AND COMMUNITIES—Parks; Specific, urban
SLEEPING
STATUES
TIME—Nighttime
TRANSFORMATION
UNITED STATES—Regions, Northeast

————. *One Small Fish.* Carol Schwartz, illus. New York: Morrow, 1993.

A girl sitting in a school science class imagines different kinds of marine life moving about the classroom.

ANIMALS—Fantasy; Marine life; Marine life, aquariums
IMAGINATION

variant.4

MOVEMENT/SPEED
SCHOOL EXPERIENCES
SENSES

———. *Sea Elf.* Michael Rothman, illus. New York: Morrow, 1993.

The reader is transformed into a young sea otter and experiences its life for a day in a cove.

ANIMALS—Habitats; Marine life, others
IMAGINATION
TIME—Cycles, day and night
TRANSFORMATION
WATER AND BODIES OF WATER—Oceans

———. *The Snail's Spell.* Lynne Cherry, illus. New York: F. Warne, 1982.

The audience is guided to experience the life of a snail in its garden habitat.

ANIMALS—Habitats; Small creatures, others
GARDENS
IMAGINATION
MATHEMATICS—Size
SENSES

———. *The Spiders Dance.* Robert J. Blake, illus. New York: Harper & Row, 1981.

The life cycle of a spider is portrayed.

ANIMALS—Cycles; Habitats, webs; Small creatures, spiders

———. *Step into the Night.* Dennis Nolan, illus. New York: Four Winds, 1988.

As night falls, a young girl steps outside her home and observes the natural world, imagining what it would be like to be a mouse, a firefly, and several other night creatures.

ANIMALS—Small creatures
IMAGINATION
OBSERVATION
SENSES—Sight; Sound
TIME—Nighttime
TRANSFORMATION

———. *Under the Moon.* Cheryl Harness, illus. New York: Random House, 1989.

Mama Mouse instructs her child to locate home through special sensory experiences.

ANIMALS—Habitats; Personified; Small creatures, mice
ASTRONOMY—Moon
SENSES

———. *Under Your Feet.* Dennis Nolan, illus. New York: Four Winds, 1990.

The habits of various creatures living under the earth's surface are explored throughout the year.

ANIMALS—Marine life, Fishes; Small creatures
IDENTITY—Relationships
IMAGINATION
OBSERVATION
SENSES
TIME—Cycles, seasons

————. *A Wet and Sandy Day*. Donald Carrick, illus. New York: Harper & Row, 1977.

A young girl discovers that one can have fun at the beach on a rainy day.
EMOTIONS—Happiness
EVERYDAY EXPERIENCES—Time of day, daytime
FAMILIES—Parents
PLAY
SAND
SENSES
STRUCTURES—Buildings, others
TIME—Specific seasons, summer
WATER AND BODIES OF WATER—Oceans
WEATHER—Rain
WORLD REGIONS—Seashore

————. *When the Woods Hum*. Catherine Stock, illus. New York: Morrow, 1991.

Jenny and her father share the wondrous sounds made by the cicadas at the end of their seventeen-year life cycle. When the cicadas appear the next time, both Jenny and her son return for the event.
ANIMALS—Cycles; Habitats; Small creatures, insects
ECOLOGY/ENVIRONMENTAL PROBLEMS
FAMILIES—Grandparents; Parents
SENSES—Sound
TIME—Across time
TIME—Specific seasons, spring; Specific seasons, summer

————. *Where Butterflies Grow*. Lynne Cherry, illus. New York: Lodestar, 1989.

Readers are invited to imagine that they are a tiny egg, growing and changing and eventually becoming a butterfly.
ANIMALS—Cycles; Eggs; Habitats; Small creatures, butterflies/moths/caterpillars
CHANGES
GARDENS
IMAGINATION
MOVEMENT/SPEED
OBSERVATION
SENSES

————. *White Bear, Ice Bear*. Michael Rothman, illus. New York: Morrow, 1989.

A boy transformed into a polar bear for one day learns what the animal's life is like.
ADVENTURES
ANIMALS—Large animals, bears
IMAGINATION
SENSES—Sight; Smell and taste; Sound; Touch
TIME—Cycles, day and night; Specified seasons, winter
TRANSFORMATION
WORLD CULTURES/COUNTRIES, Polar regions

————. *Winter Whale*. Michael Rothman, illus. New York: Morrow, 1991.

A boy spends one day transformed into a humpback whale wintering in the warm tropical waters.

ADVENTURES
ANIMALS—Marine life, whales
IMAGINATION
OBSERVATION
SENSES—Sight; Sound
TIME—Cycles, day and night; Specific seasons, summer
TRANSFORMATION
UNITED STATES—Regions, Hawaii
WATER AND BODIES OF WATER—Oceans

Rylant, Cynthia. *All I See*. Peter Catalanotto, illus. New York: Orchard, 1988.

A boy paints with an artist and discovers that painting can involve expressing inner worlds as well as representing reality.

BEHAVIOR—Sharing; Shy
FRIENDSHIP—Relationships
GIFTS
GRAPHIC AND PERFORMING ARTS—Art and artists; Music and musicians
IDENTITY—Self-worth
IMAGINATION
LIGHT AND SHADOWS/REFLECTIONS
NEIGHBORHOODS AND COMMUNITIES—Specific, rural
SENSES—Sight
SURPRISES
TIME—Daytime
WATER AND BODIES OF WATER—Lakes
WRITING—Others

———. *An Angel for Solomon Singer*. Peter Catalanotto, illus. New York: Orchard, 1992.

A lonely man wanders the streets of New York City wishing for a fuller life and some of the cherished elements of his rural boyhood home. When he meets Angel, the waiter at the Westway Café, he finds the warmth of friendship.

ANIMALS—Pets, cats
BEHAVIOR—Searching
CHANGES
DREAMS
EMOTIONS—Happiness; Loneliness
FOOD AND EATING
FRIENDSHIP—Relationships
IDENTITY—Geographic identity
NEIGHBORHOODS AND COMMUNITIES—Specific, rural; Specific, urban
POVERTY
STRUCTURES—Others
UNITED STATES—Regions, Northeast
WISHES

———. *Appalachia: The Voices of Sleeping Birds*. Barry Moser, illus. San Diego: Harcourt, 1991.

The spirit of Appalachia and its people are portrayed.

BEHAVIOR—Loyal
IDENTITY—Geographic identity
NEIGHBORHOODS AND COMMUNITIES—Specific, rural

OCCUPATIONS
UNITED STATES—Regions, Appalachia

————. *Miss Maggie.* Thomas Di Grazia, illus. New York: Dutton, 1983.

Nat's fear of the elderly neighbor Miss Maggie evolves into friendship after he helps her in a personal crisis.

ANIMALS—Pets, others; Reptiles, snakes
BEHAVIOR—Apprehensive; Responsible
ELDERLY
EMOTIONS—Fear
FRIENDSHIP—Relationships
HEALTH—Illness and injury
NEIGHBORHOODS AND COMMUNITIES—Specific, rural
POVERTY
SAFETY/DANGER
STRUCTURES—Buildings, houses and other dwellings
TIME—Specific seasons, winter

————. *Night in the Country.* Mary Szilagyi, illus. New York: Bradbury, 1986.

The sights and sounds of nighttime in the country are described.

EVERYDAY EXPERIENCES—Nighttime
FARMS
NEIGHBORHOODS AND COMMUNITIES—Specific, rural
SENSES—Sight; Sound
TIME—Cycles, day and night; Nighttime

————. *The Relative Came.* Stephen Gammell, illus. New York: Bradbury, 1985.

A family travels to Virginia for an extended reunion filled with much warmth and activity.

BEHAVIOR—Excited
EMOTIONS—Happiness; Love
FAMILIES—Family gatherings/Outings; Other relatives
FOOD AND EATING
GOALS
NEIGHBORHOODS AND COMMUNITIES—Specific, rural
OBSERVATION
SENSES—Sight; Smell and taste; Sound; Touch
TIME—Specific seasons, summer
TRANSPORTATION—Cars
TRAVEL
UNITED STATES—Regions, Appalachia
VACATIONS
WORLD REGIONS—Mountain

————. *When I Was Young in the Mountains.* Diane Goode, illus. New York: Dutton, 1982.

The pleasures of a childhood in the mountains are described.

EMOTIONS—Happiness; Love
FAMILIES—Grandparents
IDENTITY—Geographic identity
MEMORIES
NEIGHBORHOODS AND COMMUNITIES—Specific, rural

OCCUPATIONS
POVERTY
SENSES—Sound
UNITED STATES—Regions, Appalachia
WORLD REGIONS—Mountain

Sadler, Marilyn. *Alistair in Outer Space*. Roger Bollen, illus. New York: Prentice-Hall, 1984.

Throughout his fantastic space journey with outer space creatures, Alistair pursues his goal of returning his library books on time. He is relieved to return to earth, only to receive a surprise.
ADVENTURES
BEHAVIOR—Responsible
EMOTIONS—Fear
FLYING—Fantasy
GOALS
HUMOR
IMAGINATION—Imaginary creatures
READING
SPACE
STRUCTURES—Buildings, libraries
SURPRISES
TRAVEL
WORLD CULTURES/COUNTRIES—Polar regions

———. *Alistair's Elephant*. Roer Bollen, illus. Englewood Cliffs, NJ: Prentice-Hall, 1983.

Alistair's life changes greatly when an elephant follows him home from the zoo.
ANIMALS—Large animals, elephants; Zoo
BEHAVIOR—Ambitious/Persistent; Responsible
EMOTIONS—Sadness
HUMOR
OCCUPATIONS
SCHOOL EXPERIENCES
SURPRISES
ZOOS

San Souci, Robert. *Kate Shelley: Bound for Legend*. Max Ginsburg, illus. New York: Dial, 1995.

A girl crawls across a high railroad bridge during a heavy rainstorm to warn oncoming trains that another nearby bridge has collapsed.
ADVENTURES
BEHAVIOR—Courageous; Heroic
DISASTERS
HEALTH—Illness and injury
HISTORICAL PERIODS—Nineteenth Century, late
IDENTITY—Gender roles
MAPS
NEIGHBORHOODS AND COMMUNITIES—Specific, rural

SAFETY/DANGER
STRUCTURES—Bridges
SURVIVAL
TIME—Nighttime
TRANSPORTATION—Trains
UNITED STATES—Regions, Midwest
WATER AND BODIES OF WATER—Floods
WEATHER—Storms

Sara. *Across Town*. New York: Orchard, 1991.

As a man moves through the dark city, he is befriended by a cat.

ADVENTURES
ANIMALS—Pets, cats
EMOTIONS—Fear
FRIENDSHIP—Relationships
MOVEMENT/SPEED
NEIGHBORHOODS AND COMMUNITIES—Specific, urban
OBSERVATION
STORIES—Minimal or no text
TIME—Nighttime

Say, Allen. *The Bicycle Man*. Boston: Houghton Mifflin, 1982.

Two American soldiers visit a rural Japanese school shortly after World War II and win the friendship of the children.

BEHAVIOR—Apprehensive; Excited; Sharing; Shy
EMOTIONS—Fear; Happiness
GAMES/PUZZLES/TRICKS
HISTORICAL PERIODS—Twentieth Century, World War II
IDENTITY—Relationships
MEMORIES
SCHOOL EXPERIENCES
TRANSPORTATION—Bicycles
TRAVEL
WAR
WORLD CULTURES/COUNTRIES—Asia, Japan; Cross cultures

———. *El Chino*. Boston: Houghton Mifflin, 1990.

In this biography of Bill Wong, a Chinese American achieves his goal of becoming a famous bullfighter in Spain.

ADVENTURES
BEHAVIOR—Ambitious/Persistent; Competitive; Courageous
BIOGRAPHY/LIFE STORIES
GOALS
IDENTITY—Self-Worth
OCCUPATIONS
SPORTS
TRAVEL
UNITED STATES—Specific cultures, Asian American
WORLD CULTURES/COUNTRIES—Europe, Southern

————. *Grandfather's Journey*. Boston: Houghton Mifflin, 1993.

The author relates his grandfather's story as a Japanese American and then compares this story to his own.

ADVENTURES
BEHAVIOR—Searching
BIOGRAPHY/LIFE STORIES
EMOTIONS—Loneliness
FAMILIES—Grandparents
IDENTITY—Relationships
IMMIGRANTS/REFUGEES
MOVING
TIME—Across time
TRAVEL
WAR
WORLD CULTURES/COUNTRIES—Asia, Japan

————. *Stranger in the Mirror*. Boston: Houghton Mifflin, 1995.

One morning a young Asian-American boy finds that his face has the appearance of an elderly man.

BEHAVIOR—Apprehensive; Curious; Searching; Teasing
BODY—Parts of body
ELDERLY
EMOTIONS—Sadness
FAMILIES—Grandparents; Parents; Siblings
FAMILY PROBLEMS—Separation
HEALTH—Illness and injury
LIGHT AND SHADOWS/REFLECTIONS
MOVEMENT/SPEED
MYSTERY
OCCUPATIONS
SCHOOL EXPERIENCES
SENSES—Sight
SURPRISES
TRANSFORMATION
UNITED STATES—Specific cultures, Asian American
WISHES

————. *Tree of Cranes*. Boston: Houghton Mifflin, 1991.

A Japanese boy's mother shares memories of Christmas from her birthplace in the United States by decorating a tree with origami cranes and candles and wishing for peace.

BEHAVIOR—Disobedient; Sharing
FAMILIES—Parents
GIFTS
GRAPHIC AND PERFORMING ARTS—Art and artists
HEALTH—Illness and injury
HOLIDAYS AND CELEBRATIONS—Christmas
KITES
LIGHT AND SHADOWS/REFLECTIONS
MATHEMATICS—Numbers, ideas
MEMORIES

PEACE
PLANTS—Trees
SURPRISES
TIME—Specific seasons, winter
UNITED STATES—Regions, West Coast; Specific Cultures, Asian American
WEATHER—Snow
WISHES
WORLD CULTURE/COUNTRIES—Asia, Japan; Cross cultures

Scamell, Ragnhild. *Solo Plus One*. Elizabeth Martland, illus. Boston: Little, Brown, 1992.

Solo, a destructive cat, changes his ways after his encounter with a duckling who mistakenly bonds with him as his mother.

ANIMALS—Eggs; Farm, ducks; Pets, cats
BEHAVIOR—Destructive/Violent; Responsible
BIRTH
CHANGES
FAMILIES—Adoption; Parents
FOOD AND EATING
SURPRISES

Scheer, Julian, and Marvin Bileck. *Rain Makes Applesauce*. New York: Holiday House, 1964.

A repetitive nonsense verse is loosely structured on the life cycle of an apple tree, which bears fruit for applesauce.

APPLES
FOOD AND EATING
HUMOR
LANGUAGE—Sayings and special language
PLANTS—Cycles
STORIES—Predictable text

Schertle, Alice. *Witch Hazel*. Margot Tomes, illus. New York: HarperCollins, 1991.

A young boy watches as a scarecrow made from a witch hazel branch to guard his pumpkin is transformed into a living being. She tosses the pumpkin into the sky, and it becomes a spectacular harvest moon.

ASTRONOMY—Moon
BEHAVIOR—Hiding; Patient
CONSTRUCTION
EVERYDAY EXPERIENCES—Time of day, nighttime
FAIRS
FAMILIES—Siblings
GARDENS
MAGIC
MYSTERY
NEIGHBORHOODS AND COMMUNITIES—Specific, rural
PLANTS—Cycles; Seeds; Trees
PUMPKINS
SCARECROWS
SECRETS
STRUCTURES—Buildings, cabins
TIME—Cycles, seasons; Specific seasons, fall
TRANSFORMATION

Schoenherr, John. *The Barn.* Boston: Little Brown, 1968.

A skunk searches for food and avoids his enemy, the owl.

ANIMALS—Birds; Small creatures, others
ENEMIES
FARMS
NEIGHBORHOODS AND COMMUNITIES—Specific, rural
SAFETY/DANGER
SENSES—Smell and taste
STRUCTURES—Buildings, barns
SURVIVAL
TIME—Cycles, day and night

Schroeder, Alan. *Carolina Shout!* Bernie Fuchs, illus. New York: Dial, 1995.

Delia describes the sights and sounds of pre-World War II Charleston, including
the street cries of the Waffle Man, the Charcoal Man, and other vendors.

COMMUNICATION
FAMILIES—Siblings
GRAPHIC AND PERFORMING ARTS—Music and musicians
HISTORICAL PERIODS—Twentieth Century, early
IDENTITY—Geographic identity
LANGUAGE—Sayings and special language
NEIGHBORHOODS AND COMMUNITIES—Specific, urban
OBSERVATION
OCCUPATIONS
SENSES—Sound
SHOPPING/MARKETING
UNITED STATES—Regions, South; Specific cultures, African American

———. *Ragtime Tumpie.* Bernie Fuchs, illus. Boston: Little, Brown, 1989.

As a young girl, Josephine Baker danced to ragtime music, popular in the early
1900s, and dreamed of escaping poverty and becoming a famous dancer.

BEHAVIOR—Ambitious/Persistent; Competitive
BIOGRAPHY/LIFE STORIES
EMOTIONS—Happiness
FAMILY PROBLEMS—Separation
GOALS
GRAPHIC AND PERFORMING ARTS—Dance and dancers
HISTORICAL PERIODS—Twentieth Century, early
IDENTITY—Self-worth
MONEY
NEIGHBORHOODS AND COMMUNITIES—Specific, urban
POVERTY
SENSES—Sound
UNITED STATES—Regions, Midwest; Specific cultures, African American

Schwartz, Amy. *Annabelle Swift, Kindergartner.* New York: Orchard, 1988.

Annabelle's first day in kindergarten is a success even though some of her sister's
training for the big day does not work out so well.

BEHAVIOR—Sharing
FAMILIES—Siblings
LANGUAGE—Names
SCHOOL REFERENCES

————. *Bea and Mr. Jones.* Scarsdale, NY: Bradbury, 1982.

Bea, a kindergartner, and her father, who works in advertising, switch roles and find much success.

CHANGES
EVERYDAY EXPERIENCES—Time of day, daytime
FAMILIES—Parents
HUMOR
IDENTITY—Self-worth
OCCUPATIONS
SCHOOL EXPERIENCES

————. *Her Majesty, Aunt Essie.* Scarsdale, NY: Bradbury, 1984.

After boasting to her skeptical friend that her bossy aunt is a queen, Ruthie finally finds some proof.

BEHAVIOR—Boastful; Bossy; Problem-solving; Searching
CLOTHING
FAMILIES—Other relatives
FRIENDSHIP—Relationships
HEALTH—Bathing
IDENTITY—Relationships
IMAGINATION
ROYALTY
SENSES—Sight

————. *Oma and Bobo.* New York: Bradbury, 1987.

Bobo, the dog, not only wins a blue ribbon at obedience school but also the heart of Alice's grandmother.

ANIMALS—pets, dogs
BEHAVIOR—Obedient
FAMILIES—Grandparents

Schwartz, David M. *How Much Is a Million?* Steven Kellogg, illus. New York: Lothrop, 1985.

An attempt is made to conceptualize huge numbers—a million, a billion, and a trillion.

MATHEMATICS—Measurement, length; Numbers, ideas

————. *If You Made a Million.* Steven Kellogg, illus. New York: Lothrop, 1989.

Forms of money and its functions are described.

MATHEMATICS—Numbers, processes
MONEY

Scott, Ann Herbert. *On Mother's Lap.* Glo Coalson, illus. New York: Clarion, 1992.

A Young Eskimo boy's place, rocking on his mother's lap, is threatened by his new sibling.

BEHAVIOR—Sharing
EMOTIONS—Jealousy; Love
FAMILIES—Parents
FAMILY PROBLEMS—New siblings
FURNITURE—Chairs

IDENTITY—Relationships
MATHEMATICS—Measurement, mass
MOVEMENT/SPEED
TOYS
UNITED STATES—Specific cultures, American Indian/Eskimo

————. *Sam.* Symeon Shimin, illus. New York: McGraw-Hill, 1967.

Sam is too small to do many of the activities that other family members are doing. Then his mother finds a kitchen job that he can do.

BEHAVIOR—Problem-solving; Searching
EMOTIONS—Sadness
FAMILIES—Parents; Siblings
FOOD AND EATING
IDENTITY—Self-worth
PLAY
UNITED STATES—Specific cultures, African American

Sendak, Maurice. *Where the Wild Things Are.* New York: Harper & Row, 1963.

A rowdy little boy is sent to bed without his supper. A forest grows in his room, and he sails off to the land of the wild things, where he becomes king and instigator of a wild rumpus. Then he becomes lonely, he returns home to find a hot supper waiting for him.

BEHAVIOR—Bossy; Fighting/Quarreling; Mischievous; Pretending
CLOTHING—Costumes
DREAMS
EMOTIONS—Anger; Loneliness; Love
FAMILIES—Parents
FOOD AND EATING
GRAPHIC AND PERFORMING ARTS—Dance and dancers
IMAGINATION—Imaginary creatures, monsters; Imaginary worlds
PERSONAL PROBLEMS—Running Away
ROYALTY
SENSES—Sound
TRANSPORTATION—Boats
TRAVEL

Serfozo, Mary. *Rain Talk.* Keiko Narahashi, illus. New York: McElderry, 1990.

A young girl experiences the different sounds the rain makes.

SENSES—Sound
TIME—Cycles, day and night
WEATHER—Rain

Seuss, Dr. *And To Think That I Saw It On Mulberry Street.* New York: Vanguard, 1937.

Through his imagination, a boy creates remarkable experiences on his way home from school.

FAMILIES—Parents
IMAGINATION—Imaginary creatures
NEIGHBORHOODS AND COMMUNITIES—General
SENSES—Sight
STORIES—Predictable text

———. *The Cat in the Hat*. New York: Random House, 1957.

Two children's rainy day is enlivened by the Cat in the Hat's extraordinary games and tricks.

BEHAVIOR—Destructive/Violent
GAMES/PUZZLES/TRICKS
HUMOR
IMAGINATION—Imaginary creatures
KITES
MAGIC
PLAY
STORIES—Predictable text
WEATHER—Rain
WISHES

———. *Horton Hatches the Egg*. New York: Random House, 1940.

Horton, the elephant, faithfully sits on a lazy bird's egg through all kinds of danger. He is rewarded for his efforts when an elephant bird hatches from the egg.

ANIMALS—Birds; Eggs; Habitats, nests; Large animals, elephants; Personified
BEHAVIOR—Lazy; Loyal; Teasing
IDENTITY—Relationships
IMAGINATION—Imaginary creatures, others
MATHEMATICS—Measurement, mass
PERSONAL PROBLEMS—Running away
SAFETY/DANGER
STRUCTURES—Others
VACATIONS

———. *How the Grinch Stole Christmas*. New York: Random House, 1957.

When the Grinch tries to put a stop to the villagers' Christmas celebration in Who-ville, he learns that the holiday spirit involves more than receiving presents.

BEHAVIOR—Stealing
GIFTS
HOLIDAYS AND CELEBRATIONS—Christmas
IMAGINATION—Imaginary creatures, others
NEIGHBORS AND COMMUNITIES—General

———. *The Lorax*. New York: Random House, 1971.

Despite the Lorax's warnings, the Once-lers continue to cut down trees.
ECOLOGY/ENVIRONMENTAL PROBLEMS
PLANTS—Trees

Sharmat, Marjorie Weinman. *The Best Valentine in the World*. Lilian Obligado, illus. New York: Holiday House, 1982.

Having worked long and hard to create a beautiful valentine for Florette, Ferdinand is disappointed to learn that she has forgotten the special day. However, all ends well.

ANIMALS—Large animals, foxes; Personified
BEHAVIOR—Boastful; Forgetful
COMMUNICATION—Telephones
EMOTIONS—Anger; Disappointment; Love

FRIENDSHIP—Relationships
GRAPHIC AND PERFORMING ARTS—Art and artists
HOLIDAYS AND CELEBRATIONS—Valentine's
HUMOR
LANGUAGE—Names
LOST AND FOUND
SURPRISES
TIME—Clocks and other time-telling methods; Specific seasons, winter

————. *Gila Monsters Meet You at the Airport*. Byron Barton, illus. New York: Macmillan, 1980.

Preconceived notions about a new home can make moving difficult.

ANIMALS—Marine life, alligators; Reptiles, lizards/chameleons
BEHAVIOR—Apprehensive
MOVING
NEIGHBORHOODS AND COMMUNITIES—Specific, urban
PERSONAL PROBLEMS—Fearing to try something new
RANCHES
TRANSPORTATION—Airplanes
TRAVEL
UNITED STATES—Regions, Middle Atlantic; Regions, West Coast
WRITING—Letters

Sharmat, Mitchell. *Gregory, the Terrible Eater*. Jose Aruego and Ariane Dewey, illus. New York: Four Winds, 1980.

Gregory, the young goat, likes people food but learns to consume food that goats ordinarily eat.

ANIMALS—Farm, goats
FAMILIES—Parents
FOOD AND EATING
HEALTH—Health care
HUMOR
INDIVIDUALITY

Shaw, Nancy. *Sheep in a Jeep*. Margot Apple, illus. Boston: Houghton Mifflin, 1986.

A group of sheep riding in a jeep have many difficulties.

ADVENTURES
ANIMALS—Farm, sheep; Personified
MOVEMENT/SPEED
SENSES—Sound
STORIES—Predictable text
TRANSPORTATION—Other
TRAVEL

Shea, Pegi Deitz. *The Whispering Cloth: A Refugee's Story*. Anita Riggio and You Yang, illus. Honesdale, PA: Boyds Mills, 1995.

A young girl in a refugee camp in Thailand perfects her stitchery and finds a story to embroider for a story cloth.

AESTHETIC APPRECIATION
BEHAVIOR—Ambitious/Persistent; Crying; Patient

DEATH
EMOTIONS—Happiness; Loneliness; Sadness
ENEMIES
FAMILIES—Grandparents; Parents
FAMILY PROBLEMS—Separation
GRAPHIC AND PERFORMING ARTS—Art and artists
IDENTITY—Relationships
IMMIGRANTS/REFUGEES
LANGUAGE—Sayings and special language
MAPS
MEMORIES
NEIGHBORHOODS AND COMMUNITIES—Social gatherings
SAFETY/DANGER
SENSES—Touches
SEWING
STORYTELLING
SURVIVAL
WAR
WORLD CULTURES/COUNTRIES—Asia, other

Shecter, Ben. *Conrad's Castle*. New York: Harper & Row, 1967.

A small boy achieves his goal. He builds a castle in the air despite the distractions created by other children and his own brief doubts.

CONSTRUCTION
GOALS
IDENTITY—Self-worth
IMAGINATION—Imaginary worlds
STRUCTURES—Buildings, castles/palaces

Shefelman, Janice Jordan. *A Peddler's Dream*. Tom Shefelman, illus. Boston: Houghton Mifflin, 1992.

A young Lebanese immigrant, through persistent hard work, achieves his goals of bringing his sweetheart to the United States and owning his own store.

BEHAVIOR—Ambitious/Persistent; Courageous
BIOGRAPHY/LIFE STORIES
EMOTIONS—Disappointment; Love
FAMILIES—Husbands and wives
GOALS
HISTORICAL PERIODS—Twentieth Century, early
IDENTITY—Self-worth
IMMIGRANTS/REFUGEES
MEMORIES
OCCUPATIONS
SAFETY/DANGER
STRUCTURES—Buildings, stores
TRAVEL

Shelby, Anne. *Potluck*. Irene Trivas, illus. New York: Orchard, 1991.

Two girls invite friends whose names and contributions to the potluck meal represent letters of the alphabet.

BEHAVIOR—Sharing
FOOD AND EATING

FRIENDSHIP—Relationships
LANGUAGE—Alphabet
NEIGHBORHOODS AND COMMUNITIES—Social gatherings

Sheldon, Dyan. *Under the Moon.* Gary Blythe, illus. New York: Dial, 1994.

After Jenny finds an arrowhead in her backyard, she images an era hundreds of years ago. In her dreams that night, she meets the American Indian to whom the arrowhead once belonged and learns of the natural beauty of this urban place in early times.

BEHAVIOR—Cooperative; Curious; Pretending; Searching
DREAMS
HISTORICAL PERIODS—Across time; Prehistoric
IDENTITY—Geographic identity
IMAGINATION
ROCKS AND MINERALS
SENSES
UNITED STATES—Specific cultures, American Indian/Eskimo

Shepperson, Rob. *The Sandman.* New York: Farrar, 1989.

The Sandman comes at Jay's bedtime and provides him with much fun and magic.

ASTRONOMY—Sun
BEHAVIOR—Hiding
EVERYDAY EXPERIENCES—Time of day, awakening for the day; Time of day, bedtime
IMAGINATION—Imaginary creatures, others; Imaginary worlds
MAGIC
SAND
SLEEPING
TIME—Nighttime

Shulevitz, Peter. *Dawn.* New York: Farrar, 1974.

The morning gradually dawns on a man and his grandson camping in the mountains.

CAMPING
EVERYDAY EXPERIENCES—Time of day, awakening for the day
FAMILIES—Grandparents
SENSES—Sight; Sound
TIME—Daytime
VACATIONS

Shulevitz, Uri. *Rain Rain Rivers.* New York: Farrar, 1969.

A young girl hears the rain falling outside her window and thinks about its effect on nature. She looks forward to playing in the puddles it leaves.

NEIGHBORHOODS AND COMMUNITIES—General
PLAY
SENSES—Sight; Sound
WATER AND BODIES OF WATER—Oceans; Rivers
WEATHER—Rain

Silverman, Erica. *Big Pumpkin.* S. D. Schindler, illus. New York: Macmillan, 1992.

A witch grows a pumpkin so large that she must seek the help of others to pick it.

BEHAVIOR—Cooperative; Sharing

EVERYDAY EXPERIENCES—Time of day, nighttime
FOOD AND EATING
GOALS
HOLIDAYS AND CELEBRATIONS—Halloween
IMAGINATION—Imaginary creatures, ghosts; Imaginary creatures, monsters; Imaginary
    creatures, witches; Imaginary creatures, others
PLANTS—Cycles
PUMPKINS

Sis, Peter. *Follow the Dream.* New York: Knopf, 1991.

Christopher Columbus pursues his dream to find a new trade route to the Orient.
BEHAVIOR—Courageous
DREAMS
EXPLORATION
GOALS
HISTORICAL PERIODS—Exploration of the New World
MAPS
ROYALTY
TRAVEL
WRITING—Diaries

———. *Komodo!* New York: Greenwillow, 1993.

A boy who is an avid fan of dragons encounters a real one on a family trip to the
Indonesian island of Komodo.
FAMILIES—Parents
IMAGINATION—Imaginary creatures, dragons
ISLANDS
MAPS
TRAVEL
VACATIONS
WORLD CULTURES/COUNTRIES—Asia, others

———. *An Ocean World.* New York: Greenwillow, 1992.

In this wordless book, a whale who has lived in captivity since infancy is returned
to the ocean. She encounters many images that resemble whales before she finds
her kind.
ANIMALS—Marine life, whales; Personified
BEHAVIOR—Searching
ECOLOGY/ENVIRONMENTAL PROBLEMS
EMOTIONS—Love
EXPLORATION
IDENTITY—Relationships
OBSERVATION
STORIES—Minimal or no text
WATER AND BODIES OF WATER—Oceans

———. *A Small, Tall Tale from the Far, Far North.* New York: Knopf, 1993.

Jan Welzl, a Czech explorer traveling to the Arctic in the 1890s, becomes a friend
of the Eskimos. He finds a way to discourage foreigners from coming to search for
gold.
ADVENTURES
BEHAVIOR—Courageous; Tricking

BIOGRAPHY/LIFE STORIES
EXPLORATION
FRIENDSHIP—Relationships
HISTORICAL PERIODS—Nineteenth Century, late
IDENTITY—Geographic identity
MAPS
ROCKS AND MINERALS
SAFETY/DANGER
STORYTELLING
STRANGERS
SURVIVAL
TRAVEL
UNITED STATES—Cross cultural; Regions, Northwest/Alaska; Specific cultures, American Indian/Eskimo
WORLD CULTURES/COUNTRIES—Europe, Central/Eastern; Polar regions

————. *Waving: A Counting Book.* New York: Greenwillow, 1988.

In this counting book (1 to 15), Mary's mother waves for a taxi and two bicyclists wave back. Thus starts a succession of wavers in consecutively increasing numbers.

MATHEMATICS—Counting
MOVEMENT/SPEED
NEIGHBORHOODS AND COMMUNITIES—Specific, urban
OCCUPATIONS
TRANSPORTATION

Slobodkina, Esphyr. *Caps for Sale.* New York: H. R. Scott, 1947.

While the peddler sleeps, monkeys steal his caps, but he discovers a way to get the hats back.

ANIMALS—Small creatures, monkeys
BEHAVIOR—Disobedient; Imitating; Mischievous; Pretending; Tricking
CLOTHING—Hats
EMOTIONS—Anger
OCCUPATIONS
SLEEPING
STORIES—Predictable text

Small, David. *Imogene's Antlers.* New York: Crown, 1985.

Awakening one morning with antlers growing out of her head, Imogene receives much concerned attention from her family.

HUMOR
SURPRISES
TRANSFORMATION

————. *Paper John.* New York: Farrar, 1987.

A stranger takes up residency in a village, constructing his home from paper and giving paper items to the neighbors. When the devil threatens the welfare of the community, the stranger comes to the rescue through his paper folding.

BEHAVIOR—Heroic; Problem-solving; Stealing; Tricking
CONSTRUCTION
FRIENDSHIP—Relationships
GIFTS
GRAPHIC AND PERFORMING ARTS—Art and artists

IMAGINATION—Imaginary creatures, others
KITES
NEIGHBORHOODS AND COMMUNITIES—General
OCCUPATIONS
SAFETY/DANGER
STRANGERS
STRUCTURES—Buildings, houses and other dwellings
TRANSPORTATION—Boats
WATER AND BODIES OF WATER—Oceans
WEATHER—Storms; Wind
WORLD REGIONS—Seashore

Smith, Barry. *The First Voyage of Christopher Columbus, 1492*. New York: Viking, 1992.

The story of Columbus's first voyage is told from the viewpoint of a seaman. The geographical elements of the unfolding adventure are illustrated through parts of a map on the page spreads. At the end of the work, these portions can be traced on a foldout map of the entire trip.

BEHAVIOR—Courageous
EXPLORATION
GOALS
HISTORICAL PERIODS—Exploration of the New World
MAPS
OCCUPATIONS
TRANSPORTATION—Boats
TRAVEL
WATER AND BODIES OF WATER—Oceans

Sonnenschein, Harriet. *Harold's Runaway Nose*. Jurg Obrist, illus. New York: Simon & Schuster, 1989.

When Harold's mother tries to get rid of his running nose, he believes it has run away and searches everywhere for it.

ANIMALS—Personified
BEHAVIOR—Crying; Searching
BODY—Parts of body, noses
EMOTIONS—Disappointment; Fear; Sadness
FAMILIES—Parents
HEALTH—Illness and injury
HUMOR
LANGUAGE—Words

Soto, Gary. *Chato's Kitchen*. Susan Guevara, illus. New York: Putnam, 1995.

Chato, the cat, invites a new family of mice in the neighborhood to dinner. He anticipates that they will be the main course and is happy to know that they are bringing a friend. However, he must change his plans when he discovers that their friend is a dog rather than another mouse.

ANIMALS—Personified; Pets, cats; Small creatures, mice
BEHAVIOR—Tricking
EMOTIONS—Fear
ENEMIES
FOOD AND EATING
FRIENDSHIPS—Relationships

GOALS
HUMOR
LANGUAGE—Sayings and special language
STRANGERS
SURPRISES
UNITED STATES—Specific cultures, Hispanic American
WRITING—Others

————. *Too Many Tamales*. Ed Martinez, illus. New York: Putnam, 1993.

Maria fears that she lost her mother's diamond ring in the masa while making tamales. In searching for it, she asks her cousins to eat the entire batch.

BEHAVIOR—Curious
EMOTIONS—Fear
FAMILIES—Family gatherings/Outings; Parents
FOOD AND EATING
HOLIDAYS AND CELEBRATIONS—Christmas
JEWELS
LOST AND FOUND
UNITED STATES—Specific cultures, Hispanic American

Speed, Toby. *Hattie Baked a Wedding Cake*. Cathi Hepworth, illus. New York: Putnam, 1994.

Hattie accidentally beats many ingredients into the wedding cake batter that are necessary for the ceremony. She must find a way to release them and save the wedding.

BEHAVIOR—Ambitious/Persistent; Crying; Excited; Problem-solving
DISASTERS
EMOTIONS—Disappointment
FAMILIES—Marriage
FOOD AND EATING
GRAPHIC AND PERFORMING ARTS—Music and musicians
HUMOR
IMAGINATION
MATHEMATICS—Measurement, mass
READING
ROOMS—Others

Spier, Peter. *Crash! Bang! Boom!* Garden City, NY: Doubleday, 1972.

Words representing sounds made by different images are organized by categories.

LANGUAGE—Words
MATHEMATICS—Classification
OBSERVATION
SENSES—Sound

————. *Dreams*. Garden City, NY: Doubleday, 1986.

Children's imaginings as they observe cloud formations result in many fanciful images and experiences.

IMAGINATION
OBSERVATION
STORIES—Minimal or no text
TRANSPORTATION—Hot-air balloons
WEATHER—Clouds

―――. *Fast-Slow, High-Low: A Book of Opposites.* Garden City, NY: Doubleday, 1972.

Contrasting illustrations portray common concepts with opposite meanings.

LANGUAGE—Words
OBSERVATION

―――. *Father, May I Come?* New York: Doubleday, 1993.

Living three hundred years apart, two boys—both named Sietze Hemmes—report ships in trouble off the Dutch coast. In both instances, villagers work to rescue the crews, but their methods vary.

ADVENTURES
BEHAVIOR—Courageous
CHANGES
DISASTERS
IDENTITY—Geographic identity
MAPS
NEIGHBORHOODS AND COMMUNITIES—Specific, rural
SAFETY/DANGER
SURVIVAL
TIME—Across time
TRANSPORTATION—Boats
WATER AND BODIES OF WATER—Oceans
WORLD CULTURES/COUNTRIES—Europe, Northern
WORLD REGIONS—Seashore

―――. *Gobble, Growl, Grunt.* Garden City, NY: Doubleday, 1971.

A multitude of animals and the sounds they emit are depicted.

ANIMALS
SENSES—Sound

―――. *Peter Spier's Christmas!* Garden City, NY: Doubleday, 1983.

A family prepares for and celebrates Christmas.

FAMILIES—Parents
HOLIDAYS AND CELEBRATIONS—Christmas
STORIES—Minimal or no text

―――. *Peter Spier's Circus!* New York: Doubleday, 1992.

The circus leaves its winter quarters and travels in a caravan to the first site of the season where it sets up, performs, and packs to move on to the second site.

ANIMALS
CHANGES
CIRCUS
COMMUNICATION—Signs
NEIGHBORHOODS AND COMMUNITIES—Social gatherings
OBSERVATION
OCCUPATIONS
STRUCTURES—Others
TIME—Cycles
TRANSPORTATION—Trucks
TRAVEL

————. *Peter Spier's Rain.* Garden City, NY: Doubleday, 1982.

In a book without text, two children explore their neighborhood during a rainy day.

BEHAVIOR—Excited
CLOTHING—Others
EMOTIONS—Happiness
FAMILIES—Siblings
LIGHT AND SHADOWS/REFLECTIONS
NEIGHBORHOODS AND COMMUNITIES—General
OBSERVATION
PLAY
STORIES—Minimal or no text
TIME—Cycles, day and night
WEATHER—Rain; Wind

Steig, William. *The Amazing Bone.* New York: Farrar, 1976.

On her way home from school Pearl, the pig, meets a bone with amazing magical powers. The bone saves Pearl from becoming a fox's dinner, and the two become close friends.

ADVENTURES
ANIMALS—Farm, pigs; Large animals, foxes; Personified
BEHAVIOR—Crying; Curious; Evil; Heroic; Stealing
CLOTHING
EMOTIONS—Fear; Happiness
ENEMIES
FAMILIES—Parents
FRIENDSHIP—Relationships
GRAPHIC AND PERFORMING ARTS—Music and musicians
IMAGINATION—Imaginary creatures
LANGUAGE—Saying and special language; Words
MAGIC
NEIGHBORHOODS AND COMMUNITIES—General
SAFETY/DANGER
SCHOOL EXPERIENCES
SENSES—Sound
TIME—Specific seasons, spring
WORLD REGIONS—Forest

————. *Amos & Boris.* New York: Farrar, 1971.

Amos, a small mouse, and Boris, a large whale, become best friends and rescue each other from great dangers.

ADVENTURES
ANIMALS—Marine life, whales; Personified; Small creatures, mice
BEHAVIOR—Heroic; Problem-solving; Sharing
BODY—Shape and size
CONSTRUCTION
FRIENDSHIP—Relationships
HUMOR
LANGUAGE—Names
MATHEMATICS—Size
SAFETY/DANGER

SENSES
TRANSPORTATION—Boats
WATER AND BODIES OF WATER—Oceans
WEATHER—Storms
WORLD CULTURES/COUNTRIES—Africa, Western
WORLD REGIONS—Seashore

————. *Brave Irene*. New York: Farrar, 1986.

Irene travels through the fierce snowstorm to deliver the duchess's new ball gown
that Irene's mother, a dressmaker, has made.

BEHAVIOR—Ambitious/Persistent; Cooperative; Courageous; Crying; Destructive/Violent;
        Loyal; Problem-solving
CLOTHING—Dresses
EMOTIONS—Happiness; Loneliness; Sadness
FAMILIES—Parents
GRAPHIC AND PERFORMING ARTS—Dance and dancers
HEALTH—Illness and injury
IDENTITY—Relationships
OCCUPATIONS
PARTIES
ROYALTY
SAFETY/DANGER
SENSES—Sight; Sound
SEWING
STRUCTURES—Boxes and Containers; Buildings, castles/palaces
TIME—Specific seasons, winter
TRANSPORTATION—Sleighs
WEATHER—Snow; Wind

————. *Caleb & Kate*. New York: Farrar, 1977.

After a witch transforms Caleb into a dog and he is unable to tell his wife about
this change, he becomes her pet.

ANIMALS—Pets, dogs
BEHAVIOR—Apprehensive; Fighting/Quarreling; Searching; Stealing
EMOTIONS—Fear; Hate; Love
FAMILIES—Husbands and wives
FRIENDSHIP—Relationships
IMAGINATION—Imaginary creatures, witches
LANGUAGE—Sayings and special language
LIGHT AND SHADOWS/REFLECTIONS
LOST AND FOUND
MAGIC
MYSTERY
OCCUPATIONS
TRANSFORMATION
WORLD REGIONS—Forest

————. *Doctor De Soto*. New York: Farrar, 1982.

Even though the mouse dentist, Dr. De Soto, does not usually treat his enemies, he
takes pity on a suffering fox. When the fox conspires to eat the dentist, Doctor De
Soto outwits him.

ANIMALS—Large animals, foxes; Personified; Small creatures, mice

BEHAVIOR—Apprehensive; Courageous; Crying; Evil; Pretending; Tricking
BODY—Parts of body, teeth
DREAMS
ENEMIES
HEALTH—Health care
HUMOR
MACHINES
OCCUPATIONS
SAFETY/DANGER
SURPRISES

———. *Gorky Rises.* New York: Farrar, 1980.

A young frog has a fantastic flight after concocting a magic potion.
ADVENTURES
ANIMALS—Large animals, elephants; Marine life, frogs; Personified
FAMILY PROBLEMS—Separation
FLYING—Fantasy
INVENTIONS
KITES
MAGIC
ROCKS AND MINERALS
ROOMS—Others
SLEEPING
SPACE
SURPRISES
TIME—Cycles, day and night
TRANSFORMATION
WEATHER—Storms

———. *Sylvester and the Magic Pebble.* New York: Windmill, 1969.

Sylvester the donkey avoids danger by being transformed into a rock, but when the danger has passed, he is unable to return to his original state.
ANIMALS—Farm, donkeys; Personified
BEHAVIOR—Apprehensive; Foolish; Searching
EMOTIONS—Fear; Loneliness
FAMILIES—Parents
FAMILY PROBLEMS—Separation
HOBBIES
MAGIC
PERSONAL PROBLEMS—Getting lost
ROCKS AND MINERALS
SENSES—Touch
TIME—Cycles, seasons
TRANSFORMATION
WISHES

Stevenson, James. *Could Be Worse!* New York: Greenwillow, 1977.

A grandfather tells a tall tale in response to his grandchildren's assumption that nothing interesting has ever happened to him.
DREAMS
FAMILIES—Grandparents
HUMOR

IMAGINATION
LANGUAGE—Sayings and special language
STORYTELLING

———. *Don't You Know There's a War On?* New York: Greenwillow, 1992.

A ten-year-old boy contributes to the war effort during World War II.
BEHAVIOR—Cooperative
EMOTIONS—Fear; Loneliness
FAMILIES—Parents
FAMILY PROBLEMS—Separation
HISTORICAL PERIODS—Twentieth Century, World War II
SAFETY/DANGER
TRANSPORTATION—Trains
TRAVEL
WAR

———. *The Night After Christmas.* New York: Greenwillow, 1981.

Toys discarded after new ones are received for Christmas are befriended by a stray dog who arranges for them to be reclaimed.
ANIMALS—Personified; Pets, dogs
EMOTIONS—Sadness
GIFTS
HOLIDAYS AND CELEBRATIONS—Christmas
SCHOOL EXPERIENCES
SENSES—Sound
STRUCTURES—Buildings, schools
TIME—Nighttime
TOYS—Bears; Dolls
WEATHER—Snow

———. *That Dreadful Day.* New York: Greenwillow, 1985.

After Grandfather tells his grandchildren of his unpleasant first day at school, they conclude that their teacher and school experience could be worse. They are ready to give school another try the next day.
BEHAVIOR—Bullying; Revengeful
EMOTIONS—Fear; Hate
FAMILIES—Grandparents
OCCUPATIONS
SCHOOL EXPERIENCES
SENSES—Sound
STORYTELLING
STRUCTURES—Buildings, schools
TIME—Across time

———. *That Terrible Halloween Night.* New York: Greenwillow, 1980.

When the children attempt to scare their grandfather on Halloween, he tells them that nothing has scared him since a terrible Halloween experience years ago.
BEHAVIOR—Tricking
EMOTIONS—Fear
FAMILIES—Grandparents
HOLIDAYS AND CELEBRATIONS—Halloween
IMAGINATION—Imaginary creatures; Imaginary worlds

SENSES—Sound
STORYTELLING
STRUCTURES—Buildings, houses and other dwellings
TIME—Nighttime

————. *What's Under My Bed?* New York: Greenwillow, 1983.

When the children are afraid at bedtime, their grandfather tells them a story about his childhood fears at bedtime.

BEHAVIOR—Apprehensive; Problem-solving
EMOTIONS—Fear
EVERYDAY EXPERIENCES—Time of day, bedtime
FAMILIES—Grandparents
FOOD AND EATING
FURNITURE—Beds
IMAGINATION—Imaginary creatures
MOVEMENT/SPEED
ROOMS—Bedrooms
SENSES—Sight; Sound; Touch
STORYTELLING

————. *The Worst Person's Christmas.* New York: Greenwillow, 1991.

The worst person who does not like anything that anyone else likes, particularly Christmas, finds his attitude modified by his neighbors' kindness during the holidays.

BEHAVIOR—Sharing
FRIENDSHIP—Relationships
GIFTS
HOLIDAYS AND CELEBRATIONS—Christmas
NEIGHBORHOOD AND COMMUNITIES—Specific, urban
PARTIES
WRITING—Others

Stewart, Sarah. *The Library.* David Small, illus. New York: Farrar, 1995.

When Elizabeth Brown's lifetime of collecting books consumes the space in her home, she donates her house and the books to the town for a library.

BEHAVIOR—Problem-solving
BIOGRAPHY/LIFE STORIES
GIFTS
HOBBIES
INDIVIDUALITY
NEIGHBORHOODS AND COMMUNITIES—General
READING
STORIES—Predictable text
STRUCTURES—Buildings, libraries

Stolz, Mary. *Storm in the Night.* Pat Cummings, illus. New York: Harper & Row, 1988.

A boy experiencing a thunderstorm with his grandfather discovers from his grandfather's story that he, too, was afraid of storms in his youth.

ANIMALS—Pets, dogs
BEHAVIOR—Boastful; Sharing
ELDERLY

EMOTIONS—Fear
EVERYDAY EXPERIENCES—Time of day, bedtime
FAMILIES—Grandparents
MEMORIES
SENSES—Smell and taste; Sound
STORYTELLING
TIME—Nighttime
WEATHER—Storms

Stone, Bernard. *A Day to Remember*. Anton Pieck, illus. New York: Four Winds, 1981.

Detailed illustrations depict many activities of the Christmas season in a Dutch city in the late 1800s.

HISTORICAL PERIODS—Nineteenth Century, late
HOLIDAYS AND CELEBRATIONS—Christmas
WORLD CULTURES/COUNTRIES—Europe, Northern

Tarfuri, Nancy. *The Ball Bounced*. New York: Greenwillow, 1989.

A bouncing ball causes much action in the house.

FAMILIES—Babies and young siblings
LANGUAGE—Words
MOVEMENT/SPEED
STORIES—Minimal or no text
TOYS—Others

———. *Early Morning in the Barn*. New York: Greenwillow, 1983.

The crowing of the rooster awakens other animals who then make their sounds.

ANIMALS—Farm
EVERYDAY EXPERIENCES—Time or day, awakening for the day
FARMS
SENSES—Sound
STRUCTURES—Buildings, barns
TIME—Daytime

———. *Follow Me!* New York: Greenwillow, 1990.

A young sea lion in pursuit of a wandering crab is unaware of its mother's protection along the way.

ANIMALS—Marine life, others
FAMILIES—Parents
OBSERVATION
STORIES—Minimal or no text
WATER AND BODIES OF WATER—Oceans
WORLD REGIONS—Seashore

———. *Have You Seen My Duckling?* New York: Greenwillow, 1984.

When a duckling ventures away from the nest, his mother searches for him.
ADVENTURES

ANIMALS—Farm, ducks
BEHAVIOR—Searching
FAMILIES—Parents
FAMILY PROBLEMS—Separation
GOALS
LOST AND FOUND
OBSERVATION
STORIES—Minimal or no text
TIME—Cycles, day and night
WATER AND BODIES OF WATER—Ponds

———. *Junglewalk.* New York: Greenwillow, 1988.

While reading a book about a jungle, a boy falls asleep and dreams about an adventure in a jungle.

ADVENTURES
ANIMALS—Large animals, tigers; Pets, cats
DREAMS
EVERYDAY EXPERIENCES—Time of day, bedtime
IMAGINATION
OBSERVATION
READING
ROOMS—Bedrooms
STORIES—Minimal or no text
TIME—Nighttime
TRANSFORMATION
WORLD REGIONS—Rain forest/Jungle

———. *Rabbit's Morning.* New York: Greenwillow, 1985.

As the sun comes up, a young rabbit goes exploring and observes many different kinds of animal families.

ADVENTURES
ANIMALS—Babies; Small creatures, rabbits
BEHAVIOR—Curious
EVERYDAY EXPERIENCES—Time of day, daytime
OBSERVATION
STORIES—Minimal or no text
TIME—Daytime

Teague, Mark. *The Field Beyond the Outfield.* New York: Scholastic, 1992.

Ludlow's parents attempt to redirect his interests from experiences with imaginary creatures to the real-life game of baseball. But his imagination comes alive on the diamond when he makes an extraordinary performance with a team of insects.

ANIMALS—Fantasy
EMOTIONS—Fear
FAMILIES—Parents
HUMOR
IDENTITY—Self-worth
IMAGINATION—Imaginary creatures; Imaginary worlds
MATHEMATICS—Measurement, length
NEIGHBORHOODS AND COMMUNITIES—General
SPORTS

Tejima, Keizaburo. *Fox's Dream*. New York: Philomel, 1987.

A lonely young fox wanders through the forest in the wintertime, searching for companionship.

ANIMALS—Cycles; Large animals, foxes
BEHAVIOR—Searching
EMOTIONS—Loneliness
IMAGINATION
MEMORIES
SENSES—Sight
TIME—Cycles, day and night; Specific seasons, winter
WORLD REGIONS—Forest

———. *Owl Lake*. New York: Philomel, 1987.

At nightfall, a father owl comes to the mountain lake to hunt for fish to feed his family.

ANIMALS—Birds
BEHAVIOR—Searching
ENEMIES
FOOD AND EATING
MOVEMENT/SPEED
SENSES—Sight; Sound
TIME—Cycles, day and night; Nighttime
WATER AND BODIES OF WATER—Lakes
WORLD REGIONS—Mountain

———. *Swan Sky*. New York: Philomel, 1988.

Even though her family tries to encourage her, the young wan is unable to fly northward with the flock in the spring.

ANIMALS—Birds; Cycles
ASTRONOMY—Other
DEATH
EMOTIONS—Sadness
HEALTH—Illness and injury
IDENTITY—Geographic identity
IMAGINATION
MOVEMENT/SPEED
TIME—Cycles, day and night; Cycles, seasons; Specific seasons, spring
WATER AND BODIES OF WATER—Lakes

Testa, Fulvio. *If You Look Around You*. New York: Dial, 1983.

Geometric shapes are shown in scenes of children and their activities.

ASTRONOMY
MATHEMATICS—Shapes
SENSES—Sight

———. *If You Take a Pencil*. New York: Dial, 1982.

When someone takes a pencil and starts to draw, a fantasy world unfolds. In this counting book (from 1 to 12), the pencil leads the way to adventure.

ADVENTURES
GRAPHIC AND PERFORMING ARTS—Art and artists
IMAGINATION—Imaginary worlds

MATHEMATICS—Counting
TREASURES

Thomas, Jane Resh. *Lights on the River*. Michael Dooling, illus. New York: Hyperion, 1994.

A daughter of Mexican-American migrant workers is sustained through a life of hardships by memories of her grandmother in Mexico.

BEHAVIOR—Proud
FAMILIES—Grandparents; Parents
GRAPHIC AND PERFORMING ARTS—Music and musicians
HOLIDAYS AND CELEBRATIONS—Christmas
IDENTITY—Relationships
IDENTITY—Self-worth
LANGUAGE—Sayings and special language
MIGRANTS
OCCUPATIONS
POVERTY
UNITED STATES—Specific cultures, Hispanic American
WORLD CULTURES/COUNTRIES—Central America, Mexico

Thompson, Colin. *The Paper Bag Prince*. New York: Knopf, 1992.

The Paper Bag Prince, a wise, elderly man, moves into an abandoned dump and watches nature take back the land.

ECOLOGY/ENVIRONMENTAL PROBLEMS
EMOTIONS—Happiness
IDENTITY—Geographic identity
INDIVIDUALITY
MEMORIES
NEIGHBORHOODS AND COMMUNITIES—Specific, rural
SAFETY/DANGER
STRUCTURES—Buildings, houses and other dwellings

Titherington, Jeanne. *A Place for Ben*. New York: Greenwillow, 1987.

Ben resents having to share his room with his baby brother, but once he succeeds in finding a place to be alone, he realizes that he needs companionship.

BEHAVIOR—Sharing
EMOTIONS—Loneliness
FAMILIES—Babies and young siblings
FAMILY PROBLEMS—New siblings
GOALS
ROOMS—Bedrooms
SURPRISES
WISHES

———. *Pumpkin, Pumpkin*. New York: Greenwillow, 1986.

After planting a pumpkin seed in the spring, Jamie watches it grow into a large pumpkin and eventually carves it into a jack-o'-lantern. He saves some of its seeds to start the cycle again.

BEHAVIOR—Patient
CHANGES
EMOTIONS—Happiness

GARDENS
GOALS
HOLIDAYS AND CELEBRATIONS—Halloween
OBSERVATION
PLANTS—Cycles; Seeds
PUMPKINS
STORIES—Minimal or no text
TIME—Cycles, seasons

————. *Sophy and Auntie Pearl.* New York: Greenwillow, 1995.

A young girl discovers that she can fly and so can her Great-Aunt Pearl. Together they take a fanciful flight observed only by children.

BEHAVIOR—Excited
ELDERLY
EMOTIONS—Happiness
FAMILIES—Other relatives; Parents
FLYING—Fantasy
HUMOR
IDENTITY—Relationships
IMAGINATION
SHOPPING/MARKETING
TRANSFORMATION
TRAVEL

Tompert, Ann. *The Silver Whistle.* Beth Peck, illus. New York: Macmillan, 1988.

A generous Mexican boy aids the needy with the money he intended for purchasing a silver whistle for the Christ Child on Christmas Eve. He discovers that his clay whistle, representing his craftsmanship, created a miracle.

BEHAVIOR—Problem-solving; Sharing
CLOTHING—Others
EMOTIONS—Happiness; Love; Sadness
FAMILIES
GIFTS
GOALS
GRAPHIC AND PERFORMING ARTS—Art and artists
HOLIDAYS AND CELEBRATIONS—Christmas
IDENTITY—Self-worth
MONEY
OCCUPATIONS
POVERTY
RELIGION
STATUES
STRUCTURES—Buildings, churches
TOYS—Others
WORLD CULTURES/COUNTRIES—Central America, Mexico

Tresselt, Alvin R. *Hide and Seek Fog.* Roger Duvoisin, illus. New York: Lothrop, 1965.

The life of a seashore town changes for both children and adults as it is enveloped in a heavy fog.

NEIGHBORHOODS AND COMMUNITIES—General
OCCUPATIONS

PLAY
SENSES—Sight
WEATHER—Fog
WORLD REGIONS—Seashore

————. *White Snow, Bright Snow.* Roger Duvoisin, illus. New York: Lothrop, 1947.

The grown-ups cope with the snow, but the children playing in it think snow is wonderful.

NEIGHBORHOODS AND COMMUNITIES—General
OCCUPATIONS
TIME—Specific seasons, winter
WEATHER—Snow

Tsuchiya, Yukio. *Faithful Elephants.* Ted Lewin, illus. Boston: Houghton Mifflin, 1988.

A zookeeper tells the painful story of three elephants in a Tokyo zoo who perished during World War II.

ANIMALS—Large animals, elephants
DEATH
EMOTIONS—Sadness
HISTORICAL PERIODS—Twentieth Century, World War II
NEIGHBORHOODS AND COMMUNITIES—Specific, urban
SAFETY/DANGER
WAR
WORLD CULTURES/COUNTRIES—Asia, Japan
ZOOS

Turkle, Brinton. *Do Not Open.* New York: Dutton, 1981.

The courageous Miss Moody faces the evil that emerges from a bottle washed up on the beach after a storm.

ANIMALS—Pets, cats; Small creatures, mice
BEHAVIOR—Courageous; Evil, Hiding; Problem-solving; Resourceful
BODY—Shape and size
EMOTIONS—Fear
ENEMIES
IMAGINATION—Imaginary creatures, others
MAGIC
STRUCTURES—Boxes and containers
TREASURES
WATER AND BODIES OF WATER—Oceans
WEATHER—Storms
WISHES
WORLD REGIONS—Seashore

Turner, Ann Warren. *Dakota Dugout.* Ronald Himler, illus. New York: Macmillan, 1985.

A woman recalls her experiences as a young bride living in a sod house on the prairie.

CHANGES
EMOTIONS—Loneliness
FAMILIES—Grandparents; Husbands and wives

FARMS
HISTORICAL PERIODS—Nineteenth Century, pioneer/westward movement
IDENTITY—Geographic identity
MEMORIES
MOVING
STORYTELLING
STRUCTURES—Buildings, houses and other dwellings
TIME—Cycles, seasons
UNITED STATES—Regions, Midwest
WEATHER—Drought
WORLD REGIONS—Plain

————. *Heron Street.* Lisa Desimini, illus. New York: Harper & Row, 1989.

As people throughout the centuries settle near the marsh by the sea, the wildlife is displaced as a city grows.

ANIMALS—Birds
CHANGES
CONSTRUCTION
ECOLOGY/ENVIRONMENTAL PROBLEMS
NEIGHBORHOODS AND COMMUNITIES—General
SENSES—Sound
TIME—Across time
UNITED STATES—Regions, Middle Atlantic
WORLD REGIONS—Seashore

————. *Katie's Trunk.* Ronald Himler, illus. New York: Macmillan, 1992.

During the American Revolution, Katie's family is on the Tory side, which alienates them from some of their neighbors. When the rebels come to ransack their home, Katie hides in a trunk. When she is discovered by one of the soldiers, she is surprised that he does not betray her.

BEHAVIOR—Crying; Destructive/Violent; Disobedient; Fighting/Quarreling; Hiding; Loyal; Ridiculing; Stealing
EMOTIONS—Anger; Fear; Hate; Sadness
ENEMIES
FAMILY PROBLEMS—Others
FRIENDSHIP—Relationships
HISTORICAL PERIODS—Colonial
IDENTITY—Relationships
STRUCTURES—Boxes and containers
WAR

————. *Nettie's Trip South.* Ronald Himler, illus. New York: Macmillan, 1987.

In traveling to the South, a Northern girl encounters unforgettable experiences associated with the harshness of slavery.

BEHAVIOR—Evil
DREAMS
EMOTIONS—Sadness
FAMILY PROBLEMS—Separation
HISTORICAL PERIODS—Nineteenth Century, late
SLAVERY
TRANSPORTATION—Trains

TRAVEL
UNITED STATES—Cross cultural; Specific cultures, African American
WRITING—Letters

———. *Stars for Sarah*. Mary Teichman, illus. New York: HarperCollins, 1991.

When Sarah becomes uneasy about moving, her mother promises that many things will be the same, including stars on her bedroom ceiling.

ASTRONOMY—Stars
BEHAVIOR—Apprehensive
CHANGES
EMOTIONS—Fear
EVERYDAY EXPERIENCES—Time of day, bedtime
FAMILIES—Parents
MOVING
ROOMS—Bedrooms
TIME—Nighttime

Twining, Edith. *Sandman*. New York: Doubleday, 1991.

When Jack falls asleep, the Sandman beckons him into a fantasy world where he helps rescue boats at sea during a storm.

DREAMS
EVERYDAY EXPERIENCES—Time of day, bedtime
FAMILIES—Parents
IMAGINATION—Imaginary creatures, others; Imaginary worlds
MAGIC
PLAY
ROOMS—Bedrooms
SAFETY/DANGER
SLEEPING
SURVIVAL
TIME—Nighttime
TOYS (general); Bears
TRANSPORTATION—Boats
WATER AND BODIES OF WATER—Oceans
WEATHER—Storms

Tyler, Anne. *Tumble Tower*. Mitra Modarressi, illus. New York: Orchard, 1993.

Every member of the royal family is very neat, except messy Molly. When a flood causes the family to seek refuge in Molly's tower, they learn to respect her clutter.

BEHAVIOR—Resourceful; Sharing
CHANGES
DISASTERS
FAMILIES—Parents; Siblings
FAMILY PROBLEMS—Others
IDENTITY—Self-worth
INDIVIDUALITY
ROYALTY
SAFETY/DANGER
STRUCTURES—Buildings, castles/palaces
WATER AND BODIES OF WATER—Floods

Uchida, Yoshiko. *The Bracelet.* Joanna Yardley, illus. New York: Philomel, 1993.

Seven-year-old Emi, a Japanese American, is sent with her family to an internment camp during World War II. Even though she loses her friend's farewell gift, she realizes that she will never forget their friendship.

BEHAVIOR—Crying
CLOTHING—Others
EMOTIONS—Sadness
FAMILY PROBLEMS—Others
FRIENDSHIP—Relationships
GIFTS
HISTORICAL PERIODS—Twentieth Century, World War II
LOST AND FOUND
MEMORIES
MOVING
PERSONAL PROBLEMS—Others
UNITED STATES—Cross cultural; Specific cultures, Asian American

Ungerer, Tomi. *Crictor.* New York: Harper, 1958.

Madame Bodot, a teacher in a French village, receives a boa constrictor as a gift and names it Crictor. She befriends and educates Crictor, and he rescues her from robbers.

ANIMALS—Pets, others; Reptiles, snakes
BEHAVIOR—Apprehensive; Courageous; Evil; Heroic; Stealing
EMOTIONS—Fear; Happiness
FRIENDSHIPS—Relationships
GIFTS
LANGUAGE—Alphabet
MATHEMATICS—Counting
NEIGHBORHOODS AND COMMUNITIES—Specific, urban
OCCUPATIONS
SCHOOL EXPERIENCES
WORLD CULTURES/COUNTRIES—Europe, Northern

Van Allsburg, Chris. *The Alphabet Theatre Proudly Presents: The Z Was Zapped.* Boston: Houghton Mifflin, 1987.

The Alphabet Theatre presents the alphabet with a disaster that begins with each letter.

DISASTERS
GRAPHIC AND PERFORMING ARTS—Drama and actors
LANGUAGE—Alphabet; Words
OBSERVATION

———. *Bad Day at Riverbend.* Boston: Houghton Mifflin, 1995.

In a coloring book, Ned Hardy, the sheriff of a small frontier town, investigates the source of a brilliant light and shiny, greasy slime.

BEHAVIOR—Courageous; Problem-solving; Searching
COWBOYS/COWGIRLS
EMOTIONS—Fear
ENEMIES

GRAPHIC AND PERFORMING ARTS—Art and artists
HISTORICAL PERIODS—Nineteenth Century, pioneer/westward movement
IDENTITY—Geographic identity
IMAGINATION—Imaginary worlds
NEIGHBORHOODS AND COMMUNITIES—General
OBSERVATION
OCCUPATIONS
SAFETY/DANGER
SENSES—Sight
STORYTELLING
STRUCTURES—Buildings, others
SURPRISES
TRANSPORTATION—Horses; Others

————. *The Garden of Abdul Gasazi.* Boston: Houghton Mifflin, 1979.

While Alan is caring for Miss Hester's dog, Fritz, the dog runs away and enters the garden of Abdul Gasazi, the magician. Alan finds that the magician's spell has transformed the dog into a duck. When Alan returns to tell Miss Hester what has happened, he finds Fritz in his original form and Miss Hester doubting his story.

ADVENTURES
ANIMALS—Fantasy; Pets, dogs
BEHAVIOR—Apprehensive; Evil; Mischievous
CLOTHING—Hats
EMOTIONS—Sadness
GARDENS
IMAGINATION—Imaginary creatures, others; Imaginary worlds
MAGIC
MYSTERY
STRUCTURES—Buildings, houses and other dwellings
TRANSFORMATION

————. *Jumanji.* Boston: Houghton Mifflin, 1981.

A bored brother and sister become involved in a jungle board game that leads them into a mysterious, exciting adventure.

ADVENTURES
ANIMALS—Fantasy
BEHAVIOR—Bored; Excited; Problem-solving
EMOTIONS—Fear
ENEMIES
GAMES/PUZZLES/TRICKS
GOALS
IMAGINATION
MYSTERY
NEIGHBORHOODS AND COMMUNITIES—Parks
PERSONAL PROBLEMS—Breaking promises
PLAY
TRANSFORMATION

————. *Just a Dream.* Boston: Houghton Mifflin, 1990.

Through a dream, the boy, Walter, becomes enlightened about the plight of the earth if pollution and waste of the earth's resources continue.

BEHAVIOR—Destructive/Violent; Responsible

BIRTHDAYS
DREAMS
ECOLOGY/ENVIRONMENTAL PROBLEMS
IMAGINATION—Imaginary worlds
PLANTS—Trees
TIME—Across time
TRAVEL

————. *The Mysteries of Harris Burdick.* Boston: Houghton Mifflin, 1984.

Readers are asked to create stories for a collection of drawings with titles and captions that the mysterious Harris Burdick left with the publisher.

BEHAVIOR—Tricking
IMAGINATION
MYSTERY
RIDDLES
STORIES—Minimal or no text
WRITING—Others

————. *The Polar Express.* Boston: Houghton Mifflin, 1985.

A boy takes a magical train ride to the North Pole and meets Santa Claus, who asks him to choose the first gift of Christmas. He chooses a bell from Santa's sleigh but loses it on the way home. On Christmas morning, he finds it under the tree with a note from Mr. C. Although he and his sister hear the sound of the bell, his parents cannot, for it only rings for those who believe.

ADVENTURES
ANIMALS—Large animals, deer
BEHAVIOR—Excited; Sharing
BELLS
CLOTHING—Pockets
EMOTIONS—Disappointment
FAMILIES—Siblings
GIFTS
HOLIDAYS AND CELEBRATIONS—Christmas
IMAGINATION—Imaginary creatures; Imaginary worlds
LOST AND FOUND
MAGIC
SENSES—Sight; Smell and taste; Sound
TIME—Cycles, day and night
TRANSPORTATION—Trains
TRAVEL
WORLD CULTURES/COUNTRIES—Polar regions
WRITING—Letters

————. *The Stranger.* Boston: Houghton Mifflin, 1986.

When Farmer Bailey hits a stranger with his truck, he brings him home to recover. The family notices that this mysterious person has a puzzling relationship with the changes in autumn.

CHANGES
FARMS
FRIENDSHIP—Relationships
HEALTH—Illness and injury
IMAGINATION—Imaginary creatures, others

MAGIC
MYSTERY
NEIGHBORHOODS AND COMMUNITIES—Specific, rural
OCCUPATIONS
STRANGERS
TIME—Specific seasons, fall
WRITING—Others

————. *The Sweetest Fig*. Boston: Houghton Mifflin, 1993.

Marcel, a dog mistreated by his master, a French dentist, seeks revenge when the dentist brings home two enchanted figs.

ANIMALS—Pets, dogs
BEHAVIOR—Greedy; Revengeful; Tricking
DREAMS
FRUITS
MAGIC
OCCUPATIONS
SURPRISES
TRANSFORMATION
WORLD CULTURES/COUNTRIES—Europe, Northern

————. *Two Bad Ants*. Boston: Houghton Mifflin, 1988.

Two ants remain behind while the other ants return with crystals for their queen. After many misadventures, the ants are glad to return to their home.

ADVENTURES
ANIMALS—Small creatures, insects
BEHAVIOR—Searching
DISASTERS
FOOD AND EATING
MOUNTAIN CLIMBING
OBSERVATION
ROOMS—Others
SAFETY/DANGER
SENSES—Sight; Smell and taste; Sound; Touch
SURVIVAL
TRAVEL
TREASURES

————. *The Widow's Broom*. Boston: Houghton Mifflin, 1992.

Minna Shaw's neighbors distrust and plot against a worn-out broom left behind by a witch, even though the broom helps the widow a great deal.

BEHAVIOR—Apprehensive; Destructive/Violent; Evil; Revengeful; Tricking
EMOTIONS—Fear; Hate
ENEMIES
FIRE
FLYING—Fantasy
IMAGINATION—Imaginary creatures, witches; Imaginary objects
MAGIC
MYSTERY
NEIGHBORHOODS AND COMMUNITIES—Specific, rural
SAFETY/DANGER
TRANSFORMATION

————. *The Wreck of the Zephyr*. Boston: Houghton Mifflin, 1983.

In his obsession to be the greatest sailor in the world, a boy misuses his ability to sail his boat in the air and experiences disaster.

ADVENTURES
BEHAVIORS—Ambitious/Persistent
DISASTERS
ELDERLY
FLYING—Fantasy
GOALS
IMAGINATION—Imaginary worlds
MAGIC
OCCUPATIONS
SPORTS
STORYTELLING
TRANSPORTATION—Boats
TRAVEL
WATER AND BODIES OF WATER—Oceans
WEATHER—Storms
WORLD REGIONS—Seashore

————. *The Wretched Stone*. Boston: Houghton Mifflin, 1991.

A sea captain is faced with a dilemma after his crew members bring a strange, glowing stone aboard and experience a radical change.

ADVENTURES
BEHAVIOR—Foolish
FOOD AND EATING
ISLANDS
MAGIC
MYSTERY
OCCUPATIONS
READING
ROCKS AND MINERALS
SAFETY/DANGER
SECRETS
TRANSFORMATION
TRANSPORTATION—Boats
TRAVEL
WATER AND BODIES OF WATER—Oceans
WEATHER—Storms
WRITING—Diaries

Van Leeuwen, Jean. *Going West*. Thomas B. Allen, illus. New York: Dial, 1992.

Traveling to the West, a pioneer family finds a new home.

CAMPING
FAMILIES
HISTORICAL PERIODS—Nineteenth Century, pioneer/westward movement
STRUCTURES—Buildings, cabins
TIME—Cycles, seasons
TRANSPORTATION—Wagons
TRAVEL

Vaughan, Marcia K., and Patricia Mullins. *The Sea-Breeze Hotel.* New York: Willa
    Perlman, 1992.

A boy initiates kite construction and flying to promote business at a seaside hotel
suffering from low occupancy caused by the fierce offshore wind.

BEHAVIOR—Problem-solving
CONSTRUCTION
KITES
STRUCTURES—Others
SURPRISES
VACATIONS
WEATHER—Wind
WORLD REGIONS—Seashore

Ver Dorn, Bethea. *Day Breaks.* Thomas Graham, illus. New York: Arcade, 1992.

The earth's creatures respond to the break of day.

EVERYDAY EXPERIENCES—Time of day, awakening for the day
SENSES—Sight; Sound

Vincent, Gabrielle. *Feel Better, Ernest!* New York: Greenwillow, 1988.

Ernest, the bear, recovers from his illness after Celestine, his mouse friend, gives
him good care and entertains him.

ANIMALS—Large animals, bears; Personified; Small creatures, mice
BEHAVIOR—Bored; Problem-solving
EVERYDAY EXPERIENCES—Time of day, awakening for the day
FOOD AND EATING
FRIENDSHIP—Relationships
HEALTH—Health care; Illness and injury
OBSERVATION
OCCUPATIONS

———. *Merry Christmas, Ernest and Celestine.* New York: Greenwillow, 1984.

Lacking money, Ernest and Celestine rely on their resourcefulness to provide a
Christmas party for their friends.

ANIMALS—Large animals, bears; Personified; Small creatures, mice
BEHAVIOR—Resourceful; Sharing
EMOTIONS—Love
FOOD AND EATING
FRIENDSHIP—Relationships
GRAPHIC AND PERFORMING ARTS—Dance and dancers; Music and musicians
HOLIDAYS AND CELEBRATIONS—Christmas
MONEY
NEIGHBORHOODS AND COMMUNITIES—General
OBSERVATION
PARTIES
SLEEPING
STORYTELLING
SURPRISES

————. *Smile, Ernest and Celestine.* New York: Greenwillow, 1982.

When Celestine looks at Ernest's photo albums and finds no pictures of herself, she is upset. Ernest remedies this situation by photographing her and himself and creating an album exclusively of their photographs.

ANIMALS—Large animals, bears; Personified; Small creatures, mice
BEHAVIOR—Problem-solving
FRIENDSHIP—Relationships
PHOTOGRAPHY

Viorst, Judith. *Alexander and the Terrible, Horrible, No Good, Very Bad Day.* Ray Cruz, illus. New York: Atheneum, 1972.

After Alexander has had many frustrating experiences during the day, he consoles himself at bedtime by realizing that others, too, have bad days.

BEHAVIOR—Apprehensive
EVERYDAY EXPERIENCES—Time of day, daytime
HUMOR
IDENTITY—Self worth
LANGUAGE—Sayings and special language
SCHOOL EXPERIENCES

————. *Alexander, Who Used to be Rich Last Sunday.* Ray Cruz, illus. New York: Atheneum, 1978.

As he spends his gift money, Alexander recounts all the things that can be done with a dollar.

EMOTIONS—Disappointment
FAMILIES—Other relatives
MATHEMATICS—Numbers, processes
MONEY

————. *The Tenth Good Thing about Barney.* Erik Blegvad, illus. New York: Atheneum, 1971.

In the process of grieving for his dead cat, a boy thinks of ten good things about him.

ANIMALS—Pets, cats
DEATH
EMOTIONS—Sadness
FAMILIES—Parents
MEMORIES

Waber, Bernard. *The House on East 88th Street.* Boston: Houghton Mifflin, 1962.

When the family moves into their apartment they find Lyle, a performing crocodile, who becomes their friend.

ANIMALS—Marine life, crocodiles
BEHAVIOR—Crying
EMOTIONS—Fear; Sadness
FRIENDSHIP—Relationships
GAMES/PUZZLES/TRICKS
LANGUAGE—Names

NEIGHBORHOODS AND COMMUNITIES—Specific, urban
ROOMS—Bathrooms
SENSES—Sound
STRUCTURES—Buildings, houses and other dwellings

————. *Ira Says Goodbye.* Boston: Houghton Mifflin, 1988.

Ira discovers that his best friend, Reggie, does not feel happy about moving even though he has bragged about his new community. The solution to Ira's loneliness is to visit Reggie in his new home.

BEHAVIOR—Boastful; Excited
CHANGES
EMOTIONS—Happiness; Loneliness; Sadness
FRIENDSHIP—Relationships
IDENTITY—Relationships
MOVING
NEIGHBORHOODS AND COMMUNITIES—General
SURPRISES

————. *Ira Sleeps Over.* Boston: Houghton Mifflin, 1972.

A small boy finds that staying away from home overnight works better if he has his teddy bear.

EVERYDAY EXPERIENCES—Time of day, bedtime
FRIENDSHIP—Relationships
PERSONAL PROBLEMS—Giving up security objects
TOYS—Bears

Waggoner, Karen. *The Lemonade Babysitter.* Dorothy Donohue, illus. Boston: Joy Street, 1992.

In the beginning Molly does not want the new babysitter, Mr. Herbert, to come to her house, but she is won over by his active, clever involvement.

BABYSITTING
BEHAVIOR—Patient; Tricking
ELDERLY
FOOD AND EATING
FRIENDSHIP—Relationships
GRAPHIC AND PERFORMING ARTS—dance and dancers
MASKS
OCCUPATIONS
TRANSPORTATION—Buses
ZOOS

Wahl, Jan. *My Cat Ginger.* Naava, illus. New York: Tambourine, 1992.

When a young boy's cat, Ginger, begins to disappear for short periods of time, he imagines that his pet is engaged in adventures in imaginary worlds. To his surprise, he discovers that the cat is the father of a large litter of kittens.

ADVENTURES
ANIMALS—Babies; Pets, cats
BEHAVIOR—Searching
EVERYDAY EXPERIENCES
IDENTITY—Relationships

IMAGINATION—Imaginary worlds
SURPRISES

Walsh, Ellen Stoll. *Hop Jump*. San Diego: Harcourt, 1993.

Having observed the falling leaves, Betsy, the frog, leans to dance and is soon followed by other frogs.

ANIMALS—Marine life, frogs; Personified
GRAPHIC AND PERFORMING ARTS—Dance and dancers
IMAGINATION
INDIVIDUALITY
MOVEMENT/SPEED
OBSERVATION
SENSES—Sight
STORIES—Minimal or no text
TIME—Specific seasons, fall

———. *Mouse Paint*. San Diego: Harcourt, 1989.

Three white mice explore the mixing of colors.

ANIMALS—Small creatures, mice
CHANGES
COLORS
GRAPHIC AND PERFORMING ARTS—Art and artists
MATHEMATICS—Classification
OBSERVATION
SENSES—Sight

———. *You Silly Goose*. San Diego: Harcourt, 1992.

Lulu, a silly goose, accuses George, the mouse, of being the fox that will endanger Emily's goslings. When George rescues the goslings from the fox's attack, his real identity becomes known and George is a hero.

ANIMALS—Babies; Farm, geese; Large animals, foxes; Small creatures, mice
BEHAVIOR—Foolish; Heroic
ENEMIES
HUMOR
SAFETY/DANGER

Ward, Cindy. *Cookie's Week*. Tomie dePaola, illus. New York: Putnam, 1988.

Each day of the week the cat, Cookie, finds a different kind of mischief in which to engage.

ANIMALS—Pets, cats
BEHAVIOR—Destructive/Violent; Mischievous
DISASTERS
STORIES—Minimal or no text
TIME—Cycles, days of the week

Wegen, Ronald. *Sky Dragon*. New York: Greenwillow, 1982.

Having observed various images in the clouds as a snowstorm developed, the children know exactly what they will sculpt in the snow the following day.

ANIMALS—Fantasy
CONSTRUCTION
FAMILIES—Siblings

IMAGINATION
OBSERVATION
PLAY
SENSES—Sight
TIME—Specific seasons, winter
WEATHER—Clouds; Snow

Weiss, Nicki. *Where Does the Brown Bear Go?* New York: Greenwillow, 1989.

When nighttime comes, the animals return home to join the sleeping children, and the audience learns the animals' true identity. They are toys.
ANIMALS
SLEEPING
STORIES—Predictable text
SURPRISES
TIME—Nighttime
TOYS

Welch, Willy. *Playing Right Field.* Marc Simont, illus. New York: Scholastic, 1995.

A young boy finds that playing right field can be an important position.
EMOTIONS—Fear
IDENTITY—Self-worth
IMAGINATION
SPORTS
STORIES—Predictable text
WISHES

Weller, Frances Ward. *Matthew Wheelock's Wall.* Ted Lewin, illus. New York: Macmillan, 1992.

Generations later, Matthew Wheelock's descendants identify with his completed goal of building an enduring rock wall.
BEHAVIOR—Ambitious/persistent; Problem-solving
BIOGRAPHY/LIFE STORIES
CONSTRUCTION
EMOTIONS—Happiness
FAMILIES—Grandparents
FARMS
GOALS
IDENTITY—Self-worth
MATHEMATICS—Shapes; Size
NEIGHBORHOODS AND COMMUNITIES—Specific, rural
ROCKS AND MINERALS
STRUCTURES—Others
TIME—Across time

———. *Riptide.* Robert J. Blake, illus. New York: Philomel, 1990.

A boy's dog, Riptide, is drawn to the seashore, where he wins a position as the nineteenth lifeguard on Cape Cod's Nauset Beach.
ADVENTURES
ANIMALS—Pets, dogs
FAMILIES—Parents
IDENTITY—Relationships
LANGUAGE—Names

OCCUPATIONS
SAFETY/DANGER
WATER AND BODIES OF WATER—Oceans
WORLD REGIONS—Seashore

Wells, Rosemary. *Noisy Nora*. New York: Dial, 1973.

Feeling neglected, Nora creates a great deal of noise to attract her parents' attention.

ANIMALS—Personified
BEHAVIOR—Hiding; Impatient; Patient
EMOTIONS—Anger
FAMILIES—Babies and young siblings; Parents
FAMILY PROBLEMS—New siblings
PERSONAL PROBLEMS—Running away
SENSES—Sound

————. *Timothy Goes to School*. New York: Dial, 1981.

Claude finds that he is not alone in his feeling of alienation and peer rejection and establishes a friendship.

ANIMALS—Personified
BEHAVIOR—Apprehensive; Ridiculing
CLOTHING—Others
EMOTIONS—Embarrassment; Happiness
FRIENDSHIP—Relationships
IDENTITY—Self-worth
SCHOOL EXPERIENCES
STRUCTURES—Buildings, schools

Wells, Ruth. *A to Zen: A Book of Japanese Culture*. Yoshi, illus. Saxonville, MA: Picture Books Studio, 1992.

Elements of Japanese culture are introduced in this alphabet book, which is to be read from back to front and from right to left.

LANGUAGE—Alphabet
WORLD CULTURES/COUNTRIES—Asia, Japan

Westcott, Nadine Bernard. *Peanut Butter and Jelly: A Play Rhyme*. New York: Dutton, 1987.

A rhythmic text explains how to make a peanut butter and jelly sandwich.

CONSTRUCTION
EVERYDAY EXPERIENCES—Time of day, daytime
FOOD AND EATING
GAMES/PUZZLES/TRICKS
GRAPHIC AND PERFORMING ARTS—Drama and actors
HUMOR
MOVEMENT/SPEED
SENSES—Smell and taste; Touch
STORIES—Predictable text

Wiesner, David. *Free Fall*. New York: Lothrop, 1988.

Prompted by items in his bedroom, a boy dreams of marvelous adventures with imaginary creatures.

ADVENTURES
DREAMS
EVERYDAY EXPERIENCES—Time of day, nighttime
FLYING—Fantasy
FURNITURE—Beds
IMAGINATION—Imaginary creatures; Imaginary worlds
MAPS
OBSERVATION
READING
ROOMS—Bedrooms
SLEEPING
STORIES—Minimal or no text

————. *Hurricane.* New York: Clarion: 1990.

After the hurricane passes, David and George turn an uprooted tree into an imaginary world full of adventures.

ADVENTURES
FAMILIES—Parents; Siblings
IMAGINATION—Imaginary worlds
OBSERVATION
PLANTS—Trees
TIME—Cycles, day and night
WEATHER—Storms

————. *Tuesday.* New York: Clarion, 1991.

One Tuesday night hundreds of frogs fly on lilly pads throughout a neighborhood. On the next Tuesday night, hints of another strange phenomenon are in the sky.

ANIMALS—Marine life, frogs
FLYING—Fantasy
IMAGINATION—Imaginary worlds
NEIGHBORHOODS AND COMMUNITIES—General
TIME—Nighttime

Wild, Margaret. *Thank You, Santa.* Kerry Argent, illus. New York: Scholastic, 1991.

Throughout the year, a girl in Australia corresponds with Santa Claus, and learns about polar animals and the spirit of giving.

ANIMALS—Large animals, deer; Zoo
FRIENDSHIP—Relationships
GIFTS
GRAPHIC AND PERFORMING ARTS—Art and artists
HEALTH—Illness and injury
HOLIDAYS AND CELEBRATIONS—Christmas
IDENTITY—Geographic identity
IMAGINATION—Imaginary creatures
SURPRISES
TIME—Cycles, months of the year
WISHES
WORLD CULTURES/COUNTRIES—Polar regions
WRITING—Letters

————. *The Very Best of Friends*. Julie Vivas, illus. San Diego: Harcourt, 1989.

A cat named William nurtures a friendship with his beloved master's wife after the man's sudden death.

ANIMALS—Pets, cats
BEHAVIOR—Problem-solving; Searching
CHANGES
DEATH
EMOTIONS—Loneliness; Sadness
FAMILIES—Husbands and wives
FARMS
FRIENDSHIP—Relationships
STRUCTURES—Buildings, barns; Buildings, houses and other dwellings
WRITING—Letters

Wildsmith, Brian. *ABC*. New York: F. Watts, 1963.

Common images represent each letter of the alphabet.

LANGUAGE—Alphabet

————. *Birds*. New York: F. Watts, 1967.

Each page spread depicts a collective name for a particular bird.

ANIMALS—Birds
LANGUAGE—Words

————. *Brian Wildsmith's Circus*. New York: F. Watts, 1970.

The many elements of a circus are portrayed from its arrival in town to its departure.

CIRCUS
STORIES—Minimal or no text

————. *Brian Wildsmith's 1, 2, 3's*. New York: F. Watts, 1965.

The mathematical concepts of counting (1 to 10) and shapes are introduced in colorful illustrations featuring rectangles, circles, and triangles.

MATHEMATICS—Counting; Shapes

————. *Carousel*. New York: Knopf, 1988.

When Rosie becomes very ill, Tom brings a toy carousel to remind her of their favorite ride and give her hope.

CAROUSELS
FAIRS
FLYING—Fantasy
FRIENDSHIP—Relationships
GIFTS
HEALTH—Illness and injury
SLEEPING
TOYS

————. *Give a Dog a Bone*. New York: Pantheon, 1985.

A stray dog searching for a bone finds a home in a surprising way.

ANIMALS—Pets, dogs
BEHAVIOR—Searching
FOOD AND EATING

NEIGHBORHOODS AND COMMUNITIES—General
SENSES—Sound
SURPRISES

———. *Goat's Trail.* New York: Knopf, 1986.

A lonely mountain goat creates a ruckus as he picks up other animals on his way to investigate the new sounds coming from the village below.

ANIMALS—Farm; Farm, goats
BEHAVIOR—Curious; Mischievous
GRAPHIC AND PERFORMING ARTS—Music and musicians
LOST AND FOUND
NEIGHBORHOODS AND COMMUNITIES—Specific, urban
SCHOOL EXPERIENCES
SENSES—Sound
WORLD REGIONS—Mountain

———. *The Lazy Bear.* London: Oxford, 1973.

A bear discovers the pleasure of coasting downhill in a wagon, but he becomes lazy and bullies his animal friends into pushing him back to the top of the hill. The goat devises a way to teach him a lesson.

ANIMALS—Large animals, bears; Personified
BEHAVIOR—Bullying; Lazy; Revengeful; Sharing; Tricking
CHANGES
EMOTIONS—Fear
FRIENDSHIP—Relationships
MOVEMENT/SPEED
PLAY
TRANSPORTATION—Wagons

———. *The Little Wood Duck.* London: Oxford, 1972.

The little duckling with one foot larger than the other turns his disability into a heroic act and saves his siblings from the preying fox.

ANIMALS—Eggs; Farm, ducks; Large animals, foxes
BEHAVIOR—Heroic; Ridiculing
DISABILITIES
ENEMIES
FAMILIES—Siblings
MOVEMENT/SPEED
SURVIVAL
WATER AND BODIES OF WATER—Lakes

———. *Pelican.* New York: Pantheon, 1982.

The egg Paul brings home for speckled hen to hatch turns out to be a pelican that does not know how to catch fish. When his father threatens to send the fish-stealing pelican to the zoo, Paul finds many ways the pelican can prove useful on the farm.

ANIMALS—Birds; Cycles; Eggs
BEHAVIOR—Problem-solving; Stealing
FARMS
FISHING
FOOD AND EATING

————. *Puzzles*. New York: F. Watts, 1971.

The text asks questions that can be answered by studying the illustrations.
GAMES/PUZZLES/TRICKS
OBSERVATION

————. *Squirrels*. New York: F. Watts, 1975.

A close look at squirrels reveals the many uses they can make of their sharp claws, bush tails, and roomy cheek pouches.
ANIMALS—Small creatures, squirrels
MOVEMENT/SPEED
NEIGHBORHOODS AND COMMUNITIES—General

————. *What the Moon Saw*. New York: Oxford, 1978.

Since the moon has never seen what is on earth, the sun describes what is there using contrasting concepts. When the sun boasts that there is nothing it has not seen, the moon disagrees.
ASTRONOMY—Moon; Sun
LANGUAGE—Words

Wilhelm, Hans. *I'll Always Love You*. New York: Crown, 1985.

When a boy's beloved dog dies, he is comforted by reminding himself that every night he told him, "I'll always love you."
ANIMALS—Pets, dogs
DEATH
ELDERLY
EMOTIONS—Love; Sadness
FAMILIES
FRIENDSHIP—Relationships
HEALTH—Illness and injury
LANGUAGE—Sayings and special language
MEMORIES
TIME—Nighttime

Wilkon, Piotr. *Rosie the Cool Cat*. Jozef Wilkon, illus. New York: Viking, 1991.

Even though Rosie, a bright orange cat, is born into a family of black cats, she is not disturbed by her appearance and creates her own life.
ADVENTURES
ANIMALS—Pets, cats
BEHAVIOR—Proud
BIRTH
CHANGE
COLORS
COMMUNICATION—Televisions
EMOTIONS—Embarrassment; Happiness; Sadness
FAMILIES—Babies and young siblings; Parents
FAMILY PROBLEMS—Separation
FRIENDSHIP—Relationships
GRAPHIC AND PERFORMING ARTS—Music and musicians
IDENTITY—Self-worth
INDIVIDUALITY
PERSONAL PROBLEMS—Running away

Willard, Nancy. *Simple Pictures Are Best*. Tomie dePaola, illus. New York: Harcourt, 1977.

A couple being photographed for their wedding anniversary discover that the photographer's warning "Simple pictures are best" is truly advisable.

ANIMALS—Farm, cows
FAMILIES—Husbands and wives
HUMOR
PHOTOGRAPHY

Williams, Barbara. *A Valentine for Cousin Archie*. Kay Chorao, illus. New York: Dutton, 1981.

Cousin Archie discovers that the mysterious valentine he thought he had received from a lady admirer was actually half of Chester Chipmunk's grocery list.

ANIMALS—Personified; Small creatures, others
BEHAVIOR—Curious
GAMES/PUZZLES/TRICKS
GIFTS
HOLIDAYS AND CELEBRATIONS—Valentine's
HUMOR
MYSTERY
SENSES—Smell and taste
TIME—Specific seasons, winter
WEATHER—Snow
WRITING—Others

Williams, Karen Lynn. *When Africa Was Home*. Floyd Cooper, illus. New York: Orchard, 1991.

After spending his early years in Africa, Peter misses this culture when he must move back to the United States with his family.

EMOTIONS—Loneliness; Love; Sadness
FAMILIES—Parents
FRIENDSHIP—Relationships
GOALS
IDENTITY—Geographic identity
MATHEMATICS—Measurement, length
MOVING
NEIGHBORHOODS AND COMMUNITIES—General
TRAVEL
WISHES
WORLD CULTURES/COUNTRIES—Africa; Cross cultures

Williams, Linda. *The Little Old Lady Who Was Not Afraid of Anything*. Megan Lloyd, illus. New York: Crowell, 1986.

One windy autumn night, the little old lady who is not afraid of anything encounters mysterious images and sounds that give her a scare.

BEHAVIOR—Boastful; Courageous
CLOTHING
ELDERLY
EMOTIONS—Fear
GARDENS
IMAGINATION—Imaginary creatures

MOVEMENT/SPEED
MYSTERY
PLANTS
PUMPKINS
SCARECROWS
SENSES—Sound
STORIES—Predictable text
STRUCTURES—Buildings, houses and other dwellings
TIME—Nighttime; Specific seasons, fall

Williams, Sherley Anne. *Working Cotton*. Carole Byard, illus. San Diego: Harcourt, 1992.

A young African American girl tells of a day in her migrant family's life picking cotton.

BEHAVIOR—Ambitious/Persistent
FAMILIES—Parents; Siblings
FARMS
LUCK
MIGRANTS
MOVEMENT/SPEED
NEIGHBORHOODS AND COMMUNITIES—Specific, rural
OCCUPATIONS
PLANTS—Others
POVERTY
TIME—Cycles, day and night
TRANSPORTATION—Buses
UNITED STATES—Regions, West Coast; Specific cultures, African American

Williams, Sue. *I Went Walking*. Julie Vivas, illus. San Diego: Harcourt, 1990.

As a young boy encounters a progression of animals, he identifies each by name and color, eventually collecting a group of them.

ADVENTURES
ANIMALS—Farm
CLOTHING
COLORS
LANGUAGE—Words
STORIES—Predictable text

Williams, Vera B. *A Chair For My Mother*. New York: Greenwillow, 1982.

A young girl, her mother, and grandmother save dimes to purchase a comfortable chair after their furniture is destroyed by a fire.

DISASTERS
EMOTIONS—Love
FAMILIES—Grandparents; Other relatives; Parents
FAMILY PROBLEMS—Homelessness
FIRE
FURNITURE—Chairs
GIFTS
MATHEMATICS—Measurement, mass
MONEY
NEIGHBORHOODS AND COMMUNITIES—Specific, urban
OCCUPATIONS
SAFETY/DANGER

STRUCTURES—Buildings, houses and other dwellings
TRANSPORTATION—Buses; Trucks
UNITED STATES—Specific cultures, Hispanic American
WISHES

————. *Music, Music for Everyone*. New York: Greenwillow, 1984.

Rosa helps her mother with expenses during her grandmother's illness by playing the accordion in a band with friends.

BEHAVIOR—Problem-solving
EMOTIONS—Love
FAMILIES—Family gatherings/Outings; Grandparents; Parents
FRIENDSHIP—Relationships
FURNITURE—Beds; Chairs
GRAPHIC AND PERFORMING ARTS—Dance and dancers; Music and musicians
HEALTH—Illness and injury
MATHEMATICS—Measurement, mass
MONEY
PARTIES
ROOMS—Bedrooms
STRUCTURES—Boxes and containers
UNITED STATES—Specific cultures, Hispanic American

————. *Something Special For Me*. New York: Greenwillow, 1983.

After having difficulty deciding on her birthday present, Rosa hears someone making music and decides she wants an accordion.

BEHAVIOR—Apprehensive; Crying; Excited; Sharing
BIRTHDAYS
EMOTIONS—Happiness; Sadness
FAMILIES—Grandparents; Parents
GIFTS
GRAPHIC AND PERFORMING ARTS—Music and musicians
MONEY
NEIGHBORHOODS AND COMMUNITIES—Specific, urban
OCCUPATIONS
PHOTOGRAPHY
READING
SENSES—Sound
SHOPPING/MARKETING
UNITED STATES—Specific cultures, Hispanic American
WISHES

Winter, Jeanette. *Follow the Drinking Gourd*. New York: Knopf, 1988.

Runaway slaves follow the directions in "The Drinking Gourd," a song taught to them by an old sailor, and escape to freedom along the Underground Railroad to the North.

ADVENTURES
ASTRONOMY—Stars
BEHAVIOR—Apprehensive; Courageous; Evil; Heroic; Hiding; Problem-solving; Resourceful; Running away; Searching
COMMUNICATION
DISABILITIES
EMOTIONS—Fear; Happiness; Sadness
ENEMIES

GOALS
GRAPHIC AND PERFORMING ARTS—Music and musicians
HISTORICAL PERIODS—Nineteenth Century, early
IMMIGRANTS/REFUGEES
LANGUAGE—Sayings and special language
PERSONAL PROBLEMS—Running away
SAFETY/DANGER
SLAVERY
TIME—Nighttime
TRAVEL
UNITED STATES—Specific cultures, African American

Winter, Paula. *Sir Andrew.* New York: Crown, 1980.

A proud donkey who strives to make an elegant appearance finds that a stroll about town can be dangerous.

ANIMALS—Farm, donkeys; Personified
BEHAVIOR—Proud
CLOTHING
SAFETY/DANGER
STORIES—Minimal or no text
WEATHER—Wind

Wittman, Patricia. *Go Ask Giorgio!* Will Hillenbrand, illus. New York: Macmillan, 1992.

Ambitious Giorgio, wearing the hats of many jobs, becomes overwhelmed with too much work. When he attempts to limit his work activity, the villagers insist on giving him a nightcap that suggests rest periods.

BEHAVIOR—Ambitious/Persistent; Cooperative; Responsible
CLOTHING—Hats
HEALTH—Health care
OCCUPATIONS
WORLD CULTURES/COUNTRIES—Europe, Southern

Wolff, Ferida. *The Woodcutter's Coat.* Anne Wilsdorf, illus. Boston: Little, Brown, 1992.

When a woodcutter's tattered coat is stolen, its condition improves as it passes through several transactions before being returned to its original owner.

BEHAVIOR—Stealing
CHANGES
CLOTHING—Coats
LOST AND FOUND
NEIGHBORHOODS AND COMMUNITIES—General
OCCUPATIONS
SEWING
SHOPPING/MARKETING
TIME—Specific seasons, winter

Wood, Audrey. *Heckedy Peg.* Don Wood, illus. San Diego: Harcourt, 1987.

A mother rescues her seven children, named after the days of the week, from the witch, Heckedy Peg, who has transformed them into different kinds of food.

BEHAVIOR—Evil; Searching; Tricking
EMOTIONS—Sadness

FAMILIES—Parents
FAMILY PROBLEMS—Separation
FOOD AND EATING
GIFTS
IMAGINATION—Imaginary creatures, Witches
LANGUAGE—Names
LIGHT AND SHADOWS/REFLECTIONS
TIME—Cycles, days of the week
TRANSFORMATIONS
WISHES

————. *The Napping House*. Don Wood, illus. San Diego: Harcourt, 1984.

A sleeping child and several animals pile on top of a napping granny on a rainy day, but the plot reverses when a flea bite starts a fast chain reaction that awakens them as sunshine appears.

ANIMALS—Pets, others; Small creatures
BEHAVIOR—Destructive/Violent
ELDERLY
FURNITURE—Beds
MATHEMATICS—Measurement, mass
MOVEMENT/SPEED
OBSERVATION
SENSES—Sound; Touch
SLEEPING
STORIES—Predictable text
STRUCTURES—Buildings, houses and other dwellings
SURPRISES
WEATHER—Rain; Rainbows; Sunshine

Woodruff, Elvira. *The Wing Shop*. Stephen Gammell, illus. New York: Holiday House, 1991.

Matthew tries out different wings at The Wing Shop, hoping to find a pair that will fly him back to the neighborhood from which he has recently moved. When he finally finds a pair that will accomplish his goal he has adjusted to his new surroundings and no longer feels the need to go.

ADVENTURES
BEHAVIOR—Apprehensive; Searching
BODY—Parts of body
CHANGES
EMOTIONS—Loneliness
FLYING—Fantasy
MATHEMATICS—Measurement, length
MOVING
NEIGHBORHOODS AND COMMUNITIES—Specific, urban
STRUCTURES—Buildings, stores
WISHES

Yamaka, Sara. *The Gift of Driscoll Lipscomb*. Joung Un Kim, illus. New York: Simon & Schuster, 1995.

Every year the painter, Driscoll Lipscomb, gives Molly a different color of paint as a birthday gift. When he completes the set on her ninth birthday, he tells her to paint her dreams.

BEHAVIOR—Ambitious/Persistent

BIRTHDAYS
COLORS
DREAMS
ELDERLY
FRIENDSHIP—Relationships
GIFTS
GRAPHIC AND PERFORMING ARTS—Art and artists
IDENTITY—Self-worth
OBSERVATION
SENSES—Sight

Yarbrough, Camille. *Cornrows*. Carole Byard, illus. New York: Cowad, 1979.

As the children have their hair braided in traditional African patterns, their mother and grandmother share with them their special cultural heritage across time.

BODY—Parts of body, hair
EMOTIONS—Love
FAMILIES—Grandparents; Parents
STORYTELLING
TIME—Across time
UNITED STATES—Specific cultures, African American

Uashima, Tarco. *Crow Boy*. New York: Viking, 1955.

The boy, Chibi, ridiculed by his schoolmates, wins their admiration by imitating the voices of crows in a school program. He is then referred to by his peers as Crow Boy.

BEHAVIOR—Crying; Pretending; Ridiculing; Shy
EMOTIONS—Embarrassment
IDENTITY—Self-worth
LANGUAGE—Names
NEIGHBORHOODS AND COMMUNITIES—General
OCCUPATIONS
SCHOOL EXPERIENCES
SENSES—Sound
STRUCTURES—Buildings, schools
WORLD CULTURES/COUNTRIES—Asia, Japan

———. *Umbrella*. New York: Viking, 1958.

Momo, an Asian American, anxiously waits for a rainy day to use her birthday gift, an umbrella.

BEHAVIOR—Excited; Patient
BIRTHDAYS
CLOTHING—Others
GIFTS
LANGUAGE—Names
MEMORIES
SENSES—Sound
STORYTELLING
UNITED STATES—Specific cultures, Asian American
WEATHER—Rain
WISHES

Yee, Paul. *Roses Sing on New Snow.* Harvey Chan, illus. New York: Macmillan, 1991.

An Asian American girl is relegated to working in the kitchen of the family restaurant while her father and brothers claim the credit for her culinary ability. When she creates a special dish for the visiting governor from China, she finally receives the recognition she deserves.

BEHAVIOR—Greedy; Lazy; Lying
FAMILIES—Parents; Siblings
FOOD AND EATING
GOALS
HISTORICAL PERIODS—Twentieth Century, early
IDENTITY—Gender roles
IMMIGRANTS/REFUGEES
INDIVIDUALITY
NEIGHBORHOODS AND COMMUNITIES—Specific, urban
OCCUPATIONS
UNITED STATES—Regions, West Coast; Specific cultures, Asian Americans
WORLD CULTURES/COUNTRIES—Asia, China

Yolen, Jane. *All Those Secrets of the World.* Leslie Baker, illus. Boston: Little, Brown, 1991.

A young girl experiences separation from her soldier father during wartime. When he returns home, she shares with him her concept of size and distance.

BODY—Shape and size
FAMILIES—Parents
FAMILY PROBLEMS—Separation
HISTORICAL PERIODS—Twentieth Century, World War II
MATHEMATICS—Size
WAR

———. *Encounter.* David Shannon, illus. San Diego: Harcourt, 1992.

The intrusion of Columbus's exploration upon the Taino Indian culture in the Caribbean is told from the viewpoint of a native.

BEHAVIOR—Destructive/Violent
DREAMS
EXPLORATION
HISTORICAL PERIODS—Exploration of the New World
IDENTITY—Self-worth
STRANGERS
WORLD CULTURES/COUNTRIES—Central America, Caribbean Islands

———. *Grandad Bill's Song.* Melissa Bay Mathis, illus. New York: Philomel, 1994.

When a young boy asks adults what they did on the day his grandfather died, he receives different answers that reflect different emotions.

BEHAVIOR—Crying; Searching
BIOGRAPHY/LIFE STORIES
DEATH
ELDERLY
EMOTIONS—Anger; Loneliness; Love; Sadness
FAMILIES—Grandparents; Other relatives; Parents; Siblings
IDENTITY—Relationships

MEMORIES
STORYTELLING

———. *Letting Swift River Go.* Barbara Cooney, illus. Boston: Little Brown, 1992.

Sally Jane tells about the community where she grew up and how it was destroyed when a reservoir was constructed to provide water for residents of a nearby city. As an adult, memories are all that remain for her.

CHANGES
ECOLOGY/ENVIRONMENTAL PROBLEMS
FAMILIES—Parents
FRIENDSHIP—Relationships
MEMORIES
MOVING
NEIGHBORHOODS AND COMMUNITIES—Specific, rural
STRUCTURES—Others
TIME—Across time; Cycles, seasons
TRANSPORTATION—Boats
UNITED STATES—Regions, Northeast
WATER AND BODIES OF WATER—Rivers

———. *No Bath Tonight.* Nancy Winslow Parker, illus. New York: Crowell, 1978.

All week a small boy avoids taking a bath until his clever grandmother lures him into the tub.

BEHAVIOR—Tricking
EVERYDAY EXPERIENCES—Time of day, daytime
FAMILIES—Grandparents
HEALTH—Bathing
TIME—Cycles, days of the week

———. *Owl Moon.* John Schoenherr, illus. New York: Philomel, 1987.

One winter night when the moon is full, a father takes his daughter into the woods to observe the Great Horned Owl.

ANIMALS—Birds
BEHAVIOR—Obedient; Searching; Sharing
CLOTHING
FAMILIES—Parents
IDENTITY—Self-worth
NEIGHBORHOODS AND COMMUNITIES—Specific, rural
PLANTS—Trees
SENSES—Sight; Sound; Touch
TIME—Nighttime; Specific seasons, winter
WEATHER—Snow
WORLD REGIONS—Forest

———. *The Seeing Stick.* Remy Charlip and Demetra Maraslis, illus. New York: Crowell, 1977.

An elderly man teaches the Chinese emperor's blind daughter to learn about the world through the sense of touch.

BEHAVIOR—Problem-solving; Searching
BODY—Parts of body, eyes

DISABILITIES
ELDERLY
EMOTIONS—Sadness
FAMILIES—Parents
GRAPHIC AND PERFORMING ARTS—Art and artists
IDENTITY—Relationships
OCCUPATIONS
ROYALTY
SENSES—Touch
SURPRISES
WORLD CULTURES/COUNTRIES—Asia, China

Yorinks, Arthur. *Bravo, Minski.* Richard Egielski, illus. New York: Farrar, 1988.

Minski, a famous inventor, faces his most difficult challenge. He tries to develop a formula that will enable him to become a famous singer. Through perseverance, he achieves his goal.

AESTHETIC APPRECIATION
BEHAVIOR—Ambitious/Persistent; Problem-solving
GOALS
GRAPHIC AND PERFORMING ARTS—Music and musicians
IDENTITY—Self-worth
INVENTIONS
TIME—Across time

———. *Louis the Fish.* Richard Egielski, illus. New York: Farrar, 1980.

When Louis, an unhappy butcher, is transformed into a fish, he achieves happiness.

ANIMALS—Marine life, aquariums; Marine life, fishes
BEHAVIOR—Apprehensive
DREAMS
EMOTIONS—Happiness; Sadness
FOOD AND EATING
IDENTITY—Self-worth
OCCUPATIONS
TRANSFORMATION

Yorinks, Arthur. *Whitefish Will Rides Again!* Mort Drucker, illus. New York: HarperCollins, 1994.

Whitefish Will, the mighty lawman, is dismissed by the citizens of the town after he rids them of lawlessness. He returns to his former role when Bart and his gang of horse thieves victimize the town.

BEHAVIOR—Bullying; Destructive/Violent; Evil
COWBOYS/COWGIRLS
ENEMIES
GRAPHIC AND PERFORMING ARTS—Music and musicians
HISTORICAL PERIODS—Nineteenth Century, pioneer/westward movement
HUMOR
IDENTITY—Geographic identity
NEIGHBORHOODS AND COMMUNITIES—General
OCCUPATIONS

RANCHES
SAFETY/DANGER
SURVIVAL
TRANSPORTATION—Horses

Zemach, Harve. *The Judge: An Untrue Tale.* Margot Zemach, illus. New York: Farrar, 1969.

A judge discovers that the people he has thrown into jail are telling true stories about a monster.

BEHAVIOR—Destructive/Violent
EMOTIONS—Fear
HUMOR
IMAGINATION—Imaginary creatures
MATHEMATICS—Counting
OBSERVATION
OCCUPATIONS
STORIES—Predictable text

Ziefert, Harriet. *A New Coat for Anna.* Anita Lobel, illus. New York: Knopf, 1986.

After World War II, Anna's mother, with much persistence and sacrifice, fulfills her promise to obtain a new coat to replace her daughter's old one.

ANIMALS—Farm, sheep
BEHAVIOR—Patient; Problem-solving
CLOTHING—Coats
COLORS
FAMILIES—Parents
FARMS
GOALS
HISTORICAL PERIODS—Twentieth Century, World War II
HOLIDAYS AND CELEBRATIONS—Christmas
MATHEMATICS—Measurement, length; Size
OCCUPATIONS
POVERTY
SEWING
WAR
WEAVING
WORLD CULTURES/COUNTRIES—Europe, Northern

Zion, Gene. *Harry, the Dirty Dog.* Margaret Bloy Graham, illus. New York: Harper, 1956.

Harry, the dog, dislikes bathing. When he runs away, he has many experiences that leave him so dirty that he is not recognized by his family. He finds that a bath is necessary if he wants to be reunited with them.

ANIMALS—Pets, dogs
EXPLORATION
HEALTH—Bathing
PERSONAL PROBLEMS—Running away

————. *No Roses for Harry*. Margaret Bloy Graham, illus. New York: Harper, 1958.

Harry, the Dirty Dog, does not like the sweater Grandmother gave him for his birthday. After several attempts to get rid of it, he finds a happy solution.

ANIMALS—Birds; Habitats; Pets, dogs
BEHAVIOR—Problem-solving
BIRTHDAYS
CLOTHING—Others
EMOTIONS—Embarrassment
FAMILIES—Grandparents
GIFTS
LOST AND FOUND
SENSES—Sight
SHOPPING/MARKETING

————. *The Plant Sitter*. Margaret Bloy Graham, illus. New York: Harper, 1959.

Tommy is a great success as a plant sitter, taking care of his vacationing neighbors' plants.

BEHAVIOR—Problem-solving; Responsible
DREAMS
FAMILIES—Parents
MONEY
NEIGHBORHOODS AND COMMUNITIES—General
OCCUPATIONS
PLANTS—Others
READING
SLEEPING
STRUCTURES—Buildings, libraries
TRAVEL
VACATIONS

Zolotow, Charlotte. *Do You Know What I'll Do?* Garth Williams, illus. New York: Harper & Row, 1958.

A young girl shows affection for her baby brother by promising to share her experiences with him.

BEHAVIOR—Sharing
EMOTIONS—Love
FAMILIES—Babies and young siblings
STORIES—Predictable text.

————. *Mr. Rabbit and the Lovely Present*. Maurice Sendak, illus. New York: Harper & Row, 1962.

Mr. Rabbit helps a girl find a birthday present for her mother which is red, yellow, green, and blue.

ANIMALS—Personified; Small creatures, rabbits
BEHAVIOR—Searching
BIRTHDAYS
COLORS
FAMILIES—Parents
FOOD AND EATING
GIFTS

————. *My Grandson Lew.* William Pene Du Bois, illus. New York: Harper & Row, 1974.

Lew misses his grandfather, but the memories that he and his mother share of him are comforting.
BIRTH
DEATH
EMOTIONS—Happiness; Loneliness
EVERYDAY EXPERIENCES—Time of day, nighttime
FAMILIES—Grandparents; Parents
MEMORIES
STRUCTURES—Buildings, museums

————. *A Rose, A Bridge, and a Wild Black Horse.* Uri Shulevitz, illus. New York: Harper & Row, 1964.

A small boy lists for his sister the wonderful things he will do for her when he grows up.
FAMILIES—Siblings
GIFTS

————. *Some Things Go Together.* Sylvie Selig, illus. New York: Abelard-Schuman, 1969.

A series of couplets link images and express the theme of love.
EMOTIONS—Love
LANGUAGE—Words
STORIES—Predictable text

————. *Someday.* Arnold Lobel, illus. New York: Harper & Row, 1965.

A young girl imagines a world more to her liking even though improbable in reality.
IMAGINATION—Imaginary worlds
WISHES

————. *The Storm Book.* Margaret Bloy Graham, illus. New York: Harper & Row, 1952.

The progression of a rainstorm and its effects on people living in different neighborhoods is described.
NEIGHBORHOODS AND COMMUNITIES—Specific, rural; Specific, urban
SENSES—Sight; Sound
WATER AND BODIES OF WATER—Oceans
WEATHER—Rain; Rainbows; Storms

————. *This Quiet Lady.* Anita Lobel, illus. New York: Greenwillow, 1992.

By viewing photographs, a girl learns about her mother's life from the time of her own birth to that of her daughter's.
BIOGRAPHY/LIFE STORIES
BIRTH
FAMILIES—Parents
IDENTITY—Gender roles; Relationships
MEMORIES
OBSERVATION

PHOTOGRAPHY
STORIES—Predictable text
STORYTELLING
TIME—Across time

———. *A Tiger Called Thomas*. Kurt Werth, illus. New York: Lothrop, 1963.

When his family moves to a new neighborhood, Thomas finds it difficult to make friends until he goes trick-or-treating on Halloween.

ANIMALS—Large animals, tigers
BEHAVIOR—Apprehensive; Hiding
CLOTHING—Costumes
EMOTIONS—Happiness; Loneliness; Sadness
FAMILIES—Parents
FRIENDSHIP—Relationships
HOLIDAYS AND CELEBRATIONS—Halloween
IDENTITY—Self-worth
MOVING
NEIGHBORHOODS AND COMMUNITIES—General

———. *The Unfriendly Book*. William Pene Du Bois, illus. New York: Harper & Row, 1975.

A girl is jealous when her best friend associates with others and discovers the friend does not like such behavior.

EMOTIONS—Jealousy
FRIENDSHIP—Relationships
IDENTITY—Self-worth

———. *William's Doll*. William Pene Du Bois, illus. New York: Harper & Row, 1972.

William longs for a doll that he can care for even though other toys are suggested to him.

EMOTIONS—Love
IDENTITY—Gender roles
TOYS—Dolls
WISHES

Title Index

A Baby Sister for Frances. Hoban, Russell.
Baby-O. Carlstrom, Nancy White.
The Backwards Watch. Houghton, Eric.
Bad Day at Riverbend. Van Allsburg, Chris.
The Ball Bounced. Tafuri, Nancy.
A Balloon for Grandad. Gray, Nigel.
Bamboozled. Legge, David.
The Banshee. Ackerman, Karen.
The Banshee Train. Bodkin, Odds.
A Bargain for Frances. Hoban, Russell.
The Barn. Schoenherr, John.
Barn Dance! Martin, Bill, and John Archambault.
Barnyard Banter. Fleming, Denise.
Bea and Mr. Jones. Schwartz, Amy.
Bear Hunt. Browne, Anthony.
The Bear on the Moon. Ryder, Joanne.
Bear Shadow. Asch, Frank.
Bearymore. Freeman, Don.
The Bedspread. Fair, Sylvia.
Bedtime for Frances. Hoban, Russell.
The Bee Tree. Polacco, Patricia.
Ben's Trumpet. Isadora, Rachel.
Berlioz the Bear. Brett, Jan.
Best Friends for Frances. Hoban, Russell.
The Best Valentine in the World. Sharmat, Marjorie Weinman.
The Bicycle Man. Say, Allen.
Bicycle Race. Crews, Donald.
The Big Alfie and Annie Rose Storybook. Hughes, Shirley.
The Big Concrete Lorry: A Tale of Trotter Street. Hughes, Shirley.
Big Ones, Little Ones. Hoban, Tana.
Big Pumpkin. Silverman, Erica.
The Big Sneeze. Brown, Ruth.
The Biggest Boy. Henkes, Kevin.
The Biggest House in the World. Lionni, Leo.
Bigmama's. Crews, Donald.
The Bionic Bunny Show. Brown, Marc.
Bird Adalbert. Bohdal, Susi.
Birds. Wildsmith, Brian.
A Birthday Basket for Tia. Mora, Pat.
A Birthday for Blue. Lydon, Kerry Raines.
A Birthday for Frances. Hoban, Russell.
Bitter Bananas. Olaleye, Isaac O.
The Black Snowman. Mendez, Phil.
Blossom Comes Home. Herriot, James.
Blueberries for Sal. McCloskey, Robert.
Bonny's Big Day. Herriot, James.

The Circus in the Mist. Munari, Bruno.
The City. Florian, Douglas.
City/Country. Robbins, Ken.
City Night. Rice, Eve.
Clementina's Cactus. Keats, Ezra Jack.
Clive Eats Alligators. Lester, Alison.
A Cloak for the Dreamer. Friedman, Aileen.
Clocks and More Clocks. Hutchins, Pat.
The Cloud. Ray, Deborah Kogan.
Cloudy with a Chance of Meatballs. Barrett, Judi.
Clyde Monster. Crowe, Robert.
The Cobweb Curtain: A Christmas Story. Koralek, Jenny.
Coco Can't Wait. Gomi, Taro.
Color Dance. Jonas, Ann.
Color Farm. Ehlert, Lois.
Color Zoo. Ehlert, Lois.
A Colorful Adventure of the Bee, Who Left Home One Monday Morning and What He Found Along the Way. Ernst, Lisa Campbell.
Colors. Reiss, John.
Come a Tide. Lyon, George Ella.
Come Away from the Water, Shirley. Burningham, John.
Conrad's Castle. Shecter, Ben.
Cookie's Week. Ward, Cindy.
Corduroy. Freeman, Don.
Cornelius: A Fable. Lionni, Leo.
Cornrows. Yarbrough, Camille.
Could Be Worse! Stevenson, James.
Count and See. Hoban, Tana.
Country Crossing. Aylesworth, Jim.
Cowardly Clyde. Peet, Bill.
The Cowboy and the Black-eyed Pea. Johnston, Tony.
Cowboy Dreams. Khalsa, Dayal Kaur.
Cowboys. Rounds, Glen.
Crafty Chameleon. Mwenye Hadithi.
Crash! Bang! Boom! Spier, Peter.
Crictor. Ungerer, Tomi.
Crow Boy. Yashima, Taro.
Cully Cully and the Bear. Gage, Wilson.
Curiuous George. Rey, H. A.

Dakota Dugout. Turner, Ann Warren.
Dancers in the Garden. Ryder, Joanne.
Dandelion. Freeman, Don.
Daniel's Dinosaurs. Carmine, Mary.
Darcy and Gran Don't Like Babies. Cutler, Jame.

Jafta and the Wedding. Lewin, Hugh.
Jafta—the Journey. Lewin, Hugh.
Jafta—the Town. Lewin, Hugh.
Jafta's Father. Lewin, Hugh.
Jafta's Mother. Lewin, Hugh.
Jambo Means Hello: Swahili Alphabet Book. Feelings, Muriel.
Jeb Scarecrow's Pumpkin Patch. Dillon, Jana.
Jennie's Hat. Keats, Ezra Jack.
Jesse Bear, What Will You Wear? Carlstrom, Nancy White.
Jessica. Henkes, Kevin.
Jimmy's Boa Bounces Back. Noble, Trinka Hakes.
Jingle: The Christmas Clown. dePaola, Tomie.
John Patrick Norman McHennessy: The Boy Who Was Always Late. Burmingham, John.
John Tabor's Ride. Lent, Blair.
The Jolly Postman. Ahlberg, Janet.
The Josefina Story Quilt. Coerr, Eleanor.
The Journey Home. Lester, Alison.
The Judge: An Untrue Tale. Zemach, Harve.
Julius, the Baby of the World. Henkes, Kevin.
Jumanji. Van Allsburg, Chris.
Junglewalk. Tafuri, Nancy.
Just a Dream. Van Allsburg, Chris.
Just Like Daddy. Asch, Frank.

Kate Shelley: Bound for Legend. San Souci, Robert D.
Katie's Trunk. Turner, Ann Warren.
The Keeping Quilt. Polacco, Patricia.
The King's Flower. Anno, Mitsumasa.
Kipper. Inkpen, Mick.
A Kiss for Little Bear. Minarik, Else Holmelund.
The Knight and the Drdagon. dePaola, Tomie.
Knock, Knock! Who's There? Grindley, Sally.
Knots on a Counting Rope. Martin, Bill, and John Archambault.
Koala Lou. Fox, Mem.
Komodo! Sis, Peter.

The Lady and the Spider. McNulty, Faith.
The Last Puppy. Asch, Frank.
The Lazy Bear. Wildsmith, Brian.
Lazy Lion. Mwenye Hadithi.
The Leaving Morning. Johnson, Angela.
The Lemonade Babysitter. Waggoner, Karen.
Leo the Late Bloomer. Kraus, Robert.
A Letter to Amy. Keats, Ezra Jack.

Pelican. Wildsmith, Brian.
Peppe the Lamplighter. Bartone, Elisa.
Pet of the Met. Freeman, Lydia.
Pet Show! Keats, Ezra Jack.
Peter Spier's Christmas! Spier, Peter.
Peter Spier's Circus! Spier, Peter.
Peter Spier's Rain. Spier, Peter.
Peter's Chair. Keats, Ezra Jack.
Peter's Pockets. Rice, Eve.
Petrouchka. Cleaver, Elizabeth.
Petunia. Duvoisin, Roger.
The Philharmonic Gets Dressed. Kuskin, Karla.
Pianna. Ray, Mary Lyn.
The Picnic. Brown, Ruth.
Picnic. McCully, Emily Arnold.
Pig Pig Rides. McPhail, David.
Piggybook. Browne, Anthony.
Pigs from A to Z. Geisert, Arthur.
Pigs from 1 to 10. Geisert, Arthur.
Pink and Say. Polacco, Patricia.
Pinkerton, Behave! Kellogg, Steven.
The Pirates of Bedford Street. Isadora, Rachel.
A Place for Ben. Titherington, Jeanne.
The Plant Sitter. Zion, Gene.
Planting a Rainbow. Ehlert, Lois.
Play with Me. Ets, Marie Hall.
Playing Right Field. Welch, Willy.
A Pocket for Corduroy. Freeman, Don.
Polar Bear, Polar Bear, What Do You Hear? Martin, Bill.
The Polar Express. Van Allsburg, Chris.
The Popcorn Book. dePaola, Tomie.
Possum Magic. Fox, Mem.
The Potato Man. McDonald, Megan.
Potluck. Shelby, Anne.
Prehistoric Pinkerton. Kellogg, Steven.
Prince Boghole. Haugaard, Erik Christian.
Prince William. Rand, Gloria.
Pumpkin, Pumpkin. Titherington, Jeanne.
The Purple Coat. Hest, Amy.
Push, Pull, Empty, Fill: A Book of Opposites. Hoban, Tana.
Puzzles. Wildsmith, Brian.

The Queen's Goat. Mahy, Margaret.
The Quicksand Book. dePaola, Tomie.

The Quilt. Jonas, Ann.
The Quilt Story. Johnston, Tony.

Rabbit's Morning. Tafuri, Nancy.
The Rag Coat. Mills, Lauren.
Ragtime Tumpie. Schroeder, Alan.
Rain Makes Applesauce. Scheer, Julian, and Marvin Bileck.
Rain Rain Rivers. Shulevitz, Uri.
Rain Talk. Serfozo, Mary.
Randolph's Dream. Mellecker, Judith.
Rata-pata-scata-fata. Gershator, Phillis.
Rechenka's Eggs. Polacco, Patricia.
Red Leaf, Yellow Leaf. Ehlert, Lois.
Redbird. Fort, Patrick.
The Relatives Came. Rylant, Cynthia.
The Return of Freddy LeGrand. Agee, Jon.
Return of the Shadows. Farber, Norma.
A Ride on the Red Mare's Back. Le Guin, Ursula K.
Riptide. Weller, Frances Ward.
Roll Over! Gerstein, Mordicai.
Rondo in C. Fleischman, Paul.
The Room. Gerstein, Mordicai.
The Rooster Who Set Out to See the World. Carle, Eric.
A Rose, A Bridge, and a Wild Black Horse. Zolotow, Charlotte.
Rose Blanche. Innocenti, Roberto.
A Rose for Pinkerton. Kellogg, Steven.
The Rose in My Garden. Lobel, Arnold.
Roses Sing on New Snow. Yee, Paul.
Rosie the Cool Cat. Wilkon, Piotr.
Rosie's Walk. Hutchins, Pat.
Rotten Ralph. Gantos, Jack.
Round Trip. Jonas, Ann.
Roxaboxen. McLerran, Alice.
Runaway Mittens. Rogers, Jean.

Sadako. Coerr, Eleanor.
Sail Away. Crew, Donald.
Sam. Scott, Ann Herbert.
Sam, Bangs, & Moonshine. Ness, Evaline.
Sam Johnson and the Blue Ribbon Quilt. Ernst, Lisa Campbell.
Sam Who Never Forgets. Rice, Eve.
Sambalena Show-Off. Gershator, Phillis.
Sand Cake. Asch, Frank.
The Sandman. Shepperson, Rob.

Bibliography

The Booklist. Chicago: American Library Association.

Bulletin of the Center for Children's Books. Champaign, IL: University of Illinois.

The Horn Book Magazine. Boston: Horn Book, Inc.

Huck, Charlotte S. *Children's Literature in the Elementary School.* 3rd ed. Fort Worth: Holt, Rinehart, and Winston, 1976.

———. *Children's Literature in the Elementary School.* 3rd ed. update. Fort Worth: Holt, Rinehart, and Winston, 1979.

Huck, Charlotte S., Susan Hepler, and Janet Hickman. *Children's Literature in the Elementary School.* 4th ed. Fort Worth: Holt, Rinehart, and Winston, 1987.

———. *Children's Literature in the Elementary School.* 5th ed. Fort Worth: Harcourt Brace Jovanovich, 1994.

The Reading Teacher. Newark, DE: International Reading Association.

School Library Journal. New York: R. R. Bowker.

Science and Children. Washington, DC: National Science Teachers Association.

Social Education. Arlington, VA: National Council for the Social Studies.

Yaakov, Juliette, ed. *Children's Catalog.* 16th ed. New York: H. W. Wilson, 1991.